THE DAYKEEPER

THE DAYKEEPER

THE LIFE
AND
DISCOURSE
OF AN
IXIL
DIVINER

Benjamin N. Colby
and
Lore M. Colby

Harvard University Press   Cambridge, Massachusetts
and London, England   1981

Library of Congress Cataloging in Publication Data

Colby, Benjamin N., 1931–
    The daykeeper, the life and discourse of an Ixil diviner.

    Bibliography: p.
    Includes index.
    1. Ixil Indians—Religion and mythology.   2. Indians of
Central   America—Guatemala—Religion   and   mythology.
3. Koˀw, Shas.   4. Divination—Guatemala.   I. Colby, Lore
M., 1930– joint author.   II. Title.
F1465.2.I95C64   299'.78   81-372
ISBN 0-674-19409-8   AACR1

To
Alicia and Steven

PREFACE

There are not many daykeepers left among the societies descended from the pre-Columbian civilizations of Mexico and Guatemala. Fewer still are the outsiders who have known a daykeeper, heard his counsel, or seen the rituals that enable him to diagnoise a sickness or speak about the future. We were indeed fortunate when we met such a person. The man is Shas Koʔw, a daykeeper for a group of Mayans in highland Guatemala called the Ixil (pronounced *ee sheel*). We filmed his rituals, interviewed him at length, and recorded his life history, his philosophy, and his stories. The texts, our studies of them as text ethnography, and our attempt to go from these studies to a pattern-schema theory based on cultural productions are the subject of this book. It is a progression from an individual's account of his life, dreams, tales, and religious activities to a text ethnography that models some of the structures that underlie these accounts, and then from these models to a discursive general theory.

Little information is available about the lives and thoughts of Mayan peoples or of any other descendants of the American high civilizations. We hope that Shas Koʔw's texts and our study of them can help fill this gap. With these texts we are brought into the inner space of a profoundly religious person. Shas Koʔw readily spoke of ethics and rituals and of how one should honor the gods and ancestors. To his fellow Ixil he was a sage and a philosopher. As a daykeeper, he cast a handful of bean-shaped seeds on the table of his shrine to divine information about past, present, and future. The

technique is depicted in the only three hieroglyphic texts that survive from the ancient Mayans. We shall describe how Shas performed a divination, using Ixil folk narrative and his personal history
and philosophy in order to understand it. We shall also apply to the
texts analytical procedures drawn, in part, from artificial intelligence
work and the new interdisciplinary field of cognitive science. In the
process we sketch out aspects of a general pattern-schema theory
that emphasizes the dynamic interaction between the individual
and his world and combines cognitive, symbolic, and sociological
phenomena in an evolutionary perspective.

The tape recordings and transcribed texts we have collected from
Shas Koʔw will be available to scholars. It was Shas's wish that missionaries not hear his words on tape, but he was fully aware that
translations of his texts would be published and available to anyone,
and he approved this. We hope at some future time to microfilm the
original texts.

Though Shas was concerned about local missionaries who spoke
against divination, he did not want to have his identity hidden by a
pseudonym, as is often done in anthropological publishing. We
once discussed this issue at length with him. He was quite definite
that his words were to be identified as his own.

The material in this book marks the end of an epoch. An anthropologist working in Ixil country today would find that events are
moving rapidly on a tragic course. Cultural processes are now
directed by guns, not by traditional religion. The Spanish priests and
those Ixil who are active in modern Catholic religious practices
(usually the more literate), as well as the Ixil generally, have been
brutally persecuted by the national government. (See Amnesty International Paper of August 1, 1980, "Persecution of the Church in
Guatemala.") On March 3, 1980, the Guatemalan army massacred
over 40 Ixil men and women in Nebaj. On June 4, Father José María
Gran, witness of the massacre, was singled out and shot by the army,
along with his Ixil sacristan, Domingo Bats. With the pretext of carrying out a literacy campaign, the army has imposed food rationing
and tight control over most activities. The Ixil who do not have
army-issued ID cards are simply killed. The heroic stand of the
Spanish missionary priests against these and other injustices could
not withstand the systematic murdering of priests by the government and ended in their abandoning not only the Ixil area, but the

entire diocese of the department of El Quiché in June, 1980. Organizations such as Amnesty International, which work to bring public opinion to bear on the freeing of political prisoners, have no prisoners to point to in Guatemala because those who are taken for criticizing or opposing the government are shot, usually after the most inhuman treatment. The Ixil have not experienced such brutality since the time of the conquest. The material in this book was gathered before the fear and ugliness had come to the Ixil and their fellow Indians. Our analyses and commentaries were completed before the Nebaj massacre. But these new events underline the need to learn about the Ixil and to see them not merely as victims of a hypocritical, avaricious, and unbelievably cruel aggression, but as a people with richly specific thoughts, values, and feelings. Shas was a man of intelligence and compassion. It is the lack of these qualities today that is moving our history further into the darkness. The deterioration of human rights around the world calls for a renewed concern for the study of values and ethics in anthropology, for studies of cultural pathology, and for more active attempts to develop anthropological theory.

Financial support for this study was given by the National Humanities Foundation (Grant H-69-I-192) to Lore Colby, and by the National Science Foundation (Grants G.S. 2066 and 2306) and the University of California (Innovative Projects Grant) to Benjamin Colby. We were also assisted in many ways, too many to enumerate here, by our parents, to whom we cannot sufficiently express our gratitude. We also thank Friedrun Lamp, who helped us during our busiest time in Guatemala.

Among the many colleagues we are indebted to are Pierre van den Berghe and Terrence Kaufman, both of whom worked with us at one time or another. Pierre van den Berghe collaborated with Benjamin Colby in a monograph, *Ixil Country*, which was published by the University of California Press (1969). This monograph represents a macroanthropological approach and offers a general overview of social relations, particularly along ethnic lines, in the Ixil area. We are especially indebted to Pierre, with whom we have worked closely, as both friend and colleague, over many years. Some of our most stimulating and memorable occasions were in the field during the evenings, when, after a day's work, we exchanged our experiences and discussed both theoretical and methodological matters. In one sense this book emphasizes the notion of pluralism we used in *Ixil Country*, by focusing on an individual not as representing the Ixil, but simply as an interesting person who is different in many ways from other individuals in the same area.

Terrence Kaufman worked with us and our informants in 1969 and 1970 in the preparation of an Ixil dictionary, which is now on computer tape. This collaboration was in connection with the National Humanities Foundation grant to Lore˙Colby. We also acknowledge the kind assistance of Glenn Ayres, who has written a grammar of Ixil and who made suggestions for the Ixil text in Chapter 2.

Thanks are due also to Aquiles Palomino, who visited the field in 1969 with Terry Kaufman and who later did fieldwork in Chajul in 1970 and 1971. At the University of California, Irvine, Aquiles was most helpful with the two Ixil groups who visited the campus. We thank, too, Duane Metzger and the University of California, Irvine, for support through the Innovative Projects Grant to Duane and for the University's cooperation in accommodating our Ixil visitors on the campus. John Berrueta-Clement, Dorothy Clement, and Joe Harding participated in the preliminary stages of the project in the summer of 1968. John collected a number of case histories from Shas Ko²w and other informants and in addition was very helpful in arranging for the first Ixil contingent to come to Irvine.

We would also like to thank various of our missionary friends, both Catholic and Protestant, who offered hospitality when we were first getting established in Nebaj and Chajul. Padre Fernando Tirador very generously allowed Benjamin Colby to stay in the "convento" for a while in Chajul, and he also stayed a few days with Donald Lawrence and his family in Nebaj.

We are, of course, most grateful of all to our many Ixil respondents and assistants, who, in addition to Shas Ko²w, included individuals from Cotzal and Chajul as well as Nebaj. Their names are not included here because of recent events and the danger of the current irrationality in the military. Many others have given valuable data, particularly in recorded Ixil texts, of which we now have more than a thousand.

In later stages of our work other colleagues at the University of California, Irvine, have been helpful. Kim Romney provided cheerful support both in Guatemala and at Irvine, including the friendly care of our Ixil guests on flight 601 from Guatemala. We also thank our colleagues and good friends William Bardsley, Francesca Cancian, Frank Cancian, Hugh Gladwin, Jean Lave, and Ken Pierce, who all read parts of the manuscript. Barbara Metzger made many useful substantive as well as editorial suggestions. We are also indebted to many graduate students, particularly to Rodger Knaus for some stimulating collaboration during an initial analysis of the divination, which resulted in a computer program that simulated the process (Colby and Knaus, 1974); and to Betsy Rice, whose experimental work with narrative recall (Rice, 1978) has influenced our thinking about narrative processes. Waltraud Kokot, Mike Murtaugh, Carmella Moore, and Margaret Riel read parts of the manuscript and contributed useful suggestions; so also did Steve Borgatti, who assisted in the use of this book for a course on the Ixil Maya. We also thank our many undergraduate students who made suggestions after reading these materials in manuscript form in connection with the course. Emma Corrigan, Katherine Alberti, and Helen Wildman were patient and expert typists with a manuscript that was not easy.

We are also indebted to field workers who preceded us. The first person to do fieldwork in the Ixil area was Otto Stoll, a Swiss linguist who visited the area just before the initial influx of ladinos at the end of the last century. He published word lists and grammatical notes (Stoll, 1887). Later Franz Termer did a brief reconnaissance of the area (Termer, 1958). It was not until Jackson Steward Lincoln visited the area in the 1940s, however, that detailed ethnographic data were gathered (Lincoln, 1942, 1945). Shortly before we went to Ixil country, Munro Edmonson made an excursion to Chajul. We thank him for his kindness in sending us his field notes when he heard we had begun work there.

We also thank Donald Lawrence and Ray Elliot for allowing us to have a copy of Elliot's linguistic materials (1960, 1966, 1971). Elliot has since read some of the manuscript with thoughtful comments. We have had many useful interchanges with our friend and colleague Eike Hinz, Director of the Arbeitstelle für Altamerikanische Sprachen at the University of Hamburg, who spent a year at the University of California, Irvine, and visited Shas Koʔw in 1974 and collected a text from him. We also thank Eric Wanner, Harvard University Press editor, for his useful suggestions for our theory as it developed during the last revision of the manuscript.

This book is really Shas Koʔw's book, and we are grieved to report that he died just before our most recent field trip to Nebaj in June 1976. This is not the place to express our sorrow, but as the reader becomes acquainted with Shas Koʔw our sense of personal loss will be understood.

CONTENTS

THE DAYKEEPER

1
BEGINNINGS,
METHODS,
AND ISSUES

That culture shapes what we think and do is an ancient truism. Yet mapping out precisely how this happens is a task that has barely begun. There are two subfields of cultural anthropology especially concerned with this task, symbolic anthropology and ethnoscience, or more broadly, cognitive anthropology. In the past each subfield has had a widely different approach. However, in our analyses of the texts and interviews in this book we have tried to combine the interests and approaches of the two. We have used as subject matter the kind of data symbolic anthropology has focused on: myths and ritual, dreams, and a broad cultural context; at the same time we have constructed models and grammars that represent native categories of thought and that are sufficiently specified to permit different types of testing, which are all characteristic aims of cognitive anthropology. While doing this we have developed a theory that avoids the exclusively mentalistic stance of cognitive anthropology and is more specific about the locus of culture than has generally been the case in symbolic anthropology.

But more important than theory or approach is the collection and presentation of materials that are new to Mayan studies. We chose to study the Ixil because they are the most conservative and were the least studied of all the highland Maya.[1] All together there are more than twenty Mayan language groups in Guatemala and southern Mexico. Though all have links to the Mayan high culture of pre-Columbian times, the Ixil linkage retains more core elements of the ancient Mayans. Scattered through Ixil country are mounds of pyramids that go back as far as the classic period, including painted (but uncarved) stone stelae, a hallmark of the classic civilization. Even today, some of the pyramid mounds are sites of daily rituals.

One of the reasons for the continued existence of so many of the old beliefs and practices among the Ixil is the area's isolation. A river gorge and a steep ridge of mountains to the south make a formidable barrier against the more populated parts of Guatemala. To the north the land slopes more gradually to the lowland rain forests, which have been sparsely populated since the collapse of the Classic Mayan cities.

Of the three main towns of Ixil country, the principal one is Nebaj, (Naab'a in Ixil). A road that motor vehicles can travel has been open to Nebaj only during the last thirty years. The first view of Nebaj from this road comes shortly after the pass, which is almost 9,000 feet in elevation. The sight suggests to the observer what life might have been like in earlier times. Morning mist rising from streets and whitewashed adobe houses distantly suggest a sixteenth-century town. The hills and mountain slopes surrounding it are covered with luxuriant vegetation: pine and oak, maize plantings, the scrub vegetation of fallow fields, and closely cropped pasture lands. The smell of damp pine needles higher on the road gives way to that of dewy grass and recently cleared fields farther down. Here and there at lower levels are typical two-room adobe Ixil houses with the same kind of thatched roofs that Ixil houses must have had centuries before. Toward town, most of the roofs are of a darkened ocher tile. In the center the traditional Ixil houses are replaced by larger whitewashed adobe structures: church, courthouse, and the private compounds of wealthy non-Indian Guatemalans, called ladinos.

Imagine walking down the main road to town on a clear day. Distant sounds of farm animals and human activity mingle with the nearby call of a Steller's jay. Women pass by in red skirts and white blouses, some woven with elaborate and colorful designs. The women carry great jugs of steaming *tamales* and *atole*, the noon meal for the men who are planting higher up the mountain. From the road the planters form a thin line as they move slowly across the field, each with a planting stick and seed bag, just as in pre-Columbian times.

Farther down, the modern world intrudes. The telephone line rejoins the road. An old blue-and-white bus crowded with people and baggage negotiates the hairpin turns up the mountain. A small flock of sheep crosses the bridge over one of the streams that tumbles by the town. Finally, in the town center a market scene gives a mixture of old and new: vegetables and soda pop, pottery made by Quiché Indians and plastic pots of the same shape stamped out at a factory in Guatemala City. In the afternoon and evening a crowd of young people, Ixil and a few ladinos, will gather to watch television in the courthouse: American situation comedies dubbed in Spanish, commercials about refrigerators and detergent, and so on.

The thought of television in this remote town raises the matter of our reasons for being in Nebaj. What, in this modern day of fast-changing technology, can we learn from studying the Ixil that would be useful both to them and to science? We have sometimes wondered whether our work is simply an antiquarianism that today's precarious world can ill afford. This feeling is balanced, however, by the thought that if mankind does survive, many of the Ixil customs we have been studying surely will not. We have an obligation to future generations to record as much material as possible. The task has involved us in a wide range of activities—attending ceremonies, visiting other towns and hamlets, and pouring over old parish records.

Of all the experiences in our Ixil studies, the ones we enjoyed most were the times spent with the daykeeper, Shas Ko?w[2]—the man whose words are recorded in the chapters that follow. We happily recollect sitting on his porch, enjoying a cup of coffee in his house, walking with him to his maizefield. Sometimes Pap Shas joined us at our field headquarters and twice visited us in California.[3] He taught us much about the Ixil, ourselves, and anthropology—not in any single moment, but gradually, over many years. Even now, after his death, we continue to learn from the materials he gave us. Once when we seemed to be at an impasse, further analysis of these data enabled us to move ahead to part of the theoretical position described in this book.

When we first began our studies in Nebaj in 1966, anthropology, or at least anthropological theory, appeared to be at a crossroads. Although anthropology was a discipline with exciting ideas to offer, its major theoretical landmarks—Benedict's *Patterns of Culture* (1934), Murdock's *Social Structure* (1949), and various works by Boas, Malinowski, and a few others—were dated. The most interesting new development in the early sixties was the growth of a formerly obscure and tiny subfield, ethnoscience, into something now called cognitive anthropology. But the number of participants in the field was quite small. Further, by 1966 some serious problems with the approach had emerged, and not long after, the potential demise of cognitive anthropology as a viable subfield was seriously discussed (Keesing, 1972). What else was happening in anthropology then? While the public was fascinated by discoveries of early man, new archaeological finds, and even ethnographic descriptions of urban life such as Oscar Lewis's *Children of Sanchez* (1961), there was no outstanding theoretical development that would effect a major paradigm change and be of sufficient power and relevance to stimulate both neighboring social science disciplines and the intellectual public at large.[4] Though areas of social anthropology are indeed cumulative, as for example in cross-cultural studies (Naroll, 1970), no paradigm in the strict Kuhnian sense (with both a well-developed theory and a set of exemplars) had appeared. The major advances, such as those described by Pelto and Pelto (1978), had been in method rather than theory.

There is now change in the wind, much of it the result of developments in linguistics and in artificial intelligence, the new branch of computer science that attempts to model human thought. Recently areas in these two fields, along with segments of psychology concerned with discourse, have merged into a new interdisciplinary field known as cognitive science. Research in cognitive science, as well as in what we think of as "microanthropology," is concerned with how humans represent their worlds in knowledge structures, what kinds of processes they use for making inferences and decisions, how they evaluate their situation, and what kinds of feelings they have. We have used this perspective to show how some of Shas's representations can be partially formalized. But to aspire to an ethnographic understanding requires more than linguistic and semantic theories; also needed is a cultural theory that treats how experience is organized in belief systems, context-determined presuppositions, and standard behavioral procedures, as well as how feelings and emotions tie in with human activities and how this experience coupled with emotions is encapsulated in symbolic forms.

Because culture is such a complex and protean phenomenon, it would be overly austere to expect a theory to be all-encompassing at all levels of abstraction down to the actual data. If it were a very general theory, one could not expect it to be formalized mathematically with all the terms linked to the real world at a level specific enough to be tested in every particular.

Smaller, less encompassing theories have indeed been advanced. The most rigorously formal theory we know of in anthropology was proposed by Geoghegan to account for terms of personal address in Bisayan, a Philippine language (1971). Geoghegan's theory illustrates the trade-off that characterizes theory construction as it ranges from the general to the specific. In order to increase vulnerability to falsification it is necessary to have high information content. We are more interested in specific, informative theories than in near tautological ones; yet to have specific informative theories that stand up well under tests usually means that the data they explain are microcosmic, as with Geoghegan's theory of terms of personal address. Such theories are less likely to have richly ramifying explanatory value than more general ones which, alas, are less easily formalized or presented in a readily testable form. Wallace (1967), for example, has published a theory of identity structure that has a wider scope; but it is not a complete formalization even though it is stated in terms of axioms and theorems, because clear derivations of the theorems are not given. Even so, it is a step toward greater systematization. Wallace's first axiom states the widely held view that every human maintains a self-image. The second axiom subcategories the self-image into three types: ideal, indifferent, and feared. The other axioms state, in effect, that people try to be like the ideal self-image and avoid the feared one.

But formalization is not the most important desideratum in a theory. For a theory to be scientific there must be a procedure for linking the terms of the theory to empirical data so as to make the theory testable. This point has been clearly and amply set out by Gibbs (1972). Axioms and theorems without this data linkage procedure are not, in Popper's view (to which we subscribe only in part), scientific. For example, the subject of self-image or self-esteem would become especially useful if it were related to empirical results and led to an understanding of cultural or psychological mechanisms. Interesting findings in this direction have come from a cross-cultural study by Rohner (1975). Parental rejection, Rohner found, leads not only to negative self-esteem of children and adults but also to hostility, agression, emotional instability, and a negative world view.

As important as the construct of self-image is, however, it has not yet become part of a broader theory, even of the informal discursive type. It is this broader theory that we aspire to, though we feel that such a broader theory can only be reached after more work at the mid-range, or micro-level, has been done. Work at these middle and lower levels requires the writing of cultural grammars and decision models such as those we describe in Chapters 5 and 6.

Perhaps the closest approximation to an all-encompassing informal discursive theory can be seen in the summary diagram drawn by the Whitings (figure 1.1). In the Whitings' view, ecology and maintenance systems such as the economy, social structure, political

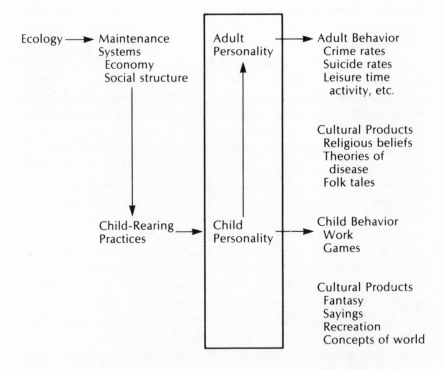

Figure 1.1.   The Whiting concept of the relation of personality and other aspects of culture.

organizations, and similar institutions provide the parameters for the behavior of people who bring up children. They see child behavior as an index of child personality, while adult behavior, beliefs, and values are indexes of adult personality. This general view has guided a large number of cross-cultural studies, though the hypotheses tested have usually been linked to the higher level only vaguely and would not be a test of a theory by any strict standard (for example, by that of Gibbs, 1972). Nevertheless, we would come close to subscribing to such a view as long as the arrows in the diagram are shown to be working in both directions; but we still prefer a theory that has greater specification and that describes the actual mechanisms of cultural processes.

Perhaps the main opponent to our approach is Marvin Harris, who espouses a kind of macroanthropological determinism. He takes a broad view of reproductive pressure, intensification of production, and the resultant environmental depletion as the main keys for understanding how family organizations, property relations, and political beliefs have evolved. So far, so good—few anthropologists would disagree. The problem comes with the word *determinism*, with which Harris seems to be enamored. In discussing historical or materialistic determinism Harris recognizes that by the term *determinism*, something would have to be shown to be the inevitable result of something else. Since human behavior has the perverse habit of being unpredictable, this term clearly will not do. He therefore speaks of a "probabilistic determinism," which is a contradiction of terms. Even with this inappropriate qualification Harris continues to make statements such as, "In my opinion, free will and moral choice have had virtually no significant effect upon the directions taken thus far by evolving systems of social life" (1978, p. xii). In Harris's view, free choice is unpredictable. By this he would have to mean either that it is unpredictable because we do not have all the information needed about a person's values, goals, and general construal of a situation to make a prediction, or that a choice is entirely random. Surely the latter is not the case; when people make decisions it is rarely done by the mental equivalent of a coin toss. Therefore, prediction is a matter of how much information is available to us. Given the limitations of our human condition, we do not have the ability to predict choices except in the roughest manner for certain types of situations. But this limited ability is not insignificant—we can anticipate some types of choices with a high probability of success. So if Harris defines free will as unpredictable, as the social sciences improve in their understanding of human behavior and are able to predict successfully an increasing (though small) amount of human behavior, free will diminishes by that amount. By that reasoning greater freedom existed before there were any successful predictions in the social sciences, which is absurd. To speak of determinism as Harris does, then, is futile. We prefer to save the term *deterministic* for rules of human behavior that have a single outcome; that is, given conditions x and y, z will always occur. Such rules can be found to hold more often in data at the micro-level of ethnography. Rules concerning language use and ritual procedures sometimes are of this type.

Harris differs from us the most in his perspective. We feel that the basis for a theory of culture must rest on the way in which the world is *construed* and must give equal weight to patterns in the external world and to internal mental structures and processes. It is the construals that we act upon, rather than upon some (non-Einsteinian) absolute reality that exists everywhere in space and time. It is not the lack of sufficient land that causes an Ixil Indian to go and work on the plantations, but rather his recognition of the fact that there is not sufficient land, plus a host of other things in his mind linking land availability to food production, family needs, and so on, which cause him to choose work on a plantation. The important thing is to account for the dynamic between the perceived external world and the mind.

The theoretical position one takes influences the kinds of data that are gathered. It is therefore useful to think about the interplay between the data-gathering process and one's theoretical position. The theoretical position that we advance here has evolved rather slowly over a long period that began before we left for the field and continues even now. Before going further into our present position, therefore, it will be helpful to describe briefly what we were thinking at the time we began our fieldwork, a time when we had not yet bridged what seemed to be a chasm between cognitive anthropology, on the one hand, and the more sociological or macroanthropology, on the other. We seemed to be wearing different hats according to the kind of data we were collecting at any give moment.

Our early fieldwork was a very open-ended situation. A typical day might have involved visits to houses around Nebaj, trips to out-lying hamlets, or interview sessions with a tape recorder. Occasion-ally we took 16-mm films. In the evenings we typed field notes about the day's activities. Rather than focusing on some particular subject, we tried to learn and record everything that came our way. It was not long, though, before choices had to be made. We were limited both in time and in resources, yet everything seemed to be changing so rapidly that we were reluctant to let anything go unstudied.

The problem was not just a matter of coverage—there were more critical questions to answer. Were we, for instance, to write an eth-nography? We were not even sure what an ethnography should be. One way to look on ethnography is as a learning experience for the writer. When one interviews three or four informants, one is doing something similar to what any Ixil does in growing up, except that the ethnographer is involved in a special kind of active writing. The experience is similar to a normal culture-learning process in that the learner, whether native or alien, is combining the accounts of several different persons to arrive at his own interpretative structure—an eclectic activity involving different processes of inference, deduc-tion, and analysis about the consistency and esteem or truth value accorded each individual source. The outcome of all this is the indi-vidual's own special cultural system, the specific variant of a culture that exists in the mind of a user of that culture together with that person's exterior cultural world.

The descriptions of the ethnographer are part of the ethnogra-pher's cultural system. The ethnographer has become to some de-gree bicultural, in the same way that linguists become to some de-gree bilingual when they study a new language. The ethnographer's production, as it exists on paper, has certain advantages in that it was written for other aliens, answers some questions that native infor-mants would not think to make explicit, and has the expository ad-vantage of anthropological training and of a perspective that is built up from a knowledge of other societies. The description is some-thing like a translation for the ethnographer's home society. Ethnog-raphers try to describe situations that many of their readers will never have experienced. The ethnographer and reader share a vo-cabulary that can be used to describe a tropical rain forest or a hunt-ing expedition in terms that will be meaningful to the reader even if that reader has never been to the tropics.

But the abstract concepts of native users of a cultural system can be quite different from those of the nonnative ethnographer's society, and there still remains the problem of different experiential backgrounds. How good a job, we asked, can the ethnographer do in dealing with such concepts and different experiences? Is there any difference between an ethnographer's description and one an observant tourist or informed traveler might write? Certainly there must be a difference, at least in the matter of accuracy and detail, but unless we had a way of assessing the accuracy of description, we were not sure we could regard ethnography as a scientific enterprise. To do so, we came to recognize, we would have to develop ways of measuring accuracy or testing observations—in other words, determining the *validity* of our observations and avoiding our own idiosyncratic biases.

The bias problem had been highlighted by some of the restudies that followed from the large increase in the number of anthropologists doing fieldwork. When Oscar Lewis restudied Tepoztlan (1951), he wrote a report that was radically different from one made earlier by Robert Redfield (1930). Which was the more valid, less biased description? By the time we were beginning the Ixil study, there was much talk among anthropologists about this need for validation, particularly validation of representations of an inner view—a view of a society in terms of native categories of thought. Traditional ethnographies were criticized as being arbitrarily organized around the ethnographer's own academic orientations, as revealed by chapter headings like "Social Organization," "Kinship," "Religion," "Economics," and so on. A simple solution some of our colleagues tried was to take native terms as chapter headings and use them liberally in the descriptions. Though that approach helped, it struck us as far from adequate to deal with the deeper levels of the problem.

This is not to denigrate traditional ethnographies. Indeed, in some respects the ethnographer's writings, even of a traditional kind, if sufficiently informed, may be superior to what might be written by an educated native on his own culture (which may have biases of quite a different sort). Much rests, however, on the expression "sufficiently informed." By informed we mean not only valid, but also conversant with scientific theory and methodology. Without a viable theory of culture, everything else, including the gathering of data, must suffer. Since a comprehensive theory of culture that is interesting and vulnerable to disproof has not been advanced, we could scarcely blame ourselves and our colleagues for what is very largely an ad hoc approach in gathering data.

Not only did anthropology lack a theory of culture that was adequate for our needs, it also lacked a precise and useful definition of culture. To be sure, there were plenty of definitions available. Most of the standard definitions stem from Tylor's: "Culture or civilization . . . is that complex whole which includes knowledge, belief, art, law, morals, custom, and any other capabilities and habits acquired by man as a member of society" (1958, p. 1). From Tylor's work and that of other writers of the period, particularly Spencer, a notion was developed that saw culture as more than the sum of individual knowledge and abilities. It was, in Kroeber's words, not organic, or mental, but "superorganic"—something over and above the sum of each individual's actions. When Kroeber used the term "superorganic," he reified it by speaking of "entities" or "substances" (1952, p. 23). His anthropological brethren jumped on this reification, rather than questioning the basic notion, and he retracted it. Even today, though, the great majority of anthropological writings on culture reflects an underlying superorganic bias. According to Bidney, "It is generally agreed among anthropologists that culture is a superorganic phenomenon" (1967, p. 34). This traditional notion of culture was useful while anthropology remained a matter of noting the presence or absence of culture traits and recording disappearing languages; but for an understanding of how culture changes through time or is located in space, it is inadequate.

One reason this concept does not work is that culture is not a well-demarcated unit. For example, some of us think of Swedes and Finns as Scandinavians and therefore as being more alike than either group is to peoples farther south, say, Italians. When we examine the components people usually think of as defining some particular "culture," however, we run into difficulty. Both Swedes and Italians speak Indo-European languages, while the Finns speak a language that is totally different. Does that mean we should not use language to define Scandinavian culture? Which cultural criteria should we use to judge similarity if not language—common values? Similar social organization? The same kind of difficulty comes up with these other components as well. If we want to delimit Ixil culture, do we include that of the Ixil who have been converted to modern Catholicism or Protestantism? Or the culture of those who have moved to plantations and have married speakers of a different language, or their children? Where do we draw the line? The traditional idea of culture is of little use for detailed study because it needs boundaries. According to the traditional definitions, cultures must have a "skin," but it is obvious that they do not.

Another problem with the traditional definition of culture is that it compartmentalizes something that is an interactive system. Anthropologists who studied the psychological side of human life described their subfield as "culture and personality," personality being treated as something distinct from culture. This separation assumed the standard anthropological view of culture as something exclusively external to the individual. The standard view is that, ideally, a well-adjusted personality must be compatible with cultural norms. Sanity is measured by conformity to a culturally standardized view of the world and to norms for behaving in that world. Pathology, then, is defined in terms of deviance from such norms. Consequently, in order to make decisions about a person's mental condition, culture and mind must be seen as distinct from each other, and culture itself is never adjudged to be pathological. Laing, Lasche, Fromm, Arendt, and many others have questioned this view, but anthropologists rarely do; for to adjudge some culture or world view as sick is to risk imposing one's own culture-bound biases. Thus the traditional notion of culture is partly shaped by our ideas about other things, such as personality, and the notion of culture in turn shapes our definition of personality.

This emphasis on what results in a spurious clarity leads to another implication of the traditional definition of culture: the matter of the "modal" or typical person. When Cora Du Bois wrote *The People of Alor* (1944) she brought together biographies, dreams, Rorschach tests, and other data from eight informants. When her monograph was published, the question of modal personality and cultural representativeness dominated criticisms of her work. The same kind of criticism was used against other life histories as well. The individuals who told their stories to the anthropologist usually were more intellectual than their brethren and hence, so the criticisms went, were nonrepresentative. The flaw in such criticisms is that no one has ever answered the question of how one discovers who a typical individual is, let alone the question of what is meant by typical, or the question of what theoretical purpose a typical description would serve. A typical individual could be identified only if the society were essentially homogeneous or if one could develop a statistical model that somehow would average a series of traits. Still, if any sizable quantity of traits were used it is most unlikely that any single individual in the group would match the model. We hope that our analysis of the materials in this book will demonstrate the meaninglessness of the expression "typical individual" and show why the selection of unusually cerebral or articulate individuals in a social group may well have a greater theoretical yield than the choice of some seemingly unremarkable person thought to be somehow more typical of "a culture."

There is one final issue we want to eliminate from our present ethnographic purpose: we are not interested in dwelling on inconsistencies or "distortions" between Shas's account and some external "objective" position. The various distortions in the way a person views space and time can be of great interest, but one cannot measure or assess them without a thorough study of the same material from an outside vantage point. And such a vantage point, though important, rests on shaky perceptual foundations. Furthermore, practically speaking it would have been difficult to trace out the people Shas refers to in his life story. Most of them are no longer alive. Nor was there much time for such a study after we began to recognize the value of Shas's texts as they accumulated.

These are just a few of the many issues we faced in considering the traditional ethnographic approach during this first stage of our work. There were other kinds of problems as well, some of which stemmed from professional demands. For example, there may be strong pressure on the ethnographer to present a single, integrated picture. Loose ends and inconsistencies are too often considered to be a shortcoming of the ethnographic procedure rather than a possible reflection of reality, so the ethnographer slips into the habit of looking for *the* belief or *the* way something is done. This pressure might explain why the older view of culture as a holistic, harmonious configuration persists in the face of the obvious fact that most societies are pluralistic and teem with inconsistencies, variations, and conflicts.

The strain toward ethnographic consistency exists for the study of single individuals as well as for social groups, and ethnographers are

not alone. Most tests administered by clinical psychologists are pred-
icated on the assumption of a pervasive cognitive coherence in the
individual being studied. For both ethnographic description and
personality analysis, unless some narrowly circumscribed behavior in
a regularized context is being studied, the phenomena described as
"clear-cut," "modal," and "consistent" are often a result of the observer's need to find regularity.

Once we free ourselves from the strain for coherent elegance and
simple statements about *the* way things are seen and done in a culture, and once we dismiss the question of whether or not an individual is typical of his social group, there still remains the question of
validity. Concern about one type of validity sometimes referred to as
psychological reality (Wallace, 1961) was responsible for the rapid
development of modern ethnoscience (Romney and D'Andrade,
1964, reviewed in Colby, 1963, 1966a). The main significance of this
approach was that traditional ethnography was seen as inadequate,
along with the superorganic notion of culture; culture was instead
defined in terms of rules and semantics in people's heads. The ethnoscience approach was linguistically oriented and consisted mostly
in mapping out the ways in which the terms of some domain, such
as plants, animals, color terms, or kin terms, were related by natives
in hierarchical and other types of structures. The most rigorous and
extensive application of this approach was by Metzger and his colleagues (Metzger and Williams, 1963; Black and Metzger, 1969). For
many purposes, cognitive anthropologists today assume that culture,
though manifested externally in cultural productions such as folktales, games, and artifacts, resides in the mind as rules and chunks of
information. This was essentially our position when we began the
Ixil fieldwork; however, it was only a partial solution to the problems
we were thinking about, and we have since rejected it.

Cognitive anthropology originally was linguistically inspired, but
linguistics had changed and was almost entirely dominated by
transformational generative grammar studies (Chomsky, 1957, 1965).
The Chomskian view ran counter to an anthropological understanding of how people thought and communicated (Colby, 1966a). Although we thought that there was a deep structure, we did not agree
with the idea of transformation. (This was all on an intuitive basis.)
Since then, psycholinguistic studies have indeed cast strong doubt
on the theory that language comprehension involves transforma-

tional rules (Wanner, 1974; Wanner and Maratsos, 1978). Furthermore, the transformational school supported the old relativistic holism indirectly through the treatment of each language as a closed, synchronic system. Diachronic and dialectal changes and contexts of speaking had been virtually ignored in linguistics, at least during the early ethnoscience phase of cognitive anthropology. The pictures drawn were static ones. Fortunately, this approach has recently changed, with increasing attention being given to performance rather than competence, to the way things are said and done in all their imperfections and variations (Hymes, 1974).

In the first stage of our fieldwork many of these issues had not been resolved in our own minds. But we were aware that even if they had been resolved, entirely new issues and solutions would surely appear in the future. We did not want to have a theoretical bias influencing the collection of our data so strongly as to render the data invalid for later scholars. Future investigators, whose more sophisticated theories would render our own ethnology obsolete, might have use for material which to us might have been of only secondary interest. We thus tried to be broad in a way that did not preclude the possibility of subsequent deep analysis of the data. To minimize the bias of the ethnographer's description, we decided to emphasize the collection of texts given to us by the Ixil themselves—texts which, for the most part, were recorded in the Ixil language on tape.[5]

Of course, there are always limitations in planning an ethnographic exploration. One must consider the cost in both resources and time as well as the ease of getting the desired information. An ethnographer can interview an informant about a particular subject and report the relevant details or he can tape the same interview; beyond that, he can tape, transcribe, and translate it while still in the field. Similarly, in the observation of rituals the ethnographer may not have the opportunity of seeing some event more than once. He must weigh and consider how much more productive a use of his own limited time or funds it would be to photograph or film some event that will not be repeated during his stay in the field. In addition to being useful for centuries hence, taped interviews, photographs, and filmed rituals are subsequently helpful to the person who has collected them: one can notice things missed during the actual event or show the record to other natives for their comment.

Ethnographic cost accounting, however, may dictate otherwise. Furthermore, if the ethnographer is filming the action he may miss important elements because of the blinder effect of looking through the camera.

In our own case, we tried to do a little of everything, always emphasizing exact recording, both on film and on tape. We had the opportunity to study many of the texts published here afterwards with Shas himself, and he clarified and amplified his recorded statements. We also collected over a thousand texts from more than thirty additional informants, and interviewed still others. Though these additional texts have not yet been published, they gave us comparative perspective for this, our first depth study. We felt that this was the best way to begin a study of Ixil life and culture.

As we analyzed the texts and field observations, we saw that work in a different area of anthropology—symbolic anthropology—was close to the task before us. Symbolic anthropology has a long history, with its deepest roots in Frazer's *Golden Bough*. After languishing through the thirties, forties, and fifties, the discipline regained vigor and visibility in the sixties and seventies. This is probably because modern symbolic anthropology is in part a response to the inadequacies of ethnoscience and cognitive anthropology, or at least to the inadequacies that had become most evident by that time. The symbolic anthropologists, in responding to areas overlooked by cognitive anthropology, were not worried about the main problem— that of validity—which had engendered cognitive anthropology in the first place. Their chief contribution was the emphasis on symbolic relevance and "thick" description (Geertz, 1973) in which observations are interpreted against a rich contextual background. One might argue that this is validity of another kind, and indeed we believe it is. But while the contextualizing of observations is surely one way of adding specificity, it pushes the question of validity back to the observation's context, which is just as subject to a biased description as the object or event itself. Nevertheless the context of situation, as Malinowski emphasized years ago, is absolutely essential, and many descriptions by symbolic anthropologists are excellent ethnographic resources because of the contextual background provided.

Perhaps the major difficulty in symbolic anthropology was a fuzzy notion of culture. In our early work we decided that, unless otherwise specified, the term "culture" should be used as an unbound variable. When precise statements are to be made, the term "culture" should be bound to a specific statement or, eventually, to a theoretical model. Binding can be done simply by specifying: "Ixil mythic culture" or "that production of Shas Koʔw's mental schemata which is recorded on tape number 30." In the first instance, a further specification of what is meant by Ixil mythic culture might be necessary, depending on the task at hand; the second is specific enough. Even now, with our pattern-schema theory of culture, this is a handy procedure.[6] Nevertheless, it begs the question. Symbolic anthropology offered no solution, so in this stage of our work the treatment of culture as an entirely cognitive phenomenon made manifest in productions such as folktales or divinatory readings had its advantages; and we thought that by studying particular domains or genres of cultural phenomena we could approximate the cognitive system that would produce them. This approximation we saw as a kind of cultural grammar, where the rules of the grammar could be tested against new samples of the genre just as a newly written language grammar can be tested with new sentences. This cultural grammar included rules for ritual and myth as well as rules for semantic domains such as kinship terminology.

We also thought (wrongly, in some respects) of culture as something that could be examined piecemeal. Indeed, cultural phenomena sometimes seemed to be closer by far to the "shreds and patches" of Gilbert and Sullivan's wandering minstrel in *The Mikado* than to Benedict's beautifully integrated configurations. Cultural patches, we believed, were passed along not only to people in other social groups but to children in one's own group. Such patches might be relatively separate cultural subsystems or minicultures for a wide variety of activities ranging from the simple tasks of recalling shopping lists to hunting and story telling. Learning a foreign language is an example of the transferability of a large cultural patch. From a perspective that is not austere we still believe the piecemeal or genre approach is viable for some purposes. Kroeber spoke of such patches as "systemic patterns." Yet one pattern or constellation of patterns, even if it is easily transportable—lock, stock, and barrel—to another society, is learned *in the context* of other patterns and of feelings about those patterns. Our view of the cultural process now spans both the inner (psychological) and outer (sociological) worlds and covers affective phenomena as well as cognitive and symbolic phenomena. While our analysis may concentrate on one simple genre or domain, the gathering of data should never be an exclusively piecemeal process. The context of the situation must also be included.

The main impetus for our grammar-writing stage came from a study one of us did of Eskimo folktales (Colby, 1973). The result was a grammar that could account for any well-told folktale from an Eskimo group that was relatively unchanged by modern resettlement and technology. The writing of a grammar that successfully accounted for new Eskimo stories from traditional groups had brought us to a very strong view of culture as a system of systems in the mind. This approach was akin to a branch of linguistic theory that has only recently begun to receive attention in American anthropology, systemic theory, particularly as represented in the work of M. A. K. Halliday (Halliday and Hasan, 1976; Halliday, 1977). Like systemic theory, the theory of culture systems we were developing then emphasized that, while each individual member of a social group thinks and behaves slightly differently from the others of his group, in certain areas behavior is so strongly conventionalized that these individual differences are much less apparent, and cultural grammars can be written to describe its regularities (Colby, 1975). Even though ethnography is, almost by definition, a description of conventionalized behavior, few attempts have been made to write (nonlinguistic) grammars. In fact, Keesing (1972) and others did not think a cultural grammar was possible.

It was during this analytical state that Shas visited us in California. The first visit, in August 1968, was in conjunction with an innovative projects grant of the University of California to Duane Metzger, our colleague in the School of Social Sciences. The purpose of this particular project was to develop alternative approaches to the teaching of anthropology to undergraduates. In connection with the project, Pap Shas brought some Ixil companions with him: a carpenter and a couple and their small child. These people acted as informal faculty for an undergraduate course on Ixil society, which included the building of an Ixil house on the campus. During this visit we recorded additional tales and sections of his life story, and we checked with him on various points in the translation. The Eskimo grammar study had just begun, and we were not yet sure whether a grammar outside the area of language proper was a realistic goal. A second visit, in 1970, had primarily linguistic and ethnographic purposes. A National Humanities grant to Lore Colby had made it possible to bring one person from each of the three Ixil dialect areas to work with her and linguist Terry Kaufman. Shas was our Nebaj dialect representative. By this time we had decided that an attempt should be made to work out a grammar for Pap Shas's divinatory system. Therefore, in addition to gathering new texts and doing further work on his life story, we interviewed him extensively on his divinations. Perhaps because he was so far out of his geographical context, where many of the gods are directly associated with local geographical features, he was willing to discuss hypothetical divinations, and we collected a good number of hypothetical readings from him.

Some time after Shas left, we moved into the last stage of the theoretical work for this book. We had wondered whether it would ever be possible for a single theory to account for symbolic and cognitive systems of individuals and at the same time include the wider context and macrosystems of the societies they live in. There was not only a "two-cultures" gap between the two subfields of microanthropology, cognitive and symbolic anthropology, but there was also a gap between microanthropology and macroanthropology. Very few anthropologists were able to bridge the gap between the two, and when they did it was in a somewhat schizoid or compartmentalized fashion. To most scholars it seemed that one had to take either an inner-view approach or an outer-view approach, but not both. Each was necessary for different purposes, and each was assigned priorities according to one's own inclinations.

Many considered the outside view, the macroanthropological approach, as the more relevant. Obviously, cultural processes and changes are often affected, if not directly produced, by events that are better described from some external vantage point rather than from what is thought to lie inside a single mind. There are hard, cold facts, such as the amount of arable land available to families, the cost of a specific economic transaction, and the scarcity or abundance of money or goods required for ritual, that can be objectively described. Soil analysis and estimates of soil productivity based on modern scientific studies may explain a great deal about environmental pressures on culture change that could not be accounted for by any native statement. Though it is helpful for such data to be complemented by native statements, the data, if well measured, are usually sufficient for some types of very basic anthropological studies. Such an external view can be made precise if by culture we include results produced through the use of the mental schemata that lead to behavior. Behavior, therefore, is seen as a physical phenomenon. Even words are physical in the sense of being carried in sound waves. This external view does not conflict with the internal one if we treat the former as productions that have patterns, the latter as schemata, and the two together as a cultural system.

A key part of our discursive theory is the interrelation of these patterns and schemata. A pattern is an arrangement of elements or events in the world that is recognized as regular by the beholder. It is the cultural patterns that give us a sense of coherence and security about the social world. Without cultural patterns our social world would be a seemingly random, senseless, atomized environment impossible to live in. Patterns are a crucial part of our lives.

But patterns have to be recognized as such, and this recognition depends on the systems of schemata that we carry around in our heads. Schemata are representations of elements, events, and relationships existing in the mind of an individual (Bartlett, 1932; Piaget, 1962; Colby, 1966b; Becker, 1973; Rice, 1980). Since schemata are not directly observable we can only speculate about what they are. Regardless of how they are represented neurophysiologically, we do have methods of approximating the way schemata are "chunked" as codings of information, the way they change through experience, and how they may be used in a larger system. One of these methods is eidochronic analysis, described in Chapter 5.

To summarize, we can say simply that culture is localized both in the patterns and the schemata. It is both external (the world) and internal (the mind). The chief dynamic is in the interaction between the two. But the external world is always mediated by the observer's eyes, ears, and other senses, whether the observer is a native or an alien.

The cognitive or schema part of the cultural system calls for an "emic" approach. This concept is based on the analogy of phonemic analysis, where in a linguistic study of a language a detailed phonetic rendering of a string of words is changed to a phonemic one. The sounds that make a psychological difference to the speakers of a language are the phonemes of the language. A phonetic rendering utilizes an overdifferentiated set of symbols brought by the linguist to study the language even before he begins working with the language. The distinction between an "etic" analysis (categories imposed by the analyst who is just beginning to become familiar with the language) and an "emic" one is now well known in anthropology and is used rather loosely to mean an outer and an inner view of culture, respectively. By emphasizing the desirability of emic analysis, though, we do not mean to exclude the external world with which an individual interacts.

The interactive dynamic involves at least three processes: selection (matching and decision or choice), creation, and generation. These are key processes in the microevolution of cultural patterns and may be visualized in the following way:

	SELECTION	CREATION	GENERATION	
Problem ------▶	Examine ------▶ situation	Modulate ------▶ Transform	Apply ---▶ solution	Store result as
	Examine solution schemata	Add		modified solution schemata

In the selection process we see each individual as existing in a particular set of circumstances and exposed to a particular variety of patterns. In any given situation, the self usually is aware of several patterned responses or "solution schemata" that he has seen other people use. To be sure, this repertoire of observed and remembered responses may consist in narrow variations on what is essentially the same pattern sequence, but it could also be a wider repertoire of different sequences. In either case one chooses what is thought to be the most appropriate response for some situation and sees what the results are. From the results the solution schemata are modified for possible future applications.

Existing cultural patterns are selected in differing frequencies partly because the people selecting them are differentially exposed to the situations in which the patterns may be appropriate. In addition to different histories, temperaments, and situation goals, there are bound to be variations in emphasis. Over time, with changes in external situations rarer patterns may become the modal ones, and common ones, more rare.

Creation concerns the way patterns themselves change and are modulated to fit varying situations. Here is where dreams may be instrumental through the process of reinterpreting a person's concerns symbolically. The metaphoric scrambling that occurs in dreams brings in fresh ways of interpreting one's life situation and responding to it. Though the neurophysiological evidence is still lacking, we think that mental activity during waking life somehow locks in ways of thinking and behaving that become unlocked through dreams, whether or not they are remembered the next morning. Myths, through providing a rich set of symbols, may have a role in making suggestions at the unconscious level for the use of symbols that are pregnant with metaphoric possibilities. In the Ixil case, dreams represent a communication from the gods. There is at least the possibility that dreams can change religious beliefs over time, and it falls upon the more rigid intermediate cultural devices, such as divination, to maintain the more conventional traditions.

In other words, it is in the nature of culture change that these cultural patterns be chosen in differing frequencies by different members of a social group according to (1) their exposure to the productions that embody the pattern and (2) their exposure to situations in which the pattern seems to be an apt model or guide for behavioral response to that situation. In sum, the people of a social group are differentially attracted to different cultural productions and their patterns.

At the same time, the *availability* of cultural patterns is important. This availability is determined by yet other cultural patterns (for example, the local political system), so we are dealing with a complex network which is partially a recursive phenomenon.

Our discursive theory encompasses more than an interaction between self and situation during some short segment of time—it goes beyond to a motivational component that is based on a history, which therefore covers a much longer time dimension. It is a biohistorical theory as well as a cognitive-situational one. The motives that push us to act are a result of our past, both the goals we have attained and those we have missed. These histories produce feelings, and the feelings attach evaluations to the events and processes we experience. Through such experiences we build up a self-image of abilities and a system of evaluation for assessing situations and determining feasible goals.

This process leads to a social and ecological contextualization which can be a point of entry to the macroanthropological analysis of a social system. The culture of such a system is the total set of interactive processes for a person or a group of people rather than the mental or cognitive system alone which each person carries in his head. The cultural system includes cultural productions, cognitive systems (including an emotional aspect), and the interaction between them (figure 1.2).

Culture thus includes both external and internal phenomena and in either case has a locus, but only in the internal case can we speak of a boundary—the brain case. Such a definition does not require reification of the sort Kroeber made nor the etherealization found in Geertz's writings (1973).

Actually, in this new view the locus question no longer seems as relevant as it once did. The cultural process is the dynamic inter-

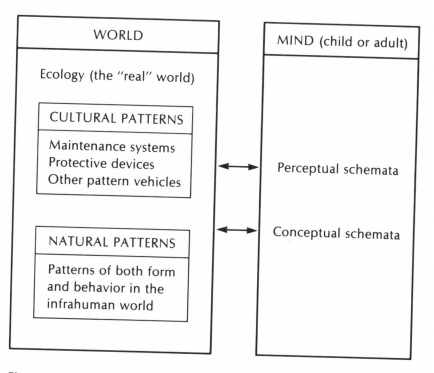

Figure 1.2. Cultural and natural patterns interacting with the mind. Cultural patterns and mental schemata constitute a cultural system.

action between inner and outer, and it is the process itself that is most important. The mind is in a fluid state, subject to continual modification as the inner systems of schemata are utilized for cultural productions (including speech) which are instantiated in the outer patterns discerned in these productions (for example, syntactic regularities discerned in a speech utterance). This process requires a definition of culture, shown in the equation below:

$$\text{culture } (G) = \sum_{i \in G} S_i, \sum_{i \in G} P_i$$

where G = a group of individuals; S = schema systems in the minds of individuals; and P = patterns available to, or observable by, individuals.

A person's cultural system has been learned through contact with cultural patterns—mostly behavioral patterns seen in significant others: parents, siblings, close relatives, and friends who act as models for the person to learn from. A person is thus a product of his history and the current situation as well as being a biological organism.

How cultural patterns are attended to, forgotten, and reconstructed has been overly neglected in anthropology.[7] In this we want to especially emphasize the idea of cultural devices and their linkages to commonly experienced situations. Though he does not use the term "cultural device," Roberts has been especially influential on our thinking in this direction (Roberts, 1964, 1965; Roberts and Sutton-Smith, 1962, 1966; Ridgeway and Roberts, 1976), and we feel that his notions of cultural models and buffered learning have received insufficient attention. Roberts, Sutton-Smith, Moore (and much earlier, Montessori [1963]) think of games and physical artifacts that children become involved with as mechanisms for teaching strategies about dealing with people and the material world in very subtle ways. This extends to other assemblages, or genres of cultural patterns. Many anthropologists, for example, have worked with the linkage of devices such as proverbs and sayings to social life.[8]

The dynamic approach requires the analysis of the "thick" context that productions such as these provide as well as the cultural grammars that approximate cognitive systems. Thick context can include different types of context—not only linguistic, but discursive, situational, and cultural (Geertz, 1973).

We think that what is needed now is a means of bringing these different strands in anthropology closer together by solving some of the problems that have kept them apart. One direction is that of emphasizing context, the other is its partial formalization. Here is where cognitive science has been especially helpful, as will be seen in later chapters, and we hope that this book will provide a useful example for anthropologists seeking to use artificial intelligence approaches, regardless of whether or not computers are involved. Though a model of divination was actually programmed and run (Colby and Knaus, 1974), the later (and very different) model in Chapter 6 has not been programmed. In fact, none of the analysis in this book has involved computers. The chief value of cognitive science for anthropology lies in its empirical contributions rather than in the ad hoc engineering decisions that are made in artificial intelligence work. Even so, the engineering is a valuable inspiration for empirical tests.[9]

It is hard to identify any single purpose as the main theme of this book. From one point of view the entire book is the pursuit of an Ixil metaphor and all its entailments: the equation of sickness and imprisonment. From another perspective it is an ethnography of a role, that of daykeeper (ʔ aaqʼ ii), and some of the knowledge and processes that are focal to that role. Or from a theoretical viewpoint this book might be seen as a primarily discursive exposition of a theory of culture which encompasses feelings as well as "rational" cognition.[10]

No matter which of the three viewpoints may be salient for the reader, all are merely adjuncts to the fact that this is a record of a single man's cultural productions, given to us on tape, edited mentally as he went along for those he was talking to and, increasingly, for the wider audience he knew his words would eventually reach, including his own descendants.

The progression of the chapters will illustrate the approach we have developed in roughly the same order in which we initially analyzed the materials, except for some additional discussion and analyses which readers of the manuscript suggested we include in the next two chapters. Shas's texts in the pages to follow are, we hope, comprehensive enough to permit the reader to "bootstrap" himself into an understanding of an alien cultural system with a minimum of explanatory promptings by the ethnographer. Rather than interposing our own viewpoint between the actual observations and the reader, we present it in notes and commentary—except for the chapter immediately following, which provides a brief introduction to the historical and religious background of the Ixil. The commentary on the texts has grown with succeeding drafts and we hope it does not overly detract from the texts themselves, which are the raison d'être of the book. The reader can be his own ethnographer by reading Shas Koʔw's own statements and deciding whether our interpretations seem reasonable. We hope that through such a first-hand experience the reader will develop some sense of personal relationship with Shas, as well as a detailed view of a different way of life.

2
HISTORICAL
AND RELIGIOUS
BACKGROUND

The task of ethnography is to understand some cultural system. This requires that we make cultural patterns explicit and try to account for their occurrence. But much of what an ethnographer sees and describes is patterned in ways which are not readily discerned and which even the native participants of a cultural system may not be able to explain consciously. The longer the period of immersion in a new surrounding of cultural patterns, the better is the understanding, even without explicit recognition of patterns as patterns. In other words, the context is fundamental for the interpretation of culture, and the contextual understanding can go a long way toward deciding whether a construed pattern isolated by that ethnographer has significance to the long-time participants—the natives.

Likewise, the reader of an ethnography will not be in a good position to judge the validity or even plausibility of formal ethnographic models unless he is apprised of the contextual background. In this chapter we describe the cultural and historical context necessary to understand Shas's testimony.

HISTORY

Preconquest

Ixil oral traditions go back to the times when the people of the first creation were thought to have built the pyramids whose ruins dot the landscape. These early people were endowed with strong magical powers that allowed them to "throw" the stones in order to build their houses, which seemed to withstand destruction so much longer than present-day houses. They thought of themselves as being equal to god, an attitude that bothered Kub'aal, the high god. He tried to destroy this first population by sending illness, fire, and water; but after hearing his plans, these strong people fought back.

They made slingshots (ʔiqaʔl) and they climbed on top of the mountains, and on top of the highest mountains they built their houses—and from there they watched the sickness arrive and they shot at it, they frightened it, they chased it, they did not let it come close, and the sickness went away.[1]

They also survived the fire, sent like a stream of lava, by hiding inside wells, rivers, and caves. And finally they survived the enormous flood that was the last punishment:

Our Father could not destroy the people with the flood, either. There were men who made boxes and there were men who made their houses; little was needed for the men to reach the sky with their houses.
   One man, a rich man, the owner of a house, climbed to the top part of the house, he almost reached the sky.[2]

Kub'aal was impressed by the resourcefulness of the survivors and asked the wind god to bring them before him. He bestowed new status and responsibilities upon them by giving them the task of watching directly over the new population to be created.
   The next creation was the present-day population, referred to as "the children of Kub'aal." Kub'aal in this context is the younger son of the high god whose creation of intelligent, well-behaved humans evokes the envy of the older sons, who only created frogs and snakes. They try to kill the younger brother, but he survives the ordeal through his resourcefulness and the hostile brothers are banned to a dark place by the old Father Kub'aal. Preconquest myths have

merged with Christian motifs in this story about the conflict of the creator Kub'aal, sometimes called Jesus Christ, with his persecutors, his older brothers. This same story without the Christian images is in the *Popul Vuh.*

The pyramids of Ixil country are fewer and less impressive than those of Tikal, Copan, or other sites in the Usumacinta Basin and Yucatán, but they show that the region participated in Classic Mayan high culture. This long tradition is one of the reasons we were initially attracted to the Ixil area. One pyramid at Nebaj, studied by Smith and Kidder (1951), yielded what may have been the cover of a codex (a pre-Columbian pictographic book), and hieroglyphic writing appears on pottery found there. Ball courts and stone monuments (stelae) that once were painted are also found at sites in Ixil country.

Archaeologists first considered the Ixil to be important middlemen in the trade between the highlands to the south and the lowland rain forests to the north (Smith and Kidder, 1951), but later work by Smith and Kidder and by Adams (1969) and Becquelin (1969) has shown that trade was minimal and confined to the life span of the great Classic lowland cities. When the cities were abandoned, the Ixil, isolated to the north by a depopulated area and to the south by mountains and a deep river gorge, seem to have carried on the Classic tradition as a kind of backwater survival pocket. The sweeping changes of the post-Classic period, in the direction of secularization and militarism, largely passed the Ixil by (see Colby, 1976).

It is possible that this isolation broke down for a time. From a brief mention in the *Rabinal Achi* (a highland Maya text transcribed in the Western alphabet shortly after the conquest), it appears that one of the Quiché rulers may have won domination over, or tribute from, the Ixil. This account has not been corroborated, nor is there much evidence that anything more than a temporary subjugation followed this incursion, if indeed it took place.[3]

In any event, the isolation of the Ixil has been the reason for their cultural conservativism. And it was the conservativism of the Ixil that was our main reason for choosing them. The isolation of the Ixil was not just a pre-Columbian characteristic, however; they continued to be isolated, comparatively speaking, even after the Spanish conquest.

Postconquest

After the Ixil had been conquered by the Spanish in 1530, there was a thirty-year period during which little was done to follow up the victory. Even with the coming of missionaries at the end of this period, the Spanish presence remained much weaker than elsewhere, but the priests did manage to effect a radical transformation in Ixil religion. Not only did they have the military power, but they also had the religious power—victory in war being seen as a sign of supernatural favor and of superior gods that it might be unwise to ignore.

However, this initial advantage was weakened by sickness. The disease and disruption brought by the conquerors caused a dramatic drop in population, which reached its lowest point in the second quarter of the eighteenth century. This drop coincided with a halt to the rapid acculturation toward the Hispanic world. By then many of the old customs had already been changed or lost. Much of this loss probably occurred because there were not enough people around to fulfill some of the roles that represented special ritual and esoteric skills. If we look upon a society as having a pool of ideas, myths, folktales, and other traditions, with some of these carried only in the heads of specialists, we can see how there might be a critical point in depopulation at which some of this information would be permanently lost. Many elements of the culture pool may have been lost more because of drastic population decline than because of Spanish prohibitions, though economic and political changes certainly played their part. Another reason for cultural conservativism after the initial period of change may well have been the reaction to the widespread sickness: if sickness was supernatural punishment, then it might be logical to associate divine displeasure with the Spanish presence. But this, of course, can only be conjecture.

From 1750 on the population slowly began to increase, but Ixil culture lagged behind the changes that were taking place among the dominant ladino peoples of Guatemala. This cultural lag existed in many other areas as well. In isolated pockets of Mesoamerica today, one still can see elements of customs being maintained centuries after they have changed or disappeared elsewhere. Guatemala gained independence from Spain in 1821, and the Indians, along with the Spaniards and people of mixed heritage, became citizens of the country. Catholic priests still visited the area, but they were very few and did not attempt, at least with any energy, to hold the Indians to orthodox Catholicism. Because of the isolation and autonomy of the Ixil region, the priests were in no position to eliminate those elements of the old religion that remained. Ixil autonomy was a consequence of the withdrawal of Spanish power, the war, and the political turmoil of the early years of independence. It was augmented by special favors granted the Ixil by President Barrios in appreciation for their help during his early revolutionary activities.

Until the 1890s, then, the Ixil remained almost completely isolated from the national life of Guatemala. This independence and isolation allowed the continued survival of those cultural features that had come down from the earlier time. Lincoln (1942) reported that, at the turn of the century, the Ixil were divided into four castes or estates: warriors, priests, merchants, and workers. We found no evidence for such a division, but there is certainly evidence for a rich culture in the late nineteenth century. The Ixil painted elaborate murals depicting rituals in homes and public buildings.[4] They also painted designs on the ceilings of the churches. Many of the designs on the church ceiling of Chajul and on the blouses woven by women are animal figures. Animal figurines were placed along the ridges of the tile roofs, too, though this practice is rarer now than before, and no known significance was attached to it by the Ixil we asked.

The Ixil still used aboriginal musical instruments—logs and turtle-shell drums—in dance-dramas and dawn ceremonies associated with important dates of the 260-day ritual calendar. Trumpets, flutes, violins, guitars, and marimbas were also used at religious ceremonies, and still are today. Mortars and skyrockets punctuated the phases of a ritual, candles and incense were burned, drinks were consumed, and ceremonial cigars were smoked. The money needed to finance these ceremonies was substantial, but many Ixil were well-off. Some of them were traders who traveled great distances; others had large landholdings.

This proliferation of art and ceremony amounted to a minor cultural florescence, but with little that was new. The syncretism of Catholic and Mayan cultural elements had all been accomplished long before and was now simply elaborated. The conservatism of this florescence is suggested by the art. The murals show a striking resemblance to a pre-Columbian pottery scene (Becquelin, 1969, fig. 59), and figures painted on the church ceiling of Chajul are quite similar to other pottery designs (Becquelin, 1969, fig. 2a).

Social control at that time included harsh punishments. Though Shas did not witness these punishments himself, he tells what he has heard from older people:

There was no fine payment; money wasn't taken from people as is done now. Now we can get out of it with money, but then the fine was the whip. The whip, they say, was used on someone, for instance, for abandoning one's wife. One would be brought to the courthouse . . . There was a stake, a pillar with arms like a cross. They would stretch out one's arms, like God on the cross, and tie them with a rope. Once tied, they brought the whip. A hundred lashes, they say, were given if the wrongdoing was great. And some couldn't stand it, because the punishment was harsh. They couldn't stand it and they just died under the whip.

As will be seen in one of Shas's dreams, the whip is still an authority symbol and was described metaphorically as a "Father."

Ixil isolation did not survive the great economic changes that took place around the end of the nineteenth century. Not only had the Ixil population increased substantially, but there was simultaneously a surge in the demand for labor in the middle-elevation coffee plantations. Coffee had become the dominant part of the Guatemalan economy by that time. Later, cotton was to have a large role also. This was a period of great change and stress for the Ixil because of the pressures involved in contracting labor as well as the pressures resulting from population increase.

Shas talks about the change:

At first there were no ladinos in our town, but little by little they came. They all heard that ours was a good place, so they came. Some of the Ixil found employers and some drank a lot. The ladinos established saloons and hired marimba bands. So little by little the wealth of the Ixil people diminished. Even young boys would do nothing but drink at the saloons. They would have the marimba playing every Sunday and every Thursday . . . people came and brought the wages they had earned from their employers. Employers gave them money then, sometimes a lot of money, like 1,000 pesos. The Ixil would take the money and go to the saloon. They would hang around the marimba and drink and spend their money.

Yes, the money disappeared. And another thing: some of them fought with their spouses. They fought with their younger brothers and their older brothers and then went to jail. And their money was all gone, so they borrowed more from their employer. The employer would get them out of jail, and little by little they became indebted to him. Some had handed over their land to their employer as collateral, so he increased his holdings. Their parcels were cheap; 500 *cuerdas* went for 500 pesos. So lots of people began to come and live among us, since they heard that there was cheap land available. Our fellow Ixil sold their lands just because of the rum, not for lack of food. How could they lack maize?

Since the beginning of the coffee market, frequent travel has been the rule for the Ixil. Coffee requires hand labor during the harvest. Most coffee is grown on the slopes of the Pacific coast at elevations running from about 1,000 to 5,000 feet above sea level. Though there are also coffee fincas (plantations) in and around the lower parts of the Ixil area, the great majority of Ixil workers went to the coast. Farm labor was regulated by provisions of the law called the *Reglamento de Jornaleros,* originally enacted in 1887 and revised in 1894. According to this law, Indian workers were classified in three main groupings. The first was the *colono,* who could contract to live and work on a plantation for four years at a time. He sometimes received a small plot of land for his own use in addition to wages. During this time he could not work elsewhere, and even after the end of the four years he could not leave until all his debts were paid off to his patron. The second group of workers, *jornaleros habilitados,* were not bound by any kind of time contract but had received money or goods from the labor contractor and had to work until the debt was paid off. Finally, there were the *jornaleros no habilitados,* who were neither under time contract nor in debt, but would fulfill any wage contract that was agreed upon. All workers had to carry with them a little booklet in which the employer wrote down the debts and credits. This was a tyrannical system for the illiterate Indians, who did not understand what was written in their books; by the contracting of indebtedness through the sale of alcoholic beverages this arrangement became particularly abusive. Previously it had not been an Ixil custom to drink heavily. The Indians drank *comiteco* made from maguey, a milder intoxicant than the present-day rum (*aguardiente*) made from sugar cane. The latter was introduced to them by the early ladino contractors, who established and controlled the trade (Lincoln, 1945, pp. 58, 62, 64). When Lincoln was in Nebaj, he counted a great number of saloons, the primary purpose of which was to build up indebtedness in contracting Indians. If an Indian ran away from a plantation, he would be brought back by the employer and his debt would be increased to cover the cost of the pursuit. It was easy for a person to build up a debt so large that it made him a virtual slave for life, and this slavery was often extended to his sons after his death.

This exploitative system was abolished by presidential decree in 1934. The Indians were grateful for the change. The new law abolished the debts, but at the same time required that an Indian not be idle. If the Indian did not work under the new law, he could be punished as a vagrant. Under this law if an Indian did not have a trade or profession, or did not cultivate a specified amount of land, he would have to work for someone else for a certain number of days per year. If he tilled less than ten cuerdas (5,000 m^2) he would have to work for others for 150 days per year; if he tilled more than ten cuerdas but less than four *manzanas* (8,000 m^2) he would have to work 100 days per year. Each worker had to carry a new kind of book with him containing his identification and any notes that might be warranted to exempt him from the vagrancy law. If he was not exempted, the book had to contain notations by plantation owners indicating the number of days worked on each plantation. If a person's book did not have a sufficient number of days, he could be thrown into prison or forced to work without compensation.

In 1933 another presidential decree required all able-bodied men to work at least two weeks each year on the public roads. Those who could pay one quetzal (dollar) for each of the two weeks were exempted from the work requirement. Since wages were very low at that time and money was scarce in the Ixil area, most of the Indians, according to Shas, had no choice but to work on the roads until they were finished.

In 1944 a liberal government with a new constitution took over in Guatemala, and both the vagrancy law and the decree for road work were abolished.

The lives of the Ixil have been constrained for centuries by a long series of exploitative political arrangements such as those just described. During the 1970s living conditions deteriorated further. The population for all of Guatemala increased from just under five million to nearly six and a half million during the last few decades, while adequate nutrition has declined. Multinational corporations, local businesses, and wealthy landowners, unfettered by the need to be socially responsible because of a repressive government, fail to pay living wages or provide decent living conditions. The cotton plantations fail to provide adequate safety for workers in their careless use of dangerous pesticides. But even more serious is the usurpation of land from the Indians. Any attempts to form cooperatives by the Indians are deliberately attacked by the government. Government military opposition to Indian improvement in the Ixcan area (not far from the Ixil region) has economically shut off 11,556 Indians after they had migrated to a remote area and purchased land, through the aid of the Maryknoll missionaries, the U.S. Agency for International Development, and the Guatemalan land distribution organization, INTA (Vittengl, 1979). In this most recent form of exploitation, Guatemalan paramilitary groups have driven into the Ixil towns and taken Ixil out of their houses at night, beaten them in front of their wives and children, and carried them away, never to be seen again. On May 29, 1978, more than 100 Kekchi Indians who live adjacent to the Ixil language area were killed by Guatemalan troops. Those killed included women and children. These families had come to the town of Panzos to discuss their claims to land that they had farmed for several generations.

The ostensible motivation for killing the Ixil, Kekchi, and other Indians was that the victims were guerrillas or sympathetic to the guerrillas, or that they had initiated violence. In the Panzos case mass graves had been dug in preparation for the slaughter two days previously (Amnesty International, 1979). The real motivation was part of a general plan of land seizure and development. Right-wing paramilitary groups, which were first formed at the suggestion of American military advisers in Guatemala (Amnesty International, 1976) and which were operating in Guatemala City when we stayed there in 1967, have begun to operate extensively in the Ixil area. The land to the north, particularly that farmed by Chajul and Cotzal Ixil, has increased in value because of plans for a highway, for oil and mineral exploration, and for other economic activities by American, Japanese, and other foreign as well as Guatemalan interests. There has been scattered resettlement of non-Ixil Indians in some Ixil areas. Guerrilla groups have operated in the area from time to time, but at first it was with little cooperation from the Ixil, who, except for some in Nebaj, were among the most unpoliticized Indians of Guatemala (Colby and van den Berghe, 1969). Where the guerrillas themselves were unsuccessful, however, the paramilitary activities are furthering the cause of the guerrillas by politicizing the Ixil through their repressive tactics. Not long ago the entire town of Nebaj was held by a guerrilla group for a day while they argued their political position in an attempt to gain more Ixil sympathy.

Though the more recent political context has enormous implications, both locally and nationally, it has developed subsequent to the time of our fieldwork, and it is beyond the scope of our present task to analyze it further. As far as Shas's life is concerned, the political situation that affected him the most existed years ago. It was a situation that required the donation of his own labor and that also denied him the opportunity for an education.

Shas's later years were less directly touched by political events; he was influenced more by long-standing religious beliefs and commitments. This is not surprising, for Ixil religion is a core institution that explains a major part of Ixil thought and activities. Religion was important not only to Shas, but to all Ixil as well. We therefore turn next to a brief orientation to the religious context of Shas's recordings.

IXIL RELIGION

Religion, like any other institution, is a vast complex of cultural patterns composed of expressed beliefs and actions. These patterns never form a perfectly integrated whole; unless conscious efforts are made at unification and codification, there are often contradictions, gaps, and ambiguities. Nor are these inconsistencies limited to oral traditions. Quotations from the Bible can be found to support a wide variety of viewpoints, some quite opposed to each other. Sometimes the contradictions are only seen as such because their context has not been fully understood, but often they are real, with texts encompassing, as they do, different time periods, world views, and so forth. Analysis of contradictions in any group of religious beliefs can reveal dynamic processes of change and cultural lag. In Ixil society political changes, missionary efforts, and economic changes all proceed differently, in different forms and at varying paces. Sometimes these differences set up tensions that influence a whole range of thoughts and behaviors. At other times there may be a compartmentalization of beliefs in particular areas of thought and activity. Such compartmentalization may even be recognized as such by users of the culture themselves, the differences arising out of usage in different contexts for convenience or expedience. For example, we say that we like to watch the sun "come up" in the morning, even though we know full well that the movement we observe comes from our own earthly turning rather than from the circling of the sun around us. A similar principle holds, undoubtedly, with many informant statements about Ixil religion. We thus make no claims about providing an integrated, coherent picture of Ixil religion, much less a complete one. In this section we sketch a general view based on the statements Shas Ko²w has made, along with our own observations.

One of the most confusing aspects of pre-Columbian religious beliefs is the tendency for supernatural beings to have protean forms, overlapping functions, and multiple names. This may reflect a situation in which the ruling elites or merchants of the society differed in ethnic origin from their subjects or customers as a result of conquest by, or trade with, groups whose deities had different names but similar functions. It could also mean that different kin groups had different ancestral deities which were melded in various ways as hegemony passed from one kin group to another. When the Spanish priests first gained control, they took advantage of the great richness and variety of deities by pointing out the similarities their saints had with some of the existing local deities. They hoped this would facilitate the reeducation process. Simply calling a local deity by a Spanish name was apparently acceptable to the Ixil, but it did not mean the abandonment of the deity's pre-Columbian attributes. The end result was often a syncretism, an amalgam mixing attributes of supernatural beings from both religions.

It is curious that in certain contexts, such as the telling of myths, deity names are not important to Pap Shas. He usually does not identify the protagonists of his myths and folktales by name, and once when he did he expressed uncertainty about which of two characters had which name. In other contexts, however, names are important; in prayer, for example, deities and ancestral souls are invoked by name.

A related source of confusion concerning the names of deities is that the honorific term *Kučučkub'aal,* literally, "our mother(s), our father(s)," is used primarily as a blanket term for all deities. The term

Kub'aal separately is often used for gods, saints, other gods, mountain deities called *ʔaanhel*, and the Christian God. *Kučuč* is used for
Santa Maria and other female deities. Alone *Kub'aal* may stand for
any deity, though it refers most often to the sun god, *Kub'aal Q'ii*, or
his Christian counterpart, Christ.

Cosmology

The Ixil see the universe as basically dual, composed of earth and
sky. The sun traverses both, traveling through the sky during the day
and moving underneath the earth at night. Pap Shas describes the
coursing of the sun in the following excerpt:

He perspires heavily; he gets very hot during his trip so when he returns
(to his heavenly abode), the sweat pours out of him. He is tired. And there
are the people, of course, who have waited for him. He sits down in the
chair and people wipe off his sweat. They too are gods, and they wipe off
all his sweat when he sits down in the chair. And then when he has settled
down in his chair, "Uush, I'm tired," he says. The people have knelt down
before him on his arrival, and after he has sat down all the people kneel
before him. Then the prayer is said with him. With prayer he arrives, and
with prayer he leaves again.

Kub'aal has an eye on his chest, and that's where the sunlight shines
out; that's where he watches from. He has an eye on his chest and eyes in
his face. So there is the sun, there is the day on his chest . . . This way he
can be seated in the chair when he arrives. And he is seated while being
carried around in the chair. Just as people do in a car or in the gondola of
a merry-go-round, he settles in his chair, and we see it only when he
moves across, while he is seated in the chair.

He has his bearers (carriers): four *ʔaanhel* who support him. Also, his
headdress, like our hats, is held by two other *ʔaanhel*. That means he has
six *ʔaanhel* who care for him; furthermore, there are four guardians . . .
because if he is frightened he may be made to drop down from heaven, if
he had no guardians—but he has guards for his well-being—four guards
follow him and we remember them when we remember Kub'aal's soul;
and if there is someone who bothers you or is envious of you: fortunately
there is Kub'aal gazing down at us and you pray to him and he will look
after us.[5]

Kub'aal q'ii, the sun god in his twenty different manifestations, is
the central figure dominating the Ixil pantheon. He is the creator of
mankind, the only god who continually cares for mankind, which
would perish without the light and warmth he faithfully provides.

His remote image becomes humanized by the attributes of Christ, also called Kub'aal, superimposed by the interpreters of early Catholic missionaries. The Father of the Sky is the Father of Kub'aal and his hostile brothers, whom he bans to a dark, distant place after they have killed their younger brother.

The mythology mentions a first creation of supermen[6] who were destroyed for their lack of respect toward Kub'aal. The people who survived were rewarded for their resourcefulness and magical power and were given the status of demigods or lesser deities, with the task of watching over the humans. These are chiefly chthonic or tellurian deities who live in mountains and springs and at the sites of temple ruins. Still others live in the sky and attend the sun god. Regardless of whether they are earth deities or sky deities, these lesser deities are all referred to as ʔaanhel. They travel noiselessly through the air, like their Christian counterparts, whose names they share.

Religious Organizations

Twelve brotherhoods (*cofradías* in Spanish), sixteenth- and seventeenth-century Catholic institutions established by the Spanish priests, care for and honor particular saints. Every year a new set of people takes over the duties of each brotherhood. The personnel change involves the selection of a *b'aal mertoma* or head or "father" mayordomo and an assistant by the elders. The b'aal mertoma and his assistant then choose eight more assistants. Each assistant is ranked, and the last is usually quite junior in age as well as in rank. The duties of higher-ranking mayordomos include arranging the clothes of the saint and supervising various aspects of the ceremony. The last assistant accompanies and cares for a higher one if the higher one is in an advanced state of intoxication. The lower assistant performs menial tasks such as (in an example given by one Ixil respondent) holding the older man's hat when he urinates. The b'aal mertoma pays for most of the fiesta expenses out of his own pocket and in the process gains prestige though not wealth.

In addition to the internal ranking, there is an unofficial ranking of the brotherhoods themselves. At least three of the brotherhoods have higher prestige than others. The greatest among these is that for the patron saint of Nebaj, Santa Maria.

After a person has served as b'aal mertoma, he then becomes a

lifelong member of the elders (*principales*). This group is also recruited from the higher ranks of the civil government, which are
about equal in prestige to the brotherhoods.

Dawn Ceremonies

Religious ceremonies are called *saqb'ičil* or "dawn ceremonies,"
because they usually last until dawn or close to it. Most often they
are family ceremonies to which relatives, friends, and neighbors are
invited; music is played, people converse, and a ritual is performed
at the household shrine. Afterwards there is usually dancing: men
dancing with men, women with women. Less often, dawn ceremonies are held by the cofradías and by the town government. Shas
laments the fact that not all the cofradías still hold large dawn ceremonies. There used to be twelve each year; now there only seem to
be four or so. (The family dawn ceremonies are called "dawn ceremony for the house," while the larger ones are categorized as communal (*komon saqb'ičil*).[7]

At dawn ceremonies as well as at most other ritual activities it is
necessary to burn incense and candles. Shas explains why in the following text:

First came the incense, first came the candle, ahead of us. Then we appeared on earth. Then came our food, our trees, and our firewood. At first
there were no trees, they say, the earth was not fertile, it was only mud. If
a seedling began to grow and it was cut down, its blood flowed. They say
they cut into the earth, and blood rose from the earth. No, no, the earth
did not like us to live on it; the earth did not want us to sow it because it
lacked strength. It was only mud.

When our Father saw this situation he asked, "What should be done?
There aren't any children to call us on their day, on their dawn. How can
we be mother and father to them if they can't survive? What can we give
to the children if this earth is not fertile? What remedy is there? How can
we nurture its strength?"

They held a reunion, apparently, just as do the principales here when
there is some task or public matter to discuss. Just so did our Father for us,
for our creation. All the gods came together.

How many gods! How many guardians! How many of our Holy Parents,
they say, he brought together in his house!

They could not think of a solution. Then our Father Saint Peter, with our
Father Saint John, said: "But really, why not call Saint Melchior, why not
call Saint Baltasar to see if they can't think in their minds of what to do?"

They brought in our Father, Saint Melchior, with Saint Baltasar just as we do [in the town hall].

They sat down on the bench; and there were all those people, all those gods in the house. "Well, pardon us, please sit down." They took their hats. It was just as they do for us sometimes: "Come in, Sir!" Then they hang up our hats. So, also, they say, they did with them. It is the custom now, surely, because of that.

So they took their hats, they hung up their hats near the saints and they sat down on the bench. "What are you going to do now that you are gathered here?" our Father, Saint Melchior, said to the gods.

"We haven't been able to do anything about the earth. Something has to be done. The earth won't do anything. The earth will not accept anything. Because the earth gives no sustenance. There is no wood, because the earth is not fertile. When we cut the wood, it bleeds, and so I take the blood of the earth. How can it then give sustenance? How do we expect to work and how do we expect to plant? There are no daughters and there are no sons."

"Why don't we calculate the light of the day," said our Father. "Between the gods, what solution might there be?" it is said that our Father said to Saint Melchior.

"But what solution is there? We can't think of a way."

"Well, let's try incense."

"But where will we get the incense? There is no wood. And where are we going to get candles because there are none!"

"No, hombre, they can be found, just tell Saint Domingo to get it and tell Saint Lucas to get the wax from the sides of his stomach and then you will see," said our Fathers Melchior and Saint Baltasar to our Father and the other saints. Well then, it was taken care of. In just a short while the incense and candles appeared. At midnight Saint Melchior and Saint Baltasar began the ritual.

When it dawned there were many great mountains and trees. How thick were the trees where the mud once was! Now the earth was dry. There was no mud, the earth had dried out. Well, there is Man, thanks to those who thought of a way. "If we had not fetched them it might have been the end of man in the day of light."

They say that thus it was left said by our Father. He gave us the benediction. Those who do ritual could remain. How can the incense be destroyed? There it is. The candle won't be destroyed. There it is. And the trees are there, too.

It is at no other place but there at Hu?il mountain. There is the god who left it sowed for us. So was the earth when it became strong, they say. There appeared the trees, we appeared ourselves, there appeared our *tortilla*, there appeared our *atole* [maize gruel], there appeared our beans, there appeared our squash, there appeared our *chayote* [vegetable pear]. All those things appeared in the world. But only the holy earth gave them to us. For that reason, there is an obligation. For that reason we say prayers for our maizefield. For that reason we give offering because the earth gives us food. That is the benefit of the candle. That is the benefit of the incense. And the incense remained and the candle remained, and it is better for us to light a little candle, to offer a little incense. It is better if one does it. So appeared the world. For that reason it remained . . .

So we are on earth, already forgiven our sins by God. Certainly we have done lots of things. That is why we have sickness. For example, there are people into which sickness has entered. If one committed a transgression, already the sickness will enter. If his time has come, already he goes. But if he stays the only remedy left is incense. If they have a healing ceremony he will get better if he has luck; if he does not have luck—even though lots of incense is consumed—time hunts him down. But sometimes one gets better because of the incense, and candles. So it is done. For that reason the incense has remained, but not only the incense.

Incense is important not only for the curing of people when they are sick (being punished for some misbehavior) but also because incense provides sustenance for the gods. Though the gods do not eat as mortals do, they must imbibe the products of human ritual, primarily the smoke of incense. To ensure that mortals do this, the ʔaanhel act as intermediaries. The ʔaanhel are a mixture, or syncretism, of sixteenth-century Spanish beliefs about angels and previously mentioned pre-Columbian deities associated with mountains and natural phenomena. They keep an eye on people. Shas explains this in a continuation of the previous text:

There remained the ʔaanhel, our keeper. He walks about. There he is! God is close to him, because there are ʔaanhel who have wings, they are the ones who come to observe, they say. There are ʔaanhel who pass at night, and they come to give blessing to us when we eat and drink. They give blessing to you from God. As did our Father, so did the ʔaanhel. Surely they walk about. But it was in old times.

Once there was a daughter and a son [i.e., mortals, children of God], they say. They were walking along the road with their food and atole when two ʔaanhel came by. "It is not good what these people do, friend, they are damaging the road. They are disturbing our road. It's better that I kill them," said one of the ʔaanhel. He drew his knife and almost killed the people for their transgression. He was just going to do it when Kub'aal wandered by and met them near the trespassers.

"What happened, what are you doing? Why are you drawing your knife against our children?" said our Father to the ʔaanhel.

"Why, they are damaging the road, when you came they already had disturbed the road," said the ʔaanhel to our Father.

"No, man, no, don't be fearful, don't think things like that. It's nothing, it's all right. They von't call you or worship you because of that. If you want to make our children disappear how will you eat, how will you drink? Your way is no good. That's your job, not mine, how will the daughters and sons multiply? You must remember: You should count how many days go by until they remember to atone for their transgression. They will call you and you will eat and you will drink right off. So shall they do it, for that the candle is used, for that the incense is used, which is offered by the children. So it is done, it will come to their minds, a person will come to leave his offering, he will feel guilty and will come to leave his offering, for what he has done. You will be called. If you kill them, then there won't be fertile days, there won't be fertile dawns. What do you say? Don't continue that." So spoke our Father to the ʔaanhel. Thus ended the destruction of the people.

There were many things in the world. It was different from the people now, whose thinking has changed. No, indeed, the law was very different then. Today people no longer pay attention to it. For example, some say that incense is useless. They say, "What good is it?" Well, it comes from long ago, we don't know who made it appear, or when they blessed it.[8]

Sacred Locations

During the nineteenth century the sacred shrine of Huʔil, located to the north of Chajul, was central to the calendrical system. It was a place of pilgrimage for diviners, priests, curers, and ordinary folk, not only from all three dialect areas of Ixil country but from neighboring language areas as well. The Ixil say that "ʔAanhel Huʔil is what holds the world together." Apparently it has a long tradition, for it is built on an archaeological site.[9]

From the outside the shrine looks like an ordinary Ixil house. Inside at one end is a long altar with crosses on it, stretching from one wall to the other. Huʔil is visited on special occasions such as the Ixil New Year and the second Friday in Lent, when some of the pilgrims visiting the Christ of Golgotha in the Chajul church make the extra trip of several hours to visit Huʔil.

According to Shas, an earlier shrine (which burned down) at the same site had the layout shown in figure 2.1.

The following narrative is an excerpt from notes written on March 4, 1966, on the first trip one of us made to Huʔil during the period of the pilgrimages to Chajul (B. Colby, field notes, 1966):

When we arrived at the Capilla . . . we were invited in and sat down just as two men from Chiul (on highway just before entering Ixil country) and a couple from Chajul came in and established themselves around a second fireplace. Of the three men from Cotzal, two of them were calendar ex-

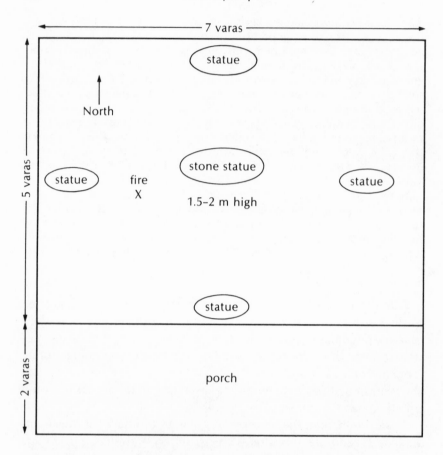

Figure 2.1.   Floor plan of shrine at Huʔil as Shas remembers it.

perts, Miguél Mendoza Velazquez from Cantón Pexla, and Diego Stuma Pacheco, from Cantón Santa Welina. Both spoke good Spanish, and Mendoza, in his fifties, told me that sacrifices of poultry, cattle, or whatever else are performed in the houses. When I asked what they did with the blood he said that the ancestors used to put the blood on the burning incense and that this had the power of removing sickness if a curing ceremony was in process, but that now this wasn't done.

The Capilla was a large rectangular adobe house with wide overhanging eaves through which the smoke of fires and incense could escape. Inside there was a long altar running the length of the room and about four feet in depth (front to back). There were eight wooden crosses and one stone cross with the top part missing. The stone cross was brought from Quezaltenango about nine years ago; the wooden crosses were only a year or two old because the *catequistas* (converts to modern Catholicism and active members of Catholic Action) had burned the crosses that were there previously. The crosses were decorated with the usual flowers; corn was laid out, and also bundles of candles and incense. When the praying for the New Year began at one point one of the Cotzal men sang from a Catholic hymnal.

The atmosphere in the house, or Capilla, was very relaxed. When I asked again about the lack of people on New Year's Eve they said that because of the Romerias, there wouldn't be any large celebration at the Capilla until twenty days later when there would be a marimba, and the padre would say mass in the Capilla for the alcaldes of the aldeas, the non-ladino authorities of Chajul and of other places in the Ixil area (this actually never took place). Something would be going on every twenty days (on the day Čee which is the entering Alcalde this year which began on 6 Čee [see later section on the calendar]), according to them. When I asked about how they would know when the New Year started they said that when a certain star (in the constellation of Orion?) dipped below the horizon it was the New Year. Another method, which they were uncertain of, was with the Pleiades (which they called the seven Marias). When it is clouded they wait until the first cock crows. Several cocks crowed at around 11 PM. They turned on the radio to hear what time it was and checked with my watch. They said that they wouldn't begin, the New Year began at midnight. In the meantime they were praying to the last day of the old year. At the time I didn't think to ask whether they meant the day before the ʔoʔqʼii (five-day end-of-year period) entered or not. Finally at midnight I showed them my watch and they said that the new day had now entered but that the ritual couldn't start until the cock crowed. In the meantime conversation continued among and between the two fire groups. Earlier the conversation at our group was dominated by Anai [the Chajul man who accompanied me], later by Mendoza. At different times those who were not praying would doze off or talk. Earlier the people around both fires ate. I was offered a large stack of tortillas with a drumstick. I turned to Anai intending to divide it among the three of us, giving him the chicken, but he misunderstood and accepted the entire stack. (In this mistake on my part I learned that food is not passed around to select from but that individual portions are passed.) Later, however, I was given chile coffee from both fires. People from both fires mixed more with one another as the evening went on.

On a second trip to Huʔil we missed a much larger crowd because we did not arrive until after dawn. We never had the opportunity to observe a 260-day end ceremony, but it seems as though there was a smaller attendance for all calendrical ceremonies at Huʔil in the late 1960s than in the 1940s when Lincoln made his trips (Lincoln, 1945). There probably is also a drop in the number of daykeepers among the Ixil (though no hard evidence was collected beyond the opinions of our informants), though the proportion of prayersayers or curers may be about the same.

In the remainder of this sketch of religious beliefs and practices, we shall focus on the calendar. From the very start we felt that beliefs and practices associated with the calendar, particularly the role of daykeeper, explain a large amount of Ixil behavior and ethics. The calendar and the role of daykeeper thus had an ethnographic priority for us. The general description that follows should provide a sufficiently broad understanding of how the calendar works for interpreting the texts in the chapters to follow.

Religious Specialists and the Calendar

There are three types of non-Catholic religious specialists in Nebaj: (1) the elected Ixil priest (*b'ooq'ol b'aalwactiiš*), who determines the days on which both communal religious ceremonies and cofradía ceremonies are to be held; (2) prayersayers (*b'aalwactiiš*), who request good providence or assist in effecting cures of sick clients and who function in dawn ceremonies of various kinds; and (3) daykeepers or diviners (*ʔaaq'ii*), who use the *mič* seed to count the days and make diagnoses. A subcategory of diviner includes those who use only crystals instead of mič seeds.

Nowhere, probably, was astrology as dominant as among the ancient Maya. Given its ancient importance, we might well wonder why Mayan astrology did not persist more strongly after the Spanish conquest than it did. One reason, undoubtedly, was that much of the astrological knowledge was held by a small group of individuals who guarded that knowledge zealously but were easily singled out for control, suppression, or elimination. Astrological knowledge was a prime source of socioreligious power and was, along with human sacrifice, the major target of the early Spanish missionaries, who quickly substituted saints' days and other Catholic ritual occasions for the indigenous ceremonies. The cofradías and the Gregorian calendar were the chief instruments for effecting these changes. Some small-scale rituals for crop and household survived. In the Ixil area, the ritual calendar persisted and was used in these smaller-scale rituals.

Mayan astrology, as represented in calendrical divination, has persisted more pervasively among the Ixil than among any of the other

Maya groups. The Ixil year currently begins in the month of March. Each year is given the name of the day in the Ixil calendar that starts it. Only four of the twenty days can appear as the first day of a new year. In 1967, for instance, the New Year began on March 5, with the day ʔEe.

The other days on which the Ixil year can begin are Noʔq, Čee and ʔliq'. These four days or *Alcalde* days are sometimes called chief days by mayanists. The chief day that begins the current year is known as the year bearer. Each time a chief day starts a new year, it is with a different number from one to thirteen. In 1974 a new thirteen-year period began with 1 Čee. For all four year bearers to run through the thirteen numbers takes fifty-two years, a time interval that before the conquest was a major marker throughout the Mesoamerican high cultures.

There are two cycles of importance in the use of the Ixil calendar: 13 times 20 (260 days) and 18 times 20 (360 days). The latter count adds five days at the end of the 360-day period for a full solar year. These five days are a time of restricted eating and behavior. A favorite food that was permissible during this time was the avocado, which in Ixil has the name ʔoo. This linkage is a false folk etymology (ʔoʔq'ii, "five days").

Because the Ixil 365-day system does not add a day every four years, it moves out of phase with the Gregorian calendar. The Ixil New Year fell on March 4 in 1971 but on March 3 during the leap year of 1972. In 1939, when Lincoln gathered his information on the Ixil calendar, the New Year began on March 12. The Ixil New Year will not coincide with the Gregorian New Year until the year 2216. We do not know whether at some earlier time the leap-year correction was regularly made. Since the Ixil New Year is known to have corresponded with the Gregorian New Year in the early 1720s, we might speculate that corrections had been made until that time. The eighteen month names seem to be related to agricultural and seasonal activities, suggesting that corrections were indeed made.

Lincoln observed that all four chief days were celebrated with special ceremonies at the altars of every house and at the mountain crosses. It was said that on every chief day turkeys and chickens were sacrificed and intrafamily confession took place. We did not observe this activity in the late 1960s, but it may be a possibility in some areas. For the new year, according to Lincoln, the two most important ceremonies were for the opening day of the year and then, 260 days later, when that chief day occurred again with the same number. Lincoln described a major ceremony on the 260th day of the year 5 ʔEe in the distant hamlet of Chel. The following year he saw another ceremony at the shrine of Huʔil celebrating the return of 6 Noʔq 260 days after it had begun the year. He reported a crowd of some 300 Indians at this ceremony. There may well have been a decrease in the observance of calendrical ritual since Lincoln's time, perhaps because of the efforts of recent Spanish missionaries and the Catholic Action movement over the past two decades. Also important, surely, is the greater exposure many Ixil have had to the outside Guatemalan-Hispanic world.

Lincoln wrote that the crosses at the four corners of town were directly associated with the four chief days but rotated according to the year bearer. However, this rotation was denied by Shas and other informants. A locality always keeps the same supernatural associations.

Association of deities with geographical location is a very strong characteristic of Mayan religion. One of the surrounding mountains, Laaw Wic, is referred to as the ʔiqlenaal, a calendrical term. Today the highest-ranking Guatemalan, the president, is also called the ʔiqlenaal.

The Ixil calendar and associated beliefs facilitate communication between people and supernaturals. Though supernaturals are very often punishing beings, they are also seen as beneficial and will sometimes send warnings through dreams and protect or reward people. While the existence of enemies may occupy the thoughts of Ixil and witchcraft is sometimes suspected, they do not take matters into their own hands in quite the same way as do, for instance, the Tzotzil Mayans of Mexico among whom we did fieldwork earlier (Colby, 1966c). The Ixil philosophy is to avoid confrontations. Further, the idea of a personalized soul that survives and is actively interested in human affairs after death provides a sense of self and control that we feel is important in maintaining social tranquillity. It is interesting to compare this attitude with that of the Tzotzil. The Huistecan and Zinacantan Tzotzil we worked with in Mexico lack the Mayan calendar. They also lack a personalized soul concept (they believe in animal souls), and any idea of the kind of two-way communication with supernaturals in which the Ixil believe.[10] Perhaps as a consequence, people suspected of being witches are sometimes killed or shot at. When doing fieldwork in Chiapas, one of us gave assistance to a Chamula Mayan man who had been shot in ambush as he stumbled home drunk in the early hours of the morning. The neighboring Tzeltal Mayans of Chiapas also have a very high homicide rate as a result of killing suspected witches (Nash, 1970). This aspect of the two religious systems, as we think it is conceptualized by their believers, can be diagrammed as in figure 2.2.

Relations between people and supernaturals in the Ixil religious view are direct, while those between human enemies are constrained by a psychological barrier against direct confrontation (as Shas's philosophy makes clear). For the Tzotzil the lines of communication with supernaturals seem less direct (though there is a direct link between the individual and an animal soul), and there is less restraint in the expression of enmity between individuals.[11] In fact, person-to-person interaction can often be quite tense (Colby, 1967).

The Tzotzil seem destined to continue in an impoverished state with insufficient land and a ladino-dominated world (Colby, 1966c; Collier, 1975; Vogt, 1969). It is a situation fraught with fears and anxieties, with individuals having little control or even sense of control—the so-called learned helplessness syndrome in no-win situations. The more creative and innovative people move out. The Ixil generally have been somewhat better off until recently. The Chajul area especially has had plenty of land and relatively little local ladino interference. Self-esteem and neighborliness seem to be significantly

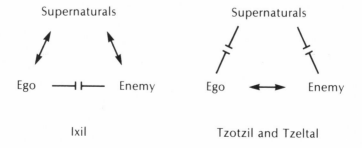

Figure 2.2.   Action (*arrows*) or lack of it (*blocked lines*) toward supernaturals and enemies.

more positive among the Ixil than among the Tzotzil of Chiapas. One can only speculate to what extent these attitudes are reflected in the religious belief system and to what extent they are caused by the belief system.

Dreams

Dreaming is of significance in a traditional Ixil's life. People get up in the morning and greet each other with: "Ma b'aʔn kušaš? Yeʔl awacik'e?" ("Are you well? Did you have any dreams?") And the answer is: "Yeʔle, yeʔškam yeʔ nunwack'a, b'aʔn kušin." ("No, I didn't dream anything. I am fine.") Dreams are the private medium for the ordinary Ixil to receive instructions and messages from the supernatural power, or from his ancestors. If danger threatens a family, various members may dream about the possible causes and seek help accordingly.

While harmless or benevolent dreams are often interpreted by the dreamer himself or an older relative or friend, more complex or threatening dreams are formally presented to the professional interpreter of dreams, the ʔaaq'ii or daykeeper. He will take the proper measures needed to reestablish the personal equilibrium of his client by searching or reestablishing vulnerable ties in the dreamer's human and superhuman *Umwelt*. The dreamer's anxiety will be reduced by the feeling that interaction with the threatening powers is possible and that a new peaceful balance in his life can be attained by reaching the offended power through prayers and offerings of incense and candles.

It is clear from our data that the traditional Ixil respond to dreams as personally and socially important events. They provide a kind of interface between individual concerns and socially shared religious activities. Since they represent a vital link to the supernatural world, it is not surprising that dreams are involved in the decision of an Ixil man or woman to be a daykeeper. This is well documented in Shas Koʔw's life history. In fact, Shas's descriptions of his dreams seem to be more vivid and detailed than the rest of his life history. Since the dreaming process figures in the recruitment into the role of daykeeper, we shall analyze these dreams in the next chapter.

Prayers

Pap Shas's speech style ranges from casual to formal.[12] The formality increases as the subject or purpose becomes more religious. This variation in speech style is generally characteristic of Mayan peoples. Gossen has pointed out that for the Chamula Mayans, "verbal expression moves in a clear continuum from lesser to greater formality, invariance, redundancy, and metaphoric heat as it moves from ordinary discourse to ancient words" (1974, p. 239). The formal style is characterized chiefly by rhythm and couplets. It is the same style found in the famous Quiché religious epic, the *Popol Vuh,* as noted by Edmonson (1971a).

One can see how the use of couplets, where two lines are semantic variations on the same idea, can enhance the ability to learn a text verbatim. Often the words of the line are identical except for the last. This tends to highlight whatever semantic features the two variants have in common. In many cases the variation centers on the names of two deities who share a particular function. The Ixil pantheon is a conceptually complex one, and each deity has many different characteristics. Thus the pairing of deities on a particular characteristic tends to focus on the function being emphasized in the text.[13]

In the prayers the mode ranges from simple calls to catch the attention of the supernaturals to strong implorations, almost demands, for their help.

Pap Shas lists seven prayer types that he has mastered: the Pedida (for the growth of maize and livestock, for marriage, and for good luck); the prayer for Kub'aal ʔAlmikaʔ; the Lawal Toŝk'al; the Tec Q'ii; the Tec Kub'aal Santo (and their counterparts in church); the Tec Kub'aal Wicil Čaq'aʔlil; and the Tec ʔAanima. A remaining important prayer which he does not use is the Cii Tiiŝ, the official prayer used in the cofradía ceremonies by the head priest of the town, the B'ooq'ol B'aalwactiiŝ. Part of a divination prayer spoken by Shas, which we recorded in a sound-synchronized film early in our fieldwork, is translated in Appendix C.

Before anaylzing the folktales and ritual texts that Pap Shas has given us, we want the reader to meet Shas as a person—as a child, a youth, a young married man, and finally, as a daykeeper of renown. The first major text we shall look at, then, is his life story in the chapter to follow.

3
SHAS KOʔW'S
LIFE HISTORY

We first made contact with Shas Koʔw in April 1966 through a friend, Kuʔ Bʼel. We wanted to find a diviner who would be willing to let us observe his divination with the seeds of the coral tree, the *bʼaqʼ mič*. The one or two diviners we contacted who were said to use the mič were unwilling to let us observe them. Those who allowed us to observe used a different kind of divining apparatus containing only quartz crystals, flint cores, and other stones, called *ʔooro* or *ʔilbʼal*. Then one day Kuʔ Bʼel announced that he was having a divination ritual for his wife and that the diviner would allow us to observe (and even film) the process. That evening he brought the man around. It was Pap Shas.

Shas was 71 at the time. He was of slightly less than medium height, as Ixil stature goes, and had kind eyes which, as we grew to know him, often had a twinkle of interest and humor. Though wrinkles were beginning to appear on his face, there was little gray in his hair. His clothes and bare feet showed that he was not a wealthy man. His face appeared to be an intelligent one; as we got to know him, we found that he was intellectually alert and curious. Although he was a small, almost frail-looking man who would sit quietly and listen to other people with great patience, his bearing was one of unassuming authority and poise. We interviewed him about divination and other rituals, and eventually he began telling us something of his history. As he got to know us, he came to share with us the more intimate currents of his thought, sometimes illuminating details that he had only mentioned in passing at an earlier time because of their personal, sometimes painful, associations.

The life history recounted in this chapter is a translation of a series of texts recorded on tape at different times, usually with an Ixil friend as Shas's audience. In some places the verbatim part of the text is interrupted by a summary of the taped text or explanatory sections derived from interviewing. The main thread of the life history is woven in an interchange between Shas and a young Ixil girl, Maʔl C'uʔč, who responded with the ideal combination of avid interest and respect to his story. Interspersed in this account are exchanges between Shas and his longtime friend Kuʔ B'el; they bear the characteristics of reminiscing man to man. Where the occasional responses of Maʔl or Kuʔ are important for understanding the text, they are shown in italics. All the rest of the texts and the summary statements and details were elicited by Lore Colby during the summer of 1970 when Shas visited us in California. In the English translation, the interjections and asides, false starts, and other features of mid-sentence revision so characteristic of spoken texts, as well as some of the repetition, have been omitted. Anyone who might wish to study the interactive patterns in detail would presumably want to use the original texts, and we plan to make them available on microfilm for such purposes.

Shas Koʔw was born in Nebaj on June 18, 1895. His father was Šaʔp C'uʔč, his mother ʔAn Siʔč. His birth was announced to the officials by a friend of the family and recorded in the town records under his Spanish name, Jacinto de Leon.[1]

Shas's ancestors had belonged to the Ixil upper class. They had owned several houses, one of them a comfortable town house facing the plaza and others on property in outlying areas, including the hamlet of ʔAk'ul. They had owned more than a thousand cuerdas of land and a considerable amount of livestock.

Shas's grandfather was an elder, having served as first regidor. He was also a prayersayer and a daykeeper. Shas remembered his grandfather praying at his own household shrine and officiating at dawn ceremonies at other people's homes. His great-grandfather on his father's side and his grandfather and uncle on his mother's side had

also been prayersayers. Here is Shas's story in several parts with titles
we have supplied.

EARLY LIFE

I cannot remember when I came into the world. I have only heard them
say that I was unfortunate when I was growing up. They say I was only six
months old when my father died, and after my father died my mother
stayed with my grandfather for six months. It was my grandfather who
made my soul appear [i.e., awakened Shas to understanding and aware-
ness].

I grew older. When I stopped nursing, my mother sought another husband. She went away with another man, and I was left with my grandfather. I stayed by my old one, and he alone brought me up. When I was
still little, perhaps only five, my "father," my old one, died, and I was left
alone. My grandfather owned houses and land; he owned cows, horses,
and chickens.

Well, I had an uncle who just traveled around wherever his trips happened to take him. He wasn't present when my grandfather died, but afterwards he came. He learned that my old one had died, and he began to
sell all the land. He sold all the houses. Nothing was left for me, and my
soul had not yet arrived.[2]

He spent the money; he got drunk with his two sisters. Do you remember the place where they played the marimba, at old Paa Toriipio's, where
he had his house formerly? Well, that's the place.

It was my father's land, but it was my uncle who sold it; they gave him
the money, and he went to dance to the marimba every Sunday. They
played the marimba at old Paa Toriipio's, and that's where my uncle went
to drink with his sisters. I didn't realize my misfortune, because I was still
a small child. I didn't understand a thing. And since my mother was too
afraid to go and complain at the courthouse, I didn't get my land. So it
was gone. The money was used up, and every bit of land was gone.

Then my uncle left for who knows where. He left to work at his business again, but without money. He was poor again: he had used it up with
his drinking. And so he died in Puerto Barrios. He didn't die in our town.
That's because he committed a crime against the earth of my father. It
isn't good that we do evil and don't give sustenance to our younger brothers, our older brothers. It angers the souls of our ancestors—and that's
probably why my uncle died of drunkenness in the Puerto Barrios prison.
He didn't die in our village, but away from home.[3]

I had nothing at all left of my own; I just wandered around, without the
least bit of my own.[4]

Shas's mother had wanted him to live with her after his grandfather's death, but her second husband did not like him, even though

the boy offered to work for him. He gave his wife the choice of doing without the boy or leaving. Little Shas went away quietly, and while he stood crying on the street corner a relative, Liš, came by and took him home. He found a place where the boy could stay and work with his brother Shas Č'ib' in the mountains, at Čila Matom, a rugged area about 5.5 kilometers southwest of Nebaj. It was a wealthy family, and Shas had to take care of the livestock in the mountains, where cougars and other wild animals had to be kept from the herds.

I just stayed with people. I grew up. I had my thoughts. I began to look for a living in order to eat. I grew up with some wealthy people. There were Ixil who owned horses, and there was a man who owned cows. I lived with him. I tended his sheep, and I herded his cows. I herded his pigs and fattened them. But I earned only my food. They didn't give me clothes; they gave me only their ragged discards. My body was black from the sun.

But where could I possibly have gone? Who would have cared for me? I had no mother; I had no father. My mother was dead [to me], and that's why I suffered all the things that befell me.[5]

For two years Shas stayed with the herd in the mountains. He had a gun, and when he was afraid he would fire a shot into the air, causing his dogs to bark. It was his way of keeping cougars and coyotes from attacking the herd. Then Liš, who had helped him before, persuaded the boy to work for him. He lived in C'alb'al. When Shas was about twelve years old he moved to Ci? Hul Čee, outside C'alb'al, and worked for Lu? C'u?č for the next four years.

It was during this time that Guatemala City was damaged by an earthquake,[6] and the President, Manuel Estrada Cabrera, ordered people from all over the country to come and help reconstruct the damaged capital. Each department was requested to send men, food, and building material. Three hundred Ixil men carried beams, poles, cordage, and thatch under the direction of two Ixil leaders. It was a long and tortuous trek over mountains and across valleys. Shas, a slightly built boy, had to help carry a pole measuring 7 varas (12 feet) in length. Once the men had arrived, it took around three days to construct a simple ranch house. While some of the men carried water from a distant water hole in their drinking jugs, others wetted adobe mud and mixed it with their feet. It took many trips to the water hole to finish the work. After the roof was thatched, the house was turned over to one of the victims of the quake. Shas remembers the groaning that came from a large tent where the wounded were cared for.

After the house was built the Ixil returned home. They had been pressed into service by means of a law that applied to men between the ages of twenty and sixty years. These age limits were often ignored, however, and boys and old men suffered equally under unreasonably heavy loads from the strenuous work they had to perform at the road construction camps. Shas, at thirteen, was really too young for compulsory service, but he did not have the means or the support of a ladino patron to buy himself out of his obligation as non-Indian citizens usually could do. As a result, he had to carry another heavy load to Quetzaltenango shortly after returning from Guatemala City. It took him ten to fifteen days to make the trip for a token wage that was not even enough to buy food for the trip. Shas remembers this period as one of "great punishment."

[Finally] I began to think for myself. It was just as it is with everyone: I grew up, and I looked for an employer for myself. I took work as a servant, and it was good because my employer gave me food and paid me by the day.

I bought my own clothes. I bought my own wool blanket from my earnings, and slowly I matured. I acquired money in hand, because there was food and there was pay—a peso a day, because it was a long time ago. It was in the money of that time. You wouldn't remember that there were peso coins. I earned thirty pesos a month. It was enough, because I could buy my things, whatever they were.

I stayed two years as servant to this employer, and then I entered manhood.

This first employer was Arturo García from Aguacatán, who had been appointed to a two years' office as municipal secretary in Nebaj. He was also a *habilitador*; he got paid for recruiting Indian laborers for the coffee plantations. After his official stay in Nebaj was completed, he returned to Aguacatán. He tried very hard to persuade Shas to go with him. He offered him ladino clothes to wear and gave him a very small load—a cage of birds—to carry during the day's journey down the mountain to the warm valley of Aguacatán. He wanted to keep Shas in good humor. But Shas felt very foreign and lonely in the strange town, and he decided to return home after three days.

His stepfather had died, and Shas rented a small house from his maternal uncle, Šun ʔOʔš, for his mother and his half-sister Sin ʔAwil, who was six years old. His mother did his laundry, and he began renting land to grow maize. When they were settled, his older sister, Maʔl ʔAnay, left her husband and came to live with them. She often quarreled with her mother and made life troublesome. Shas became restless.

I became an adult. I sought my own way of life. I searched for a new employer. I went to an employer at a coffee plantation[7] and completed thirty *tareas* [a month's work] at the plantation and then returned to the village.
     I didn't have a wife yet.[8] I walked all alone to the plantation.
     They were still using money of former times, for what was my day worth? It was only one *tuštuun* [from the Spanish *tostón*, a coin], only four *riaal* that the boss paid us in those times. We borrowed thirty pesos from him and it was a month's work: we had to repay it with thirty tareas. Thirty tareas for thirty pesos—a peso for a tarea in those times; but in those times we got our clothes cheap. We could get a *wiʔ šokomil šiʔ*, [chamarro, a woolen outer shirt] for thirty pesos, fifteen if it was loosely woven—only fifteen pesos, which isn't much. That is how I lived. Slowly I matured and became strong, but that was all. How much better [it would have been] if I had had a little of my own land! But I could only think about the boss: I completed my work at the plantation and returned home. But sure enough, I came home and borrowed more money, and slowly I increased my debt. I drank a lot in those times, so that the rum became very accustomed to me.
     I borrowed money from the boss;[9] I kept on drinking up the money, because what else was it good for? I got used to the liquor, and the liquor got used to me.
     I entered manhood and looked for a wife. I found a wife who was in the same state as myself: she was poor, too.

Shas's first wife was ʔAn Siʔč. When she moved into the house where his mother and sisters lived, Shas suggested they keep two fires burning in order to prevent arguments between the women. They lived together in one household for a full year, and it went well. ʔAn was as poor as he was, and her parents were dead. She was quick at work, and she loved the sunny lowlands and the work on the plantation. As long as they lived there, they lived happily and often enjoyed drinking together and with friends. Shas described her some fifty years later as very good at her work, but more strong-willed, or even mean, than some of his later wives.

So it was. We were the same, and so we went to the plantation, and without delay we set out to seek our livelihood. Soon we came to the town

K'aqb'al Čee.[10] We spent a week working there, but the wages weren't fair and we looked for another employer.

We met a woman. She was a widow but of great wealth. She may have had a hundred cattle in her corral. She had coffee fields; perhaps a hundred cuerdas of coffee, and I cultivated these for her. When the work was finished, it came to a hundred tareas. Then I did some tareas of wood. I finished in good time with the work, since I was young and nimble, and then I was free to wander around a bit.

The woman noticed that I had good character. I got out of the [difficult] work, and instead I only had to look after the cattle. There were animals in the corral, and I herded them. I milked them and then came home for breakfast. And there I was, I didn't have to work much more. When I judged it to be around noon, I went to change the animals again. I watered them, and that was all the work I had to do. I earned a hundred pesos a month—no, every two weeks I earned a hundred pesos. I got paid every fortnight. I had cash. Then she also gave me land, a place for my maizefield.

I sowed my maizefield. I sowed all kinds of things, because the spaces between the maize plants were wide—perhaps a single space between the plants was from here to the table.[11] I sowed a row of chile, and we wondered what else we could sow because there wasn't anything that soil couldn't grow. Whatever we wanted the earth would produce. One row of chile grew alongside the row with the maize plants and continued in the next row. We sowed *yuca* in other furrows, and the earth produced everything.

After I had harvested the things I had sown, I went to sell them on Sundays, and there was my money. My maizefield grew for me, and my day was paid too. Everything was fine. I stayed there a long time. I spent perhaps five years in Mala[12] with the woman employer.

I thought to myself: "I won't go back to our village. I'm estranged from the place, and since I have food and my salary, I have no wants." I had my clothes. I didn't lack anything and neither did my wife.

"It is better if we don't go back up to our village, for what would we do there? There isn't anything for us there. We don't have a house, we don't have land. I don't have a mother, and you don't have a father or a mother, and we'll be sad. At least we're equal—the land is neither yours nor mine, but equally ours—so let's die here," I said to my woman.

"It's all right," she answered. "We are alive. We have no worries. We have our pigs, chickens, and everything; for us it's like our home. Nothing is lacking. We have all the food we need, and we have money."

All this had happened because I had sold my soul[13] there in Mala. "Once and for all I won't leave," I kept thinking. "Rather, let us always live here."

But it happened that I had a dream.

In my dream I saw a ladino[14] appear. A woman was walking ahead of me. Have you seen women like the ones from Cotzal?[15] She was quite tall. She was walking ahead of me on a wide road, like that road there. She went before me; I was following her, it seemed, and it was under the trees. It was a beautiful place. There were coconuts and bananas above. We passed under them, just like under decorations made for the road [during a fiesta]. The woman went first, and I followed behind. Perhaps about as far as from here to the monument with the statue over there[16] was the ladino. He was mounted. I heard him whistle; he raised his hand and cried: "Stop!"

I stood still. I was watching the man, and when I turned, the woman had disappeared. Who knows where that woman went? She was no longer there, and when I looked around the ladino came up to me. He was riding a little horse, and he held a whip in his hand. I approached, and he came to a halt.

He said to me: "Where are you going?"

"Nowhere. I was going with the woman," I said.

"Ah, you thoughtless man, why do you follow after that woman?[17] Do you think she might be yours? She isn't yours at all. You have your own. You are very thoughtless, and I've been searching for you. It's been quite a while since I left to look for you, and I couldn't find you. Turn back! Don't follow that woman, turn back!" urged the man. So he said to me in my dream.

"Thank you," I answered him. The woman was gone, where could I go? The woman was no longer there, she had left. Only the man remained standing before me. "Well, never mind, I'd better go, then," I said to him.

"That's the road you shall take—not the wide one, but that narrow one."

He directed me down a small path; it was narrow as it went through the underbrush. It wasn't a trail; there was hardly any place to set my feet.

"Go along, and this way you'll reach the foot of the mountain. Then you have to ascend. You have to climb to the top of the mountain."

But what a towering mountain! It was of enormous size and great height.

"You shall climb the mountain, and when you arrive at the top of it your place awaits you, it is yours. There you shall build your house. There is your land. There is your house," said the man. So he said to me in my dream.

For a long while I spoke with the man.

"Thank you," I said to him.

"That is all—if you agree to go. If you don't obey you'll need the whip in my hand to teach you. This is your father, who will educate you if you don't obey. So you'd better go along," said the man to me. [He threatened me] with the whip he held in his hand, but all in the dream.

"All right," I said to the man. I went down the path. I arrived at the foot of the mountain and climbed up. Yes, there was a path, but it was very narrow. And how steep was the mountain I beheld! I climbed and climbed up the mountainside and when I was halfway up the earth rumbled under my feet, sending me plummeting to the bottom of the mountain. "Christ! What is this?" I cried, and climbed up again—the same:

When I got halfway up the earth slid underfoot and I fell to the bottom again. Ah, it was such trouble for me! There were roots of trees, all the things that grow in the underbrush. The mountain was thickly wooded, and there were vines, and I grabbed the vines to scale it: from vine to vine I climbed. After a third attempt I reached the top of the mountain. I had arrived.

What a huge plain! There were trees just like those tall ones on top of the mountain. I had arrived; I had reached the mountaintop—but what a huge mountain! Do you know the mountain K'aʔlil Caa? It was like the Čočol mountain but much higher. I arrived, and it was open country. Who knows where it ended? What a vast plain! And there were many trees like those trees [out there]. They grew in groves, and beneath them a broad meadow stretched out. There was grass, tall grass, but that was all. There were no maizefields, nothing. The earth was naked.

Ah, my eyes grew wide. But where should I go? At that moment, a ladino appeared before me. He just appeared and said, "Have you come?"[18]

"I have."

"Very good, you did very well. Don't waste your life, because this place is for you alone; it is yours now. The whole place is yours. It's up to you where to build your house and where to plant your maizefield, for the whole land is yours alone. You will have no trouble at all," he said.

I woke up with a start from the dream. What could it mean? I had dreamed perhaps half the night.

I woke up my wife. "I had a dream," I said to her.

"What did you dream?" she asked.

"My dream is full of punishment. It seems that we shouldn't live here, but should leave," I told her, "because of my dream."

"Well, what shall we do when we go?" we thought. "This is our maizefield, and these are our animals. Now what can we do with them? What shall we do?"

I wondered, I searched my heart. I wished the daylight would come. It dawned, and because I had many friends in town I knew of an old man, Juan, who owned the sacred bundle.[19] What's more, the Earth God[20] visited him. Not only did he divine as I do but the Earth God visited him. So I went to tell him of my dream.

"What shall I do? I had a dream. This is what I dreamt!"

"Ah, do come and see me, but come in the afternoon, and bring a big bottle of liquor for us," he said. "We'll consider the matter, and then we'll go," said the man.

We came to a large tree, a ceiba, and we arrived there at night. Perhaps half the night we had walked together. The place was familiar to us. It was far. We walked a long way, and at night we reached the tree. And the man got down on his knees to burn incense—just as I do. He began to burn incense, and then he called the Earth God. That was all. He finished with the prayers and snuffed out the candles.

I heard a sound—*tlin*—arise from the earth, and the ceiba trembled, and the ground shook. The earth moved, and then we heard, "Well, then, have you come?" A man's voice spoke to the old gentleman, Paa Huan Laʔn, the daykeeper.

"Well, have you come, Juan?" he greeted us.

"Yes, indeed I have come, I have come," answered he.

"Has Jacinto come?" he asked. How did the Earth God know my name? He talked the way we talk, just like the radio.

"Well, so you have come."

"I have come."

"Very good, and where is Jacinto?"

"There he is."

"Ah, look here, it isn't for him to live here any longer. This isn't his own place. Even though he may find wealth, he may live only six months longer and then die. He shouldn't live here, because this place here isn't for him. Instead, you must tell him to go back to his home village, to go back and remember his home village. His grandfather is greatly displeased with him, because he has looked all over for him but he is never in town.[21] Therefore, he must return. If he does not leave, he may ride a horse [= he may become wealthy], but it will be only six months more that he will be alive, and then he'll die. But if he returns to his home village he will grow very old, and he will enjoy his work. Likewise, his calling, which is the same as yours, will become known to him. Only in his home village will he fulfill his calling. There is no call for him here," said the Earth God to the old gentleman who burns incense.

And I listened to what he said. I understood, since I knew their language (because it wasn't in Ixil, but in Quiché that they were speaking), and I was listening.

[Afterwards, old Paa Huan said,] "That's what you have to do: you must leave, fool. Don't waste your life! You'll have land; you'll build a house. Now you have no land, but little by little it will appear—if you leave. If you don't leave, you'll die, for this isn't your place. Another man is the owner of this place here. That's all. There won't be any trouble. Go, and perhaps a year after you have arrived in your village the Day[22] will give itself to you," said the man. "Perhaps in a year the Day will come and remain with you, and later on the [knowledge of the] *meeša*[23] will manifest itself to you, but you must wait for it. You must not seek it out; just wait and see. You will receive your orders what to do. When you have counted the Day for two years, it will come, and there is where you will fulfill your office," he said to me.

"Very well," I answered. I just listened.

Shas and his wife obeyed the word of the Earth God. They left their comfortable life in the lowlands, sold their livestock, and returned to the mountains. And Shas continued to dream. It was during the first year after his return to the highlands that he received with certainty the knowledge of the day count.

THE CALL TO OFFICE

A man becomes a prayersayer by dreaming the twenty day names of the calendar. If the dreams occur repeatedly, he will seek professional analysis of them by a prayersayer, who will determine whether he has truly received the call. If someone comes from a family that has produced other prayersayers, it is easier to become accepted as an apprentice. Since Shas's family had produced prayersayers for at least two generations, his credentials were perfect.

The head prayersayer Pap We?l was Shas's personal counselor during the intensive period of dreaming. After a period of apprenticeship with him, Shas had a dream which made it clear that he in fact was also chosen to receive the sacred bundle.

Because the call to be a prayersayer comes from the day gods, one has to offer prayers to their counterparts on earth, the Alcalde crosses associated with the four year bearers of the calender and the saint statues (tiiš) in the churches. The call to use the b'aq' mič comes with the help of the earth or mountain-and-valley gods and of the departed souls of previous daykeepers. Special ceremonies are required to acknowledge their wishes. It is at the mountain shrines and in the cemetery that one offers prayers and gifts of candles and incense, but one should also offer candles to the Our Mother (the Virgin Mary) in the village church, to announce one's new status and to ask for blessing of one's difficult new profession.

No one instructed me about the Days; I just dreamt of them, and I went to ask the prayersayer what the dreams meant.

"Ah, but it's the Day who is giving himself to you. Don't worry. What you should do is offer something of yourself, present yourself before the Days. Perhaps you should offer gifts, perhaps you should offer prayers for it, so that the Days will give you some further knowledge of how it can be accomplished. It's the Days who will bestow the blessing on you, so remember the gods for it. Offer your candle, offer your prayers. Let's do that," said the prayersayer.

"Do me the favor, Pap," I answered. And it proved to be correct, because after my prayers, more dreams came. I dreamt all manner of things:

I dreamt that I was flying. I rose into the sky, and I looked down with the birds, and I flew around. I crossed a mountain, flying—in my dream.

It was because your vocation was given to you, I suppose.

So it was. Perhaps it meant that there would be a long life for me, I guess. And this was what I dreamt one time:

I had lifted myself into the sky by flying, and then I made many turns, just the way airplanes do, many turns in the sky. I soared up and down in the sky the way the black vultures do. And then I lost my desire to fly, but since I didn't know who had lifted me up I went on wandering in the sky. I came over a mountain. Well, it was one of our landmarks, Wiʔ Suʔl ʔA.[24]

Over there in our mountains?

Yes, in our township. I came to Wiʔ Suʔ ʔA in my flight, and then I came to Şeʔ Kampaano Wic[25] as they call it.

Yes, Suʔmal district.

That's it. There I went. And I descended into a valley surrounded by mountains. It was suddenly flat country. Well, the old gentleman is still there—you know him, don't you? Paa Meʔk Paʔl, who lives in ʔUčuč, and he performs the office of calendar priest.

Yes, of course, I know him.

Well, it was he who was seated in a ravine when I came. And I had a companion—old Paa Meʔk Kʼubʼ, who has since died, the one who served in the village government as . . .

Čusul and ʔalkaalte?

Yes, that was the man who accompanied me when I came to the old gentleman's.

"Have you come?" he greeted me. So said Paa Meʔk Paʔl to me.

"Yes, I have come."

"Ah, but that's it: How did you manage to get here? There's hardly a path to come on—there just isn't any," he said.

"Oh, there's no road, but it didn't bother me, because I was flying. And I didn't feel what I did. I didn't see anything," I told him, in the dream.

"Very good. Your ways are good indeed, because you will become knowledgeable. You will not become worthless. There will be a certain knowledge[26] with you," said Paa Meʔk Paʔl to me, in my dream.

When old Paa Meʔk Kʼubʼ heard that he said: "Ah, be quiet, Meʔk, you shouldn't talk that way. You shouldn't utter such words. Look here, you're [really] jealous of him, of what the young man does. You're envious of him. But the boy is good. He will prosper. There will be blessings for him in what he undertakes, because he is good. He will be capable of removing large tree trunks from the road, but you're not: while you can place the trees across the road, you're not capable of removing them. You're not good for anything. The boy, on the other hand, whatever there is, maybe a large tree trunk on the path, he'll take it away. So don't say what shouldn't be said because you're jealous. You heart is envious of him and of what he accomplishes," said old Paa Meʔk Kʼubʼ to him.

And while I was looking on, he [Meʔk Paʔl] lifted his hand to his forehead, and from his sitting position he disappeared into a ravine.[27]

That's right, because he talked too much.

Yes, that's what the old man told him, and he fell into a ravine. When he heard the word, he tumbled into the ravine. That was all.

"Forget it," said old Paa Meʔk Kʼubʼ. "Don't worry, this old man can't win over you. He's good enough to sprinkle lime, but what counts is to remove it. There isn't anything he can do to remove it, but as for you, whatever it be, like some large trees that have fallen down on the road, you will take them away. But he didn't say so, we did," said old Paa Me?k K'ub' to me.

So he told you.

Yes.

Because he perceived what you would accomplish.

That's it. But while he was talking like this, I woke up, and it was only a dream.

Then there was another dream I dreamt. It was this:

I saw a metal cable hanging down from the sky. It came down from the sky, and I held on to the lasso in my hand. How I went swinging—the way we do in our childhood, for fun, when we swing! That's what I was doing—and as I went backwards, who knows where the cable went, where it went up with me. And I came back down once more, but at every swing I went a little higher, and the cable went up higher and higher into the sky, where I remained. Little by little I went up.

"But what shall I do? I cannot jump down, because if I jumped I would surely die," I thought.

Perhaps four swings the cable took, with me swinging back and forth, and the fifth time it lowered itself gradually and I tried to let go. Then it happened again. It had lowered itself a little bit when off I went again with it. Then it lowered itself a little and the same thing happened again. The fourth time I landed, and there were some corral fences just like those walls there [of the room]. There was a corral, and when I went over it the fourth time I grabbed the side of it and let the lasso jump up into the sky; I let go of it.

You held onto the corral?

It was a corral I held onto, after I had gradually descended over it. I was back on the ground.

I woke up.

"Christ, what does that dream I had mean?"

I went to tell an old Paa about it who was also a prayersayer.

"What should I do? What is the significance of the dream I had? What I have dreamt is that I fly up into the sky and balance myself in the sky. Why do I do this?"

"Don't worry, it's all right. It isn't that you might die; you won't die. Rather, it means that your lifetime rises high, and it's certain that your destiny is the Day. It is yours—that is your vocation. It isn't that you will lose [your life]; rather, your life span will be long before the gods. Perhaps it's because you honor Our Father, you love the gods, you fold your hands [in prayer] regularly; so God will give you wisdom. But when God gives you knowledge you won't die soon after. Rather, you will grow old. Your life span will rise high; you won't die," said the prayersayer to me. That was it.

And he wasn't just saying so, but spoke from experience.

Yes. He knew why it was that way. And so my heart rejoiced. For what could I do if I had had to die soon—if I had been going to die tomorrow or the day after tomorrow, as I had thought? My heart had been frightened by the dream. That was what I [had feared]. But it was true that gradually my knowledge increased. Gradually I began to burn candles [perform ritual] along with my prayers. I was burning candles and praying. I didn't see the face of Our Father in the sky, nor did I see the faces of the gods, but slowly they revealed themselves to me.

Also, the old men, the prayersayers, recited their prayers, and I listened to what they did. I went to meet them at the places where incense is burned and in the cemetery; we met in front of the Alcalde cross of Our Father Kaqay.[28] I listened to their words—to what they said when they burned incense—and gradually they stayed in my head; slowly I learned them.

I didn't study the Days. While there are those among us who study the Days, sickness strikes us for it if we do. I dreamt of them, I just dreamt the Day.

You dreamt of it?

Yes, I dreamt our Lord ?liq' and I dreamt our Lord Čee. "This is the day we have today," they said. But it wasn't the Days themselves who told me, but an old man I dreamt of, or a ladino I dreamt of: "It is this day today. Keep it in your head," they would tell me, the [spiritual] old people in my dreams. And I went to see the prayersayers, the old men who are burners of incense, and I told them my dreams.

"It's the day gods who are giving themselves to you," they said.

"Really? Thank you."

And I kept it in my mind. I said nothing about it.

I went to the plantation, and I met a Chajul friend in the bunkhouse. I slept next to him. And I dreamt the Day, and the Day I dreamt was K'ač, I dreamt of 1 K'ač while I slept next to my compatriot from Chajul, and I told him of my dream.

I woke in the night: "Are you awake, wec-k'aol?"[29] I asked the man.

"Yes, I'm awake."

"What is the meaning of a dream I had?"

"What did you dream?" he asked.

"Nothing much, except that an old man came to me. 'Keep the day of today in your head. It's 1 K'ač today,' he said to me. What does that possibly mean? Which day is it today?" The Day hadn't appeared in my head yet; I had only dreamt about it.

And the man gave me advice: "Ah, it is the Days who are giving themselves to you, wec-k'aol! The Days will reveal themselves to you! Since you have dreamt the name of the day, you won't forget it. But I'll give you some help, because I know the day count. I'll give you its essence. Here is one *Tačb'al q'ii* [= one 13-day count] starting today: 1 K'ač today, tomorrow 2 Kan, the day after tomorrow 3 Kamel, the fourth day is 4 Čee, the fifth day is 5 Q'anil, the sixth day is 6 Čoo, the seventh day from now 7

Č'i?. 8 B'aac' will be on the eighth day," said the man to me. "8 B'aac', 9 ?Ee, 10 ?Aa, 11 ?I?ş̌, 12 C'ikin, 13 ?Aama will come forth, and so we'll have finished one count of thirteen days."

"And we carry on with another day count: With 1 No?q, you begin all over; [from] 1 No?q you carry on until thirteen. Thus you begin with 1 No?q, 2 Tiaš, 3 Kaoo, 4 Hunaapu, 5 ?Imuş̌, 6 ?Iiq', 7 ?Aq'b'al, 8 K'ač will come to pass, and this is the way the days shall come to pass until 8 K'ač comes around. On the twentieth day from today, 8 K'ač will come up. Don't forget your knowledge of it," said the man.

That was all he told me about the day names and once and for all they stayed in my head, all of them.

And also:

"If, when you begin to count the Day, there is no chapel on the plantation where you happen to be, go and pray before the gods' images [after you get home]. Say: 'The Days have surely given themselves to me, but don't hold me for it, don't punish me for it, for here is a little candle that I light before you. Don't let me get lost, don't let evil befall me. Don't hold me for it, for it wasn't I who asked for it. It happened in my dream; that's how it was given to me.' This is what you are to say. Go pray in the place of the gods, go light your candle, and choose a day, a good day, one of the chief days, and offer your candle. That's what you must do when you return, when you get to your village. There are prayersayers in your village. Go tell one of them, if you don't have your own," he told me.

"Very good, I'll do that."

I finished praying to the days on K'ač. Then I passed through the count once more. And after I returned to our village, having come up from the plantation, I went to speak with my prayersayer. I had one who always offered my gifts to the gods, and I told him that the Day had given himself to my mind.

"But what shall I do? What is necessary to serve the Day? The Days themselves are completely in my mind. I am capable of completing the count," I said to the prayersayer.

"Ah, what are you worried about? It's your destiny, indeed, that the Day has given himself to you. It's by no means everywhere that the Day offers himself; instead we are selected. It's your destiny, indeed, if the Day offers himself to you. What are you worried about? But the thing to do is to buy something [to offer]. The thing to do is to present yourself to the day gods. Before the Twenty Days you must present yourself. You must have a prayer session every day, every single day. When the twenty-day period is completed, we will celebrate a dawn ceremony. You must buy candles and five pounds of incense, and we'll offer the gifts to 8 B'aac'," said the prayersayer to me.

"All right then," I replied.

And I presented myself to the Days, to the Twenty Days. After this was done, a dawn ceremony took place, and we went to shield the candle—I had bought one for ten pesos—and keep watch over it (sitting up and praying all night). We celebrated the dawning of the day as proof that I had entered as one of the counters of the seats, the counters of the altars—that I was to be the guardian before the people. I entered before the Day.[30] This is what the Day bestowed on me, when I entered before the Twenty Days: now I was the one to burn the incense with my own hand. Whatever the prayersayer did, I repeated in my turn, and I carried through the count from the day when we had finished celebrating the dawn ceremony; I repeated once more whatever the prayersayer had done; where he had gone, there I went, too: before the chief crosses, the four chief crosses of the village I went alone to worship by burning candles and incense. But how afraid I was, for there were many people!—it happened that I arrived with many people—and at times my prayers came out correctly and at other times they didn't. But there were the Days [to be attended], every Day, every single Day—the same way until I completed [the count] before the Twenty Days once more. And only then had I finished.

Slowly the people began to hear that it had been almost a year since I had first received the Day in my mind. I already performed ceremonies. After another year had passed, one year later, the meeša was given to me. But one can't just get it somewhere; I had to find it little by little. I still had my dreams; there were always the dreams. Every day there was something I dreamt. After the twenty-day period had come to an end, I dreamt again.

What I dreamt was that officials (*mayuul*) of the town government came to get me in my house. They came to fetch me:

"We have come to take you, Pap," they said, "because the ʔalkaalte wants you in the courthouse." So said the officials to me in my dream.

"Let's go, then," I replied, and straightaway I left with them.

But I didn't arrive at the courthouse first. Instead, suddenly I was at the cemetery. I had come to the *Wiʔ Kamnaq* it seems, and there was a man who stood in the door—just the way the *b'aṣa mayuul* (first *mayor*) in the courthouse does. When I got to the *Wiʔ ʔAama* a man was leaning against a pillar, in my dream. He stood in the doorway and guarded it. He held his staff in his hand. He held his staff across the doorway when I arrived. I greeted him: "Čaʔš pap."[31]

"Tii," he answered, and he removed the staff from the doorway and I entered.

There were four old men beside the cross. They were seated; there were four of them. Their head shawls (*suʔt*) were very white; they wore *kotoon* jackets like this one, and in their hands they held a *paanyo* (handkerchief) just like this black one here, but very white. Similarly, their chests were wrapped in white material—not black, but white, and the headshawls they wore were white.

"Čaʔlaaṣ pap," I greeted the men.

"Čaʔlaaṣ *kumpaale*," they answered.

So I was already a "kumpaale." I didn't answer them.[32]

"Čaʔlaaṣ kumpaale. How are you? Have you come?"

"I have."

"Sit down in the chair. Come in, kumpaale, come close," they said.

They brought a chair. One of them stood up, and I sat down in his seat.

For heaven's sake, what was I doing? I was nowhere near the age of the old men who seated me in the chair. "And I hardly know anything," I said [to myself], and I stood up. But there was the man there at the door, the guardian of the entrance. I was going to go out, but he said,

"Wait, stand still! Stay there! Wait! You must watch what they will do. Only this little we will show you." So he spoke, the doorkeeper.

"Thank you," I replied.

There stood a man against the wall, before my eyes, and how the water streamed over the man! His body was green because of the algae—just as in brooks, that's what the man's body looked like. The water fell on his head—it streamed over him as he leaned against the wall. How the water poured over the man! He was drenched. I looked at him.

Was it the man at the door?

No, the man was surely a prisoner of the gods; he was dead, but he was a prisoner, a man who had practiced witchcraft [in his lifetime]. They are the ones who are kept in eternal punishment. That is what I came to witness in the Wiʔ Kamnaq. And I saw him leave. I saw him get out of the water and leave it.

And also, there was fire there. There was fire, and he entered it. There was a section of a metal grating laid across some stones; the iron was this thick. It was laid across the fire, and I saw the man walk across the fire. Slowly he crossed over the metal; it was the metal he walked on. But at each step, the skin of his foot stuck fast, and when he lifted his foot the skin remained on the metal, right on the metal. And while I watched him, the flesh of his foot stuck fast. He took two steps, and then with the third step he came to the middle of the fire, on top of the iron grating. The fire was burning fiercely. When he got to the middle of the fire, the grating turned over under him and he fell into the flames.

Well, he came out, but like a pail of syrup for candy—it was a huge pail that came out, it boiled over like soap (made from boiling bones), bubbling all over. That was what I witnessed. Well, I had seen enough and was ready to leave once more.

"By God, I've got to leave," I said to myself, and I started out. But the man at the door, the guardian, questioned me:

"Well, then, is it good what you've seen? Which will be your profession? Do you like what the old men did to you who seated you in the chair? Well, that's your profession. That's the calling you will follow. But you'd better not follow it as that man did. That's the little we will teach you; that's the little you will remember," said the man.

Well, I didn't answer. I just listened to his speech.

"Go along, go along," he said, and he removed the staff and gave me a slap on the shoulder, and I went out into the cemetery again.

I went to get the man—the official who had come after me, the messenger. Surely he was still guarding me, so I went out and went before him. We went down the hill and we came to the courthouse. Straightaway I came to the courthouse of the ʔalkaalte.

And again: when I got to the courthouse, I went right into the office where they hold their hearings. I entered with him, and there again I said "čaʔlaaṣ pap," I greeted the man on my arrival.

"Čaʔlaaṣ kumpaale. Well, then, have you come?"

"I have come."

"It is good, indeed, that you have come, very good. You shall remain as my replacement. I will leave my chair, but you will stay in it—you will get to know the daughters and sons now," said the man.

"But no, Pap, how can it be that I stay in your chair? I have no knowledge, I have no experience. I haven't held even a small office, not even as mayuul have I worked in the courthouse. I shall have little knowledge of the work. I certainly won't do. And the people know that I am really poor; they won't give me an office," I said.

"Oh, not at all, that's not what is said: all the people have given their vote for you. It's an order that you enter here; it's not for your own pleasure. But wait, don't pay attention to any of the people's gossip about you. Don't pay any attention. The only word you must obey is what I tell you," he said.

There was a bell near him and he rang it. Like the church bell he shook it: *tsilin* sounded the bell, and the first mayuul came running in. He had summoned the first mayuul by ringing the bell.

"Where is the key you carry with you?" he asked the first mayuul.

"There it is, hanging on the wall."

"Go bring it here," he ordered.

"Very well." The first mayuul went to get the key from the wall.

"Hand it to him—not that he seeks it, but hand it to him, and go show him the jail. Let him see what the jail is like and whether he is able to open it or not. Watch," said the ʔalkaalte. So spoke he to the first mayuul.

"Very well."

We left. We arrived in front of the courthouse of long ago; the present courthouse had not yet been built. The courthouse of that time was quite small. And so I went to open the jail—also, the jail was on the outside [of the courthouse], in daylight. It wasn't the way it is today, inside. Rather, it was outside, alongside the porch. A prisoner could look out over the marketplace. Before us was the marketplace, and we watched from the window. Today, how much can we see? But in the old days [the jail] was ancient, a thing of the forefathers.

Well, I came to the jail and I went to open it. There was no one, only silence in the jail; nobody was there. I peered inside: nobody—there was no prisoner inside. After I had looked inside, that was it. I locked it again, and then I left to report to the ʔalkaalte—but in my dream. I was walking along, but behind me followed the first mayuul, and the key which he carried I was now carrying. When we got back to the ʔalkaalte, he asked the first mayuul: "How did it go? Was he able to open the jail?"

"Yes, he opened it and closed it again."

"Ah, very well, then, Pap, what more do you want? You're free now. Go ahead, there isn't anything to worry about. Go and walk around now, see if there isn't someone a bit drunk out there, or someone quarreling. Bring them and put them into the jail. That's the way prisoners are taken. Don't worry about it," said the ʔalkaalte. So it appeared to me, but this was in my dream.

I answered, "Very well," and I walked out, putting the keys into my [pocket]. There were keys of this size and there were others of that size; there were small ones—and the chain that held them was this thick. I put them into my pocket and left the courthouse. After I had passed the marketplace, I suppose, I went down to my house. And I was already holding the staff of office under my arm. How the tip of the cane glistened!

I got to my house. My grandfather, who raised me, had been dead a long time—he was long dead when the Day gave itself to me—but when I arrived home he was there, sitting in the chair. It was in my house, and this is the way the table that was the altar was placed.

"What could it be, Pap?" I said. "What is it that those men have done to me? They have given me the staff! What shall I do with it?" I said.

"Ha, ha, ha, they've already told me. They spoke to me, but I didn't like the idea, because surely it will bring difficulties. What has happened to you isn't an easy thing. You will hear both good things and bad things because of it.[33] But what can you do? It is surely your destiny. What can you do about it? Lay down the staff on the altar," he answered. So he spoke to me in my dream, and I placed the staff upon the altar.

When I awoke, there wasn't any staff, but that's how it began. The staff was the b'aq' mič that had come to me. But it was only later that I thought of what I should say and do. Meanwhile, I went to tell the prayersayer about the dream, and he said:

"That's nothing to worry about. Probably it refers to the office which the ʔaanhel will send. Probably it refers to your work, which the holy souls [of previous daykeepers] will send. Perhaps the sacred bundle will come to you. There isn't anything we can do, but since you dreamt the holy souls and the ʔAlkaalte, we should go and make your offering among the souls (Komon ʔAama), for it is the souls who will give you your work, whatever you have to do. The only thing we can do is to go and speak [to them], and to make your offering: say that your calling has appeared and ask what is to be done, what is the message that the gods are sending you. It is the gods who know, and it is the souls who know, so we shall offer your candles to Our Mother and to the souls. We shall call the ancestral souls, because they are the ones who entered the plea for your office," said my prayersayer.

"Please, do me that favor, Pap," I said to him. And he went to give my offerings again for whatever my calling was—the calling that had been given to me in the dream. That was what he went to pray for among the souls [aṭ Komon ʔAama]. He returned from the cemetery and went to the Kučuč; he went to the ʔalkaalte Tiʔ Kaqay in order for me to receive instruction concerning my work.

And then many dreams came to me. I kept on dreaming, nothing but dreams appeared to me. Slowly the sacred bundle came to me; slowly came the measure, the stones for me to gather.[34] I didn't buy them, rather I had to collect them. Little by little the day count began; I saw in my dream that the sacred bundle was put before me. There was the *tal suʔt*[35] placed before me, and I was already weighing [the fortunes of] the daughters. I already was able to see the transgressions of some daughters, which they came to speak to me about. I did it already in my dreams.

"You must not do it, you must not tell [the people]," I thought. But I went to tell the prayersayer about it.

"This is what I dreamt again, Pap. What does the dream mean?"

"Ah, don't worry, the dream is a good one, for it's about the office the gods will give you. But follow the call! A sick person may come to see you, and you will see what his offense is: whether he's sick because of an offense or whether he has an enemy [performing witchcraft] against him. And so you will take his trouble away." The prayersayer showed me what needed to be done and which was the Day I should ask about, which was the Day that would answer.[36] That was all, and he showed it to me.

Little by little it happened. Gradually the people heard what it was that I had and they came, just as [the dream said]. They came asking, "Please, do us a favor if—as they say—you have it, and give us our 'destiny-reading,' because we have a problem." It went slowly, and it came out correctly. Whatever offense it was they had committed, it came out clearly, and they understood. "That's true," they would say. So that was when the divining began. People heard it, and many of them came to me. And I kept on dreaming.

I dreamt I was flying like an airplane. I felt I was ascending into heaven. I was flying back and forth, all over the sky. Then I descended to the ground. At times it was above a corral, and it was the corral I held onto when I descended; it was the corral I reached for and I slowly came down to the ground—in my dream.

But it was the *piadoor* again who gave good advice, the prayersayer who had the knowledge. After I dreamt the dream, I went again to tell him.

"Certainly, your life will rise. You will grow old in your work, but do it straightforwardly! Don't do what someone may tell you to, because it must not be: 'Lay down an offering against someone. This is what we've been doing: we have a quarrel. Can't you cast a sickness on him?' they may say. Don't answer them or pay any attention. Only for a sick man should you perform offerings. There may come to you another who says: 'Do me a favor, Pap, and perform an offering for me that will bring me money.' Those words are all right, and that's what you'll ask about. That's your task. Don't lend your hand [to harm] one of our younger or older brothers because—poor you!—you'll only find a chain lowered around your neck, and perhaps you won't benefit from your office," said the prayersayer, because he knows how to warn and how to counsel, whatever is necessary.

That is what happened, and gradually people heard about it.

WIVES

I had begun with the calendar count; the Days had come into my mind. So it came to pass. But I still hadn't seen any good fortune, because it wasn't my own land where I planted my maizefield. I was only renting the land, that was all. Sometimes it was good soil that I was given, and at other times it was very poor; it didn't produce any maize. So I stayed at the plantation. Only there could I make any money. And then the woman I was married to died [for me].[37]

Just living at the plantation with her was all right. She didn't complain; it was her wish that we stay at the plantation. But then my heart didn't like it any more. Besides, one after the other our children were born. I had two children by her. I talked to her; it was all right for her, because she was content with our trips to the plantation, but I was tired of it.

It is easy now because we go by truck, but in former times . . .

Yes, indeed, on foot it was, and what a sorry situation: we carried our food—we suffered so much under the burden of our food—and, besides, there were the children on top of it! We didn't make much progress, and that was what made me think. I told her: "Never mind, don't you go to the plantation anymore, but I'll plant our maizefield." I had always planted a maizefield before leaving when we went together, but when we returned from the plantation, sometimes the beans we had sown with the maize or the little *chilacayotes* underneath were not there anymore; they had been stolen. The same with the maize: sometimes it had been depleted by robbers. We would search and search for the last bits and would only carry away some two nets full. So I said to her: "Ah, what we're doing won't do. We'll have more children, and then woe be unto us. We'll only cause their souls to wander.[38] You'd better stay while I go alone down to the plantation. You must look after our maizefield. You should be the one to eat what they've been stealing. Certainly, you should be the one to eat it. You must stop going to the plantation. You mustn't borrow any more money for yourself.[39] Instead, you must watch our maizefield," I said to her.

"If I didn't know how to work, then such words would be justified. But I'll never say: 'What a lot of work!' I'll never say: 'What a lot of grinding!' because I know how to work.[40] No indeed, I'm not staying behind," she said.

That's what made me angry: "Your way of thinking won't do!" I said.

Gradually we began to quarrel. I separated from her, and she remained alone.

Only because of that you split up?

It was only for that reason that we separated. She didn't agree. There was my maizefield. I planted it—sometimes I sowed twenty cuerdas, sometimes twenty-five—but it just got robbed, because they would see that we had gone to the plantation. A lot would be stolen, because the maizefield was left unattended. No one was taking care of it; it was neglected. When we returned, we would only harvest a few [ears of maize] that were left behind. If we were lucky, we would fill two little nets with what hadn't been taken by the robbers: all the beans and the chilacayotes would be gone, lost to thieves. That was unacceptable to me. But when she didn't agree, I said: "Too bad. If you don't agree, then it's better that we separate. Since you don't agree with my words, it's useless. Besides I don't want to do it anymore because it's very troublesome to carry the children. It's reasonable what I tell you: that you stay close to our maizefield, that you guard it and eat from it with the children. As for me, I'll go. And another thing, you mustn't borrow any more money. If you really want to go with me to the plantation, you can just help me. Who knows if tomorrow or the day after tomorrow I'll die, and then who would be your companion? You would have to go all by yourself to the plantation [to repay your debt]," I said to her. But she didn't agree.[41]

    ʔAn liked the life at the plantation. She could not reconcile herself to staying in the highlands alone. She and Shas had been traveling back and forth for almost six years. In the highlands, they rented a house at Wiʔ C'al for two years, another at Şeʔ Wic for three years. Finally, they bought land at Şeʔ Suʔmal, twelve hours by foot from Nebaj. It was during this last period that Shas began visiting a second woman in Nebaj. He describes the second woman as attentive and friendly, with the prettiest face of all his wives. Her name was Siʔt Pop. He would have married her, but her mother did not want her to leave the house, expecting her to marry a man who would move in with her. Shas had a daughter by Siʔt. Even after he stopped visiting her, he sent money to her for their child Maʔl K'ub'. Siʔt married someone else some time later.

    The separation from ʔAn became final when Shas was called to visit a sick person in Salquil which meant an absence of four or five days. ʔAn did not want him to go, and he never returned to her. While he was in Salquil, a man from C'alb'al with a sick wife offered to take Shas into his house while he was attending to his wife's case. So Shas stayed for another five days, even though he already had been gone for fifteen days. On the day 8 Q'anil he had a dream about Sin K'ač, who lived next door to the couple he was staying with. In the dream, the woman put on a shawl and came to the fence to talk to him: "I'm waiting for you. Don't you want to come and see me? Here is a present for you," she said, and she handed him a tal suʔt. "Don't be sad, I am here!" she said to him.

When he awoke, Shas thought about the dream. He could not decide what to make of it. He told it to his host, who said, "Well, if it weren't for your wife . . . ?" Asking about Sin K'ač, Shas found out that she was a widow; he had known her a long time ago. He kept thinking, "The dream does not get lost [= the dream must be right]. Perhaps it's good!" By coincidence, the woman came over shortly afterwards with some b'ošb'oʔl (a special dish of cornmeal mush wrapped in leaves with a hot sauce) for Shas. He came in and found the food in the kitchen. His patient teased him, saying, "Your sweetheart brought your breakfast." He went over to see Sin K'ač, because he was curious to hear what she would say. Although the man he was staying with did not approve, Shas told her that he was always quarreling with his wife. They talked for a long time, and Shas proposed to come and live with her for a while. But she said: "If you only want to come for a while, I won't like it." She kept saying: "Too bad you have a wife; otherwise I'd think about it. I have to stay here, because it is my mother's place and I have to take care of my brother." (Shas's friend had warned him already of Sin K'ač's younger brother, who was part of her household.) "Too bad that my parents are dead, or I'd ask them for advice . . ." In the end Sin persuaded him to stay with her. When he asked his friend to go along with him to get his things from Šeʔ Sumaʔl, the friend declined, saying: "That's no good. You have children, and if you leave them they should at least get your property." He never returned.

Shas's daughter, who was six or seven years old, left her mother a month later and walked all the way to Nebaj to ask at her aunt Maʔl ʔAnay's house about her father. Maʔl sent a message to C'alb'al, and Shas and Sin went to fetch the little girl the following Sunday. The child was happy to stay with Sin. Six months later, ʔAn remarried and moved away to Seʔ ʔAmaq' with Shas's young son. There, eventually, she died. His son has always been a stranger to him, even though Shas has offered him an inheritance.

I searched for a replacement for her [ʔAn], and I found another woman. I was married to her perhaps four years—no, five years. I moved in with her. She was good-natured and pleasant, but she had a younger brother, and he didn't like me. I was working a lot in those days. There were many jobs to be done—just as now—and I had obtained a loan, I had money. It was all right. Since her house was small, I said to her: "Let's make it nicer," since I was getting a loan. "Let's make it pretty. Let's collect the wood; perhaps we can change it," I said.

"Very good, if you can manage. It would be nice to change it," she said.

It was a great pleasure to talk about it at first. Unfortunately, it disturbed the man [her brother]. When we decided to improve the house, there was a person who was envious of me, and he counseled the woman's brother against me. And having been counseled, her brother accepted the advice. When I wanted to build the house, he wouldn't work with me, but sought his own work. I was the only one who was interested in working. When I noticed this, we talked. I had sought a man to work on the house—I had hired a carpenter—and he saw that after the foundation was laid down my wife's brother wasn't there to work, but sought work on his own.

"He doesn't approve of our wanting to rebuild the house," said the carpenter.[42] "Why not ask him? It's useless for us to continue alone, because he must not approve of our work if he isn't working with us. What is happening that he doesn't like it? Go ask the woman, and ask him, too, why it is that he doesn't work, because it's for all of you, not only for [you alone]. Even though you are building the house, after you've built it you can't carry it away! If the woman should die, it would belong to him, since the land isn't yours," said the old man.

"All right," I said. I asked the brother about it.

"Ah, it must not be; you shouldn't build the house. It's up to you— build it, since you have the money—but I won't give you my approval, because this land is mine. What if, after building the house, you should buy some property of your own? You'll try not to leave it behind; you may try to take it away. I'm telling you right now that you're only borrowing it," he said.

And when his sister was there, I said: "This is what he told me," and I asked her, "What shall we do? Shall we build the house or not? What your brother said is something else. Why should I make myself suffer needlessly? I'll leave it up to you, but wouldn't it be possible [to divide the land]?" Because this is what the carpenter had told me:

"Her situation isn't good, because the land is owned jointly; she doesn't own a piece by herself. She doesn't have any claim to inheritance for herself; it isn't divided. She ought to consider what you tell her—that the land should be divided, so that she knows what is hers and he knows what is his, and whatever is her part, that's where you should build the house. It will be your soul's remembrance after you die, because it will be left to her," said the carpenter.

And so I told her, but she didn't like it. She didn't agree.

"It can't be: after I divide the land, he may run off." (Her brother didn't have a wife yet, he had been living with us.) "Who knows where he might go? And this can't be. My mother's soul will get angry at him. Even worse, she'll take me," said the woman. She feared her death.[43]

Ah, well, I went to talk to the carpenter again.

"Well, then, forget it. This thing isn't for you. Let's stop the work. The work you do will be in vain. It doesn't make sense. Perhaps it's already been decided by them; perhaps they are just watching. Just leave it alone. Let's abandon the work," said the old man.

So it was left. Perhaps we had finished two rows of the foundation; so it remained.

You had laid down the foundation of the house?

We had put down the foundation of the house. We had thought of improving the house, but the man didn't like it, and so it was left unfinished. All my efforts were wasted—I had cut the wood, I had prepared it for the construction of the house, except for the roof—because they didn't support me any more, I guess. And my soul wandered:[44] "The hell with it all, it doesn't matter."

And little by little we began to quarrel. After I had moved in with her, we had been successful in what we did; we had our maize together, we had acquired cows and a horse together. But once her brother placed himself between us, the arguments began between us, and we separated—and she took the cows away from me because I had come to live there. I had three cows and a horse, and when I had to leave her house the animals stayed with her. She took all of them. Only one animal did I get, and only because I went to complain [at the courthouse].

[At first] she went to complain about me at the courthouse—she told them that I shouldn't have anything, because I didn't know how to work. She said I wasted my days entirely with ritual and came home only to eat. I went out all the time to worship, she said, and came back to scold her about my food; that's what she said to the ʔalkaalte. And he believed her, and I was called to the courthouse:

"What is it that you're doing? Why do you punish the woman? Why do you scold the woman?" he said. "Is it true? When you came to live with her, she said, she gave food to you, but you only go around wasting time, and then you come to scold her about your food. Any why is it that you keep bothering her? If you've left her, leave her alone. Whatever animals there are at the woman's place, will remain, she says, because they are hers. They're her mother's and her father's, she said; they remain with her. And you're thinking of taking them, when they aren't yours?" said the ʔalkaalte. She had prepared a letter and put it into the hands of the ʔalkaalte and he didn't know what I had been doing with her.

Was it true?

Well, no, but what happened was that I just waited [without offering my side of the story]. Later, one of my employers did me the favor. I went to tell him:

"Please, since you know about what I've been doing with the woman: true, I did come to live with her, but she had nothing whatsoever when I came, absolutely nothing. She had no maizefield when I arrived. She had a small maizefield, but it was full of underbrush. After I married her, I cleared the maizefield, but it produced little. On the other hand, mine, which I sowed together with her, produced well. We fattened a pig and sold it, and that's how I bought the cow. Granted, the pig was hers, but I bought it; I bought the maize and fed it. It grew fat, and we sold it. We didn't sell it alive, we slaughtered it and made soap the way it was made in the old days. We made soap from the animal together, and I went to sell it in K'usal. I brought back the money and simply handed it to the woman. We counted the money. It was 600 pesos we received for the pig, from the soap we had made. I worked with her, and with the money we earned we bought the cow."

It happened that the old man from whom I had bought the cow was still around, and he went [to the courthouse] to tell the true situation. It contradicted what she had said: "It was my mother's and my father's, the cow was there when he came, he had nothing . . . I was only feeding him," she had said. So she had told the ?alkaalte, this was in the document she handed to the ?alkaalte.

I told my employer: "This is what I did, maybe you noticed? You didn't see me just lounging around and going for walks, as she says? Of course, I do walk around, but there is a hired hand who comes to work. It isn't as if I didn't plant my maizefield. The maizefield is there, and so are the hired hands I pay—which is why I wasn't working, as she said. Nothing, not even a little bit, she said, will she return. I left the maize with her, a full granary, and she took it. And there are three cows; she isn't giving me my share of those either. 'It's mine,' she keeps saying, but I paid for it.

"Also, I was the one who rented the pasture for the animals. She hardly knew where the pasturage for the cows came from. It was I who rented it. I rented the pasture for them from some men. She didn't even know what I talked about with them, how much I paid them per month for the pasturage for the animals."

Well, it was my employer, Paa Q'es Kandelaario—he's dead now—who prepared the document for me. He wrote my document, because he remembered when I worked for him. True, I took up with the woman, but I always went to the plantation. It wasn't that I didn't go to the plantation. I hadn't sold myself to the woman. This is what I told him: "You know that I always go to the plantation. Even though I went to live with her, I still went to earn money at the plantation. And she has two children, and I take care of them well. They're hardly without clothes; I clothe them. So it isn't as she says, that I don't work for them and only live there. And she won't even give me my cow, she says."

Well, he made out a letter for me. It was well done, what he wrote. "Go take it to the ?alkaalte." And I went to leave it in the ?alkaalte's hands. So that's the way I prevailed over her so that she gave me one of the cows; two stayed with her. I took it away, and that was all. It was all because of her younger brother, who didn't like me because I married her. He didn't accept me, just because of the house I was going to build. That is what bothered him—that I came to live there and the land was his. "He'll build the house, and then he'll drive you out. But why should you give it to him? He'll build the house on your land, and it's your mother's and your father's property," so they had said to the woman.

And the ʔalkaalte did the favor of telling her: "Leave me alone. You're just a liar, because here are the words his employer writes. He has his employer, I see. How is it possible that you say he is lazy while this here is a testimonial to his work? He has his employer; he worked for him, it says, and you don't say that. 'The man does not work,' you say; well, you're deceitful, you're a thief. It isn't our fault but yours if you don't understand: If you don't give up the cow, you'll go to jail. Give it up. Tomorrow the posse will go and bring it in from your fields," the woman was told.

So the animal was brought in by the posse.[45] She lived in C'alb'al; that's where they went to fetch my cow. Well, I got only one animal and two stayed with her when I separated from the second woman.

The separation from Sin is the only one in Shas's life that involved confrontations at the courthouse. Shas thought that one of his enemies had counseled Sin and her brother against him; the letter with the untruthful statements about him was written by Kat C'uʔc', a friend of Sin's. The separation from Sin was the one in his life that hurt Shas deeply. He had been full of good intentions and very much in love with Sin. He had one son with her, Ŝaʔp C'uʔč, named after Shas's father. The little boy was a year and a half old when Shas had to leave C'alb'al. He was brought "buenamente" (freely) to stay with his father after he had stopped nursing and Shas had settled down with his last wife.[46] Sin never married again. She died some nine years later during an influenza epidemic and was buried in Wiʔ Košoʔ together with one of her daughters. The second daughter, Sin C'uʔč, often visits Shas and brings small gifts. She considers him her father, since she cannot remember her own, who died when she was very small.

When Shas left Sin, he sold his cow and bought land in Ŝeʔ K'aʔŝ. Then he went to look for another woman to take care of his own and his little daughter's needs. He remembered Taa, whom he had met during his travels. She was either widowed or unmarried and had a small daughter. Taa moved in with Shas. This was a less formal relationship than his previous ones; she cooked and washed for him and his daughter and went to the plantation with him when he needed her.

The third woman, I think, was Taa, old lady Taa. She's dead now. She didn't do anything against me.[47] We went to the plantation, and she left me there. There is a plantation at Mușan, and some workers worked at another plantation called Montancia. She had friends among them, and they took her away when they came up from Montancia. Yes, they agreed upon it during market day at Mușan. They saw each other at the market and came to an agreement about when they planned to go back, and she told them she would be ready. I didn't know anything about what she was thinking, but—of course—it was Sunday, and I changed my clothes, and she didn't go to do the laundry. Instead, she was laying in a store of tortillas, a lot of them, for her trip. She had prepared a lot of dough. I just watched her; I didn't say anything to her. She put on the griddle and cooked the tortillas on it. She must have made a whole basket of tortillas.

"What is all the food you're making for?"

"It's nothing. We'll probably come back late from work, and then I'll only have to reheat them," she said to me.

"Perhaps she's right," I thought. "Ah, that's all right," I said. That was all. I just listened to the words.

When it dawned Monday, I said: "Hurry, we have to go. The time passes quickly, it'll soon be noontime. Let's go right now."

"I'm not going to pick coffee beans today. Yesterday I didn't wash, so I'll go wash today; tomorrow I'll go with you," she said to me.

"Oh, indeed?" I said.

"Yes."

"All right, never mind, go and rest a day." And I left. I went to the coffee harvest. She saw that I had left, and when the workers came up—a group of workers from Montancia—the men took her along, they say. She was ready with her food, and they took her with them.

Then the foreman came to me among the coffee trees. It was noon. He came to ask me: "What happened to you?"

"Nothing happened to me," [I said], since I didn't know what the woman had done. "I didn't do anything."

"Didn't you fight with her?"

"No, I didn't."

"And where is she?"

"She didn't come because she didn't do the laundry yesterday. 'I'll go wash, but tomorrow I'll go with you,' she said, and stayed behind."

"Oh, it isn't good what's happening to you, for the woman has left," said the foreman.

"Oh, I didn't know that. It must be true, because yesterday she began to make tortillas. She had her food all ready, and I asked her and she said, 'Why, sometimes it's late when we come home from work, and I may be tired, and then we can just reheat them.' 'Perhaps she is right,' I thought. I didn't know what she was thinking."

I stayed behind alone. The foreman told me that the boss had said: "Go ask the man, what are you going to do? Are you going to let her go, or shall we go and stop her? What did the woman do? Did he beat her? Does he want her to leave? It's possible to bring her back. There's a plantation called Horizonte; she barely reached there to sleep, because it was late when they left. I saw them leave."

"So," the foreman asked, "what are you going to do? Do you want her to just leave? If you don't, we'll go and bring her back. We'll go with the alcalde, and the boss will give us horses. There's no problem. He'll give you a horse. 'And ask the woman,' he said, 'why she went away and who scolded her so that she left.' What you did to her, that's what he wants to know. 'And we'll go and bring her back, tell him,' said the boss."

"Very well, then, if you do me the favor, let's bring her back. As it is, I haven't quarreled with her; I haven't had a fight with her. Who knows what she did, why she went? If you'll do me the favor, if he'll do the favor, let's go and get her back," I said to the foreman.

"All right, get done early and leave your coffee, and then we'll go to the boss and see what he says," said the foreman.

"All right," I said. But I didn't feel like a person. My soul just wandered. My heart was sad, because I hadn't quarreled with her; my heart was sad about what it was. "What shall I do?" I was thinking to myself. Well, then the time came for me, sometime past two o'clock, maybe almost three, and I returned from the coffee grove and went immediately to leave my coffee to be weighed. I went by to turn in my coffee at the ranch and went to see the foreman. "Here I am, I've come," I said.

"And your coffee? How are you going to turn it in?"

"I already turned it in."

"Ah, very good. So let's go, let's go and see. But what are we going to do? I'm thinking . . ."

And wasn't it far where she had gone?

No, there was a plantation up the way that she had gone to, just as we do when we go back [to Nebaj].

"We'll get there to sleep tonight. It's no effort on horseback, so we'll get there in time, even though it may be after eight o'clock when we reach the place where they sleep in their bunkhouse. That's where the boss said we should meet the alcalde[48] who'll go with us." That's what the boss said to the foreman, and the latter gave me advice:

"Think it over well, because I was wondering myself. The boss says, 'Why, damn it, if a man persuaded her, catch him and tie him to the tail of the horse and bring him down immediately; and likewise the woman: tie her and bring her down. And if something happens, if the man who took the woman turns on you, here's a gun. There's no problem, just shoot him. That's an order. Wherever you end up [in jail] I'll go there and give [the explanation]. I'll come and free my hired hand,' said the boss.

"But I was thinking it over, and it seems to me it can't be done. It seems useless to do this. In the end, the boss will be all right, because he is a free man, but as for you, you may end up a prisoner because of the woman. Who knows if it really happened, if it was really a man who took her?—

and then we'll become prisoners, both of us. I'll be mixed up with you. All of us will go to jail. Anger is dangerous because . . . Perhaps you'll get hurt by the man in his anger . . . How much is the woman worth? Would it be possible to let her go? Let's leave her alone—let her go! It isn't as if there weren't any more women in town! Don't be sad! Go look for another one for yourself because it's very dangerous what we're planning to do, and what the boss says is dangerous. No, no, no . . . I'm thinking it mustn't be done. It is wrong. We won't come out well with the [boss's] plan," said the foreman.

And so I thought it over: "Ah, what's the importance of her? Never mind, forget it, sir. Let her go. She isn't important to me. What you say is right, and it's hardly for yourself that you're speaking. Let her go, since that's her wish. I'd only feel embarrassed facing her if I went to bring her back. Also, she would repeat it to me: 'You ran after me,' she'd say. No, it's better to forget it. Let her go. I have only six tareas more to do. It's only another week I have to complete and I'll be finished with the tareas and I'll leave, so never mind, let her go," I said to the foreman.

"All right, let's go and stop the man [= the boss]. I'll tell him that we won't go, that I asked the man about it [and he said] 'No, let her go, because it's her wish. Forget about it. If we go and catch her, I might beat her, and she might do something to me. I don't like fights, so let her go, since it is her wish. There wasn't anything—I haven't beaten her, I haven't done anything to her, but it's of her own will that she left. So let's leave her alone. Maybe she is sad. Let her go. It's up to her,' he told [me]," said the foreman. He went to tell the boss.

"Ah, damn it, man, what a weakling! Well, then, let's forget it," said the boss. And so it was left. I didn't go; she went back. Nobody held her back. She went back, and she went to her house. It may have been a week later that I returned. I didn't go to see her. That was all. That's how I separated from her, the third woman.[49]

Taa had not left with another man, but with a couple she was friends with. Shas stayed with his sister when he returned to Nebaj and avoided Taa, but she sent her uncle over with a gift of rum, and he persuaded Shas to talk to her. Shas was half drunk when he went to see her. She was very happy and cried when he came, but he was angry: "How did I injure you? Did I hit you? I'm only here to greet you; I don't have any desire to be with you. Why don't you go back to your friends who took you? If you were homesick, why didn't you tell me?" They proceeded to get drunk together, and Shas went back to her. He could not forget the insult he had suffered, however, and his anger returned from time to time. They did not get along anymore. After another week, Taa left town and found another man to live with. She died only a few years later and was buried in Pulay.

It seems that Taa resented Shas's absences during his ceremonial activities just as Sin had. She would not say much when he left on his praying missions, but she would be angry when he came home. Furthermore, Shas insisted on sexual abstinence during curing ceremonies. Nine days of vigil were usually required, but sometimes the time span was twenty days. "God doesn't like it for one to arrive before him *mojado*," he explains.[50] In earlier times sexual abstinence was observed not only by the prayersayers and daykeepers during ceremonies, but by everyone involved when the fields were being planted, when the wood for a new house was being cut, and during the final five days of the Mayan calendar year. Shas reported that one reason houses do not last as long as they used to is that people do not observe this custom any longer. Most of his wives did not like Shas's faithful observance of this custom either. In retrospect, this was for him final proof that they had not really been destined to be his companions for life.

During the time he lived with Taa, his mother died. He tells his friend, Kuʔ Bʹel, about it:

Fortunately, I didn't have to bury many dead; I buried only my mother. As for my father, I was so small when he died that I didn't realize it. And there was my grandfather—I buried him, but I don't remember it; my soul hadn't arrived yet. But I saw my mother die, since I lived for a while near her.

Well, my mother went to the plantation. The only reason she went was that my younger sister had promised to marry. She separated from the man after he had paid the bridal money to my mother, I suppose, and, of course, my mother had spent the money. When my sister didn't keep her word and separated from him, he demanded his money back. My mother went to get the money from old Paa Sayiʔ at Manantial; she went away to work at the plantation.

It was a miracle, indeed, that I found myself together with her. It was only ten days after she came to the plantation that she died. She became sick about the seventh day, and there she remained, on the plantation Manantial. Fortunately, I was with her, and so it was I who buried her.

There in Manantial?

In Manantial.

So she didn't die in her own house? Didn't they bury her again?

No, she's there, in Manantial. There she remained because of her sickness. But it was my younger sister's fault, with the expenses demanded for her. She didn't keep her promise to the man; she separated from him, and he demanded his money back. So my mother borrowed the money from the plantation owner and returned it [to the suitor]. So it was my sister's fault, and my mother died at the plantation. My mother whispered when her soul was about to leave, "Go find him!" and so they went to get me from the coffee grove.

I was harvesting coffee. The foreman sought me out: "Go see your mother, because it looks as though she is dying. 'I have to speak with him,' she said, 'because I won't survive this illness. I'm going.' Go, go see her," said the foreman.

And I went. I left my coffee in the patio and went in to her.

"How are you, have you come?" she asked.

"I have come, Mother," I said to her. "How do you feel?"

"Let it be, my son. Don't worry. Go deliver your coffee, then we'll talk. It's better if you go and turn in your coffee. If you don't, something may happen and you may be delayed. Go carry it in first, and then we'll talk," she said.

"All right," I said, and I went to deliver the coffee.

"I'm back, see, I'm back," I said.

"Good. Don't grieve. What can I do about it? I shall remain here, but it's clearly your younger sister's fault. It isn't because I'm a widow. It's hardly for lack of food. Rather it has to do with the money that was given for her.[51] It's because of that. I went to borrow the money from the plantation owner, and I paid it, but I haven't earned it back. So it goes; it can't be helped. It's her remembrance that I shall remain here. But never mind, it's all right, because you at least are here. A thousand thanks to the gods that you can take care of me! You have an older sister, but thanks be to the gods that she doesn't see me, for she quarreled so with me, she argued so with me! A thousand thanks to the gods that she won't bury me, and thanks to the gods that you will bury me. But don't get drunk, don't go into debt. Thank you for burying me. And do wake up: don't get drunk any more!

Also: you have your obligation. You burn incense, because that is what your ancestors did. They were burners of incense, and they went for their worship just as you do," said my mother. "But don't grieve about it, it can't be helped: I must remain here," she said.[52] "You will bury me for good, because I'm going." She had barely spoken these words when she died.

So she must have felt her death?

She did feel her death. I held her in my arms, and she put her hand on my chest, and then her soul went away. Slowly I put her down, I saw that she had gone. That was all; she was buried while we stayed at the plantation.

I went up to the boss: "What will you do for me? Since my mother has died, some expense is called for. Here I am at your plantation. What shall be done? Perhaps there are friends of mine around. It's our custom [on such occasions] to come together and see each other.[53] Couldn't you give me some money? What shall I do? I don't have any money, but I'll pay you back, I'll certainly pay you back," I said.

"Oh, very well, it's all right, it's all right. If you don't bury her—because she's your mother—who will? If it's your mother, of course I'll give you the money. How much are you asking for?"

That was in the old days when they had paper notes of a hundred. I asked him for three hundred.

"Ah, what do you need three hundred for? But never mind, don't worry. I'll give it to you, since it's your mother. But you must repay the money promptly, I'll tell you right now: it'll be deducted from your tareas. You'll have to repay it immediately with your tareas, and since it is your mother, God will bless you," said the boss. And he gave me the three hundred.

We had many friends at the plantation. There were friends of mine, and there were many onlookers. With three hundred I buried my poor mother at the plantation. There she remained. I repaid my debt with my tareas. I repaid the money, and I went back home.

She had said: "Don't grieve, it can't be helped. Forgive me, because it's my fault that there's no land I can leave you. I'm the one who is at fault. This is what some of my younger relations and some of my older ones said, everyone told me: 'Get your son, go and see that the land won't all be taken. Take him to the courthouse. Look after his share of the property.' But I was afraid to go to the courthouse; I couldn't muster the courage to go before the ʔalkaalte. So it's because of me, it's my fault that you don't have your property. Just because I didn't go to the courthouse, you have no land; you have nothing of your own. It's only because I couldn't take heart to go to the courthouse that you lack property to enjoy. But the gods, my son, are with you. God is with you; don't be sad! It won't take you long to begin to acquire things of your own. But you must remember this: don't drink liquor—don't get drunk! Wake up!" said my mother.

"As for your younger sister, just watch what she does, but leave her alone. She isn't your responsibility. Here is one of my skirts. Give it to her. There is a napkin and a headband she may have. It's all right, it can't be helped, it's all right. But just watch what she does. Don't tell her: 'This is what she said.' Keep the words in your head," said my mother. Thus she counseled me.

"As for your older sister, she had many arguments with me. She gave me many hard words. Never mind, it can't be helped, just watch her.

When it comes to you, there are no problems. You are poor now, but the gods will quietly bestow blessings and grace. Without much effort, you'll acquire possessions. I say so," she said. "It may happen that—without your noticing it—your place in life will appear."

Only my mother did I bury, but how fortunate that I buried her!

So that must be how it happened: you did the favor for your mother, and therefore you're still alive. Your mother is returning the favor, and you live well today.

That's the reason. "Thanks to my son there," she said to some *Kučučbʼaal.* "I had only one son, but he cared for me. He loved me. Therefore, won't you see that he finds a place where he can eat, where he

can sustain himself? Would you grant this favor?" she said. It was her soul
that spoke at a distant place [to the gods].

*That's the reason that you're healthy, that you eat and drink well. You
haven't been sick recently, have you?*

No, not at all. I'm fine.

*And if you were to become sick, it would be because your time had
come and you should go.*

Yes, that's right.

*For it's our mother who must speak for us. If there is no one who speaks
up, neither food nor drink will reach our hand.*

Very true Pap.

*But it's because your way of life is correct. If you were evil, who knows
where you'd be now?*

So it is.

*You'd be living either at the plantation or with the ladinos. But things
are the way they are because of the merit of your mind, for your mind is
good.*

No, this is the remembrance of my mother's soul!

*It's your mother's favor to you; it's thanks to your mother. "Thanks to
my son," she must have said, and this must be her gift, that you're living
comfortably now.*

Yes, that's why there's nothing the matter with us.

And you eat well, and you're not without clothes.

It took several more years and two more wives to come and go
before Shas reached the state of relative happiness just mentioned.

His memory of Sil B'am, his fourth companion, is not as negative
as that of Niʔl Chiʔw, the fifth. Sil's main problem was her unwilling-
ness to "live in the mountains" at Ṣeʔ K'aʔš. Her small boy, Domingo
Bernal Santiago, liked the place. He still visits Shas from time to time.

Now, the next woman, the fourth woman [Sil B'am], had no faults, but
she didn't stay in my house: every Sunday she spent in her [own] house in
town. My little house that I shared with her remained closed because of
her on Sundays. And I gave her spending money:

"Go get some chile, go get the things you need, and bring a pound of
meat for us. Here is the money," I said to her.

"All right," she said.

"But come back right away so that you can cook it, and we'll eat when I
come home. Whatever time I return, you must be here, and our food must
be ready."

"All right," she said. But if only she had complied! Sometimes she
would arrive and sometimes the house would be closed when I got back.
There would be no fire; she would just stay in her own house. So one
time—it wasn't so good: I always went to the plantation—I went down in
May, and she stayed home. There was my maize. There may have been

forty nets of my maize left, and she remained at home. Only I went down [to the plantation]. There was a pig that was being fattened. It was late when I left, perhaps after San Antonio, or during the fiesta of San Antonio, and therefore I got back two days after the fiesta of Santa Maria.[54] When I arrived—it was right on the road, where her house was, like this road—I went to her house, thinking to stop in and rest a little. And if she wasn't living in her house! She had left my hut closed up, and she had carried over all of my maize. There had been maize in the attic and maize heaped up in the house, and the maize was here now. The pig, on the other hand, she had already sold, and bought a skirt. She didn't say how much the pig went for. I didn't know about that; I had just arrived. There were her chickens, clustered together in the yard.

Well, I arrived and put down my load and went in. The woman was by the hearth in the kitchen. "So it seems that you've moved?" I asked her.

"I've moved,because I was very sad there. I can't get used to the countryside. I didn't grow up in the countryside. I grew up in town, and I can't adjust, so I moved."

"But why didn't you leave the maize locked up there? Nothing can happen to the granary, because there's a beam on top of it. No one can open it. Why didn't you just leave it locked up? Why did you take it out?"

"I just took it out. If you want to, you can carry it back again. I don't intend to use up your maize," she said. This wasn't kindly spoken; it was with anger that she answered me.

"Ah, I didn't have an agreement with you to move the maize. I didn't tell you that. If you're the caretaker who stayed behind, why did you take it out? You're useless. But never mind, forget about it. You must move it once more, since it won't be of use to you. And whoever was your helper in moving it, go pay him to return it to its proper place. That's all I have to say to you. But never mind, forget about it. If this is what you want, never mind, forget about it. We'll stay right here," I said to her. And so we used up the maize. And that was her offense against me. It wasn't without reason that I separated from her; it was because she took away [the maize] and because she sold the pig and bought a skirt with it; she obtained her *huipil* with it when it was really I who had bought it. Finally our maize was used up, and I left. She stayed behind in her house, and I went back to my house to live alone.

Many people scolded me: "Why don't you come? Isn't this your place? There's your house, and it's always locked up. What do you think you're doing? She's hardly the only woman in town. Do you just follow her around? People [looking for you] think that you live in your house. You just make people walk there for nothing. It isn't good." They had looked for me, but the house was always locked up. And therefore there were many people who told me: "Can't you find another one? If you'd look for another woman, there would be no problem," they said.

"All right, no matter. It is true what our younger and older brothers say. My god! They hardly want it [the advice] for themselves. It doesn't matter to me. Let her stay here." I went away, and she stayed behind: "I have to go, because I can't stay here. You're the one who can't adjust. This isn't my place. No, I have my own house, and I shall live in it. But you can stay, it doesn't matter. The maize is used up, so let it end between us. It's hardly my wish to leave you, but if you can't get used to my house—I didn't make an agreement with you that I would come live with you. I told you that you had to live with me. You did come [to live there]. If you don't like it, then we can't do it by force," I said to her.

"Never mind. If this is what you say, it doesn't matter. It's up to you," she answered. That's how she stayed behind.

Then I met old lady Niʔl Chiʔw, the one who left me just before my present wife came. I was searching for another woman, and I met her. But it turned out worse: she was an insane person. What temper tantrums she threw! It wasn't my fault. It certainly wasn't true that she had no food; she had her food, she had her clothes. She carried off all the clothes when we separated. She carried away all the blouses, all the skirts, all the head-bands, all the belts, all the napkins, everything. It was empty! Five acres of maizefield I gave her, and she carried away all the utensils and the grind-stone. She didn't leave anything at all behind. I stayed behind, and the inside of the house was left like [that empty corner over there]. The only things left were broken utensils, that was all.

It wasn't for anything. I didn't have fights with her—of course, I quarreled with her, but that blew over. What happened was that she had two children, and the little boy had a dream. It's dangerous when we quarrel with you [women]. It's dangerous because we bother the Mountain God's head; we bother the place where we live.[55] It was the little boy—I knew about the dream because when he dreamt I wasn't asleep. I had stretched out, but I was awake, and I heard him call: "Mother! Mother!"

"What is it?"

"I dreamt, Mother."

"What did you dream?"

"Nothing much, but there was a ladino, Mother. He was above the house. How the gun glistened in his hand! And he said: 'Now I'm going to shoot you!' and he held the gun pointed at me. 'Go away, go away. You'd better understand that you must leave, because you make my head ache. Why should you? I've lost patience with you for causing me so much headache. Go away right now, and if you don't go I'll shoot you,' he said. And there was his gun—how it gleamed! It was of pure silver, the man's gun. But I'm very frightened, Mother. I feel his words are true," said the boy. So he told his mother, and I overheard.

Then the boy's mother woke me up. "Are you awake?" she said.

"What is it? I was asleep, you woke me up," I said, but I was awake.

I had heard what the boy told his mother, but I didn't say anything. "I was sleeping. You just woke me up," I said.

"Why, the boy had a dream."

"What did he dream?"

"This is what he dreamt: that there was a ladino on the roof of the house, and the ladino wanted to kill him. 'Go away right now. Disappear from my face. My head aches because of you,' said the ladino. This is what the boy said," said his mother.

"Ah, but it isn't good, it isn't good what you do. Why do you think it is that the ladino will shoot except for the quarrels we have? It's the Mountain God, the god of this place, whose head we have hurt, and he will make us sick, and perhaps the boy will get sick," I said to her.

"Ah, you're not good. You're dangerous. It will be your fault if my son dies. You will bewitch my son!" she said to me.

"Ah, what you say won't do, it's evil! Instead of saying 'What shall we do? Can't we light our candle or remember the gods because the sacred place has lost patience with us because of the quarrels? What can we do?' You don't say that at all. You don't ask for advice from the gods. Rather, you show your anger quite openly. Forgive me, but it will make things more difficult. What needs to be done is that you'd better go. You all can leave, because I don't like it anymore. I've tried. I've counseled you. I wanted to tell you with my own mouth and I have told you by asking my friends to counsel you. But once they've given you advice, you're even more persistent in mistreating the people who do the favor and the kindness, the people who give you good advice. You simply don't understand. What is the answer you want me to give you? What is the remedy I can give you? I've tried the bitter and the sweet in telling you, but you don't understand. What other advice shall I give you? The only thing is to forget it. Let's separate.

"I tell you the truth seriously, because I'll be blamed if your son dies. Then you'll say it was I who did it. It's the spirit of this place whose head hurts because of us. It's the Earth Spirit who'll do it, but you can't understand that. Instead, you've shown the anger inside; this is how your heart is. But never mind; don't bother yourself with me, and I won't concern myself with you. Even if you marry a ladino, even if you're on horseback, when you pass in front of me I'll only change my direction. Who knows if I'll find a wife for myself or not? Never mind, I'll buy my tortilla in the market. So listen, go and leave. Also, if I should marry another woman, even a Chiquimula woman,[56] whatever kind the woman may be, it isn't your concern. Never mind me, and I won't mind you, as that's your wish and mine. It's all finished here," I said to her.

"Ah, I'll go. It's all right if that's the way it is. I'll go. But whatever is mine I'll take."

When the big fiestas come, I always take part as skyrocket shooter, so I had bought a napkin for wrapping the skyrockets the women carry in their arms. I had bought it because the fiesta was close, and I had said to the woman: "Let's join as skyrocket shooter again.[57] Maybe I'll die. Let's do it once more, if you like. You'd better buy another napkin for us, a new one, and get yourself a belt and another headband, and buy another blouse for yourself," I had said to her.

She knew how to make the *q'e?na?q*, but the *količ* (huipil, an Ixil blouse with colorful woven designs) she couldn't make. I bought the količ; she had one, but it was worn. It was the wife of this man [Ku? B'el] who made it; Ni?l Č'e?n made the količ. I commissioned her, and she made it. And after the količ was finished, the sleeves got put in. It was ready, and it was a huge pile of clothes she took—all her skirts she took with her.

"I'll take everything!"

"Take it. Never mind, take it. What good is it to me? Am I going to wear it? No, we'll see if it can be gotten for another person, if I should find a wife. If not, I'll be wandering about, but that is none of your concern. Take it with you. If I don't give it to you, you'll regret it and you'll cry about it, and they're your clothes. Why not? Once I've spit my saliva out, it's hardly possible for me to get it back. No, go and take it all. Whatever is yours, take it."

"Well, there are all my utensils; also, we shall divide the maizefield," she said.

"All right, let's divide it. Very good, take it. Never mind, take it. It's my pleasure to give it to you. Take it, take it, never mind. We'll see how I can acquire property again," I said to her.

And sure enough, she carried away my grindstone—two grindstones I had bought—with her. All her clothes, all the utensils, the pots and the griddles—she picked up everything and carried it away. Only the things that were broken, useless, remained in the house, and I was left alone.

And she said, "Let's divide the maizefield," and so we divided it.

"It's all right. I have a small patch in Kamb'alam, and sometimes it produces well and sometimes—it seems when the weather is bad—it doesn't do very well. And so I'll give you the one in Kamb'alam. It's thirty cuerdas you'll get."

But I also had a little patch in Soc', forty cuerdas. It was very good land, because the earth is loam, and the maize is very good, and she wanted to take this. She didn't want the Kamb'alam field:

"No. Why should I take the patch in Kamb'alam? The ears that grow there are empty. I'd rather take the one in Soc'," she said.

"It's all right. We'll see what can be done. We'll see. I'll give it. I can't take it away from you," I said. And I thought about it.

Do you remember old Pap Liš, who is married to old mother Še?p—the father of the Kulaš boys, Pap Liš who became ?alkaalte a long time ago? Do you know his children, the three Kulaš boys who live near Šo?lanay?

Not the Pap Kulaš who was foreman for Laapo?

Yes, his father. He was an elder, the Pap, and I was good friends with him—the way I am with him here [Ku? B'el]. I served him as prayersayer. He had gone to talk to her, to counsel her, the woman who was with me. He had said [to her]:

"Why, man, what do you want? It isn't just his worship he is attending to; he's earning his living, too. Also, it's certainly true that he has the calendar in his head. He is hardly offering himself to the people; it's the people's wish that he attend to them. Why shouldn't he like it? It's his calling. And you surely have your mouthful to eat: there are daughters and sons who have good hearts and give gifts and it's hardly he alone who eats it and not you, too," he said to her.

But she didn't pay attention, and afterward she said: "Of course he talks that way. Why doesn't he give you one of his daughters?" She couldn't take it. She didn't understand well-meaning advice. It wasn't good for her. She didn't know how to obey. She was just like an animal.

And so I went to tell him. "What shall I do, Pap? I've thrown the woman out. What do you think I should do? 'I have to have my maizefield,' she says. The utensils, all her clothes—all that she has carried away. But what shall I do now that she is asking for the maizefield? I have a little patch in Kamb'alam and another patch in Soc'. It's the one in Kamb'alam I want to give her, but she doesn't want it. What she demands is the one in Soc', and my maizefield over there is much better," I told him.

"Well, she's smart. Her thinking is very shrewd, indeed. And you're thinking of giving it to her, you say?"

"No, but this is that I came to ask you: what shall I do? Should I give her a little bit or nothing at all?"

"You should give her some, because there are your children by her to care for. Who will feed them?" he said.

"But I have no children by her."

"None?"

"That's right."

As we were talking, she arrived; she came to meet me at his place.

"Well, then, here she comes," he said. "Why do you give the maizefield to the woman? You have fed her and her children. She has two children, and they've grown; I know it's been a while since they came to stay with you. They have clothes—they are hardly naked—and where do they come from? The woman hardly has a machete, a hoe, an axe. It isn't as if she were speaking for her children, so it really won't do. Why does she want to take the maizefield when you don't even have children by her? Not at all. The woman has no rights according to the law. But wait, if that's the way it is it's better that . . . Give her five cuerdas of the Soc' patch if she doesn't like the field in Kamb'alam, but only five cuerdas. If she doesn't want it, then we won't give her anything. Let her go to the courthouse, and then I'll counsel that since you don't have children by her, you're doing her a favor. You've supported her and her children; how is it that she wants to take your field and everything else? It can't be."

And while he was saying this, she appeared and went straight down to his wife.

"Send the woman over. She can't sit down with you!" he called to his wife. And she came over to us.

"What are you two doing, young woman?" he said.

"Well, we've been separated."

"And what have you talked about? What do you think? Should he give you a bit of your own property? You've left him already?" he asked.

"I've left already."

"Well, and did you take all your things, or did you leave some of your clothes behind?"

"No, I took it all away."

"Ah, and how many clothes do you have?"

"Only two *čik* [skirts]."

"And do you have a *qʼeʔnaʔq?*"

"I have two."

"And your *ʔišbʼuʔq?*"

"It's the same, they finished making my *ʔišbʼuʔq* [for the fiesta]."

"Ah, and do you have a *siinta?*"

"Yes, I do."

"Do you have a *tal suʔt* [shawl]?"

"Yes, I have."

"Ah, all is well."

But there was the *količ*. She hadn't mentioned the *količ*.

"Pap, she has a *količ*."

"Very good."

"Also, there's another *količ*. It was perhaps fifteen quetzales that went for the *količ*, and she has taken it. It's new, she hasn't worn it yet," I said to him.

"Ah, really, it's very nice what you are doing. But never mind, forget it, since it's your desire not to live with him anymore. Is it for good that you've left him?"

"Yes, because he said 'Go away!' Why should I force myself on him?"

"Well, and is it really your wish to let her leave?"

"Yes, Pap, because she doesn't obey. It's not as if she didn't have clothes or food: she lacks nothing. If she had to carry loads, if she had to sell things—but instead, every Sunday I give her her spending money, and she takes it along when she buys things, when she goes out. I eat with her, that's it."

And so the old man thought about it: "All right, then, if it's final, and you have your clothes, it's all right. You've already taken them away. What do you want the maizefield for? It's only recently that he's been able to acquire his own maizefield. He didn't own one before. Leave it to him then because it doesn't fill your stomach anyway. That's why it bothers you—because it's only our stomachs we worry about with you [women]; it's only your stomachs that you worry about with us. There's hardly anything else to worry about with us if what we eat is enjoyable, if our drink is good. But what is it: you eat well, you drink well—what bothers your heart? Really, there isn't anything to bother your heart. Well, leave him. What can we do about you now? But you can hardly receive the maizefield; you can hardly demand it now. What is it you want? Who's driving you out? Is there another woman in his life? Have you seen or heard of anyone trying to drive you out? This is what I want to hear, and we'll put her in jail," said the Pap to her.

"No, no, it's only my hot temper."

"Well, never mind. See whether it's your hot temper or whether there's someone else turning you away from him—but then you will have your necessities with him. It's a pure favor we're doing you. It isn't right for him not to give you anything; that's a sin, because you have worked a little bit for him. So never mind, but we'll only give you five cuerdas. This is all I'll tell you; and it's only in my house that I'll make this judgment; if you don't like it, I'll give my opinion to the ʔalkaalte, and then you won't get anything at all, that I'll tell you for certain. That way you won't get anything because he supported your children, and he has no children by you," said the Pap; so he spoke to her.

"Well, never mind, I'll take it," she said.

"Very well, it's all right. But words never settle anything so once and for all let's go today and see. Let's take my measure. After we've measured [the field], we'll leave your boundary marker," he said to her.

"All right."

We went to measure the maizefield, and the same day she left. She took all of it, five cuerdas of the maizefield, and so it ended. "Don't touch her part, and she mustn't touch yours! If you touch her property, she'll go and complain about you, and you'll go to jail. But likewise: if she touches your part, then you'll go and complain and she'll go to jail. There are your boundary markers so you'll know where the corner posts are to plan your furrows; and this finishes it," he said.

"Thank you," I said, and that was how I split up with her.[58]

That's what kept happening to me: I didn't accumulate anything. I was so miserable that I got drunk. It was because of the rage that I got drunk, because of the anger: "Why? What do I do to women that they treat me this way?" I wondered. My heart kept searching. At times I got drunk for two or three days.[59]

It was my mother, they say. My father (my real father) owned sheep, and they were left with my grandfather. And my grandfather didn't let go of the sheep; he didn't give them to my mother. My mother wanted to take the sheep away, and my grandfather wouldn't let them go. So my mother went to complain about my grandfather at the courthouse. My grandfather was summoned to the courthouse, and he must have had to go to jail for a day or two. And that's the trouble, they say; that's what I've had to pay for by women not staying with me.[60] It isn't only that women have done this to me but that I've been driven towards troublesome women: I'd find one and then she'd leave again.

I hunted and I hunted for the one who is with me now. Ever since that time we have remained married, but only because I always paid reverent homage to the gods when each woman left. I went to complain before the souls. I went to light a candle before Our Mother: "What is it that I do? What is my offense? Why? I don't steal. But why is it? What is the secret of the trouble I have, that women don't stay with me?" I kept saying. I went to ask forgiveness from Our Mother. And that was all. Slowly my offense against the souls was erased, and I met her through the dream I told you.[61]

I always prayed. When each woman left, I went to ask forgiveness before God, I went to light my candle before Our Mother for whatever it was I did wrong—or whether it was my fate. God was with me, for another man dreamt about me. A young man who lived in Wi? Pešlaq dreamt about me. He was waiting in front of my house when I came home. My present house wasn't built yet; only wooden sticks were there before. I had been away traveling and when I arrived I was quite drunk. The poor man was sitting in front of the house and he said: "Have you come, Pap?"

"I have come."

"I dreamt," said the man.

"What did you dream?"

"Where is the keeper of the house, I wonder? Nobody is here. It's quiet; your house is closed up."

"Of course nobody is here, because I separated from her," I said.

"Oh, perhaps that's why I had the dream. This was the dream, Pap, that I came to tell you about. It wasn't just a trifle, it was a *señora*[62] I dreamt about. I passed by a house, and I saw a señora come out.

'Where are you going?' said she.

'I am only taking a walk,' I said to her.

'Look, come here, come in,' said she.

'Thank you,' I said. I went in with her. The house was all made of metal! It was a big house. And she wore robes that swept over the floor. Her hair flowed down her back and swept over the ground. How tall she was!

'It isn't much that I want to tell you, but since you're a friend of my son, please go tell him that he should come to get his chair. This is his chair, but I've been keeping it for him. It was only because his penance had not been completed. Now that his fine has been paid, this is his chair; he should take it now,' said the señora to me," he said. So she said to the man in his dream.

[He went on:] " 'Yes,' I replied.

'And here it is. I just want to show you that I'm not lying about what I told you. Look, here it is. This is what he should come and get,' said she.

Pap, when she brought out the chair, it was of pure silver, and the brilliance of it was dazzling. She brought it out to show to me; then she took it away again.

'He should come and get it from me,' said the woman," the man told me.

"Oh, but what could it be, young friend? Perhaps I won't find a wife, I suppose. Perhaps I'll stay in the chair alone," I said to the man.

And then I got some rum, a quart of it, and we drank together.

"Thank you very much. I have listened, and thank you very much."

Then I thought and thought about it: "But who is the señora? Surely it's Our Mother—who else but Our Mother?" I thought.

I went off. It came to my mind to go and light candles for nine days in front of Our Mother. There are special prayers for that, just as for you women who are looking for a husband—you honor the gods a little, and for nine days we place candles in front of Our Mother, but every day, every day, until the count of nine days is completed. So when I went to perform the *b'eluwal q'ii* rites I went to light my candles, and I left an offering in the cemetery.[63]

When I came out of the prayerhouse at Wiʔ u Kamnaq, there stood an old man in front of it, waiting for me. Who knows how he knew about me? But I saw it with my eyes; I didn't dream it, I saw it. I had finished with my prayers, and that old gentleman stood there—he has died long since—but there he stood before the prayerhouse. He had come to meet me at the cemetery I presume—who knows how he knew of me—and he said, "I see you were praying?"

"Yes, I left an offering," said I.

"By the way,' what happened to you with that woman? Is it true that she is no longer with you, that she has left, as they say?" said he to me.

"It's true, man, she has left me. What about me? Where do you think I should go for a woman who is good? What is it, supposedly, that I do that I can't find a good woman? Ever since my first woman disappeared, the others have treated me the same way, so that I always lose what I have," I told him.

"It seems I have heard," he said, "of a woman over there. Perhaps, if you like, you could go and see. Go and see first if she'll do, and then come back and tell me. We'll help you a little. [My wife]—your aunt—will put in some good words [for you]. But go, go and see first how it appears to you. Although she does have a husband, she is separated from him; also, we have asked her word that once and for all she won't go back. She surely won't go back to him. It is certainly this man's fault," said the man.

"Very well, then. Thank you very much," and after he had finished his speech I remembered to ask: "The fact is that I don't know where she lives. Which is the house where she lives?" said I.

"No problem. You go straight ahead; it's that house."

"Thank you." It was true. I went on my errand. I knew the house. When I arrived, she [Šiiw Koʔt] was in the patio, but she had a visitor; there was a woman with her. They were talking on the porch. I took courage and walked in.

"Would you do me a favor, young woman [to the visitor]? I want to light my cigarette but don't have a match. Perhaps I could borrow a twig of your wood," I just said to her. The words came slowly to my mind.

"Yes," said she, and she went in to bring a firebrand. And I entered a little further into the patio, as it was there that the woman was sitting on the porch. "I do have a reason [for coming]. I do have some business with you. Perhaps, if possible, I'll come by to see you in a while? It's only for you that I've come here; the woman there is lending me a firebrand—but I do have some business with you. Is it possible to see you?" I said to her.

"It's all right. It's better if she leaves. She'll go home, and if you like, come back. Come and see me in a little while," said she.

I went only once around the corner and came back again, and the woman [visitor] wasn't there; she had left. I went in. Only she was there. I went in and said: "Did your visitor leave?"

"She left. It was only for a moment; she had an errand with me," said she. "What is your business? Do come in," said she to me.

"Thank you." I went into the house and pulled out a bench and sat down on it.

"Tell me, what is your errand?"

"It's not very much of an errand, but I did hear about your separation, so they say, from the old man. Is it true?"

"Yes, it's true."

"Well, just as I was thinking. That's the way I am [= separated], because they haven't died, those women. Who knows what my sin is?[64] I'd tell you the reason, but it's nothing except that it's difficult because of what I'm doing,[65] and they leave me, and where shall I go? This is my business with you: Isn't there a possibility that we could get married?" I said to her. Slowly my words came out.

"Well, perhaps, if this is all you've done with the woman. I'm listening, and I understand your problems with them and what you've done. You've separated from her, but you may take her back again. What if you should do that, because you have gotten used to her?" said she.

"Oh, no, man, we've split up once and for all. We've already been to the courthouse.[66] She has her portion of maize, and she took all her things and all the utensils. But never mind, because I know that I can buy them [again], so do consider it."

"Look; I'll think about it. It's all right, I'll think about it. The day after tomorrow, come and see me again; today you'd only come back in vain. It's useless until the day after tomorrow."

"Thank you," I said, and with this we ended the conversation and I left.

From then on, my heart could hardly wait until I came to the end of the second day, and it was exactly on the second day that she gave her answer:

"It is all right if you agree that in a month I'll go with you. I have quite a bit of weaving to do, and after I've taken it off the loom we'll get married. Also, my ex-husband still comes here. That man keeps coming; for him it isn't yet forgotten. If only he would stop—but he still wants to marry me again. As for me, I'm sure; I would never consent, because I've seen the kind of injustice he has done to me. I won't agree. He's finished. For me it's over, but it isn't over for him. It could happen that you'd arrive and meet him! Also, if I go with you right now, you will become burdened because you will get involved and he'll say that you are the one who takes me away from him; therefore, let us wait a while. Patience," said she to me.

"It's all right, but my life is hard because I don't have my little girl with me anymore. I have two little lambs, a pig, a dog, whatever, and there won't be anyone to take care of them. That is what saddens me," I said.

"Oh, well, it'll be all right. You can bring your things and your laundry and leave them with me, and you can bring the maize, too, and I'll prepare feed for the animals. Whatever is necessary, bring it and leave it. And then simply come and take it and feed them," she said to me.

I agreed to her proposal: "This is a good thing. God, don't worry. It doesn't matter. If you'll favor me, it's all right, I'll wait a month."

A month later she came to me; she had come to stay. There wasn't any more difficulty. She came for good. I was drinking, and I went about my ritual business, but nothing happened. It was all right. There was my food; there she was waiting for me. Nothing happened; we were married for good. And perhaps a year after we had married, we were chosen for third *mertomail* (mayordomo) of the Kurus ʔlšoq ceremony.[67] There was no trouble. We aren't burdened by any debts. Everything is fine, great is her blessing. We obtained money, and there we are. We have our food, nothing is amiss, everything is fine. We served as mertomail and we built the house. It was thanks to her that we built the house. For good she arrived when we got married, and therfore for good we are married. We'll never split up. It's a long time that we've been married, perhaps thirty years. There is no trouble, all is well.

Such are the things that have happened to me in this world. She who is with me now was the sixth one I married. She was the sixth one, and the one I had split up with was the fifth—and only because we didn't communicate very well.

There was another thing they [the other women] did to me: Since I knew the calendar, since I had the Days in my head, I had to go out for my prayer sessions. But [they would say that] I wasn't attending to my praying but visiting other women. They accused me of having many women "in my hand." Sometimes I only crossed my arms [in exasperation]—but there were times when I cried in anger because they accused me. It wasn't true, but I was blamed; there wasn't any woman I was seeing. There wasn't any truth in their words. They only were searching for some wrongdoing on my part, that's how they started out—and only because I went to my prayer session and got home late: "And you, haven't you been sitting down with some people? You didn't say a prayer for your ceremony, it's a woman! You have a mistress, that's what you went to see." They would start out against me, and slowly the fight would begin between us. After that, we split up when I couldn't stand it any longer. How they made my head ache! I knew what was wrong, and it didn't matter. We split up, and sometimes I divided my maizefield with them for their good fortune; we didn't go to the courthouse, because I didn't want to. They only asked me, and I complied: "I'm going to take this," they said. "Take it, why not?" I said. And they would carry away all the pots and pans—I didn't take anything away from them. So it happened. But I didn't experience that with this woman. It may be thirty years now that I've been married to her.

There has been no problem since she arrived. We haven't separated. We sometimes quarrel a little with each other, because sometimes I get drunk and scold her. But after I come to myself it blows over. After I come to my senses, she tells me: "You scolded all the time. This is what you said. You speak straightforwardly when you're sober. Is it only the liquor that makes you speak to me like this? You said mean words to me: that I'm crazy, and that I'm bothering you, and, worse, that we always fight." So she tells me.

"Not at all, man, forgive me. It must be only the liquor that clouds my head, and I say all kinds of nonsense to you. Please, forgive me. Don't pay any attention. Have I ever told you so when I was sober? Have I scolded you or said bad things to you when I was normal? Why is it then? It's only the liquor that affects me and I scold you. Let's forget it, may it end there," I said to her.

"All right, let it be," she said, and with that it ended. We were married for two years when we took on the duties of mertomail. We entered as mertomail for Kruus ʔlšoq and from then on we had no problems, everything was fine. Even more since God did us the favor and we built my little house, the one we live in together. Thanks to her it was built.

It was with her that you built it?

She was the one I built it with.

So there wasn't any house [before]?

No, there wasn't, because it was my employer, Paa Yeermo, who gave us the land. It was his land. But no, there wasn't any house on it, only trees.[68] I didn't get along with any of the women until she arrived. So we built the house. Everything is good now. We don't worry about anything; we're equal. We don't have children. We are just the two of us. Our stomachs are satisfied. I plant my maizefield, and when I go out for one of my prayer sessions and come back, she's waiting for me with my meal. Would I be foolish if I were to argue with her! She makes a good wife for me. What else do I want? I'm happy.

Things are good, thanks to the gods. God showed favor towards us and we accumulated a small store of maize. Sometimes there isn't anything—I would be telling lies, that's a sin, I would only be lying to say that I'm working in the fields. But God sent good fortune so that I can plant my maizefield. And sometimes I sell a small load of maize and another time perhaps there's a little pig to be fattened. It buys a few clothes for her and provides some of mine, and that's fine. I just begin something and it turns out fine—but only since she came to be with me did God send good fortune. That's what happened, that's all. Before I saw a great deal of poverty; what a poor man I was, wandering about! But thanks to God—because it was God who did the favor—everything is in order. Now I have my clothes. I am comfortable. Yes, indeed, there isn't anything amiss. God bestows the blessing and the favor of my food, thanks to God. You just fold your arms because it's all over. What you don't know is whether she'll be first or you'll be first, because it's all finished, you've grown old. There isn't anything amiss. It's only death that you're awaiting. We'll just wait for our time to arrive. What I talk about with her now is poor me! I remember how very good her ways were. I would be drunk, and there would be my food.

"Eat your food, man! Leave the liquor alone," she would tell me.

"Yes, thank you," I would say; it's good, it's fine.

Sometimes I say to her: "Oh, man, poor us. Who knows which one of us will go first? Will it be you who goes first, or will I be the one? We shall see poverty again for sure, who knows when? We don't know which one of us will go first to our death. Perhaps it'd better be you, as I would say the prayers. It would be good if you went first, because I would bury you. I know how to perform your burial. If only we had a daughter, a son. But what can be done? If it's I who goes first, who will bury you? I have a daughter, but who knows who will care for you? But what can we do about it? If only God would do the favor so we would go together! But what can we do? Be it as it may. Also, if you go away, after everything we have done together, what good would it be? If you go first to your death, who will take care of me? What woman would do all the things you are able to do for me? If I find another woman—because I do have to look for another one—this is what she will certainly do: she will take all your work and sell it. The way we live is good, thanks to God. You take good care of our belongings, you take care of our well-being. But what will happen when God separates us? What shall we do? Which one of us will go first. Who knows when we shall complete our count?" I say to her.

That's all we can do, because there's no solution for that, and no sacrifice can be offered for it. What happens is that one's time arrives, and then it can be suffocation or a small illness, but that is unknown to us. Nobody can forsee it. The count·will be completed.

Don't worry about it, Pap, because it's finished when one has become old. But let it be, because all your efforts will be finished; you have worked, you are tired, she is tired.

God has bestowed the favor. Let it be. When we have finished, we resign ourselves to our fate.

But Our Father has left word for certain that we shall return. We don't grow old, but rejuvenate. When we have finished, we just await our count—perhaps a day, perhaps several days—and the word will come true that some ancient people have left: "Perhaps it is a week only that we remain,"[69] some people say.[70]

COMMENTARY

Pap Shas was dedicated to his calling. He was a seeker of wisdom who devoted his life to using his abilities to help others, and he did so with an open and intellectually curious mind. (Indeed, if it were not for these qualities we would not have been taken into his confidence as we were.) His character was all the more remarkable when we consider his handicaps, beginning with his lack of close family as a boy. His father died when he was an infant, and his mother abandoned him shortly after weaning. His grandfather, who had taken him in, died when he was only five years old. A history of loss and rejection, of going from one family to another and carrying out the duties of lonely shepherd at an age before one's "soul had arrived," seems enough to mark anyone's adult personality. Children brought up without love have been found to have psychological deficits that are difficult to overcome. The poignant scene Shas describes of wandering aimlessly in the streets in tears before being taken in by an uncle seems symbolic of his entire childhood. Yet the scars hardly show in the texts, except perhaps for his problems with women. While Shas's life was not easy, it is by no means certain that his problems were primarily the result of a stressful childhood, though the fact that he was rejected by his mother may have had something to do with his marital difficulties.

Spitz's classic studies comparing the growth of infants in a nursing home cared for by their mothers with that of infants in a foundling home who did not receive much care showed the tremendous importance of love and affection or simply of frequent human interaction in an infant's development (Spitz, 1945). Since then many other studies have confirmed Spitz's findings. We now know that even at the level of the individual neuron there is greater dendritic branching, as well as more growth in the surrounding glial cells and other neurophysiological changes, when there is an optimal degree of interaction between an infant and the environment. The cross-cultural study by Rohner (1975) mentioned in Chapter 1 has shown how childhood rejection has adverse effects on adult personality. Work in life-event studies has shown in a different way (that is, with the focus not on development) the relationship between general health and negative life events in a person's recent history. But in spite of all these findings, very little attention has been given to the differential effects of these negative situations on particular individuals in terms of different coping responses (an exception is Antonovsky, 1979). Why do some survive while others do not? Why do some people live happy, productive lives while others end up in mental hospitals or jails? Freud has not been of much help in answering these questions because, as Popper has written, Freudian theory is not falsifiable and hence cannot be tested. According to

Kandel, psychiatry received its main intellectual impetus between
1920 and 1960 from psychoanalysis; since that time psychiatry has
derived its main influence from biology—psychobiology, neurophy-
siology, and psychopharmacology (Kandel, 1979). But in this shift toward science there has been a gap. The molar-level phenomena that
psychoanalysis has sought to explain are still not covered by a major
theory meeting the usual criteria for scientific status. It is just possible, however, that a new psychological anthropology might develop
to meet this need, where analyses of texts can be followed up (as we
are unable to do here, unfortunately) with more field observations,
interviewing, and other data-gathering procedures performed over
an extended time period—that is, in longitudinal studies.

We know very little about the ways in which individuals adjust to
the situations Shas grew up in. The focus of most studies is on the
pathological—on case studies of people who are unsuccessful in
making repairs. But the crucial issues in psychological anthropology
today require that stress pressures and coping with these pressures
be differentiated and more carefully analyzed. The texts Shas has
given us would provide an excellent opportunity to investigate some
aspects of these insufficiently studied issues if only we could have
had more opportunity to interview Shas before his death. In fact,
most of our analysis was done after the last texts had been collected.
Though we had earlier opportunities to question Shas on the details
of his texts, it was too late to ask the questions that arose during our
subsequent analyses. We will have to do the best we can with the
texts at hand.

Not only did Shas survive his childhood, but he survived his calling. The hazards of the prayersayer/daykeeper roles are formidable.
Perhaps the most serious is that of alcohol; it is necessary to drink
often during rituals. One of us filmed a dawn ceremony at Shas's
house at which a different prayersayer was to officiate. A prayersayer
must not officiate at a dawn ceremony for his own house because
part of the reason for a ritual is to make some expenditure, to give up
something (such as a gift to the prayersayer or expenditures for the
candles and incense consumed). The prayersayer, a man in his thirties, was so drunk that he could not go through the ritual, and Shas
had to do it, first asking forgiveness from the gods for the breach.
Shas later told us that the man died of alcoholism the following year.
We occasionally observed Shas when he was heavily under the in-

fluence of alcohol (a gentle person with us, even in that state), though not during rituals. McClelland and his colleagues (1972) have suggested that a common reason for heavy drinking by men is a need for power and that if this need is directed toward helping others, the situation is less likely to get out of control. Perhaps the seriousness of Shas's calling helped him to manage the problem. Another hazard of the role is sexual abstinence; prior to some rituals, a daykeeper must refrain from intercourse. The text shows that this was a source of difficulty with some of Shas's wives, who would accuse him of sleeping with other women when he was away overnight.

Shas's life shows how a good choice among available cultural patterns supports survival. One might go so far as to suggest that it was precisely Shas's childhood experiences that made him a seeker—that caused him to invest such authority in the supernatural world and to become a daykeeper. We know from many studies that children normally learn about roles through the observation of a parental figure of the same sex. We know, too, that this learning occurs not just through immediate imitation, but also in some latent manner through which roles that cannot be acted out by children (unless perhaps in doll play) are mentally stored away for later use. Shas's seriousness about his role as daykeeper was a dominant factor in his life. The approval of the ancestors, the gods, and the prayersayers was tremendously important to him. To some extent they may have taken the place of a parental figure for Shas. His emphasis on dreams reflects this need for guidance, a need that was perhaps amplified during some periods of his childhood.

At a very broad and abstract level the Ixil tend to think of roles along the dimensions of wealth, ceremonial-civic stature, and degree of indigenousness. These were the dimensions found when Ixil were asked to compare the similarity of such role terms as b'aalwac-tiiš, ʔaaq'ii, and catequista (Harding and Clement, 1979).[71] In pursuing the Ixil conceptualization of roles, however, we must range from the broad and abstract to very concrete particulars. Different dimensions or attributes for a role are likely to surface according to the concern and context of the moment.

The concept of role occupies a pivotal position in the study of cultural processes. This concept is a meeting ground for the two major perspectives one can take, the microscopic perspective of the individual—his personality and cognitive systems—and the macroscopic perspective of the social group and of social institutions. For example, an individual can be characterized by the roles he occupies in his life, and an institution can be characterized by all the roles usually entered into within the scope of that institution. It is curious that the concept of role has not been developed in anthropology. The most extensive and useful anthropological treatment of role is Nadel's *Theory of Social Structure* (1957).

A problem involved in studying roles is that if they are at all important, they are by no means simple or easily described. We will show how complex the role of daykeeper can be by analyzing the texts and divination cases that Shas has given us and by showing how those texts interrelate in different ways, and especially how the knowledge structures derived from these texts are likely to be drawn upon in the focal activity of the daykeeper: divination.

Sometimes a role activity is so routine and stereotyped that it can be described in terms of a script. The notion of script has been used in artificial intelligence to mean a cognitive structure that lays out a particular sequence of events appropriate to a special context or situation (Schank and Abelson, 1977). It is a predetermined sequence of actions. But as artificial intelligence has leaned more toward empirical studies in cognitive science, it has been recognized that such a view is inadequate. This lesson was actually first taught us years ago by Bartlett when he found through the recall of folktales that memory is basically a reconstructive process. If behavioral sequences contain similar components—that is, if there is some kind of overlap of components in scripts—it would be an unnecessary burden to have a separate script for each sequence. It would be more efficient to break scripts into cognitive "chunks," some of which could be shared in more than one stereotyped kind of behavior. Schank has recognized this in a recent paper (1979).

The process of building up knowledge structures occurs through generalization from particular situations and also through the learning of cultural patterns in which aspects of a situation are already interpreted and chunked by others. And the chunking is done in some way that is visible to the unconsciously learning mind, just as phonemes and syntactic rules of language are. Thus, instead of a predetermined script we refer to a constructed sequence built from chunks as required by particular situations.

A typical situation that Shas encountered, first as a client and then later as a daykeeper, was the consultation. As a client, Shas went to several daykeepers for interpretations of dreams and advice. Later as a daykeeper himself, he gave advice to others and interpreted dreams and also determined the cause of sickness.

During a consultation with a daykeeper the sequence of events that takes place is as follows: Go to the daykeeper's house; call outside; be invited to come in; sit down; describe the problem to the daykeeper; have the divination take place; be given instructions on the necessary ritual; leave some gift; depart. There are also various optional events that can happen during this time. For example, if the diviner is temporarily absent from the house, waiting may be done inside or on the porch outside until he comes, depending on what the daykeeper's spouse or some other person in the house may say if present. Another option is to receive a cup of coffee from some other member of the household.

But there are other occasions for visiting someone when some of the same kinds of events take place. Thus it is useful to think of a general "House Visit" macrosequence with variations according to purpose, as shown in figure 3.1. Several other macrosequences are shown in this figure which tie in with the lower-level stereotyped sequences for a house visit.

When a person feels himself to be sick he enters a higher, more abstract—yet routinized—sequence. We shall call this a general *thematic sequence*. A thematic sequence is a recurrent sequence of ideas, a chain of events, a motif, or simply a proposition about the world that occurs frequently in a variety of statements, is especially significant in the cultural system, and is part of a rich contextual web of relationships. As will be discussed later, sickness is shown to be one part of a sequence which begins with a transgression or sin and is followed by an appeal to the supernatural being angered by the transgression. A successful appeal requires the performance of the appropriate ritual (itself an extended macrosequence), which in turn requires a determination of the transgression, the reason for the sickness. Consultation with the daykeeper provides this information, and a house visit is usually part of the process.

The main purpose of figure 3.1 is to show how a cognitive structure consists of an enormous network of actions and relations, all chunked at different levels of organization. The levels of cognitive

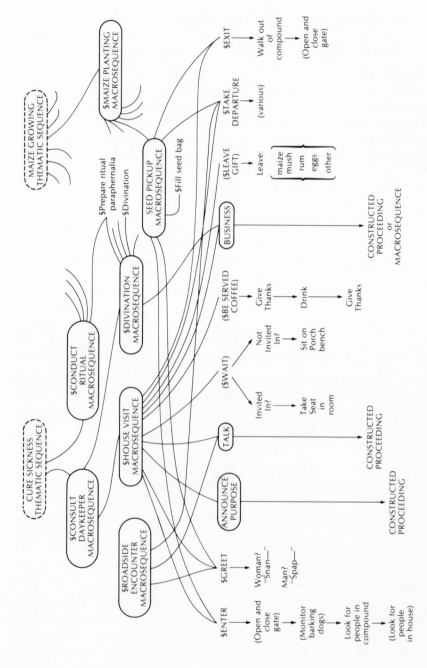

Figure 3.1. Macrosequence for a house visit and other stereotyped sequences including eidons (prefixed by dollar sign).

organization are immensely problematic, but a very small beginning has been made with single lexical units in the taxonomic studies that have characterized the early phase of cognitive anthropology.[72] Berlin (1972, 1976) has suggested that lexemes for folk biological taxa form different evolutionary ranks from general to specific terms. The evolutionary sequence from one level to the next tends to be universal, since the people who use the language utilize the terms under changing circumstances and frequencies that are similar. Evolutionary change of this type has also been examined by Brown (1979). The development of a taxonomic vocabulary usually begins around a middle level of abstraction, which is the most basic. "Oak," "pine," "maple," and "hickory" are examples of this middle level; they are generic names at a level of abstraction that has the greatest utility in most contexts. A man who wants to find good firewood that will produce the most heat for a long time will look for oak or hickory trees rather than pine or hemlock. To merely go out and get "a tree" would fail to make the required distinction. However, more specific names like "white oak" or "shagbark hickory" are less necessary than simply the generic "oak" or "hickory." The generic term, then, is the most basic, most utilized or frequent term.

For actions and events (in contrast to noun concepts like oak or hickory) the most salient level of chunking is the event level that emerges in distributional analyses of folktales.[73] This type of event unit we refer to as an *eidon,* which, by definition, is an emic unit. In figure 3.1 we conjecture eidons to be those units preceded by a dollar sign; but we have no way of going beyond such a conjecture without doing an analysis. We have done such an analysis in the study of Shas's folktales in chapter 5.

Numerous problems arise in mapping out the processes of figure 3.1. Determining levels of abstraction, degrees of stereotypy, and other features that enter into the definition of different kinds of sequences is initially (without distributional analysis) quite arbitrary. These are essentially engineering decisions based on admittedly naive psychology and anthropology. Only with certain forms of systematic analysis can we claim greater validity or culturally real determinations. But if we leave aside the matter of how we label these entities, sequences, and arrangements, another problem arises that has important implications: it is simply that virtually *any* human behavior can be modeled now by a computer program in some fashion, crude and inadequate as the model is likely to be. This possibility of bringing any ethnographic phenomenon to a semiformal understanding through greater precision and specification opens up Pandora's box. It can be likened to the situation in linguistic science that came about with the development of phonetics: phoneticians became proficient at representing such a vast number of human language sounds that they did not know where to draw the line. Sound spectrographic analysis has shown that even the same individual never pronounces the same word twice in exactly the same way. The same problem of endless variation exists in the phenomena modeled in an artificial intelligence approach to anthropology. There is no limit; description can proliferate in an infinite number of directions. Even the smallest area of ethnographic study can occupy a lifetime of investigation and analysis, given the fine-grained attention to detail that is now developing. Thus as ethnography becomes more sophisticated, it is increasingly important to deal with the question of ethnographic relevance, of deciding which among a virtually infinite number of cultural elements and relations should be singled out for attention.

The answer in linguistics, of course, was the discovery of the phonemic principle. And even though there was a time when distinctive feature analysis assailed the psychological reality of the phoneme, it has survived as a psychologically valid unit. In the analysis of cultural materials the answer is to look for salient cultural patterns (which, by definition, are emic). Texts like folktales and Shas's philosophy text in Chapter 4 represent native models or constructions of the world with patterns that are both simpler and more ethnographically relevant than the continuum of actual human life as it unfolds in the real world. These cultural productions organize experience in ways that are useful to the people involved; they take the buzzing, booming confusion of the world and reduce it to essential patterns. Those patterns that are especially important are highlighted or made salient in a variety of ways.

Why not consider the task of ethnography to be the analysis of these essential patterns, the isolation of those patterns that organize other patterns and that have special relevance for the people involved? Like the phoneme, such salient patterns are the ones that are psychologically important, that make a difference to the people involved. This is the strategy we follow here.

Salience must not be confused with stereotypy. The House Visit macrosequence is indeed a stereotyped set of actions, as is the Maize Planting sequence, which will be discussed later. They are important simply because they are part of major daily life activities. But these sequences are so routine, and normally so unproblematic, that they do not occupy much of an Ixil person's thought.

These stereotypical sequences, therefore, do not find much of a place in Shas's cultural productions. They are part of the underlying presuppositions that the readers of Shas's life history are assumed by Shas to have, or at least those of us who were with him when he recorded the texts; they are not the processes that command Shas's interest when reviewing his life. What is really interesting to Shas is his role as daykeeper.

Shas's life history is centered on *recruitment* to the role of daykeeper, whereas the philosophy text in the next chapter centers on the *performance* of the role. Part of the recruitment process involves dreaming about events that are interpreted by an established daykeeper as constituting a recruitment dream. To do this requires the use of interpretative knowledge structures, including metaphoric, metonymic, and causal linkages. For the subsequent performance of the role of daykeeper, other knowledge structures and construction mechanisms are required. Knowledge about facts and processes, the need to maintain a good reputation, and the behavior that maintaining a good reputation entails, are encapsulated in the philosophy text.

We begin our analysis of Shas's role as daykeeper with a discussion of his dreams, including those in which he was recruited into the role of daykeeper. Guidance by dream is one of the most striking aspects of Shas's life history. In his view, dreams were key determinants in his decisions about where he was to live, whom he was to marry, and what his social role was to be.

We can classify the dreams Shas has told us about into four types: *sky* dreams, *conferral* dreams, *calendar* dreams, and *living-decision* dreams. His sky dreams have themes of swinging on a great cable or flying through the air. Such a motif is probably universal. Henry Murray calls such dreams "Icarus dreams" and interprets them as expressing a need for attention or recognition (1955). If the sky dreams express the need for attention, the conferral dreams express its attainment. In conferring the office of daykeeper, they assure Shas of the attention of the deities and ancestral souls, certainly a far loftier reference group than any he might have in this world. The calendar dreams do not seem so elaborate, but they are very important because a daykeeper must never lose a day. Sickness or inebriation may throw a person's sense of time off balance, but a daykeeper always has divine guidance which keeps control over the days in his head. Finally, the living-decision dreams concern matters of current preoccupation—where to live or Shas's relationship with his wives.

The two dreams Shas describes at greatest length and most vividly are a living-decision dream and a conferral dream. They have a number of common features. In the first, Shas is walking behind a woman and is confronted by a figure on horseback. The figure is described as a ladino. Deities are often identified as ladinos, and a ladino in a dream can, at least for Shas, be a sufficient signal that the figure is a deity. That the ladino is on horseback is a further indication of authority. (At one time it was prohibited for Indians to ride horses, and even in Shas's day it was not a common sight.) The figure stops Shas and instructs him to leave the broad path he is following to take a narrower one that leads to the summit of a distant mountain. The man's power is indicated by the whip he carries, which he refers to as Shas's "father." Shas obeys. Instead of following the woman along the broad path, he sets off for the mountain. When he arrives, he encounters another ladino who tells him that the place he has come to is where he should settle—build his house and cultivate his fields.

This sequence can be analyzed as consisting of an *initial situation,* and *encounter,* an *instruction,* a *second encounter,* and a *second instruction.* The *terminal situation* of the dream is Shas's possession of new land for his house and fields.

In the second dream, Shas receives a summons and goes to the cemetery, where he is admitted and briefly seated. He is then given a graphic demonstration of what happens to those who misuse the office of daykeeper for sorcery. Next he goes to the courthouse, where he is given a demonstration of his newly acquired ability to release prisoners. In the end, he is presented with his staff of office, and the dream is interpreted within the dream by his departed grandfather.

Like the first dream, this one can be analyzed abstractly. In the initial situation, Shas follows the messengers to the cemetery. There he has an encounter with the four ancestral prayersayers, who give him his first instruction. His second encounter is with the ?alkaalte, who gives him further instruction. The terminal situation is his possession of the staff of office.

A very strong element of authority can be seen in these dreams: in the ladinos, one of whom has a whip; in the ancestral daykeepers and the guard who stands with his staff across the door; in the authority transfer symbolized by the seating of Shas; in the threat of punishment if he does not carry out his office correctly; in the giving to him of the keys to the jail, meaning the power to release clients from their sickness. (Also implied is the power to imprison them, by informing the appropriate gods.) The instructional component is also particularly strong, with two separate instructional episodes occurring in each dream. In the conferral dream, both demonstrations are about captivity. The first, in which the sorcerer is captive, ends in his destruction. In the second, the captivity ends in release, symbolized by Shas's opening and closing of the jail door with the keys given to him.

In the conferral dream there are three chief settings: Shas's home and household shrine, the dream-world *komoon* in the cemetery, and the dream-world courthouse with its jail. Because there is a very close conceptual linking of supernatural beings and activities with the political and religious institutions of Mayan societies, we can have a good understanding of these last two settings simply by looking at what exists in the real world at Nebaj. In fact, Shas himself verifies the close parallel between dream-world and mundane setting by explaining that his dream took place in a setting that paralleled the layout of the courthouse of earlier times. There is some question as to whether there was indeed a parallel dream world somewhere or whether the mundane settings were actually occupied by supernatural beings.

Eventually as important as settings are the dream symbols and their interconnections. Authority symbols such as the *staff* and the *whip* are prevalent. Even today, as Shas mentions, a guard sometimes stands in the doorway of the courthouse holding his staff across it. In addition to representing governing authority, the staff also denotes the divining bundle. (The word for "staff," *vara*, is a loanword from Spanish.) The *seat* is again a symbol of office; taking the seat of the prayersayer is symbolic of taking office. In prayers, among the deities invoked are ?Ana Siila and ?Ana Meesa, from the

Spanish *silla* and *mesa*, and referring to the seat and table (or altar) used during dawn ceremonies or divinations. The four daykeepers in white kerchiefs and shrouds may be a remnant of a former ranking of daykeepers. Though there is no such ranking in Nebaj or Chajul today (save for the head prayersayer we have mentioned), there are four ranked daykeepers in the third Ixil town of Cotzal. The *jail* symbolizes sickness, the *keys* the means of releasing prisoners (sick people) from their captivity by the gods. *Ladinos* signify sky gods and saints. The saints in the church have light skin and ladino clothes. Pictures of (ladino) presidents are often placed over the household shrines along with calendar art showing saints and other figures. We can only speculate about the *corral* or *fence;* perhaps it is a symbol of divine control, or perhaps, given Shas's experiences as a shepherd, it signifies a sense of responsibility.

The analysis of sequence, setting, and symbol is a general procedure that will be used with increasing elaboration and formalization in succeeding chapters. A main purpose as we progress through these chapters is the delineation of the knowledge and behavior involved in the daykeeper role. We have begun with the dreams that officially inaugurated the following of that role. Their importance is shown by the amount of attention Shas gives to them. We have chosen to discuss particular aspects of these dreams which, at this point, seem to be primarily intuitive choices. Much of what we have selected, however, will be shown in our study of myths and divination to be important.

Although we have talked about two dreams that are similar enough in some respects to suggest a pattern, we believe that most dreams are not good sources for finding patterns generated by some single system. Instead, we see the dream system as being normally a scrambling device by which concerns, either momentary or enduring, are transformed into symbols which are brought into metaphoric juxtaposition with other symbols in a way that usually does not occur in waking life. Though the recall and recounting of dreams are subject to influence by cultural schemata, most dreams represent man's more creative moments and are a key process in keeping people from being locked into the kind of stereotyped behavior and thought that is modeled by cultural grammars.

Our main analytical task in this book is to go through the texts that Shas has given us and determine those salient patterns that form part of a complex that can be represented by a cultural grammar, a decision model, or both. The dreams are not sufficiently stereotyped, nor are they numerous enough, to do this. However, they are enormously important as a key to the symbolic relations in Shas's life. In this and the next chapter we will attempt to build an understanding of these symbolic interpretations, for they are prerequisite to the development of cultural grammars and the decision model that follow.

Other aspects of the cultural context we must learn about are those that are presupposed in Shas's texts. They are the kinds of actions we have already seen in figure 3.1. The thematic sequences, macrosequences, and eidons of that figure represent a conjectured cognitive network concerned with those actions. But the cognitive network that we know exists (even though we only conjecture about its form) should not be confused with our analytical approximations to it. To keep the two separate in our discussion it is helpful to use different terms; we therefore will use an analytical device called a *frame* to work with our analytical approximations.

The concept of frames was developed in artificial intelligence by Minsky (1975) and, under the term "stereotype," by Hewitt (1975), as well as by others. We see the use of frames as a way of formalizing ethnographic description for both the texts that an ethnographer might write about a society and those that natives of the society might write. We do not suggest that an entire ethnography be formalized with frames but rather that key aspects be so treated for special purposes.

An ethnographic frame is the analyst's approximation to the way a person represents the world, either as perceived at some particular time and place or as a more generalized scheme, perhaps as a datastructure containing a set of categories, relations, or procedures. The categories of ethnographic frames are preferably native-based, linguistically or semantically determined, or validated in some way appropriate to the theoretical purpose of the analysis. Minsky describes frames as having markers that indicate a slot as being appropriately filled by some class of objects, relations, or actions. For example, a frame for *hitting* or *striking* actions would have slot markers for different cases: the person doing the hitting, the object hit, and the instrument, if any. Frames can be linked in networks or systems; they can be embedded or transformed; they can also share slots.

Slots can be filled with the most typical, salient, or frequent value. Such a value can be assumed in the absence of some statement of the contrary. Thus with frames we can model the presuppositions that lie behind elliptical statements. This is an important feature, and one that is of special anthropological interest, since the unmarked values, where obtainable, constitute a powerful ethnographic statement in themselves.

In the process of interpreting the sentences of a story, for example, certain cultural expectations tend to guide the interpretations and fill in the missing information. If the story is about a person being sick because of another's envy and we read "the enemy performed a ritual," we know that the enemy tried to persuade the gods to punish the sick person. Representing this situation with frames would involve the use of a generalized frame for envy and various frames for typical actions, characters, and settings. One would be a "jealousy of wealth" frame, which would include all the stereotyped situations in which this type of jealousy occurs.

A great advantage of frames is that they allow us to use any linguistic relation. Rather than being restricted to the impoverished set of relations in mathematical and symbolic logic, we have available the full gamut of any natural language. Just as natural language has the flexibility to deal with many different levels of abstraction and with complex embedding of ideas, frame networks can do likewise. The chief advantage of using frames, then, is to take ordinary language statements or chunks of discourse and convert them to a more visibly systematic framework that can constitute elements of a formal model or lead to the construction of a formal model. Frames also have the advantage of being amenable to use in computer models, should that be desirable.

If we wanted to model the single most important economic activity engaged in by Ixil males, that of growing maize, we could begin with a high-level "role frame" for the role of maize farmer and then include the various actions that typically make up such a role (figure 3.2). Since the actions for maize farming are quite stereotyped and represent a common part of the Ixil *eidos* or cognitive culture (in contrast to the *ethos* or affective aspects of cultural phenomena), we can speak of these actions tentatively as eidons. The relationship between such a role and its associated eidons is shown in the frames in figure 3.2. In the top frame the role of maize farmer is shown as con-

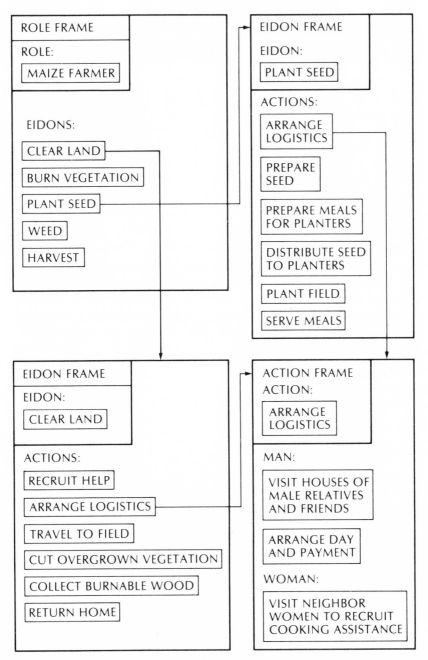

Figure 3.2. Frames of common Ixil activities.

sisting of five eidons or routine actions, from clearing land to harvesting. If we had a reason for it we could also include a number of membership criteria for the role of maize farmer, such as being male (the usual or "default" condition), being over about twelve years of age, being in a state of good health and physical strength, and so on. Then each particular slot can be thought of as a frame within a frame or else as having a pointer to another "subframe." Such a more detailed frame is the bottom frame for clearing land. Each of the actions in turn points to still another frame.

One of the advantages of a frame network is that some frames are used by a variety of different eidon or action frames, as we illustrated in figure 3.1. For example, the arranging of logistics for a work party in the field involves mobilizing several women, estimating how many tamales and how much atole should be made, and purchasing ingredients if they are not on hand. These activities are virtually the same whether the action is that of clearing the field, planting the maize, weeding, or some other field activity (differing chiefly in the number of workers involved). Thus the CLEAR LAND frame and the PLANT SEED frame would both point to the same ARRANGE LOGISTICS frame.

The separation of actual or inductively postulated cognitive structures from our crude first approximations to them by using the concept of frames for the latter is illustrated below:

cognitive structures	analytical approximations
kernels	slots
schemata and eidons	frames and slots

systems of schemata
   thematic sequences
   macrosequences
   eidon networks
	grammars, frame networks
	decision models

We know so little about how the brain works. Psychologists are still a great distance away from linking up synaptic conditions, neurotransmitter processes, and other neurophysiological phenomena to the chunks or codings of thought processes that we experience in language and other areas that are sufficiently patterned to permit the writing of grammars.

But as ethnographers, we are most concerned with externally observed patterns and the ways in which they are used and transmitted. Thus we need to look for patterns that are easily recognized as such, and thematic sequences are a good beginning. With the availability of a frame approach the possibilities are limitless, and, as we suggested earlier, the question of what to select for ethnographic attention assumes a new urgency. We therefore speak of a "motivated" description. Though all descriptions are motivated, even if at some trivial level, we emphasize the selection process and bring it to the foreground in order to highlight our theoretical purpose. This is hardly a radical idea, but we have seen too many instances in the social sciences in which analyses are done simply because the procedures are available and recognized as professionally legitimate rather than because a theoretical goal motivates them.

In working with Shas's life history, we have begun by focusing on the relationship between important life decisions and dreams. Though we see dreams as primarily a source of creative integration (as well as a memory-enhancing device), we have found two dreams with similar patterns that will later be seen in the myths Shas told us. We are thus moving toward the identification of a number of patterns that are fairly conventionalized for Shas and, with variations, for many other Ixil as well. The study of conventionalized cultural phenomena is for anthropologists what controlled laboratory experiments are for psychologists. The constructs or cultural patterns in conventionalized texts and other cultural productions provide the individual user (consumer) of those patterns with tried-and-true reference points, means of predicting and regularizing one's situation to make the world more manageable and interpretable. To show how these reference points emerge in analysis and are used by people like Shas, we have organized the texts in a progressive order of conventionalization. Not unexpectedly, the life history is the least conventionalized, though perhaps less expected even here is its extensive linkage to the later patterns.

It is crucial to an understanding of our theory, however, that our intention in demonstrating this conventionalization is not to cast Shas as a typical Ixil. The systems we approximate through our grammars are Shas's own systems, developed through his own selection and modification of cultural patterns.

4
SHAS KO?W'S
PHILOSOPHY

In the past some have argued that peasant, herding, and foraging
societies have no philosophers. The reason usually offered in such
arguments is that the people in these societies are thought to be
more primitive in their thinking ability than are those in modern civilizations. Another reason given is that the natives of simpler societies
are so caught up with the exigencies of daily life that there is no time
for reflective thought; still another is that they are so submerged in
their group that thinkers and philosophers, who always diverge
somewhat from commonly held ideas, could not exist. In *Primitive
Man as Philosopher*, the anthropologist Paul Radin (1927) attacked
this mistaken idea. In doing so, he was taking on a prejudice held
not only by the general public but also by a number of his colleagues. The earlier work of Levy-Bruhl (1910), for example, had
supported the idea of a lower intelligence among primitive groups.
This widely held misconception was passed on by Ernst Cassirer and
numerous others; so there was much for Radin to refute. To do so, he
published verbatim texts from preliterate societies which contained
the kinds of ideas that we would normally classify as philosophical,
ethical, or intellectual. These texts clearly demonstrated that there
were "intellectuals" in a great number of economically and technologically undeveloped societies and that the ideas these people discussed were of much the same sort as the philosophical and religious ideas of people in technologically advanced societies.

Since the publication of Radin's book, the trend has been toward recognition of the intellectual side of life in the simpler societies. Whorf, for example, spoke of the Hopi language as being an ideal one in which to state Einstein's general theory of relativity. Modern ethnoscience has emphasized the intellectual sophistication of various language domains of such societies. Horton (1967) has shown that, though there is indeed more magic and ritual in the simpler societies than in our own, this is no evidence of a difference in intellectual ability; in many respects the same kind of thinking occurs with magical practices and observances as with scientific observation.

Pap Shas's philosophy text, given to us (in one sitting) in California in 1970, represents a further contribution to the body of evidence for intellectual accomplishment in simpler societies. It is valuable not only for what it tells us about Shas himself, but for the glimpse it gives us of earlier Mayan and mixed Mayan-Christian thinking. It helps to clarify the ritual texts and may provide valuable insights for interpreting earlier pre-Columbian systems.

The text moves in and out of a ritualistic, poetic style in transitions that are sometimes not easily perceived. To preserve some of this quality in the translation, we have printed parts of the text line for line to bring out the imagery, parallelisms, and rhythm. Even in the parts of the text that read more like prose, the reader will find repetitions that underline the special character of the material. In the introduction to his translation of the *Popol Vuh*, Edmonson (1971a) discusses similar poetic and stylistic features. The fact that so many of the phrases were in couplets was helpful to him in his translation. Of course, a more formal style such as this makes a text easier to learn as well as providing poetic enjoyment.

The didactic component in the text that follows is quite clear. It is a philosophy of daily living, a compendium of typical advice and explanations that Pap Shas gives to his clients, but it is updated by reference to the circumstances under which he was telling it. He begins by praising God and then his mentor, Pap Weʔl, and then points out that his own long life is testimony to his good behavior, for those who attempt to do harm through ritual have their lives cut short by the gods. All these preliminary statements establish the authority for the advice that follows.

THE TEXT

Only this shall I say,
Only this shall I speak,
Some words shall I leave behind
About what I do in this world:
Suppose there is a daughter [of God][1]
Suppose there is a child [of God],
Someone who is ignorant,
Who has no thought,
Who has no knowledge,
So he asks guidance from me.
And I will speak to him, I will give him advice;
Because I have knowledge, but only for serving the days.[2]
I have thoughts, but only for serving the gods.
I have wisdom, but only for serving the ʔaanhel.
I have skill, but only for serving the ancestral souls,
This all for honoring the deities.
I haven't achieved much.
I never became mayuyil,
I never became rišitolil,
Because I was poor.
I didn't have money,
I didn't have land.
I exist merely to fill my stomach.
I exist merely to obtain my food.
But that is all I do.
I don't scold.
No one do I scold.

There are men who mistreat me. They'll say anything. "That man lies, he is a daykeeper, what a lying daykeeper," a man will say. But when I hear it I never rebuke the man. What would I say to him? Instead I just listen. It is up to the gods to decide whether I am false of word, whether I am a lying daykeeper, for it was God who entrusted me with his word.

It was God who provided my thoughts.
It's for God alone that I speak.
It's God I honor.
It's certainly not just anything
That I recite before a believer.
I don't speak [pray] just for any man,
Even though he be ʔalkaalte,[3]
Even though he be ʔaacib' [scribe],
Or even though he be chief.
I need not say the prayers.

My chief is God.
My chief is Our Father of the Sky,
My chief is Our Mother, Our Father, and Jesus.
My president is the Eternal Father,
Because he gives me my tortilla,
Because he gives me my drink.
This is what I am trying to say.

You will hear only a few of my words, because it may not be long before I die. It was God who placed me on earth, so God will take me. It was not a daughter, it was not a son who placed me on earth.

Many men envy me. There are men who perform evil rituals against me. There are men who send moisture to me.[4] There was a man who sent his *win* [animal spirit associated with witchcraft] to my house. But who knows why, they can't succeed.

I am alive.
I walk.
I earn money.
I work.
But it is God who decides
What my work is,
What my thoughts are.
It was God who gave them to me.

It wasn't just any man on earth who showed me my way of life. The man who did it was a prayersayer, a good man with good thoughts and good laws. Good were the laws that were in the mind of the man. He gave them to me long ago—Pap Weʔl.

He gave me my knowledge
When I burned the *pom.*
When I took up the day count,
ᐧHe taught me the *ʔuq'iib'al.*[5]
When I took up the day count,
He taught me about the Days.
When I took up the day count,
He taught me about the *ʔaanhel.*
He told me the names of the saints,
How many saints there are.
He told me the names of all the souls.
He grouped them.
He said to me:
"Thus are the souls;
Thus are the Days;
Thus are the *ʔaanhel.*"

That is everything he told me.
It was he who gave me the wisdom.
An ancient man was he who gave it.
He was an old man.
He had fulfilled his office.
He was an ancient prayersayer.
He accompanied the ʔalkaaltes.
He consecrated the staves,
He consecrated the staves for the *b'aal c'aq meertoma*[6]:
Indeed, an ancient man was he who gave me my wisdom.

What a long time since I grew up! When he died, I was still young. I was
still a young man when he left me enlightened by wisdom. Now I've
grown old. But so be it, because it's my destiny, my fortune with God. So
far I've survived. There are many prayersayers who are young when they
go. They are young and they die; their lifetime is shortened. Sometimes
the prayersayer shortens his own thread [life] because of some man who
has envy for a fellow man, and he loses his head because of money; he
loses his senses because of money!

Suppose there is a daughter or son who has a disagreement with some
other son or daughter [and he says to the prayersayer]:

"Please, do me a favor: do some ritual, do some witchcraft, because he
rants at me, because he took my wife."

"All right, if you can afford my price, I'll do it," the prayersayer will answer, and he loses his head because of the money.

But what if the man still has time before God, and he only does harm?
He will shorten his own days. He doesn't know what is happening. Perhaps because of that the man goes early.

Men like that are on a par with dogs that hunt deer, that hunt rabbits,
that kill the animals of the ʔaanhel.[7] The dog dies very soon. He may
overcome the animal, but he won't enjoy it. The dog doesn't live long because he doesn't see what he is doing. This is his nature. But our lord, the
ʔaanhel, is concerned about his animals, so the dog dies soon. So also is
the way of the sorcerer. If one's intentions are evil, one goes early.

But I'm not like that. Many men have talked about me. Many are the
men I have heard say: "That old man is no good; he's a man without
worth. Not like me, because I have wisdom. My thoughts are not the same
as his. I have magical chants," they say.

I have no magical chants, but God forgives me my sins, whether what I
do before God is good or not. It is God who pardons my faults, because it
was God who gave me my wisdom. It was our Father in heaven who gave
me my wisdom, and he is the one who knows me. He is the one who pardons my sins; and they just utter their words—"The man is of no use,"
they say.

Who knows? Surely God knows whether my words are useful or not,
but God forgives me my faults. God doesn't say anything like, "That man

isn't useful, so I won't listen to his words." God would hardly say that. On the contrary, since he exists God pardons my transgressions; because I always perform the rituals. I do ritual for my maizefield. I do ritual for my animals.

The children say many things. I just reply, "It's all right."

There are those who pay me, and there are those who don't pay me, but let them be. God is with them, and God is with me also, because perhaps there is one person who doesn't pay me and perhaps there is another who pays extra. That is the only way I live. I don't demand anything of people. I don't ask for anything, I don't ask for money. I don't ask for more, because it's like a sin. Money is hot. Money isn't good. I have it in my head, so I don't ask for more. I don't ask for money, nor do I ask for rum.

There are men who say, "You hardly meet my price, give me rum then. Why don't you buy a liter of rum for me?" And people will provide it, because they want to win—they want to kill the person or do whatever it is they intend. Perhaps they will wish him poverty. "Well, I'd like to see him die before me," they will say. Hardly will he die, hardly will he disappear. Rather, it's the one who speaks who will die. Without forewarning, he will go prior to his intended victim, the man whose days he has tried to shorten, whose light he has tried to shorten. The victim may remain on earth while he [who wished the evil] dies because he has committed a sin before God.

Not I, because I've already grown old; but who knows whether my words are useful, whether my words are real, the words I say before God? Perhaps they are not—who knows? May God pardon me my faults, but that is all I do.

Suppose there is an unfortunate person, a child who has no mother, no father, and he asks me for advice. Then:

"This is what you should do, because I did it. I had no mother, no father when I grew up. I just grew up alone with some rich people. That's the way I got where I am. I haven't done anything wrong. To be sure, I haven't held an office. I haven't been ?alkaalte. I was only a mertomil. I have been third mertomil for *Kruus ?Išoq* and fourth mertomil for *Kruus Winaq* (both cofradías or religious brotherhoods in Nebaj). That is all I did, only twice. I didn't enter the courthouse because I have no money, I'm poor. Yet at the same time I never touched anything."

"Well, here I am," [says the other person;]. "I don't own a thing. I'm poor. If only I had animals. If only I had cattle. If only I had horses. There isn't anything, only a small *milpa* [maizefield] that I cultivate, just that. I haven't stolen anything, I haven't touched anything. Here I am, nothing more."

"This is what you must do," I will say. "Think a little about God. Place a few candles, help yourself a bit; perform ritual in the mountains; leave an offering before Kučuč; leave an offering on your father's place [grave]; honor the soul of your father; honor the soul of your mother," I will say to

the man. Because that's the way we live in the world: we exist to honor
God:

We earn our money and honor God.
We receive a little animal.
We place our candles.
We receive some of our maize.
We ask pardon of God.
We seek pardon before Kučuč,
We seek pardon before Kub'aal: the Holy Land, the Holy Earth—
We use machetes, we wield machetes, we cut [the brush].
    But what is their fault?
It's our offense.
It's our fault alone.
It's ours for fault of our stomach.
It's ours for fault of our food.
Because there are trees that grow.
There are trees that sprout.
There are trees that appear.
Let them be.
How happily they sprout!
Perhaps it is a resting place for Kub'aal ʔAanhel.
Perhaps it is a sleeping place of Kučuč Kub'aal the ʔaanhel.
Perhaps it is a place of rest for the birds.
Perhaps it is their place of frolic.
Perhaps it is their nesting place,
And we cut it. I cut it.
I sharpen my machete and I cut it.
But what offense is there?
The tree is not at fault.
How handsomely it grows!
It is full of desire to grow.
What is its offense, then?
It is the urging of my insides
For food, for drink.
Because there is no other place to get it from;
That is surely its service.
Our pom was left to us,
Our candles were left for us
By Our Father.
Our candles were left for us
By Our Mother of the Sky.
That is why I seek pardon,
I offer my atonement,
Because I sharpened my machete
I'm very content,

I sharpened my machete and
I'm very happy.

I do a cuerda of work [clear a cuerda of land], happily clearing land, and
I say, "All that is my work." Well, those are many souls; it's a cuerda of
souls that I've killed because I've cut the trees. Perhaps there was a small
animal. Perhaps there was a little snake. Perhaps there was a little bird.
Lord, have mercy, perhaps it was his roosting place. Perhaps it was its nest,
and I moved it. I cut the trunk, the tree disappeared, the bird disappeared
because it fled, it no longer stayed in the tree. All for the offense of my
stomach.

But that's what pom is for.[8] That's what the candle is for. That's what
Our Father left us instructed about. I honor God. I sprinkle my pom, I
place my candle on the ground before the Earth. That's all that lies in my
power. That's all I can do.

Suppose there is another—another older brother, another child. Because I've seen poverty, I can give him counsel. There are children who
have no mother, who have no father. If it is a man:

"Young friend, this is the way to do it: sow your maizefield; put in your
maizefield! If you have no fields, you must rent them. There are fields that
belong to your fellow Ixil. Go ask for them. Well, go sow your maizefield,
because the maizefield is very good for you, because the maizefield has a
soul. It isn't like the plantation. The plantation is no good. What if we get
sick at the plantation? Who will come to fetch us? It's so far away. We can
no longer come back here; we stay and die at the plantation. We are indeed unfortunate.

"But if instead we have our own maizefield, it's always good. Once you
have your own maizefield, soon your own maize will appear. Once you
have good fortune in the maizefield, there will soon be a little pig. There
will soon be a woman; you will seek a wife. She will raise chickens; she
will raise a little pig. But you must have a milpa. You must have maize,
and she will store your maize in the granary and feed it to the animals.
Then money will come your way. Perhaps your wife will sell some animal.
With that you can buy chile or salt. That is why it is worthwhile for you to
have a maizefield. Otherwise, although the woman raises chickens, you
won't have maize. Where will she get it? She can hardly go look for it
herself. That's what it's good for. Your wife will need to eat. Your wife will
need clothes. That's why she seeks a husband—she wants clothes. You
must plant your maizefield and work. You mustn't sleep. Little by little
you will awaken.[9] Little by little you will buy small parcels of land. Perhaps in a short while you'll get a little house of your own.

"That's what I did when I was growing up. I was very poor. I didn't have
land. I didn't have anything for myself. I only rented my land. But it was
all right. Now I own my house. I have a little land that I've bought. It's not
very much, but at least it's something. Since I sleep in my own house, no
one scolds me. No one berates me about it. Not so if it were rented. When

we rent a house, they argue with us. We can't even defecate out back.
Well, ordinarily no one can scold us, but if the house is rented the owner
will complain. It's a delicate situation. Suppose a child knocks a hole in
the house: "You're no good, because your son made a hole in my house.
Look for another homestead, get out!" he will say. Well, what can we answer, because we are only renting? So we go. Suppose a woman wants to
grow her patch of č'imay. She wants to plant some q'ooq'. They have to
remain behind when we go. It's not like having our own place that no one
can take from us because it's ours.

"So you must do just as I have. When I rented my land and house, whatever I sowed was always left behind. I couldn't dig it up and carry it away
when I left. It just stayed there. Now I have plants in my yard, I have animals in my yard. No one bothers me. They're mine. No one bothers me
about them because they are my property. But with renting it's a headache. Renting is precarious. I had to rent out of poverty, but one gets tired
of it," I will say to one of our brothers, I will say to a daughter, to a son.
Who knows whether what I say is good counsel or bad? There are those
who say, "That man gives too much advice. What good is he? He's hardly
God. He isn't equal to God," they will say. But my words are counsel:
they're the truth.

Suppose there is another man, and he says to a friend:

"What are you doing, boy? You're just hanging around in the street.
You're just wasting time. You aren't looking for a living, you aren't looking
for a job. Let's go to the plantation, my friend, for the hell of it. Let's see
what they tell us we can do. We'll have money at the plantation. We'll
have an employer."

"All right," the friend will answer, thoughtlessly following the advice.
He'll believe such words, and there you are. But it's no good, because he's
going to be lost, the poor man. He may sicken and die at the plantation.
That is a great danger. It's risky. Such words aren't good.

There are foolish men, good-for-nothing men, who say: "Why, that is
how I live. It's not true that I don't eat, it's not true that I don't drink at the
plantation, not at all. You should do the same. Our mothers argue too
much. Our fathers scold too much," they will say. The other young man
gets excited. He listens to him with interest. But it's wrong, because he's
going to be lost. His mind is already ensnared. Perhaps he'll die. He won't
see the death of his mother and father. So it isn't good. It's his mistake.

On the other hand, good advice would be this:

"We die in our home village. Our mother dies, our father dies before us;
we bury them, because we're there. Or we are buried by our mother, our
father. That is the belief; so you must do. Don't go out on the road." Thus
I will say to a young man, a man who isn't fully grown. "Thus you must
do, young man. Don't do silly things. That's the way to do it. That's how it
is done. Here is how you should make a living: you should buy some land,
but you must work! Little by little you will raise your piglet and sell it, buy
a few clothes, buy clothes for your wife," I will say to him. Who knows
whether it is good advice for him or bad?

Well, if the man is a good, polite person: "Thank you, Pap. You gave me good advice," he will say. Good, he will take the advice when he sees that my words are true. If the man follows my advice then perhaps—who knows how long afterwards—when he remembers that it was my advice he followed and that it was good, when he realizes that what I told him came true, he will say to me: "Thank you, Pap, for giving me advice, for giving me wisdom; thanks to you forever. It's true what you say. There it is, I've experienced it. There it is. I am living well thanks to you, Pap. Take a little rum, take a little rum. It's just for my pleasure that I offer it to you. It's a pleasure for me to talk to you," the man will say, just because of the favor that I did for him. They were good words, correct words; they weren't useless words, dangerous words, but rather words of Our Mother, words of Our Father of the Sky, words of the tiiš.

Then to another man: "You mustn't strike a woman. You mustn't scold a woman. You must speak to a woman with goodwill. You must speak straight; you must speak truthfully to a woman. Otherwise you're only going to torment her. If she has good thoughts, the offense will be yours. You will be lost; it isn't good. But even if she is the one who commits the offenses, if she doesn't pay attention to your words, your thoughts, you mustn't beat her, you mustn't bother her, because it's a sin. It isn't good to hit a woman; it isn't good to scold a woman. If she is the offending one she should go quietly without ceremony. We must stay at peace. We should just go to seek another wife for ourselves, and she should seek another husband. Maybe it's her destiny not to find a husband. Maybe that's her fate. The same with the man: maybe that's our fate. Perhaps it's our destiny that the woman not remain ours. There's no evil in that; there's no harm in that.

"There may be some other man, however, who, when he separates from his wife, will bewitch the woman. He will place pom. He will place a candle against her so that she will have trouble. He will curse her: 'Let her not find a husband,' he may say. 'Let her suddenly die,' he may say. Without doubt, God will hear those words. Well, perhaps the poor thing will run into difficulty, but she may still have time left. She may stop being sick; she may not die. She may recuperate through penance. She may do her penance for God and recover. Perhaps it's he who will have died before her, if he tries to do evil to her.

"There should be no evil before God. There should be no foolishness before God. If there are shortcomings one can leave, but in honesty, with kindness, without argument, without so much scolding, but gently. One can also send the woman to the courthouse, but it wasn't the court that gave us the woman. Instead, it was we who made our agreements with her. So in the same way we should speak our words before separating, if our destinies do not coincide.

"If you speak well, it will be all right. You will have your food when you come from the steep fields; you will have your drink when you come from the steep fields. That way is good. It will turn out well. You'll see food in front of you because of her, and you'll have drink to enjoy because of her.

It's the same way for the woman. She gets her clothes from you. Her desire to be adorned is why she seeks a husband and if you don't clothe her, that surely isn't good. It's wrong."

Some woman may ask, "What should I do, Pap? My husband does nothing but scold me. He criticizes me too much. I can't live happily with him."

So I reply, "What is there between you and him? What does he say? Does he give you your food? Does he give you your clothes? Does he provide for you or not?"

"Well, yes, he provides for me, but what happens is that I get angry every little while and I feel like leaving him," she will say to me.

"Ah, but no, that's not good, just leaving him. You have clothes from him; you have possessions from him. What do you want, then? You have nothing to complain about. Give him his tortilla. Give him his drink. Besides, perhaps you aren't honoring the soul of your mother or your father.[10] Place your candle. I'll do you the favor, if you want me to, and place one. I will hold two rituals for you. Let's look for a good day.[11] I will go to do your ritual on that day.

We shall ask forgiveness among the souls.
We shall ask pardon before the Kučuč.
We shall ask pardon before the ʔAlkaalte [cross].
We shall go before the hills.
We shall ask for pardon,
For tranquillity in your soul.

"Perhaps you have an enemy. Perhaps there is some man who fell in love with you when you were a girl, and perhaps he did you wrong. Perhaps he cried out in anger[12] about you, and you weren't thinking of God. That may be why your soul isn't attached to your husband.

"What is lacking if you have food, if you have clothes, thanks to him? What is it you want? If you lacked food, if he didn't give you tortillas, well, then, that would be sufficient to make your soul wander. That would be what would do it to you, not [an enemy]. What is it, then? Because what you want is to eat. What you want is to drink. And so does the man. He wants to eat, to drink, to make a living. That's what he wants. If you don't like to cook, he will become angry. The same goes for you. If he doesn't give you clothing, if he doesn't give you your qʼeʔnaʔq, if he doesn't give you your čik, that just won't do. But if you have clothes and sustenance, then what more do you want? It's better that you think some about God. It isn't good that you lose yourself in the streets.[13] It won't do. No man is perfect. We're all alike. You, too, none of you is perfect. How can it be otherwise? Instead, we must seek pardon in the face of destiny so that we can eat, so that we can drink." That is what I tell her.

"Thank you, Pap, that was my errand that I came to speak with you. Be it so. Thank you."

"Well, this is what you do: just ask pardon before God. Make two offerings," I will say to her.

"Ah, good, but Pap, do me a favor, would you perhaps grant me a consultation? Would you perhaps look at my destiny—see what the root is, what the motive is for what I do, why it is that I get angry when nothing is being said to me, when I'm the one who's unreasonable?" she will say.

"All right, we'll take a look," I will tell her. And I'll take a look, I'll question [the seeds]. Then, if her offense is revealed: "It says that this is your offense, before your mother, before your father. Or, it says there is a man. He cried; he called for you; he performed ritual because he was in love with you. Or, it says, here is a man who gave money [bride price] for you, and you didn't return it to him."

"Yes, Pap, that's true, that happened to me," the woman will say.

"Ah, but that's what hurt him, and he did you wrong," I will say to her.

"But do me a favor then, Pap. Where can I turn unless you yourself do me the favor?" she will say.

And I will do her ritual, so that she becomes reconciled, that she remembers (the gods), that it will enter her mind.

Later she will say: "Thank you, Pap, for the favor you did me. Now I live well. God is with you: here is a little gift of food for you," and she will leave some maize mush for me. That is all. That is their recognition of what I have done.

Only thus do I speak to them, I hardly tell them: "Ah, it's all right, leave the man; it's all right, leave the woman." I only enlighten them: "There you are. I don't have legal authority, since I'm not the ?alkaalte. I'm not the courthouse. It's only the justice of God that I can give you," I say to them. And little by little they become reconciled. They compose themselves.

But there are younger brothers, there are older brothers, and after we save . . . some ignorant person from the wrong path—"Ah, but it is good what you are doing," we might have said without giving him advice.

But it isn't good. It's a mistake, Our Father would say, that's not the way. Instead Our Father says this:

"An ignorant person doesn't think, he doesn't know anything. So you give him advice from what you know, from what you have done. You tell the daughter, you tell the son," says Our Father. Our Father left the words behind, he left the words in parting. That is all I say to the poor person. Some people are ignorant. I just give them guidance, and little by little they improve. That is all I do, because I have myself experienced it: I have seen poverty. I have experienced life with women. We live in poverty and we may separate from our wives, as I did. In my case it may have been my mother or my father whom I had offended. As of now, everything speaks in my favor. I have my tortillas; I have my drink. This is it: I do favors. God does favors. I walked in poverty for a long time; that's how I can give advice.

I'm poor, but I've never robbed anybody. I've never stolen an animal or a single ear of maize. I've never gone into anyone's maizefield. Nor have I stolen money. I've never stolen a single thing. Perhaps I did before my soul had arrived, when I was still a boy, but once I awoke I no longer did anything wrong. Then I earned my money through work. I have many things, but through work: I climbed steep uphill roads, I descended steep downhill roads. Perhaps my sweat cleansed me to obtain them.

Well, it's the same way you all will do, only I have done it already. It's no trifling matter that I give you advice about. My words are not just empty words after I have said them. I'm helping you out of trouble. Then, after I've given you my advice, you'll say, "Why, Pap, you've done me a favor."

There are some I counsel who may no longer speak to me. Perhaps some of you will no longer talk to me. You will just pass by me; no longer will you recognize me. There are others of you, children of God, who may remember and may offer me rum. "It's your choice; I'm not asking for it," I will say.

So there are some who receive my words well, and there are others who receive them poorly. But I just speak my words kindly; I don't scold anyone.

It's all because of the things I did, because of what happened to me when I grew up. I was ignorant. Some of my older and younger brothers, some of God's children awakened me. They gave me advice. They taught me my work. Since I was an infant when my father died, I never saw him; but so much for that. I grew up. I didn't have a mother. I didn't have a father. But I ate well, I drank well, and it was God who blessed me. "That's what you will do. You must think of God," I will say to the poor person.

Because thus spoke Our Father.
Thus said Our Mother.
Thus said God.
Thus said the ʔaanhel.
Thus said the Earth.
If we have a younger brother
Or if we have an older brother
Who is ignorant,
We give him advice.
Suppose we have a younger brother
Or we have an older brother
Who is ignorant, but
The god who created him [one of the day gods][14] was equally ignorant,
The one who created him to live on earth.
Suppose we have a younger brother, or a daughter,
Or a son who is mute.
But Our Father in the Sky [another day god] was mute
When he gave him as a present.

There is a younger brother, there is an older brother
Who is blind,
Who doesn't have sight,
Who has his eyes closed.
But again, Our Father gave him.
Our Father blessed him
Then certainly Our Father didn't have eyes when he gave him as a gift,
So he looks after him.
Well, there is another one,
Another child who is a sinner,
Who is a drunk,
Who has a mistress.
He is good for two or three wives.
But it's his fortune, it's his fate,
And we cannot scold him.
We can't reprove him.
We can't ridicule him,
Because it's a sin [to do so].
A blind man:
We must not laugh at him.
A mute man:
We must not mistreat him.
The blind man:
We must not abuse him.
Because why should we abuse him if he has done no wrong?
Because it is a god who did it to him.
It's his fate to have no sight.
It's his fate to have no speech.
But he, too, has thoughts inside,
Even though he has no sight.
He, too, has ideas inside
Even though he has no speech.
It is not as though he were completely useless.
On the contrary, he has knowledge.
He has thoughts in his head, in his soul.
He may have more knowledge without speech.
He may have more thoughts without sight.
We, on the other hand,
Who have our mouths open,
Who have our eyes open;
We will often mistreat someone.
We will often mistreat our younger brother
We will often mistreat our older brother
When he is foolish in what he does.
A man may be a sinner,
And because of it we may mistreat him.

Well, too bad for us!
Because perhaps it will happen to us,
Or to one of our daughters or sons.
Perhaps it will be a daughter of ours
Perhaps it will be a son of ours
Who will see it,
Who will experience it.
What can be done?
The giver of sight,
The giver of speech,
We don't see him.
We don't behold him.
It's a sin to stare at our younger brother,
Our older brother, whose bare skin is showing.
Unfortunate is he.
He has no clothes.
What shall we do?
We certainly shouldn't scold him.
We certainly shouldn't mock him;
Because it's his bad luck,
It's his fate,
Bestowed by God.
Because we have clothes, thanks to God,
We live well.
But we must fold our hands [in prayer].
"Whatever it be, Christ, God,
Forgive us," we must say.
But we also must give more advice:
"Be it my younger brother,
Be it my older brother,
Be it first for him, be it first for him.
May I follow," we say.
Even worse, if we really do something (like killing him):
That is quite surely what will happen to us!
Because really, we are asking for it when we talk this way
"Would that our younger brother die first,
And I may follow," we say.
"Ah, he's asking for a little punishment of his own.
Let's give him a little," says Our Father.
So say the gods; so they agree.
And we'll get what we deserve.
But Our Mother has her own prayers.
Our Father has his own prayers.
"God, forgive the daughter.
God, forgive the woman.
God, forgive the man.

God, forgive me.
Forgive whoever the children of god may be," we say.
These are beneficial words.
These are holy words before God.
Only these, they say, will help.
Only these I will talk about here.

It's evil to say, "Let's steal something." It's evil to say, "Let's steal a bone," "Let's steal a cocoa bean," "Let's steal an animal." It's a great offense, because perhaps the man who owns the animal is suffering from hunger. Perhaps he is starving. He keeps going out to care for his animal, and we watch it grow and then take it with our hand. It's a great sin, because the animal may be intended not just for the man, but for something else. Perhaps he has debts, obligations; perhaps he lacks something, or he may need it simply for his own sustenance. We who take it away with our hands, we just want to steal it. We shall just eat it, when it isn't ours; it's not of our labor. What we do is all the more wrong because we do it willfully. We just take with our hands while our eyes are open, our mouth is open. We have our hands and feet. We have our eyes. We are able to obtain our own things with our money. We must earn our money or else it's no good.

Here is some further advice: We may say [of someone], "He's lazy." But that's not right, because it's his fate to be lazy. It's not for us to mention it, because that's a great sin. It's forbidden to speak of laziness, because it doesn't matter. "God may forgive him," that's all we can say. That's all that has been left decided by God. So if we mention laziness, woe be to us! We may be all right, because it's our good fortune, but perhaps some of our [own] children will be that way.

There are people who mistreat me. There are men who say all manner of things about me. There are people who gossip about me. They blame me for many things. But I only listen, I don't answer. I don't talk back; I just walk by such a person.

"You're good for nothing. You don't know a thing," he will say.

"Too bad, what can I do about it?" is all I say; I tell the man I can't talk back to him. If I should quarrel with him, if I should strike him, it would only be because I had been drinking. When the liquor goes to my head, I might not control myself. But if I'm sober and I meet the man, I only change my direction before him, because I mustn't reply. I mustn't lower myself to being his equal because of the words he has spoken. That's all I can do. That is my way of living, because God's words, as I well know, are that it's a sin to reply to such a man. If he's bad, if he's crazy, never mind him. We'll just change our path ahead of him. Let him say what he wants to say over there. He is of no consequence to us, even though he scolds us, even though he mistreats us. We won't come to an end because of his mistreatment. That is all I abide by.

There are many men who scold me. Some mistreat me when they are drunk. I just pass them by on the road. I merely excuse myself. I just walk by them cautiously. I can't say, "Ah, but you're so angry, what's the matter with you?" I can't hit them. It would be a sin if I should hit them. Therefore I just listen to their words.

What's more, there's no reason for their anger. It's only because they see that people seek me out. It makes them jealous. Even my neighbor—his soul is disturbed. But who knows why? There's no reason for it. [It would be different] if I should steal, or if I myself solicited the people that came to me: "Help me, man, because I lack money. Can't I get some money from you? There is something I possess."

But it's without my seeking that they come. There are times when I'm sleeping. Sometimes it's midnight when a person comes to me. Perhaps it's a sick man: "Please help me." Thus it's not I who calls on them. It's hardly so that I say to them: "I have some advice, don't you want it? Won't you come to consult me? I'll give you counsel." I never say that, yet who knows why they come? Perhaps God is the one who causes it. But the people know about it. They come to me. So that's all. It's all right. Even though there are other people who don't come to me, but mistreat me, never mind them. Let them gossip. I won't meet my end because of their words. I don't rob them. I don't steal from them. I don't take their wives. I don't take their maize. I don't steal their livestock. But who knows what their motive is, why it is that they should feel envy for me? "Never mind them, may they lose their desire [to bother me]," I say. I just ask forgiveness of God.

That's all I am capable of,
That's all I do.
These alone are the thoughts I have,
Because I know Our Father's words,
Our Mother's words.
Indeed, it is surely God who bestowed such words on us,
And only in that way,
And perhaps partly for that reason
Have I reached this position.
Thank heavens.
I was poor when I grew up,
But now, fortunately, it is all well thanks to God:
God grants the favor.
God grants the blessing,
Just as he has done already.
I am the one who came here.
I came to this place [California].
I came to this blessed world. Fortunately:
I hardly could have planned that.
I hardly could have known that.
I hardly could have seen it.

I hardly could have heard it.
Who knows, for surely it is God who gave me his blessing
That I came here.
For certainly it's my luck.
It's my fortune, because of God.
But thanks are due also to the children who do the favor.[15]
I came to visit,
I came here,
Thanks to the children.
They give me money.
Here I eat,
Here I drink.
But it's God's command.
It's God's order.
It's not just happenstance.
It's not I who asked for it.
"This is what I have,
Don't you want me to come to you?"
Hardly did I say that.
Rather, it was certainly [divine] justice.
So it isn't that I steal.
I don't do anything.
But God knows, it is certainly for the worship of God
When I speak.
Clearly, they just want me to give them counsel.
So there it is, I've given it.
There it is, I've said it.
So that's what you must do.
That's the way you must do it, too.
Whoever of you should read these pages,
Whoever of you should listen to the tape,
So also must you do.
So also must you do, only obey!
Don't do anything wrong, don't disobey.
Don't scold your younger brother.
Don't scold your older brother.
Don't scold a daughter.
Don't scold a son.
Don't plan just to hoard your money
So that a poor man seems worthless to you.
These are my observances.
Here is what I do.

Yes, I'm poor. I'm needy, but when there is another person who is destitute I always take pity on him. I always give him a little money. Take an alcoholic ready to die of a hangover: "Do me the favor, Pap, give me a little money. Don't you have some money for me?"

"It's all right, here it is," I will say. If I have any, I'll give it [to him]. Because I've experienced drinking liquor myself, I will take pity on him. I will give him his dime, or his fifteen cents. I give it once and for all. I don't ask for it back. It isn't possible that I should tell him, "Remember what you did? This is what I did for you. I gave you money. I gave you money as a gift." I could hardly say such a thing. It's a great sin before God for us to speak in such a manner. Once we give it, we give it; never mind, it's nothing, we won't ask for it anymore. We won't be envious of it. That's the way my thinking goes; I pity him. It's because I experienced poverty myself; I suffered misfortune when I grew up, and there it stays in my mind. And so I take pity on a poor man. I feel sorry for another person, because our poverty is the same. Only one [and the same] God is our Creator. It's not so that his God is poor, that his creator is a different one from one who is rich. He is the same. The God who created him is certainly not different. Rather, one and the same is Our Mother God, Our Father God. It's just that things are that way because it's *his destiny*.[16]

When a person encounters goodness, well-being, it's because he has good fortune. We mustn't covet his land. We mustn't covet his animals. You say: "If only I had some!" We mustn't say that. We mustn't covet them, because it's a sin. It's his good fortune, and it's our fate, no matter how much we kneel before God and no matter how much we cry out before the Earth. It's our fate that God does not bestow gifts on us. What can we do? It's our destiny. Why should we complain? Rather, it's possible that it's our good fortune! It's surely a blessing for us that we are poor. Even though we are poor—we hardly have anything to eat, we hardly have anything to drink—God knows how we eat, how we drink, where our food comes from, where our drink comes from. It is God who has to do the favor. But possibly because we worship God even though we are poor, it won't be hard. We will eat. We will drink. Because we worship God we will eat. Poverty is in order to worship God.

Poverty doesn't exist without reason. The poor person doesn't exist without reason. The poor person is a better worshiper of God. The person who has money, who has animals, the rich one, he doesn't worship God, because he is content; his stomach is full. But the poor person remembers God, because where will he get his sustenance today? And how much will he have to eat tomorrow? Worse it is if he has children. What can he give them? It's because of that that he worships God.

Perhaps he will kneel at noon.
Perhaps he will kneel when it dawns.
Perhaps he will kneel at sundown,
But it's because of his poverty.
On the other hand, when there is money, animals, and seed
We do not remember God.
That is not good.
It's a sin,

For we have our property, thanks to God.
God gives the good things.
God does the favor.
We have our animals.
We have our seed.
And we remember God for it, too.
Thanks be to God,
Because no one else gives.
Be it your animals,
Be it your cow,
Where else does an animal eat?
It can't very well gnaw on your leg.
It is only [from] the ground that it eats;
It eats the grass,
But that is the hair of the Earth.
Even if you have only a horse,
What does it eat?
It only eats the grass
Until it is satisfied.
We are the animals,
Because we, too, eat what the Earth has given us as our food.
Then we go and soil it.
We walk over its face,
We go and urinate,
And it sustains us.
And what do you think?
If that were done to us, we would scold,
We would most certainly punish,
But what does the Earth say instead?
We trample it,
We cut it,
We slash it,
And what is its offense?
What is its disgrace,
Its difficulty?
How beautiful is the Holy Earth,
And we carve it up for our stomach,
Because of our stomach,
But that's what it's for.

This is what Our Father of the Sky said. He went through the suffering, they say. He went through the pain, they say, for us. I have heard the stories that he went through the suffering for us: thirty years he suffered. Our Father was tied up by the early gods, by Our Uncles of old.[17] And why did he fight for thirty years? Well, it was for us. It was our fault. The reason was that when the earth appeared, he then made the people; after the world appeared, we appeared. And it was only for that reason; it was surely because of us. "That man is very smart, because all alone he managed to create the world. He managed to create the children. It's better that we kill him. Let's kill him. It's better that his face should disappear. We are the ones who shall remain on earth. We shall remain among his children," Our Uncles of old said about Our Father. After they had agreed upon it, they attacked Our Father and hit him. They kept watch over Our Father, and Our Father knew it. He had to flee. When Our Father first came to the earth, it is said, when he was perhaps only a day or two old, he began to reason, he began to have strength. He did many things. He cut a tree and made his cross, and when they passed before the cross they immediately fell down because of it. They became more upset; they became more angry. "This man is very strong, he is very powerful. He must be the owner of the earth, the savior who will appear, the master of the earth as it is said! But wait, we must listen. Let's get to know him, and we'll kill him," they said. And so Our Father fled. He went away, that's all. Well, it was on our account that they seized Our Father. It was on our account that they beat him. That is what I have in my memory, that is what I think, and that is what I believe.

Simply because I'm poor, because I'm needy, I don't refuse to help another poor person. I help him, I do him a favor. Also, some patient who may be sick, I do his ritual, and I cure him, too, because I have my little remedies. Some person who has been cheated, who has been enchanted by Our Uncles of old, when he comes to me, I have a remedy. I have a snake's tooth; I apply a snake's tooth; I hold it over the smoke. Well, then, after holding it over the smoke, I give the remedy to him. He gets well; he is already better. At times he heals in five days, at times in six days, at times in ten days, but he is already better. Little by little the sickness leaves his body, it's all right. Well, it's really a favor that I do for him. But also, it isn't entirely a favor, because they always pay me; they always give me a few cents.

Once he is well, I say: "Although you're well, although I've cured you, it won't remain so. You must offer a ritual for yourself, and also one for me, because I don't know if you have an enemy. I don't know if it's your fate. If I just receive payment from you and don't give it to God, what will happen? I'll do the favor, the service, but you must offer a ritual for me."

"I agree, certainly I shall offer it. There is no problem. I'll offer it," the man will say, and he will give me a few cents, a little rum. I don't insist on it; it's his desire, once he is well.

There are some who have boils appear on them, who have boils wished upon them, who have been bewitched, who have some enemy who has cried [to the gods] about them and the Day God has heard and seized them. They come to me and ask about it: "Do me a favor, do me a ritual for it." I do perhaps two, perhaps five rituals for them. Little by little the boils subside; they recover. That's all there is to it.

Then, little by little, news about me spreads among them. "That old man is really good. He possesses real knowledge. We went to him, and we certainly got better immediately. He isn't just telling us lies; we really got better. Also, he says that if one doesn't improve right away, there's no payment. He's the only man who's really good," they say. Gradually others hear about it. That's the way I gain my reputation with them, which is a good one.

It's hardly my favor. I scarcely speak to Our Mother. I rarely see the face of the saints. Rather, it's the Holy Day alone whom I ask for blessing. That's all I do.

I will always help an unfortunate person. There are some who are very poor, who no longer have any money, who have spent their money because of sickness. Such a person may say: "Pap, would you wait a little? I don't have money. Do me a favor. I'll try to get it. I'll pay. I'll give you money, but little by little, so forgive me and do the ritual for me."

"Well, that's all right, I hardly need to see my payment beforehand. I'll do you the favor," [I say].

And after he gets well, he doesn't pay me. But never mind. I can't demand it of them, because it's God whom I serve. So much for that.

So there are times when they do pay me, and there are times when they don't pay me, but [in the latter case] someone else [God] does the favor for me.

Another man might say, "Ah, I'm certainly perfect. No one can match me. My thinking is complete, my knowledge is complete. I possess magic power," he might śay. Who knows? I wouldn't know, because we don't know what he is capable of doing. Why, so he's perfect! What does he accomplish being perfect? What is his work while being perfect? It's not that way. He's hardly like our Father, because he is the only one who is perfect.

Our Father who passes above us in the sky,[18]
The Holy Day, the Holy Dawn,
He is the one who is perfect,
Because it is a perfect accomplishment
That each day rises with precision at dawn.
There's hardly a son, there's hardly a daughter
Who tells him how. Well, then.
If there is a man who is ignorant, without knowledge,
Leave him alone. Let him do as he wishes. Let him say
What he wants to. If he's insulting,
What are his words to insult?
It's Our Father whom he insults,
Our Mother whom he insults.
How good is he, indeed—
"That man doesn't know anything. He's not good at anything,
Not like me, because I'm perfect. I have knowledge,
I have ideas in my mind, I have many things.

No one else matters to me," the man will say [boast].
But what is he like, to be perfect?
If he didn't need to eat,
If he didn't need to drink,
If he didn't need a woman,
If he didn't need a wife . . .
But he *does* eat,
And he *does* drink,
And he has his wife
And he has his children
And he says "I'm perfect"!
Where does he show his perfection?
Only Our Father of the Sky is perfect
Because he comes forth, he appears with precision, when he rises,
And suddenly at noon, clouds appear,
And in the afternoon there is a downpour.
Yes, but nobody has heard of it.
Our Father hardly announces
What he is going to do:
"That's what I'll do in a while,
You'll see, I'm going to send a downpour. I'll bring frost.
I'll bring hail!"
If Our Father would say that! If we would know!
But rather, we are destined to be only humans,
Because we only see
That the face of the sky changes,
That clouds appear,
That a rainstorm comes,
That hail appears.
We just have to accept it.

We just wait and see if it's hail that comes, or perhaps a wind that comes. We just wait; we don't know [in advance]. So only He is complete. It is only He who is perfect in his thinking, because we don't know what is being done. What grounds do we have to say we are perfect? Where do our thoughts come from? Who gives us our thoughts? Perhaps the man's thoughts are perfect, but where did he get them? Where would he have gone to purchase them? It hardly could have been an authority who gave it to him, unless God himself gave it to him.

So all right, when he has knowledge then he is most disobedient. He becomes very proud. He thinks he is superior to God. That shouldn't be. Patience. It isn't good.

It's a sinful statement.
He is superior, because he is satiated.
He is superior, because he eats some meat.

He is superior, because he eats some bread.
He is strong.
He strikes a younger brother.
He can even strike his mother;
He can even strike his father
Because he is disobedient.
But only in that lies his superiority.
He is not like Our Father,
Not like Our Mother,
Not like Our Father of the Sky,
Our Mother of the Sky.
Because they have great patience
Even though we say many things,
Even though we speak many things.
Many things we might say in church,
Those of us who invent sins against our older brothers,
Those of us who invent sins against our younger brothers.
If only Our Mother would say something.
If only Our Father would say something.
But he doesn't say anything to us.
But afterwards, when we die,
We go to pay for our sins,
For what we do on earth;
Not until after we die.

Even though we don't pay while on earth, when we die we receive our punishment from God. God is just.

This is known to me, it is apparent to me. It wasn't just anyone who told me. It wasn't any mortal who told me, it was a departed soul, or a God or an ʔaanhel who gave me my thoughts. I had the dream, you see, so I know the law through God. It isn't lenient; that I understand from the dream. It happened that I dreamt the dream. It isn't good that we do so many things against our brothers. Just because the thought is there, just because our intelligence is perfect, with a magic formula we know everything Our Uncles know. Ah, but after we have become knowledgeable according to Our Uncles[19] we are unfortunate indeed, because it's all right [with them] that you strike your younger brother. It is not good.

"One is only there for one day,[20]
One is only there for two days,"
We will say.
Perhaps it's our luck,
Perhaps its our destiny
When the sentence has been completed,
Whatever tasks have been assigned us.
It is we who shall pay for it:[21]

We shall enter the fire.
We shall enter the water.
We shall come out of the water.
We shall go directly into the fire.
They will punish us:
You will see, they will turn us into soap,
They will turn us into sausage,
Because we have committed evil against our brothers.
But I will tell you now:
On the other hand, those of us who behave well,
We who keep only God in mind, we are known,
Whether our words to God are numerous or not,
And likewise to Our Mother,
Likewise to Our Father,
Likewise to the gods,
Likewise to Our Father of the Sky.
Because before Our Father there isn't much discussion.

What does the ʔalkaalte do on earth? We hardly say many words to him. He'll just listen to two or three of our words; already he has written it down, and thus it remains. God is hardly that way. Even though you haven't said it yet to God, even though you haven't spoken the words that you have in your mind, there they are already with Our Father. They are already with the gods. They are already with Our Mother in the Sky.

Well, even the judge has his law.
How could the gods be without law?
How could Our Father be without law?
That is what I thought about,
That is what I explained,
That is what I understand,
Because of the dream:
It isn't good that we do evil against a brother
Because we shall go to the fire, we shall burn.
We shall go into the water, we shall die in the water,
When our souls arrive [at the place of judgment],
If we send out strong words in order to have
A brother die,
Then we shall go to Our Uncles. There we shall arrive
And they will eat us,
They will swallow us,
They will do many things to us,
Because we are already their daughters,
We are already their sons,
And we will no longer see the face of God.
So here it is, this I will leave said:

It isn't good to wish sickness,
It isn't good to wish imprisonment.
It isn't good to wish a chain on a younger brother, on an older brother.
If we have knowledge, we begin to think
Thus as I do.

I have the Days in my head. I have the ?uq'iib'al in my head, that is what matters, and I can recite it, whoever of our brothers, whoever of our daughters, whoever of the children asks for it. "Pap, please tell me the ?uq'iib'al," a daughter or son will say, and I will answer because thus is the word of Our Father of the Sky. "Forgive us, please, Pap. What are the Days like? Would that you could teach me!" "Very well, I will teach you, because I have dreamed the Day. Only this is its use; only this is its power. Thus begins the day count and thus ends the day count," I will answer one of our brothers. "Thus you must do. Thus one prays to the saints, thus one prays to the ?aanhel, thus one prays to the souls," I will tell a daughter, a son.

That's my knowledge that won't disappear. It isn't good not to give advice to our brothers, just to be content because we have wisdom, because we can think, and when we are ready to die, not to leave our knowledge with some other poor soul, some other child; for when we die we disappear once and for all. We leave no trace; no seed (*qial*) nor sign (*qešlal*) of us remains. But if we leave our teaching with some younger brother, some older brother, our wisdom will remain. "Thus have I done, thus have I spoken, and that is how you should speak," we'll say and we'll pass on our knowledge. Perhaps if we die and he is still alive, then he will remember our soul: "Thanks to you, Pap, holy soul. You are spoken to just like a god; you are remembered like a god; you are attended like a god: thanks to you for leaving my knowledge," he will say. And so our thoughts won't be lost. Whatever our thinking is, it will remain on earth. We'll give it to him, you see. That's good, because he will remember our soul and our words won't disappear. If our teaching is lost, if we say nothing, if we just conceal it, it isn't good, because we shall die. There will be no seed of ours, no mark of ours left; once and for all our face will vanish.

This is what an old man I knew did. He was a cantor by profession. He would retire for only a year before taking on the job again. At times he would serve for two years, because he could play the organ; I saw it when I was a boy. It wasn't like the organs of today; now they move it by foot, now it's the same as a machine. Now it's the ladinos who play the organ. There is no longer a compatriot [Ixil] who knows how to do it, because that man didn't teach us. Pap Pil knew how to play the organ. It is said that he went to school, and he must have studied it and learned it. So every now and then he went to do the Mass at the church. There was a priest, and the man would accompany him with the organ. Now that no longer happens; it has disappeared because he died. When questioned [about it], he didn't answer. He didn't share his knowledge. He didn't leave his soul's remembrance, and now no one remembers him. He didn't leave his knowledge for some other daughter—there must have been some other children who desired it. If only he had left instructions—which were the numbers[22]—the knowledge wouldn't have disappeared. His memory wouldn't have vanished. The reputation of our town wouldn't have been lost. Instead, the organ is no longer played, because the man disappeared once and for all.

It was the organ that was there in the old days. There was also a man who could make it work. They called him ʔOlin C'uʔm,[23] because he made the organ move; if one didn't move it, it wouldn't sound, so they called him ʔOlin C'uʔm. He was the other of the two men. There was also a third man, the fiscal, who accompanied Pap Pil. While Pap Pil played the organ, the fiscal, who was charged with the praying, responded.

This will happen to us, too, if we don't leave a skill for our brothers, if we simply remain content [with possessing it]. Take what I do, for example. I have the Holy Days in my head. I have the prayer in my mind, and if someone should ask for it, I tell him, because it isn't good for me to hide it. If one of the sons or daughters should ask for the ʔaanhel,[24] of course, why shouldn't I tell him? It was God who gave it to me. I know the ʔaanhel prayer; it's right there [in my head]. The same for the meeša, what I do with the ʔooro.[25] I'll teach it; I'll explain how it's done—where the Day answers, where the Day speaks out. These are the teachings I'll leave behind; thus they won't fail to remember me. The seed [of my thought] will remain on earth. If I don't leave my teachings behind, I'll disappear, and once and for all the word will disappear. The knowledge of what I do will disappear.

But it [the meeša] isn't for everything. I don't do it for stealing, but for a sick person. If someone has stolen something, they come to ask. It's all revealed [in the divination], but we mustn't talk about the robber. "Tssah, what have I done to that old man? Why does he complain about me?" the man [thief] will say. Perhaps he will await me along the road to attack me, because he's ruthless, he has "thief" for a label, he's a bandit. So it isn't good, and I won't discuss it. On the other hand, if it's a sick person, either God did it or some person placed a ritual and it was ordered by God, but that means it's all right; only that do I reveal.

This way your ritual is offered.
This way you must carry it out.
At that mountain you must do your ritual.
You must go to the ʔAlkaalte cross.
You must go before Kučuč.
You must go before Kub'aal in the komoon.
You must go before that mountain.
You must go to Kaarsa Wic.
You must go before Č'iʔlaaʔ.
That is what you must do in order to get well.
"All right, it is good, thanks to you."

This is all I say.
So I have my thoughts.
I will tell my thoughts,
I will leave my wisdom.
I will not fail to be spoken of. My seed will remain.
Perhaps my seed will endure, perhaps not;
Only God knows that.
It's only just a little that I am sharing with you.
It's only just a little that I am teaching you.
Only thus, whoever of you will review the tape recording
Whoever of you will listen to the tape
Shall see whether these words of mine you hear are clear
Or whether the words you hear won't be of use;
It's good that we kneel when the sun comes up,
That we kneel when it is noon,
That we kneel when the sun sets,
That we say a few prayers.
That's it.
If we say a few prayers.
That's it.
If we awake at midnight,
We shall think of God.
When we awake at dawn, we shall ask for blessing
Before Our Father, because Our Father is the one who
Gives us our sustenance.
Because it's for us; it's our fault.
And so Our Father goes forth.
But if Our Father were no longer to rise,
We would no longer eat.
We would have to perish,
We would have to die.
So that is the reason,
Only for us Our Father rises.
Only for us Our Father travels.
Our Father is poor.
What we give Our Father is hardly
Everything that we eat on earth:
We eat bread, we eat some meat
We eat all kinds of food.
We will take a drink, forgive us,
Our poor Father.
And what do we give him?
What do we give to Our Father?
What do we offer to Our Father?
What does Our Father say?
On the other hand, we immediately will say
If we discover a brother who is eating,

"Oh, I had to look on and they wouldn't give me any,"
Because we are humans.
On the other hand, Our Father,
Because he cares for us, tolerates us.
It is our fault, so
We must remember God at noontime.
We must remember Our Father when he comes up.
We must remember God at dusk.
We must remember the soul of Our Father at midnight.
We must remember the soul of Our Father at dawn.
We are children of Our Mother and Our Father.
We will die.
Perhaps we'll enjoy the days a little, the light,
And perhaps we'll grow a little old
If our soul is correct.
That is what I will leave said for you.
Only that is what my heart says,
I wish only that some of it be heard,
What it is that I do.
It's not a big thing at all.
It's not a scolding
Nor is it a complaint that I make;
It concerns only what I have experienced.

Simply that I'm poor is no reason for not giving aid to my brothers. There might be some other poor person who eats only with great effort and difficulty. Even though I'm poor, I will take it from my mouth and give it to my younger brother, to my older brother. I will give it to the unfortunate one. I will give it to Our Mother's unfortunate one, to Our Father's unfortunate one, because surely God was his maker. It's a blessing that he is poor. We can't mistreat him, and if he's poor, we shouldn't tell him, "You're poor." That isn't good. It's a great sin, because we don't know how it came about—whether God is the cause of his fortune or whether it is his fault. Perhaps it was his mother or his father whose counsel he didn't heed, whose teaching he didn't obey; perhaps that's why he is poor. Perhaps that's why he eats only with the greatest of effort and difficulty. Or it might be that he stole, and the man [the victim] called poverty down upon him, complained to the gods. That's what we can't know. And if we say such words, if we scold him, if we mistreat him, it's a great sin. It's not the way God speaks. It's not the way Our Father of the Sky speaks.

God, ʔAanhel, forgive me, Our Heavenly Parents,
The strong words;
The day is borrowed.
The light is borrowed.

The earth is borrowed.
The world is borrowed.
We are destined to die.
We are destined to disappear.
Never can we avoid death.
Never can we avoid extinction.
Forgive us,
We're only borrowing the world.
We're only borrowing the earth.
That's what our candle signifies.
That's why we offer our pom.

We're content as long as we can eat. We're content because we eat and our stomachs are full. Our happiness lies only in eating; our happiness lies simply in drinking. We talk a lot, we scold; we scold a younger brother, an older brother, a daughter, a son: "You're worthless to me," we may say carelessly. He may not mean anything to us, because our stomachs are full. Food gives us strength, you see; a person doesn't matter to us. On the other hand, if we must experience hunger, if we must experience poverty, perhaps a younger brother, an older brother, might mean more to us.

Suppose a man grows up rich. His father is rich. He has shoes, he has clothes, he is well dressed thanks to his father. Good, it will end well. Some land will be left to him by his father. Some property will be left by his father. A cow, a horse will be left to him; a house will be left to him. Well, it will end well if his father was a good man—if he thought a little about God, if he helped a poor person, gave him some clothing or an *almud* of maize. But if all he wants is to achieve more, he may scold the poor person, if he can't work, he may scold him or beat him. The poor man needs money, and we must give him money when he asks for work. What he wants is to eat, to drink. If we don't help him, it's a great sin. He will cry [to the gods]; he will become sad. We are the ones; perhaps we ourselves will experience it. Or next it might be a daughter or a son of ours who will suffer for it. It's a great sin.

Then perhaps there is another man who is simple-minded and boasts a lot. He has a lot of land, a lot of money, but since he doesn't honor poor people, it will happen to his daughter or his son.

There's another thing: he may be miserly with his wealth. He may just hoard his money. Perhaps he won't even smoke a cigarette, won't even take a drink, won't even think a little about God. He is satisfied just because he has money. He is content just because he has animals. There are no problems; he has land, he has his own place. He is all right. But if he doesn't give to a poor man, the poor man will become sad. He will cry, "What about me? Am I not poor? I have no land, I have no money. I am so poor, the man is well-off. He has land, he has money, Lord, but he scolds me, he abuses me," the man will say of the rich man. Then he will fold his hands.[26]

The rich man doesn't smoke
And he doesn't drink rum,
But his daughter, his son,
One of his grandchildren, one of his heirs, his offspring, perhaps
His daughter will be the one who will suffer poverty,
Unfortunate one!
Because though they inherit the land
Perhaps his daughter will come to know it.
His son will start drinking
Or eat some bread, some meat.
There are some rich people who won't eat meat,
And there are some rich people who won't eat bread.
There are some rich people who don't take anything,
Who won't drink any rum.
But now there will be his daughter, now there will be his son,
Perhaps there will be a ladino
And the man's daughter will sell the land to him,
The man's son will sell the land to him.
His son will be the one who will want to drink rum.
His son will be the one who will want to eat cake.
His daughter will be the one who will want to drink a little rum.
His daughter will be the one who will want to drink,
Who will eat meat, who will eat cake
With his land
And he is the one who just wasted his efforts
By not eating.
Nor would he buy any clothes.
But it is because his soul dictates it,
And it isn't good.
He could be a good person
If he showed respect toward a poor person,
If he helped a poor person,
Because he has the money.
He has the maize,
He has food,
He has drink,
He has animals,
So he will help a poor person.
He will give him a share.
He will help the poor man.
He will give him an almud of maize.
He will give him a little *mulco*.[27]
He will give him some beans.
Ah, then the poor man may say:
"What is it, Christ, listen:
If it were not for what that man gave, what would I have eaten?

Thanks be to him,
He helped me, he gave me food, he gave me drink.
May grace fall on the daughter, may grace fall on the son.
I would recompense him in some way,
But what could I do?
What do I have?
I am poor.
But there is always Our Father,
There is always Our Mother,
There is always the Sky
Who will return the favor, the charity.
May they recompense him. Help, O Lord.
May he receive blessings for his fate,"
The poor man will say, on folding his hands.
He will kneel on the ground.
He will kiss the earth.
He will fold his hands toward the sky. So it is.
Now the man has departed; he has gone far away.
Here is his daughter, there is his son.
They will see a good life,
Even though he died.
Just as he ate, as he drank,
So also will his daughter eat, so also will his son eat,
Even better: his son will buy another small parcel of land.
Even better: his son will gain a little more money.
Even better: he will buy another animal.
Even better: he will buy another horse.
Because it is through the beneficence of his father
Who earned the blessing of a poor man.
But if he didn't show kindness toward a poor man
It is certain that his son will be the one to use up his land.
Perhaps it will be a ladino who will encroach upon his land.
Perhaps it will be another man, even though he be poor,
Perhaps he will be the one to buy the land
Because he has passed through his misfortunes.

That's what I will tell you.
That's the little bit I have to say.
Those of you who will examine the content of this tape:
That's what you ought to know.
That's what you ought to think about.
Not just because you will earn money,
Not just because you are good
At reading the pages—
You can understand the pages,
You know how to read—

Not just because our younger brother, a daughter or a son
Doesn't know how to read,
Are we allowed to say: "He isn't worth anything.
He isn't like us, because I know how to read.
I know about everything, I can go where I wish."
No, it's a great sin.
It isn't true that simply because
He doesn't know how to read,
He doesn't have knowledge,
He doesn't have wisdom.
God is the one who knows about him.
He may not have the eyes for it.
He may not be able to read the pages,
But all right, he has his thoughts in his mind.
He has his knowledge in his memory,
Whatever it be that he does, whatever work he may do.
All right, here he is, it's his luck, it's his fortune.
There may be another of you who will look at the pages,
Who will understand the pages,
But won't believe what they say.
The words of God are on the pages.
The words of Our Father are on the paper!
That's what you should think about.
That's what you should heed—
What God says,
What Our Father in the Sky says on the paper,
That's what you should follow.
That's what you should know.
It's very valuable.

But there might be another of you
Who seeks to learn a spell that is on some paper,
A spell to strike your younger brother with,
To strike some older brother with,
To strike your son with, a magic prayer.
It's evil. You see,
Once you have knowledge,
"Ah, I have knowledge. I know how to read.
I'm not like him, for he isn't worth anything.
Wait, we'll arrange it;
We'll make out a document for his land,"[28] you will say.
You rejoice.
You have hands, you have eyes [you can write, you can read].
You have younger brothers, older brothers.
You won't give anything; you'll take it away.
Soon you will make out a document for him.

You will take his land away.
You will have won!
But you won't have gained anything before God.
That's the law.

Here I am. What did the children do?
Here I am!
I came here, I came to another place, another state.
Too bad: because I also don't know how to read, I'm not worth anything.
Would that I could read, would that I had talents . . .
But all I know is God's prayer.
All I know are the prayers.
All I know is the law.
What the law of God is,
That's what I tell our brothers.
Is it that the daughters listened well?
Is it that the sons heard what was good?
I arrived; I was brought here.
There are many prayersayers.
There are those who have many prayers,
There are those who kill their fellows,
There are *ʔaakun* [witches].
There are those who know many prayers.
They may have the doctrine completely in their minds, all of it.
They know all the doctrine,
But where are they? They haven't gotten here.
Why? Because it's not their destiny,
But it is surely my destiny; it is surely my fortune
That I came here. I certainly didn't ask for it:
"Man, please take me with you,
Because I know those words. I am proficient in the knowledge.
I have that information in my mind. I'll say it among you."
I hardly said that to the daughter, to the son.
Who knows why it happened? It's fate, it's fortune.
But thanks be to God,
Thanks be to Our Father of the Sky.
It must be the gods who give me their blessing.
Here I eat, here I drink.
They give me food.
He gives me my meals, Paa Micolaš,
She gives me my meals, Çu Lol.[29]
They care for me here.
Also they gave me a few clothes.
Thanks to Our Father, thanks to God.
Perhaps it's God who gives me his blessings,
Because I was poor when I grew up,

But now I live well.
Thanks to God.
It must be God who blesses me,
So thanks be to God then. It is no one else.
But I'm not taking advantage of anyone.
There isn't anything that I'm stealing.
Rather, it's only for my thinking;
They must consider it worthwhile, and I came here.
Who knows if my words will turn out well or not?
Thanks to the daughter, thanks to the son.
I don't say, "I'm repaying the children,"   °
There is no way.
I'm hardly God.
I'm hardly the Father.
I can hardly obtain something, I can hardly give anything
To the daughter, to the son.
Rather God, Our Father, is the one who will bless them.
Thus it is, that's what I'm trying to say.
That's what I do; you will think a little about it.
Because here are the children doing a kindness,
Here are the children; they give me food,
They give me drink.
I came with them; here they care for me.
They gave me my *čoʔunši?*, I have my *čoʔunši?*, I have a bed.
You see, it is good
Indeed, the children will reach a summit, again
Because, thanks to the daughter,
They are doing a favor, a charity.
The land has been doing me a favor.
So the children will indeed reach a summit.
The children will benefit from their kindness.
They will benefit from their gift,
Daughters and sons of Jesus, daughters and sons of Christ.
He is barely a foreigner,
No matter if he be from [another] state,
No matter if his mother is different,
No matter if his father is different,
Even though it is another country where he is,
Even though the place is different,
Even though it is a different place where
He is on the earth,
Nevertheless it is the same dominion of God,
It is the same land of God
Where he lives.
It is the same Father who created him.
It is the Savior of the world who created him,

It is Jesus Nazareno who created him.
It is Maria Guadalupe who created him,
Our Mother, Our Father, Queen Concepción were those who created
    him.
We have the same Mother, the same Father.
We mustn't mistreat him, and he isn't going to mistreat us.
Thanks be to God, because we mistreat him and what is his offense?
Rather, it's only our language that differs.

It is said that Our Father said that if we had a single language, then we
could kill each other, because if someone quarrels with us, if someone berates us and hurts us, we will revile him—we will only kill each other on
earth. But it isn't like that. What about *kastiiya*?[30] The kastiiya of the ladinos isn't so difficult, yet not all of us understand it. The kastiiya I know
isn't so much. I don't know how to read. I don't know how to write. Be
that as it may, it's only the doctrine of God that I have in my mind. Only
that is what I can do. I don't know much kastiiya, but what more could I
do if I learned it? It's not that. I don't know much, and I came here, but it's
by the grace of God. God did the favor that I could come here. And just
the same are the children, because it's the same language, the same
thinking, the same way, if we mistreat him, it's God whom we will be
mistreating. If he mistreats us, it's Our Father whom he mistreats. No, they
don't believe in mistreating [us]. It's only a little that the man lags behind
God. It's little that his thought lags behind [that of] Our Father, because
in the end that's where the thought was. That's where the law was. That's
where the order for him was.

It is said that they loved Our Father.[31] It is said that for them Our Father
was most important. It is said that possibly Our Father came here among
them, it is said that what they wanted most was that Our Father would
show them the way to him—where it is that he goes and where he appears. They wanted to go and see [him], it is said: "Show us the bridge.
Place the bridge for us over the water and we will cross over it to see you,
Lord. We will come to leave you your meal, we will give you whatever you
want," they said. Thus was their thinking. It was very good what they said,
but Our Father didn't show them the path. Instead, he left them his
knowledge. "No, there is wisdom; there are thoughts. There is another
way of thinking, which is this way. That's what you must learn, that's what
you must know. That will be your task to carry out," Our Father said to
them. Well, they did it. They learned it all. That's why they have money,
because they loved Our Father so much. It is said that they placed Our Father in the chair. It is said that they gave Our Father his meals, not like us.
It is said that once Our Father appeared as a *muʔs* and another time as a
ʔulaʔ.[32] Another time, Our Father changed into a sick person, it is said, one
who was very sick, who couldn't walk anymore. Another thing he does, it
is said, is that he breaks out with boils, when he passes by a person: "Ah,
what kind of man might that be? What an ugly man! He stinks!" we say.

And Holy Ave Maria, it's Our Father! That's why it is said, we're poor, because we have no grace bestowed on us. For them it's different, because he went among them and they gave him food, they gave him drink, they gave him sustenance, they found a bed for him, a good bed. That's why they have a good bed, why they have good clothes to wear—because Our Father left them his blessing.

That's what I tell you.
That's what you must know.
That's what you haven't seen.
That's what you haven't known.
Whoever among you sees the paper,
Whether you are adults,
Or whether you are young people,
You shall know it:
Thus is the justice of God,
Thus is the justice of Our Father.
Thus is the law that Our Father made there with the gods.
On the earth of long ago
Our Father walked.
Thirty years Our Father had to fight
With Our Uncles
But it was our fault.
It was for us.
Because it was only for the formation of the earth.
It was only for the creation of the world.
It was only for our creation.
It was only for our appearance on earth.
That's why Our Father exists.
That's why we're here on earth.

But what if they had defeated Our Father, if Our Father had died, if they had killed Our Father? Well, yes, Our Father died, but only for three days. Our Father died at eight in the morning, on Maundy Thursday, and on Good Friday Our Father went in the funeral procession,[33] and on Glorious Saturday Our Father revived, he was well. That's why we die.[34] But in the end Our Father was well because he revived, he was alive [again], but we, on the other hand, we shall die. We shall never return. We go for always, once and for all our faces disappear. We shall never return. Thus am I: whatever I look like now, on dying my visage will disappear once and for all. Whether my appearance is good or bad, once and for all I shall disappear. It's different with Our Father, because Our Father will never disappear. There he is. He is the one who watches over us. If he had disappeared, then we wouldn't exist. We would have disappeared once and for all. Thanks be to Our Father, because here we are, alive, and we shall honor him.

We shall remember his soul.
We shall honor the soul of the Savior.
We shall honor the soul of the Eternal Father.
We shall honor the soul of Jesus of Nazareth.
We shall honor the soul of Our Father Kayiita.[35]
We shall honor the soul of Father Jesus Christ,
Of the Father Celestial,
Of the Queen of the Sky,
Of the Queen of Glory,
Of Maria Santisima,
Maria of Jesus,
Maria Santisima,
Maria of the Glory,
Maria of the Child Jesus,
Of the Child of Bethlehem,
Child of Atocha,
Child Kapetal,[36]
Of the Child of Grief,
The Child of Succor,
Of the Glory of the Sky,
Where Our Mother,
Our Father resides.
They are the ones whose souls we must honor,
Whom we must ask permission of: we ask for food,
We ask for drink,
For a daughter,
For a son:
"Thanks to Our Father,
We're alive."'
That's all we can do.
But not with some evil deed:
If we only mistreat others,
If we only berate others,
If we do evil,
If we kill some younger brother,
If we kill some older brother,
It's a great sin.
Because if you shoot him,
Then you will be shot also.
If you cut him with a machete,
You will be cut down with a machete also.
It's the commandment of God.
It's the same commandment that will protect you,
But you must follow it honestly.
That's all,
So much for that,

Be that as it may,
That is all I will say to you
You must excuse me,
I must be giving you a headache
I must be giving you an earache with these words.

Only that I will leave said to you,
Our Mother,
Our Father,
Their daughters,
Their sons,
The saints,
Our mothers,
Our fathers,
The children,
Thanks to the daughter,
To the son,
I came to rest a little.
I came to rest.
It wasn't any work that I came to do with them,
I just came to rest.
Two months did I come to rest,
So thanks, then, to them. Listen,
He gives me food.
He gives me drink.
Thus have I spoken a little.
You will know it.

COMMENTARY

The beauty of Shas's philosophy makes us reluctant to analyze it, yet analyze we must if we are to seek further ethnographic understanding. First, though, we shall briefly recapitulate some of Shas's ideas. Several things stand out quite strongly. Patience, humility, and generosity are the virtues to strive for. There is a love for all living things. We must be careful about them, but we cannot always avoid harming them. If we clear land to plant maize we have to cut living trees and plants; we may disturb a bird's nest or some small animal. But the need to "fill our stomachs" compels us to go on. This capacity to harm other living things is a tragedy of our existence, which is rectified only in part by rituals asking forgiveness which are performed before undertaking any life-destroying action such as clearing a field or cutting timber.

This empathy extends to our fellow humans. We must be non-judgmental of others, for we never know fully what predicament or history another person has to contend with. And though the gods themselves are punitive of wrongdoing, humans should never be so. The empathy predominates. Rather than saying that one should not steal because thievery is punishable, Shas says that one should not steal because the victim may need the stolen item much more than the person who would steal it—and who knows what sorrows and problems the victim may have as a result? Being nonjudgmental of others extends to everything from laziness to drunkenness. Shas counsels against drinking too much but does not condemn the drunkard. At Shas's dawn ceremony that we filmed, where the prayersayer in charge of the ritual was too drunk to officiate, he was never refused whenever he asked Shas for another drink. Then when the time came for the ritual and the prayersayer was obviously too drunk to perform, there was no word of rebuke.

Empathy extends to all people, especially the poor and the physically handicapped. Here the protection of the deities comes in. After the fashion of Greek gods, Kub'aal may take on the disguise of a poor human—so one never knows. The day gods are also protectors. Apparently one of the day gods is mute (Shas did not know which one; furthermore, it would be a transgression to identify which one if he did know), and a mute person is under that deity's protection. This is also the case for other handicaps.

Shas describes a kind of ritual therapy that has psychoanalytic overtones, as in the scrutiny of the client's past history to understand some undesirable behavior. For instance, a wife who is concerned about getting angry too easily must examine her past history to find why her "soul is not attached" to her husband.

Some of the other salient themes of Shas's philosophy text are the following: (1) man's physical, social, and material disabilities or advantages are determined by his fate; (2) if you should make someone (living, dead, or supernatural) angry, he may persuade the gods to punish you or your children; (3) if you should seek to punish another through witchcraft, you shorten your own life and perhaps the sorcerer's as well; (4) you can avoid some punishment by remembering the gods. However, these themes as described briefly here hardly do justice to such a rich text with so many other observations and opinions—about why it is good to have poverty in the world, why it is desirable to have many different languages, why death is necessary, how education and literacy are no measure of native intelligence, to mention a few.

Major components of Shas's philosophy must have been passed down from generation to generation, with modifications, emphases, and innovations that were adjusted to suit individuals needs and differing situations. Of course, without looking at comparable texts by others it is not possible to separate the idiosyncratic elements from those that are shared. But since we see so much in common between Shas's gentle behavior and his advice, we feel that his own stamp on this philosophy text is strong. The text reflects his own selection, emphasis, and change of a rich set of cultural patterns. Presumably the survival of cultural patterns over generations is some indication of their utility; in fact, they may represent a condensation of typical life problems to those conceptualizations that have the widest applicability and economy. In this respect the philosophy is a gold mine of information. If one were to collect similar texts from other Ixil over many years, it would be revealing to keep track of which statements survive, which fall by the wayside, and which seem to be new or transformed as the pace of sociocultural change quickens. The selective process winnows out those statements that are inappropriate or ineffective. This is not to say that what survives is necessarily the best; cultural systems, like biological systems, are full of imperfections, contraditions, and anachronisms.

The patterns that appear in Shas's philosophy text have been molded and created over many years during his time as a daykeeper. It is part of Shas's role to give this advice—not as he did to us in an extended tape recording, but in shorter segments, appropriate to the occasion, to the many people of different age, sex, and circumstance who came to him for help.

The beliefs, expectations, and values that lie behind Shas's philosophy text feed into a highly complex role performance system. Shas must not only give advice, he must undertake the religious psychotherapy of his patients. He must assess their situations, their behavior, their concerns. He must also himself lead an exemplary life, or at least try to. Doing all of this requires self-analysis as well as an empathic viewpoint for understanding others: it requires an updating, a revising, and a repairing of one's self-image; it requires a conceptualization of others which is added to and revised—a conceptualization that includes attributes and relations which one's client's and their families and friends maintain with each other; it requires an understanding of the goals and values that motivate people and of the way in which the context of situation can modify those goals and intentions.

Such a complex set of considerations is best handled ethnographically in a systematic fashion, and one way to be systematic with such data is to use frames. In considering how ethnographic data should be organized into frames, we might start with five high-level categories: viewpoint, process, process relations, context of situation, and goal.

1. *Viewpoint.* Given the social context of role, we must include the image· that the role performer has of the role-relevant social context. A daykeeper keeps clients in mind while praying. Clients have certain views and expectancies concerning the daykeeper. There must also be some monitoring of the self in this context in a kind of feedback system; the self must have a view of what others must be thinking during some interaction with them. This need not always require the presence of people. A notable characteristic of Ixil society is that some of the significant others, in fact perhaps the most important ones, are ancestral ghosts, particularly recently deceased relatives known to the individual.

2. *Process.* A key part of role, of course, is the process or action involved. These actions have what linguists call *aspect.* For example, among the attributes that are commonly associated with role behavior are those of purposiveness and constancy (recurrence, repetitiveness) of behavior. Since actions normally carried out in the performance of a role are part of a sequence, several different actions might be phases of what is conceptualized as a single role process, as, for example, a client at a divination. In such a conceptualization, one role process might serve as a cue for another. A sequence of actions thus can be part of this category. The appearance of any one role component in a text might lead to presuppositions on the part of the observer as to what has already happened or what will happen in the future.

3. *Process relations.* Part and parcel of the actions that are typically carried out in performing a role are the relations among those actions. We follow linguistic convention here and speak of *case* relations. The role of thief, for example, includes the process of steal-

ing, which requires that the agent (the thief) take an object from a victim. These three cases—agent, object, and patient—are crucial for role description.

4. *Context of situation.* It is the context of situation (together with goal or motivation) that evokes role action. Role is a social concept. Many of the activities we engage in are procedures that require no reference at all to other people. The procedures involved in eating, for instance, are a set of activities necessary for the ingestion of food that are independent of social context. Eating can be done alone or together with other people. It is not until one places the procedure of eating in a higher-level context—say, the role of a disciple during a reenactment of the last Supper in Nebaj, or the role of a customer in a restaurant—that the procedure of eating becomes incorporated into a role. Most roles have contingent properties that concern the appropriate or facilitating settings for role performance.

5. *Goal.* Any human action, of course, has to be motivated. Rules have purposes or goals that must be included in the theoretical machinery we want to set up. At times this motivational component can be most diffuse or general. Thus it is difficult to think of some of the more perduring roles, such as president or mother, in terms of a single, clearly stated goal. Instead, there is a whole series of goals, some of them in hierarchical systems, others in heterarchical or mixed networks. There are also motivating attitudes and feelings which are tied to the success and failures of prior goal-attaining efforts. In any case, goal—or more broadly, motivation—is obviously an essential part of role behavior.

Role frames are just one of many kinds of ethnographic frames. They are more useful in the initial stages of an analysis, before the investigator has acquired a stable series of results or before he has worked out a means of testing his model. Since there may be uncertainty as to which kinds of slots and frames should be used, it is useful to have a global set of categories as a working base. The following list includes and expands the five categories in a different partitioning and is helpful as a kind of etic grid for initiating studies of role behavior:

1. Setting (context)
   Space
   Time
   General ambience

Behavior setting
Expected actions, roles appropriate to the setting
2. Participants, entities
   Animate
      Motivations, attitudes, attributes (including potentialities)
      Current state
   Inanimate
      Attributes, location
3. Processes (events, actions)
   Case relations
   Event hierarchy and sequence relations
   Multiple (reciprocal, nonreciprocal, simultaneous, nonsimultaneous, embedded, etc.)
   Goal linkages
4. Goals, motivations, problems, and states
   Unfulfilled goals
   Lacking attributes
   Mismatch of existing situation with desired situation
5. Viewpoints and perspective
   Self-image
   Other image
6. Focus and Salience
   Identification
   Position
   Choice
   Reason
   Process
   Contingency
   Attribution

To show how this set of categories can be translated into frames, we can take item 4, "Goals, motivations, problems, and states," and choose a state or condition that is mentioned with some frequency in Pap Shas's philosophy—namely, envy. There are several process relations and participants to consider. To begin with, there needs to be a *subject*, a person who is in a state of envy or who envies someone. There must also be a *target*, a person or group of persons that causes the subject to be envious. Subject and target, therefore, are two principal categories to put into an envy frame. Further, there has to be a *reason* for the envy; this usually has to do with a mismatch between what the subject would like for himself, what he has, and what someone else has. These relations can be diagrammed in a frame, as shown in figure 4.1.

There is no need to elaborate further the building of frames without a specific ethnographic or theoretical purpose. Again, we emphasize the importance of a motivated description. Because we are working with a formalization of textual information that can cover an overwhelming number of possible entities, attributes, relations, and situations, we must conserve our formalization for what seems to be the most relevant and useful kind of analysis. We cannot expect to cover everything, just as linguists no longer expect to write definitive grammars of a language that cover all there is to know about the language. The wisdom of our decisions, however, very much depends on our having had access to a rich contextual background, which is why we emphasize the collection of native texts in large numbers.

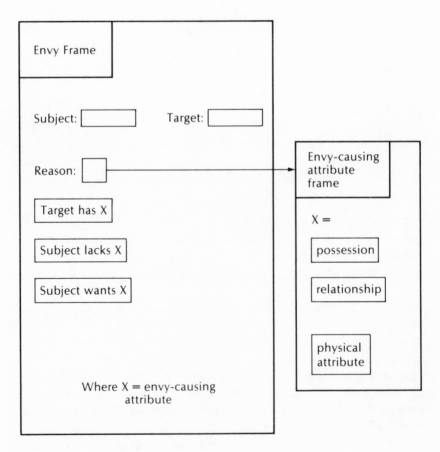

Figure 4.1.   Envy frames.

In the chapter on divination we will have a purpose for an envy frame, a more expanded one than the frame shown in figure 4.1. We may also wish to arrange conventional data in such a way as to facilitate question answering with regard to decision making in divination. Seven basic aspects of focus and salience can be activated by questions: (1) identification, (2) position, (3) choice, (4) reason, (5) process, (6) contingency, and (7) attribution.

Patterns for the *identification* slots for nonhuman participants, objects, concepts, or processes are invoked by "what" questions, for persons by "who" and "whom" questions, and for both persons and nonpersons by auxiliary verb questions. These questions are all easily identified linguistically in English because the key words come first. Patterns for *position* frames are determined for space, direction, and situations by "where" questions, for time and sequence by "when" questions, and for both by auxiliary verb questions. Patterns for the *choice* slot are determined by auxiliary verb questions, for the *reason* slot by "why" questions, for the *process* slot by "what" questions, for the *contingency* slot by "would" questions, and for *attribution* by "what" and "how" questions. If, in the case of the envy frame, we wanted to ask, "Who was envious?" or "Why was the man envious?" we would pick the answer out of the appropriate slot.

A challenging ethnographic task for the future might be to take Shas Koʔ w's philosophy text and organize it into a frame network. As will be suggested in Chapter 6, such a frame network would be useful not only as input for a model of Ixil divination but for numerous other models as well. Though the number of possible ethnographic frames that could be made up is infinite, it is not inconceivable that by sticking to salient patterns and by taking advantage of the fact that a single frame (such as ARRANGE LOGISTICS in Chapter 3) might serve for many other frames (such as those modeling dawn ceremonies, curing rituals, and other types of work parties), one might be able to cover much of the text with a manageable number of frames. In other words, we envision a new type of ethnographic procedure in which much of a cultural system can be represented by frames. While most of the data would be in etic form, a cultural pattern, by definition, is emic. Since most routinized or stereotyped behavior is highly patterned, a frame approach will also capture some emic formulations. However, knowing which items are emic—formulating the cultural grammars and schema systems that produce them—requires more work.

Using frames might, in the future, have two advantages. First, instead of reading a book with traditional ethnographic information in it, an investigator could use a data retrieval system that would retrieve only those frames that were of special interest to him. That process would by no means replace written materials such as those in this book or even traditional ethnographic descriptions by anthropologists. The frame approach would require traditional materials as a primary data base (or else it would require an informant to be on hand for answering questions at a computer terminal). Such a data base, representing thoughts formed directly by natives who use the cultural system being studied, is irreplaceable. To this day, the best ethnographic data base ever collected was done in the sixteenth century by Fray Bernardino de Sahagún, who interviewed priests and rulers and recorded many volumes of extended discourse from them in their own language (Anderson and Dibble, 1950–63). We still have something to learn from Fray Bernardino; but with data as good as those he collected, a frame network computer retrieval system can speed the analysis.

The second implication for the future involves the testing of non-quantitative formal theory. The arranging of ethnographic data in a frame network demonstrates how different elements exist at different levels of generality and act as components to more than a single sequence of processes. Since a major problem in anthropological theory involves the level of contrast specification, not to mention the generation of testable hypotheses, the casting of ethnographic information into ethnographic frames should make it easier to formulate theories grounded in the data so organized.

Frames represent something like a scratch pad. Unless they are used in a computer retrieval system, they need not be used in the final description if emic units have been found and confirmed. Once cultural patterns have been confirmed as such, they can be described as the cognitive structure or cognitive system rather than as some unanalyzed ad hoc approximation. Once we can talk about eidons, thematic sequences, and other knowledge structures that have been shown (through analysis) to be emic, the frames that were used in their discovery can be discarded like scaffolding on a building.

In our analysis of Shas's divination we shall have to retain some of the frame scaffolding, for we unfortuantely can no longer interview Shas on the special topics that our analysis now would indicate are important. In the analysis of the folktales, however, we have enough of the right kind of data for a preliminary narrative grammar with a tentative listing of tale eidons. This analysis is all on the basis of distributional study alone and can be done without the use of frames.

The great advantage of working with extended discourse, whether it be something like Shas Ko?w's philosophy text or his myths and folktales in the next chapter, is that we can have our cake and eat it too—that is, we can attempt to find what structural formulas or mental organizations were used in the production of such texts, and we can also enjoy the discourse for what it says, as a work of art or an interesting communication.

5
FOLK
NARRATIVES

Myths, folktales, and other traditional stories reveal much about the values, goals, and life-styles of the people who tell them. One need only think of the Bible, the Koran, the Upanishads, and other great religious works to appreciate how much stories can reveal about a people. Stories can also tell us something about how culture has been changing. Further, the quality and availability of narratives in a social group say something about the "richness" of the cultural systems being used in the group.[1] There is something more they may be able to tell us, however, and that is what we shall explore in this chapter.

The narratives Pap Shas told us substantially improve our understanding of his world view. Further, they reveal the underlying links between myth, on the one hand, and ritual and other matters, on the other. But our analysis has yet a wider purpose: we seek to discover the behavioral logic that underlies Ixil stories as well as other Ixil cultural systems. Though some aspects of this logic are presumably specific to the Ixil, other aspects are universal or nearly so. We therefore expect to get results that can tell us something about general narrative and, more widely, cultural processes.

We already have a good idea of how to begin. In an earlier study by Benjamin Colby, a grammar was written that accounted for the plot sequences in two samples of Eskimo folktales (Colby, 1973). Now we want to show how one goes about writing such a grammar and to give the historical background for this kind of analysis. We will begin by looking at one of the first stories Shas told us, "The ?Aanhel."[2]

The ?Aanhel

There was the *?aanhel*. But he wasn't a god, only a guardian for us on earth. Formerly he was a mortal, in the beginning of an earlier people that was destroyed before we were created. With the end of those people the flood subsided.

It wasn't without reason that they died there. It was because they always went to eavesdrop on Kub'aal. It was just as if we were to follow Kub'aal around wherever he went. They wanted to listen in on the words Kub'aal spoke—what he said about them, which of them he was going to destroy, whom he was going to support. That's what he talked about. When they eavesdropped by the window, they began to offend Kub'aal so the flood came to finish them, to end their lives. But he couldn't succeed; Kub'aal couldn't succeed in destroying the people by the flood when it came.

There were people who made boxes, and there were people who made tall houses. From the houses the people could almost reach heaven.[3]

Now one, a rich man, the lord of the houses, almost reached heaven from the top of the house.

Well, it was seven days and seven nights that the water covered the earth in order to destroy man, in order to make man die once and for all, as Kub'aal had commanded.

And the water came, but it didn't destroy man, because there were some who nailed themselves into boxes. So they just stayed in the boxes; they kept food with them. They just floated on top of the water, just bobbing along as people do when swimming. They were floating on top of the water and bobbing up and down in their boxes.

After the flood subsided, after the land was dry, they were left on the ground in their boxes. Some landed on the ground, some in ravines, some in the branches of trees; they were left stuck in their boxes.

After the water subsided, the rich man climbed down and began to free the people whom he had locked in the house.

Then the daughters and sons in the house went to hunt for the people inside the caves, amidst the trees, the ones who needed to be freed from the boxes. The people were all right; they hadn't perished. They were alive in their boxes. The water didn't conquer them.

Well, they overheard Kub'aal's words again: "Better take precautions, because sickness is coming." When the sickness arrived they made a sling and they shot and shot and shot. So the disease just fled; indeed, no sickness could come among them. That's not how we live, because we die of sickness. But those people never died. They were real people but they were also like God, because sickness would never harm them. And so they continued in their customs without end.

Well, then there was a liquid at the edge of heaven, which is lava. It is said that this liquid came down, but as fire. It came down like a rainstorm, but it was fire. The word of Kub'aal got to the people: "It's better if the liquid comes down to destroy the people." And the liquid at the edge of heaven poured out. It came to destroy them; like a thunderstorm it came down, with great pounding. After they overheard the word [they said to each other]: "Imagine, the liquid will come down here, it is said, but as fire, it is said. It will come down on top of us. We will surely die; we will surely burn. Two varas deep it will enter; two varas deep the fire will penetrate the earth."

"Two varas will destroy them," Kub'aal had said. Those were the words, they say for certain, that Kub'aal spoke up there to the other gods.

"Therefore, two varas deep, comrades, we will go," [they said]. "It will be one vara deep, comrades, that the fire will penetrate the ground. Don't worry, it is better that we go down two varas deep," they said. Then they made caves. They dug up the ground. They made containers and got into them and went into the earth. They dug caves and went inside. They went in two varas deep.

But three varas deep went the fire into the earth to burn them, to destroy them, once and for all. Three varas deep, they say, went the fire into the earth, just like the flames of a bonfire; it spread out all over. Wherever it hunted it destroyed man. Thus it destroyed man. They disappeared, they died; all the people perished. Thus might it happen to us if a trial comes to us such as an earthquake. Then our house will fall on top of us and we'll be caught under the house; we'll be destroyed for good, just as happened to them.

The only people who weren't destroyed were those who went inside the springs; they stayed alive. Some, they say, went and hid in the rivers where the current runs swiftly. Some others were saved, they say, who owned the hills, for example, like the hill I mentioned which is Še? Tiiš, because they surely were their dwelling places. Since it's stone, where could the fire get to the inside? Those were the people who survived. They weren't destroyed, because the fire was extinguished at the edge of the water; the fire didn't penetrate the water. For that reason they stayed alive. They are the ones who remained as ?aanhel, they say. That's the reason they came back as ?aanhel. This is a mountain now, but once it was a person. They took office as ?aanhel because they had survived the destruction and their sins were forgiven.

The dying was over when the fire went out. And, they say, Kub'aal himself spoke to Kub'aal the Wind: "Look here, come look, come hunt around to see if all our children are destroyed, and if there are still some left, bring them right away. Wherever it be, be it in the water, be it in a cave, be it in a mountain, bring them, gather them up, all of them," said Kub'aal to the Wind.

"All right," [said the Wind], and he left.

And it was true, there were some inside the caves, some inside the mountains, some in the river currents. All were lifted out by the Wind; the Wind carried off all of them, and they came to Kub'aal. He asked them: "What did you do? How did you survive?"

"Why, this is the way we did it," [they answered]. "We hid ourselves in the river, or in the mountains," wherever they were; they told the truth.

"All right, then, my children, all right, it doesn't matter. Forget it! You were able to withstand the trial; you didn't die. All right, then. But your work will be different, because you will stay on earth. You won't be destroyed anymore; I won't do any more to you. Since you've won, you'll get other work. But don't repeat what you did earlier when you came to just overhear my words. Why, I didn't go out to you, and you kept eavesdropping on me. Don't listen to my words anymore; don't come anymore. Messages will be sent down to you from here, from heaven; only messages will get to you. Others will appear on earth; other daughters, other sons will appear on earth. Just wait until they come. You will live on earth, and you will be the ones to watch them; you will send messages up to me. But don't come anymore; just send up messages. That's what will happen; that's how it will be done. There will be a daughter or a son who commits a sin on earth. You must tell me; you must send me the message. If they seek you out, if they give you food, if they give you a little *atole*, then tell me. If they don't remember [honor] you, if they don't serve you, send me a complaint. I am the one who knows what to do, not you; you only have to be there. But you must live there; you are now the keepers of the children. You don't have to disappear from the earth; you will stay, you are ʔaanhel now." He had given his blessing to them.

Well, they were once real people, perhaps, but we will never see for ourselves because they appeared as persons in old times. Now they are gods. They are gods now because of Kub'aal's blessing. One can scarcely notice when they go by; the way they pass is sometimes like a star or like the moon that crosses the sky. The reason they walk is that they are people. The ones that flash, that make lightning, are ʔaanhel too. The ones that make noise, that thunder, are ʔaanhel, but they were people before. Since Kub'aal blessed them to be our keepers, they are now lords over our affairs; they watch us and see what needs we have. We have to remember the ʔaanhel: a thousand ʔaanhel in heaven, a thousand ʔaanhel in the gloria, a thousand ʔaanhel on the earth, our keepers, eavesdroppers on us. But we will never see them face to face, because only their words are left; their names are the ones that are written down. There is ʔaanhel San Miguel, there is San Rafael, there is San Gabriel, there is San Vicente. And they're our keepers; they're everywhere. Just like the Wind, because the Wind is their carrier. That's what the ʔaanhel do. But they're not God. God, Our Mother and Kub'aal God who created us on earth, he's different because he's high over our heads, he's truly different, high above us. Whether he's high above us or at the edge of heaven, we'll never know;

we just hear the word that it is so. There are some who own books in which it is written what Kub'aal says.

So it is that the ʔaanhel appeared.

In very general terms, we can think of this story as dealing with misbehavior or transgression (as judged by Kub'aal), followed by a series of punitive actions by Kub'aal, followed by a change in the circumstances of the protagonists. The motivating actions are performed by the protagonists, the responsive actions by a higher power; and the results concern the circumstances of the protagonist. As will be seen, this pattern is basic. It is a pattern of social control by a higher power, usually in the form of punishments, followed by forgiveness. This already begins to tell us something about Ixil culture. To see the deeper interrelationships, however, we need an analytical procedure for decoding the significant units in some reasonably close approximation to the inner, or native, view. To approximate the native reality, techniques need to be developed to analyze the distribution of elements. Through distribution study the key elements or units in the native construction can be revealed.

UNITS OF NARRATIVE ANALYSIS

The first approach to the discovery of the key elements or units of folktales was made by the Russian folklorist Vladimir Propp, who showed that elements of fairy-tale plots operate in a regular fashion above the level of the sentence (Propp, 1968). These units are good clues to native constructions of reality. Propp worked with basic plots or "moves." A move can be thought of as consisting of a motivating problem and the events that lead to a solution to that problem. Propp defined a Russian fairy-tale move as any development out of "villainy" or a "lack" (the motivational actions) through various intermediary actions to terminal actions such as "marriage," "reward," or "liquidation of the lack." Every new villainy or lack creates a new move.

Many of the Russian fairy tales he examined had only a single move, but others had several. Though the moves might be interwoven in different ways, they could always (in Propp's sample) be identified unambiguously. Propp demonstrated that any move in a Russian fairy tale could be described in terms of only thirty-one basic actions or "functions." Each function had a relatively fixed sequential position. If the action category "pursuit" occurred, it was always prior to "rescue"; again, villainy or lack, typically beginning actions, would not occur at the end of a story. No single tale used all thirty-one basic functions, but the functions used usually followed the inventory sequence. The chronological position of a function with respect to all other functions in the inventory was therefore a defining criterion. Propp's sequence accounted, with minor variations, for 100 Russian fairy tales.

This stereotyped sequence was thought by Propp himself (and many folklorists at first) to be universal. In actuality, much of it was specific to time, place, and genre. Propp failed to see that different cultural groups have different combinatorial elements and rules. Though he did note that some of the expressive characteristics and attributes of the dramatis personae were culture-specific, he argued that the structure of tales of the same genre was everywhere the same and that the functions he had identified would describe the action of a great many other tales of dissimilar peoples. Thus when Propp suggested that his Russian fairy tales reduced to a single tale, many folklorists took him to mean that all myths everywhere were basically the same and that his thirty-one functions were universal.

While some of Propp's functions do appear to be part of the inventory of other narrative cultures, there are other functions elsewhere in the world that are not included in the Russian inventory. Moreover, when similar functions appear, they are different in important respects. For example, in the Russian stories one function is "difficult task," which is regularly followed by "solution." In the Ixil stories, however, the "difficult task" is sometimes never accomplished, so instead of a "solution" we must speak of "task outcome." In addition to these differences, there are cultural differences in the sequence of functions.

Rather than testing Propp's statement that culture makes no difference, most folktale analysts have simply accepted the statement as correct. One writer has tried to apply Propp's sequence to the folktales of an entire continent; another has attempted to fit it to the trickster theme in folktales scattered about the world. These and similar efforts have led many people to overlook the real significance of Propp's work. Another reason Propp's work was not sufficiently appreciated was Lévi-Strauss's clever subsumption of Propp as a primitive forerunner to his own structuralist approach. Actually the two are radically different from each other: Propp's analysis can be empirically tested, whereas Lévi-Strauss's cannot.

If we leave aside the theoretical confusions, there are two key characteristics of Propp's discovery. The first of these is replicability. His basic units do indeed fit the Russian fairy tales (and they do not fit random samples of non-Russian fairy tales). They are well enough defined that even untrained analysts, if they proceed carefully, can do reasonably well in analyzing Russian fairy tales as Propp did. The second key characteristic is exhaustive accountability: *all* the major events of a story are accounted for by the sequence (with the exceptions here and there which Propp dismissed as "transformations"), and *all* the stories in the sample are drawn from the same population.

In our own work on narrative units, we have replaced Propp's term *function,* which can be used in as many as four other ways (linguistic, mathematical, computational, and anthropological) in the study of narrative culture, with the new term *eidon.* The term comes from Bateson's *eidos* (1936), which covers the cognitive aspects of culture and comes from the prefix *eid-,* "pictorial" or "imaginary." We think of the eidon as a cognitive chunk coded in a way that, if not entirely "pictorial," is close to what might be called pictorial imagery in the brain.

Eidos, for Bateson, was "a standardisation of the cognitive aspects of the personality of the individual" in a particular society (1936, p. 220). It included the premises or generalized assumptions and implications that are recognizable in cultural behavior—the logical system that people use in their day-to-day living, particularly in intellectual activities. It contrasted with *ethos,* the standardization of the affective or emotional aspects of culture. Although this distinction is useful for some purposes, it obscures the fact that there is a major informational or cognitive component in the emotions as well, and it should not be overlooked. By eidos and eidons, then, we do not wish to exclude linkages to evaluations and feelings.

The eidon is a pattern, or element of a pattern, which can be an action, process, arrangement, scene, or circumstance. It can be thought of as having linkages or "pointers" to more general patterns at a higher level of abstraction and to more specific patterns at a lower level. It forms part of a hierarchical network.

Eidons that function as plot elements and that form a string or sequence in the story line are *sequence eidons*. The discovery and analysis of these sequence eidons we refer to as *eidochronic analysis*. We see the sequence eidon as the basic analytical unit of folk narrative and as having an important additional component which Propp's function lacks—government by higher-level categories and rules. Eidochronic phenomena in traditional narratives usually systematize, at a cultural level, matters that are of major concern to the people who use the narratives. This eidochronic systematization includes codifications of the world, of role playing, and of concerns that are typical in the cultural systems of the people who use the narratives. It ties in to a behavioral and situational logic. The basic pattern-organizing rules that govern eidochronic phenomena can be described in a cultural grammar.

CULTURAL GRAMMARS

A cultural grammar is, in one sense, a theoretical model. It must account for all the cultural productions of a specified type in some time period and location. Because formal approaches and testing have usually not been applied to narrative structures, it is hard to separate the genuinely insightful descriptions from those that reflect the analyst's own habits of thought. Clearly, only a systematic approach can be used in working out a cultural grammar for narrative. The key element in such a procedure is the testing of the grammar with new stories as the analysis proceeds. By bringing in the elements of prediction and testing, we place eidochronic analysis on a scientific footing.

By prediction we do not mean prediction of the exact words a storyteller might say from one moment to the next; what we are talking about is prediction of the *class* of events to which the next event mentioned will belong. Just as in sentences we can predict for some types of words that certain other types of words, say nouns or verbs, will follow, so also can we predict events in a stereotyped narrative genre that we are familiar with. We can predict that after some event *E*, one of perhaps three or more events, all of the same class, *F*, or perhaps a few other event classes, say *G* or *H*, will almost inevitably occur. We "know" this because we have a schema system that is like a narrative grammar for the genre in our heads. Once this system has been analyzed and described, real tests of the model can be made. As predictions go in the social sciences, the prediction of an event class is not as strong in itself as the prediction of a specific event; but with repeated successes of a complex of predictions organized by a schemata system, we have a powerful theoretical model.

The work done on Eskimo folktales can be mentioned briefly as an illustration. With two samples of Eskimo folktales, it was possible to work out a grammar that accounted for well-formed Eskimo folktales. Since the number of Eskimo folktales published is quite large, one can easily draw new samples of published Eskimo tales from *traditional* Eskimo populations to test the grammar.

Each eidon of the Eskimo folktale grammar is a class of events defined and represented by a number of varieties. For example, the eidon Magical Engagement has two varieties: (1) "The protagonist engages in a magical contest," and (2) "The protagonist engages in a unilateral magical action against the adversary." The eidons, in turn, are subcategories of higher-level components. Magical Engagement can form part of the Main Action component and is positioned between other eidons by the following rule:

Main action → (Attack, Fishing/Hunting, Retrieval Attempt, Persuasion, Transaction, Magical Support, *Magical Engagement*, Elimination, Struggle, Discovery, Deception)

The complete grammar (Colby, 1973) requires eleven rules:

Grammar: Rule 1: Move → $M^\frown Resp^n$

Rule 2: Resp → $E^m {}^\frown R$

Rule 3: M → $\left\{ \begin{array}{c} VM \\ \\ IM \end{array} \right\}$

Rule 4: E → $(PA \emptyset MA)$

Rule 5: R → $(IR \emptyset VR)$

Rule 6: VM → $\left\{ \begin{array}{c} FI \\ SI \\ MI \end{array} \right\}$

Rule 7: IM → $\left\{ \begin{array}{c} VI \\ Bt \\ Sp \end{array} \right\}$

Rule 8: PA → (En◊Hs◊Ch◊Cn)
Rule 9: Ma → (Ak◊Fh◊Rv◊Ps◊Tr◊Me◊Ma◊El◊St◊Ds◊Dc)
Rule 10: IR → (Vc◊Rl◊Po◊Rs◊Es◊Re◊Mr)
Rule 11: VR →(Gr◊Se◊At)
where: { } indicates one and only one item is selected
 (◊) indicates at least one of the linked items must
 occur
 ⌒ indicates linkage of obligatory categories.

These rules are shown in derivational form in figure 5.1. on p. 201.

The events of any particular Eskimo story, when coded into eidons, will be represented by a string of symbols that conforms to these rules. For example, the Eskimo story "The Three Kings" has the following eidochronic sequence, starting with variety 7 of Villany (Vl), variety 5 of Facilitation (Fc), and so on:

Vl-7 Fc-5 Fh-3 Gr-3 Pc Hs-1 In Ch-1 St-1 Vc-2 Hs-2 Ds-1 Ch-2 St-2 Vc-1 Re-3 Rt

The numbers indicate the particular variety of the eidon. Eidons without numbers are secondary eidons, which are largely involved in highlighting functions that serve to emphasize the primary eidons.

Analyzing the sequencing of key ideas in narratives can lead to a grammar for a particular narrative genre among a group of people using the same cultural systems. That these key ideas approximate some underlying cultural reality is indicated by successful prediction from a given cultural grammar to new samples of the same narrative genre from the group of people being studied (Colby, 1973a, 1975).

In working with Shas's myths and folktales, we do not have a large enough sample to proceed in the same manner as in the Eskimo study. However, the Eskimo study was made without any reference to ethnographic data beyond the stories themselves. With the Ixil material, we have a much greater depth and richness of ethno-graphic context immediately available to us. We also have another advantage: working with stories produced entirely by a single person means that we do not have interpersonal variation to contend with. Finally, we have the advantage of a developing theory and the find-ings of the Eskimo study to assist us in doing what Propp, for lack of comparative data, was unable to do: to begin to separate universal or widespread characteristics of narrative logic from culture-specific ones.

In speaking of cultural grammars, the notion of a generative system comes to the fore. Indeed, the study by Lord and Parry of ancient and contemporary epic singers (Lord, 1960) has emphasized the generative idea in the production of narrative. Those who remember their Homer need only be reminded of phrases like "the rosy-fingered dawn." This is as though the storyteller had a stock inventory of story parts which were plugged in at the right places with only minor variations—in short, a formulaic system. Lord describes similar processes among Yugoslav epic singers of the 1930s. After hearing variations of the same song, epic singers learn to abandon the rigidity of the rote procedure for something more flexible. The singer learns how to expand and ornament his songs and how to add thematic material at the appropriate places whenever desirable.

One would expect more "variations on a theme" in societies in which storytelling or epic singing is frequently done—where there is a rich production of narrative. Yet there is a problem in cases where the epic has religious and ritual significance. In such cases, there are constraints that operate. For example, a myth that is closely linked to a particular ritual is less likely to change over time than one that is not. Different cultural production systems may "resonate" when they produce similar sequences. A narrative system and a ritual system producing similar sequences may intensify each other and also act as restraints on creative divergences, thus leading to greater conservatism for the social group using the systems that produced those sequences.[4]

One of the critical problems in analyzing tales is that of scale. Sentences can represent entire stories, and the case-relation values in a particular clause can be expanded to an eidochronic unit spanning several paragraphs or pages of text. To illustrate this problem of scale, we might reduce "Goldilocks and the Three Bears" to a single sentence: "A girl who had entered a house belonging to bears, eaten their porridge, sat in their chairs, and fallen asleep in one of the beds, was suddenly awakened on the return of the bears and ran out of the house in fright." Thus a story can be expanded or contracted, and in the process information is added or lost. Nevertheless, even a single-sentence story can consist of several eidons, as is undoubtedly the case in the example just given.[5] Sometimes this process is governed by an expectation that the audience has enough contextual understanding to fill in the gaps; the more people have in common, the less needs to be said. The narrative analyst must always be alert to this question of meaning and must be careful not to throw away relevant information.

EIDOCHRONIC ANALYSIS OF IXIL TALES

To see how one might begin an eidochronic analysis of Ixil stories, we will consider two more of Shas's tales. The first is about a man who was transported to the Underworld; the second is about a man who was carried to the Skyworld (published earlier in Colby and Colby, 1974). Like the story with which we began this chapter, in which people annoyed Kub'aal, were punished, and then were forgiven, these two stories portray wrongdoing followed by punishment and then by the restorative action of a god.

The Abode of the Mountain-and-Valley God
(synopsis)

Once a wild pig raided a farmer's maizefield. The supernatural shepherds who are in charge of wild pigs come to the field to assess the damage and discuss how the farmer might be recompensed. Just then the farmer rushes out in anger. He flails wildly about with his machete, cutting the maize stalks. In the process he just barely misses cutting the shepherds, who are invisible to him. The farmer repeats the action several times.

As a result the farmer finds himself transported to the underground house of the Mountain-and-Valley God. In the temporary absence of the god, the farmer is questioned by the god's attendants. He is unable to explain how he came to be there. Eventually the god arrives and also questions the farmer. Again the farmer replies that he does not know how it was that he came to be there. The god then tells him to sit down and await the return of the shepherds to see if any of them has an explanation. With the dawn's coming, the farmer is given food. Then the shepherds of all the different animals begin to return. The god questions each one. Finally the wild pig shepherds come. They explain what happened. The man is being punished for his lack of respect for maize and animals.

By this time the farmer's wife, family, and friends start to look for him. They go to the edge of the field and beat a drum. The wife cries out so loudly that she can be heard in the house of the Mountain-and-Valley God. But the god forbids the farmer to answer her or escape. This injunction is enforced by a snake and a jaguar who guard the entrance of the house.

But the din of the farmer's wife and of the drum begins to give all the deities a terrible headache. Finally the wild pig shepherds decide to let the farmer return. The farmer is enjoined not to mistreat wild pigs again or to cut the corn stalks. He closes his eyes and finds himself back at his field with his family and friends.

We can represent the plot of this story in the following abbreviated form:

Crop damage
Farmer's wrongdoing
Transportation to Underworld
Interrogation by deities
Hospitality
Explanation by shepherds
Wife's appeal with noise of drum
Instruction by Earth God
Release of farmer, allowing him to return

The second story, "The Fish Merchant," follows and has some similarities to the previous one:

The Fish Merchant
(synopsis)

There once was a traveling merchant and his wife. One time when he was away, his wife took up with another man. The two of them decided to get rid of the absent husband by witchcraft. They go to a sorcerer and request that magic be done. A ritual is performed with incense and candles. This magic causes the man to be swallowed by a large animal of the sea. The animal takes the fish merchant to a place inhabited by the gods. The man cuts his way out and finds himself in a land of bountiful crops. Because he is hungry, the fish merchant tries to pick the corn and fruits growing there. The food cries out, betraying his presence. The local people rush out and seize the man. Being immortals, they find that the man smells bad to them. They ask how he came to be there. He answers that he doesn't know. He tells them about being swallowed.

He is identified as one of the earth children. The people take him to a higher official, the alcalde. They report how he tried to eat the food. The alcalde questions the man, who answers with the same story. The alcalde now orders new clothes and commands that he be bathed. After this purification, the fish merchant is left among the flowers near the house of Our Father. Our Father arrives. A procession goes to meet him. He asks about the "son" and interrogates him. The fish merchant answers again by saying that he does not know how he came to be there. Our Father answers that it was the fault of the fish merchant's wife.

Our Father takes him to a window in the sky. Through the window the fish merchant is able to see his wife eating with her lover. The fish merchant is then instructed not to tell anyone of his visit to the Skyworld and is told that on his return to earth everything will be well and that he will get a new wife. He is told to go first to his neighbor's house and ask to marry the neighbor's daughter. He must leave his former wife alone, and must stay away from a ceremony that will be taking place on his return.

The Father tells the man to rest and stay awhile. The fish merchant is given food. While he is eating, some of the immortals marvel at his ability to ingest food. They request that he cut openings in their bodies to serve as anuses so that they too can eat. He complies, but as a result, they die. The Father scolds him and shortens his stay in the Skyworld.[6]

The fish merchant is finally transported back to the shore on earth where he was first captured by the sea animal. He leaves for home. When he arrives at his village, he finds that his former wife's lover has died. The ceremony taking place is the lover's funeral. Doing as instructed, the fish merchant goes to his neighbor's house. He is given food and remains there. The neighbor's daughter becomes the wife of the fish merchant. In the meantime, his former wife loses her mind. The fish merchant's new wife asks him to fetch the old wife as a servant. He brings his old wife. She is bathed and cleaned, is given instructions, and finally gets well but remains only as a servant.

The plot of this story can be represented as follows:

Absence of protagonist
Wrongdoing or transgression of protagonist's wife
Capture of protagonist by animals under spell of witchcraft
Transportation of protagonist to Skyworld
Discovery of protagonist
Preliminary interrogation
Purification
Interrogation by Sky God
Explanation by Sky God
Instruction by Sky God
Hospitality
Task performed by protagonist
Ill consequence of task
Release from Skyworld
Hospitality by neighbor
Marriage to neighbor's daughter
Mental sickness of former wife
Purification of former wife and hospitality
Instructions to former wife
Partial release (i.e., release from mental sickness)
Partial reunion (bondage to protagonist and his new wife)

A still more abbreviated description can be made in terms of event types that have occurred often enough as recognizable "chunks" of action to be considered as candidates for eidon status:

"Mountain-and-Valley God"
Transgression — Transport — Interrogation — Hospitality — Explanation — Appeal — Instruction — Release

"Fish Merchant"
Transgression — Capture — Transport — Discovery — Preliminary   Interrogation — Purification — Interrogation — Explanation (or "revelation") —Instruction — Hospitality — Task — Consequence — Release — Hospitality — Marriage — Sickness — Purification — Hospitality — Instruction — Release — Reunion

If we eliminate the actions that are not common to both stories we get the following strings:

"Mountain-and-Valley God"
Transgression — Transport — Interrogation — Hospitality — Explanation — Instruction — Release

"Fish Merchant"
Transgression — Transport — Interrogation — Explanation — Instruction — Hospitality — Release — Hospitality — Instruction — Release

With the exception of Hospitality, the order is parallel up through the first Release. In the sequence that leads up to the second Release in "Fish Merchant," the order is the same as in "Mountain-and-Valley God."

These elements will be tentatively labeled as eidons. The events not common to both may be eidons also, but other stories must be examined before we can determine whether they are eidons or not. In the study of Eskimo folktales, tentative eidons were studied in two different collections of folktales and revised in a series of successive approximations until the eidons and rules remained stable as new stories were tested. With Shas's smaller sample of Ixil stories, we must take full advantage of contextual references in other texts and of our own personal field experiences with the Ixil. Further, in considering the content of the eidons it is especially important to see what the overall significance of the action is. Each eidon must be considered with respect to its overall plot function.

The importance of function cannot be overemphasized. For example, one might think that the fish merchant's trying to take some of the maize in the land of the gods represents a further Transgression. The main function of this event, however, is to act as a sign to the listener that the fish merchant is in a supernatural land, as well as a signal to the deities that the fish merchant has arrived. These functions are secondary to the main plot action; they serve only to highlight the action. That the action is not an instance of transgression here is confirmed by its consequences: the fish merchant is not punished for attempting to satisfy his hunger in the maizefield. One can see that the determination of eidons is a kind of "bootstrap" operation. It is not entirely a circular process, however, because eidons are only *partially* defined in terms of their sequence rules.

This bootstrap operation can utilize the secondary or highlighting functions as a means of honing in on the primary eidons. Highlighting is a device for increasing salience. It appears that the highlighting eidons and elements are more universal than the primary eidons. Highlighting is the common function of the various narrative devices discussed at the beginning of the century by Axel Olrik, a Danish folklorist (Olrik, 1965). These devices were expressed in the form of "laws," one of which was the law of contrast: if a rich man appeared in a folktale, then there was also a poor man. This binary opposition extends to many attributes—young and old, good and evil, large and small. By this means, single-attribute dimensions that have special meaning for the story are highlighted. Repetition is another kind of highlighting which builds tension and focuses on a particular action sequence. For example, if the hero tries to do something difficult and fails several times before succeeding, the failures are just another way of telling us how difficult the task is. When the hero finally succeeds (in European fairy tales, it is usually on the third attempt) we appreciate the difficulty of the feat. There are other kinds of highlighting and plot-support elements, which we will discuss later.

In this initial stage of the eidochronic analysis of Ixil myths, we are helped by two things: first, by an emerging idea of plot function at a fairly high level (higher than the eidon level). We have just touched on this concept briefly in discussing the first story in this chapter, "The ?Aanhel." Second, we are aided by an understanding of certain thematic sequences. We have indicated that one thematic sequence of the Ixil deals with the nature of sickness, which is believed to be caused by a transgression, either by the person who is sick or by someone (usually a relative) closely associated with him. The release from sickness, symbolized in Shas's dream by releasing people from a supernatural jail, is only at the pleasure of supernaturals and is a result of a ritual appeal. The same sort of sequence seems to hold for the folktales. In the stories we have so far examined, it runs as follows:

Transgression — Transport or Captivity (symbolic of sickness) — Appeal — Release (health and life)

Since this is not the full eidochronic sequence, in a sense it can be considered to be at a higher level than the eidon; each eidon becomes a metonym standing for a more general idea than the particular action or event class designated by the eidon. Stated differently, some elements of an eidochronic pattern can be more salient and frequent (in the stories) than others. A string of very salient eidons that omits more variable eidons in between can be conceptualized either at the eidochronic level or, as just suggested, at a higher level. In either case we are calling such a sequence a *narrative thematic sequence.*

One might next ask if a thematic sequence such as the one just described has variations. For example, what might happen if Release does not occur? Sick people do not always get well. Is there a sequence that leads from Transgression to Death? Indeed there is. The following story, "Maria Markaao," not only proceeds from Transgression to Death but dwells upon Death and, through it, provides an explanation for the origin of some of the animals.

Maria Markaao
(synopsis)

ʔOyew ʔAči, a god, became enamored of Maria Markaao, the daughter of Mataqtani, another god.[7] Mataqtani would not allow ʔOyew ʔAči to visit his daughter, so ʔOyew ʔAči changed himself into a hummingbird to gain access to the house compound of the family. When Maria asked for the bird to use as a pattern for her weaving, the bird was gathered up in her basket and brought into her room. She locked the door, and the two lovers spent the night together in her room. In the morning when it was time to eat, Maria did not come out and her father found that the door was locked.

The father sent the louse to investigate. When the louse went in he found blood and began to drink it. He became so full that he could hardly walk and failed to return to the father. As a result the louse was made to inhabit the streets forever, drink blood, and eventually die.

Mataqtani then sent the flea to investigate. The flea also found the blood and gorged himself with it. When the flea failed to report, Mataqtani condemned him always to be useless and to keep people from sleeping.

Finally Mataqtani sent the firefly. The firefly was instructed to enter through the roof and light up the room; if he succeeded he would be given the light for use at night to see with. The firefly did so and reported back that Maria was sleeping with the hummingbird in the form of a man. On hearing this the father tore at his hair, but nothing could be done.

When morning came Maria opened her door and came out. Her father asked her why she had locked the door. She answered that the bird had turned into a man, that they had made love, and that now he wanted to marry her.

The father was very disturbed, but resigned himself to the fact and said that they should go to the priest to be baptized.

So they went to the priest. First they had mass and then they were baptized.

Afterward the father told ʔOyew ʔAči that he must build a house and plant a maizefield. But he wanted the maize ears immediately. ʔOyew ʔAči had to grow ayotes, chilacayotes, and beans as well. But he did not know how to do it so quickly.

Maria told him to buy six machetes and measure out a cuerda of land. He then was to leave the machetes in the middle of the cuerda and go back to sleep and rest. Then she called upon an insect like an ant. This animal did all the work of clearing the field. When ʔOyew ʔAči awoke he found the work all done. Then he sowed maize, chilacayote, ayotes, and beans and went to sleep again. When he awoke everything had grown and he began to harvest it and brought it to his father-in-law. That is when the ant appeared. Maria created it.

Then they ate.

Afterward the father told ʔOyew ʔAči to get the beams and other materials to build a huge house.

Her husband did not know where to get the lumber, because there were no trees close by. Then Maria gave him some of the milk of her breast to sprinkle over a hill. He was instructed not to look, just to sow the milk and then return to sleep as before. And he left the machete on the ground. When he awoke there were great quantities of trees. He cut the trees and made lumber out of them, and prepared the adobes, and overnight the house was built.

The father was exasperated by the success of his son-in-law at tasks he did not think could be done. So finally Mataqtani asked him to build a sweat house. Once the sweat house was built, ʔOyew ʔAči was told to go bring dry wood for the fire. But where could he find dry wood? Maria told him to leave his machete on the peak of a mountain where there were large stones and then go to sleep. When he awoke he had dry wood.

When he returned with the wood to the sweat house he was instructed to start a fire. When everything was prepared, Maria told her father to bathe himself. The father answered that it would be better for them to bathe themselves first in case there was not enough wood. When they went inside the father sealed the entrance of the sweat house and also the opening for the smoke. The man cried out, what could they do, perhaps he should leave, her father was too much for him. But a mole helped them to escape by digging a tunnel out from under the sweat house. They escaped and traveled quite some distance. Then they got to a very narrow place, a window. The man could get through because he was very thin, but the woman could not, she was too fat. Her father saw her and struck her with a lightning bolt. There was nothing but the bones of Maria left. Her husband gathered up the bones in his handkerchief. He traveled along the same direction but on a different level. He cried as he gathered up the bones.

Then ?Oyew ?Ači went to his aunt. There he left the bones in an urn, and closed it with a cover. He told his aunt he had to leave for a while and instructed her not to touch the urn. When he was gone there was movement inside the jar. The aunt went to open the urn to see what was inside. The bones turned into animals which jumped out of the urn and ran in all directions: deer, rabbits, wild pigs, squirrels, and others. When the man returned he cried. He wandered along the road in a dazed condition looking for his wife. He heard a woodpecker, who asked him why he was crying. ?Oyew ?Ači replied that he was crying for his wife. The woodpecker said he knew where she was; but the woodpecker would only show him for a price. All the man had was a red handkerchief, which he offered to the bird for its head. The woodpecker accepted and that is how it got its red head. The man was told to return at noon and listen for the bird. When he returned he heard the bird singing like a person. The woodpecker hammered at a tree and caused some bees to come out. "That's your wife," said the woodpecker. ?Oyew ?Ači asked the bee, "Is it really you?" The bee answered that it was and upbraided him for abandoning the urn. If the aunt had not interfered Maria would have returned to life in her original form. Now she was a bee and she also was the wild pig, and her body had turned into the rabbit and deer as well. She asked ?Oyew ?Ači to call all of them. So he called her bones. They came, all the animals: deer, rabbits, wild pigs, birds, and bees.

The man asked, "Are you all my wife?" They all answered yes. The man was downcast at his fate. Then to the deer he said he would give shoes because she was so unfortunate, having to run from dogs, and having to run through canyons and jump over logs. Now the deer has shoes and can run without difficulty.

For the rabbit he put hair on her feet so the scent of her feet would not stay on the road. That way the dogs would not be able to smell her so easily.

For the wild pig he said that she would have the maize of the fields as her food and would live in caves to avoid the heavy rains.

Some of the key actions of "Markaao" might be represented in the following sequence:

Transgression — Contest — Death — Transformation — Bestowal

Except for the first action, these categories are different from the earlier ones. To be sure, they are simply rough labels. One might wish to question the Transgression label; perhaps it should be distinguished from the kind of transgression that leads to direct punishment in the form of imprisonment (the symbolic form of illness). On the other hand, the closing off of the sweat house with the two lovers inside might be a form of imprisonment. At this first stage of approximation, we have to allow ourselves leeway and be ready to redefine our terms.[8]

So far we have discussed thematic-sequence variations on the consequences (Release or Death) of a sequence of actions that began with what can be called either Transgression or Wrongdoing. Might not some stories start out with an opposite action like "Right-doing?" Indeed, Shas gave us such a story, "The Snake's Treasure." It is interesting, however, that the story starts out as though it were about a transgression—as a story about a "boy who didn't want to fetch wood." We discover immediately, however, that the reason the boy did not want to fetch firewood was not so much laziness as it was the fact that trees in those days—or in that supernatural realm—were sentient and would cry out if cut. To this day, for any Ixil to cut down a tree before carrying out a ritual asking pardon is a transgression against the Earth God, so we could hardly describe this failure to cut firewood as a transgression. Shas's beginning in a "transgression" vein suggests that for him, at least, the Transgression cultural sentence was one that was frequently used and came readily to mind. Such a tendency might be expected in someone whose primary activity focused on ascertaining the transgressions of sick clients.

"The Snake's Treasure," then, looks as though it represents a departure from the usual pattern. We give the full story rather than a synopsis:

The Snake's Treasure

There once was a boy who didn't want to work. He didn't want to fetch firewood.

He had a mother. His poor mother had difficulty in getting something to eat for them.

"Go cut some firewood for us, because we have none. Here I am cooking your dinner, but wood is needed. How can I cook a meal without your going to cut some wood for us? We must make a fire and start cooking dinner," she told him.

"All right," said he, and he left. But he just went to stroll around. There wasn't any wood, and he just wandered off. Certainly there must not have been enough fertility [in the earth]. Certainly the world had not yet appeared, and there were no trees. That is, there were some trees, but when he cut one the tree would cry out. That made him afraid, so he just went to rest under the trees and fell asleep. Then he went home. He didn't carry any load back.

"And where is the wood?" his mother said once again to him.

"There are hardly any trees. When I cut a tree it cries, the blood flows out, and then I get worried. So I can't bring any firewood," was all he said on his return.

That was all; she just listened to him.

When the next day came, he went again. He must have returned to his sleeping place when he met a man. The man was standing in the road. There was a snake in front of him. He had a huge stick in his hand, and he would have killed the creature if the boy had not arrived just then. He had just found the stick when the boy came. The animal was motionless in the road.

"And what might you be wanting to do? What do you want to do to that poor creature?" the boy asked him.

"I'm going to kill it, because it's not a good creature. It bites. It's poisonous. That's why I'm going to kill it," he said.

"Ah, no, that's wrong. What sin has it committed? It's just passing by, so let it alone. Don't kill it. I'll protect it. Don't worry, if you wish I'll pay you. I'll give you some money so you won't kill it," he said.

"Very well, very well, then, if that's the way it is, all right."

So the boy gave him two *reales*. He must have had some money in his pocket, and he took it out and gave it to him. Then the man gave up killing the creature. Now it wouldn't die.

On the following day, the boy went out again, and he met the snake again under the trees.

"What are you looking for?" it asked.

"I'm just wandering around, looking for firewood, that's all. It's very difficult. There aren't any trees. My mother scolds me: 'Go bring firewood,'

she tells me. That's why I'm looking, but trees aren't to be found," he said
to the snake.

"Ah, that's nothing. Don't worry. Don't you worry about that. Buy your
firewood. You've done me a favor; thanks to you I wasn't killed. If you
hadn't come just then, I would have died. He was very close to killing me,
but you arrived just in time. Thanks to you I didn't die. So I'm going to do
a favor for you in return, as a remembrance of my not dying. I'll do you a
favor, so come with me if you want. I'll show you something. I've seen
something over there. I'll go with you to show you so you can fetch it.
Come with me, I'll show it to you," it said.

"Very well, then, let's go see it," he answered.

The creature went ahead, and he followed. It came near a fallen log; it
got to the log.

"This is it. Dig it up and take it with you. What is there is money. Now
there will be no more problems. You can buy your wood. But don't take it
now. Come and get it later. Wait until nighttime before coming to fetch it,
until eight at night. Then come and get it. That way no one will see you
come. No one will see you with it. And when you come, put it in a box,
and you'll see what happens. You'll just see what happens," it told the
boy.

"Very well, many thanks."

"Only this is what I've come to show you, because I didn't die. If I had
died, who would have done you the favor? You did me a favor, so I'll do
one for you. Now you won't have to search for firewood, but can buy it
instead," the creature said to him.

"Very well," he answered.

He turned back. He didn't go on looking for wood. When he came back
again to his mother [he said],

"There is no wood, I have gone to look, and there is none. What shall I
do? There are no trees. I just wandered around. There were no trees. Yet I
found a fortune! A fortune has come to me. But that part I haven't yet told
you about. Yesterday I came upon a man. There was a snake in front of
him, and he was about to kill it. He already had a stick in his hand when I
got there. 'Don't kill it, because it's a sin,' I told him. I felt sorry for the
poor creature. Sad was his face; distraught was his expression. 'Don't kill
it,' I told him. So he didn't kill it. I met the snake again on the road, and
the snake showed me, as a favor, where there was a fortune. When it
showed me, I wanted to take it but couldn't. Instead the snake said, 'Wait
and come fetch it later, at eight at night, and by nine you'll be back at
your house.' But at night I'll be afraid to go alone. Who will accompany
me? What if I run into something? I'll be afraid. But wait, I'll ask a friend
of mine, so we can both go. It'll be better that way. We won't be afraid if
he comes with me. I'll pay him for it, if he goes with me. I'll tell him so,"
he said to his mother.

"It's up to you if what you say is true, but you're just lying. You just
don't want me to scold you," she said to him.

"You'll see, then, if I'm lying. You'll see. Anyway, I'll go tell him." So he left. He went to ask his friend:

"Wouldn't you like to come with me? I've seen a fortune; let's go fetch it. Let's go at eight tonight. Come by for me; I just want you to keep me company, but I'll pay you for your time. Do me a favor and come with me," he said to him.

"Very well, I'll go. What time shall we leave?" he said.

"At eight."

"All right. Wait for me, then. Wait, and I'll stop by on the way. But wait for me. Don't go anywhere, wait and watch for me to come," said his friend.

"All right."

He left and must have returned to his house in the afternoon. Then he was already waiting as the day grew dark. He waited, and the man didn't come. He waited and waited. It was already quite late at night when he finally heard the man speaking outside the house.

"Boy, are you in the house?" he said.

"Yes, I'm here. Come in," he answered.

"I already went to see what you were talking about. What good will that do you? There isn't anything in there. It's just charcoal inside. You'll see, here it is. Watch it come into your house," he said.

The man opened the window and threw a little jar inside. He hurled it right through the window. The jar landed in the middle of the room and burst open. A great heap of money fell into the room, good money. How the money jingled when it poured out into the room! But the man who had gone to fetch it had looked inside the jar and seen only charcoal there; there wasn't any money. "Well, I'm going to take it and show him, because he said it was money. This is hardly money. What does he want charcoal for? Just wait till I go show them," he had said. He just wanted to go show him, and all he saw was charcoal, while it was money that it held. But surely this was to confuse him. Because it wasn't his fortune, it wasn't shown to him. But when the little jar reached the boy's house, the jar broke and the money fell out. So he became content.

"Thank you, man. You did me a favor, you went to fetch it. Thank you. Well, then, I'm going to see what to do," he said. Then he began to gather up the money.

Having left it, the other man just went on. He returned to his house angry.

Well, after gathering up the money the boy put it in a box. Then he went to look at the money again the next day, and there was the box full of money. Plentiful was the money in the box! So it was that he grew content. He bought some land. He bought a house. He began to live well. He was rich. His mother was contented with him. As to the firewood, he no longer had to go look for it. He could just buy it, since now he had the money. So it was all because he did a favor for the snake. It didn't die, and it bestowed the blessing on him.

This story reiterates those parts of Shas's philosophy text that call for the care and protection of all living things. In this story, as in the previous one, there are three main characters and a series of actions in which one of the characters tries to do wrong to one or both of the others. This leads to an engagement or contest in which there is a winner and a loser. In working out a tentative eidochronic variety sequence for "The Snake's Treasure," it is again helpful first to map out the more abstract eidon level. At this early stage, levels of abstraction can be just as fuzzy as the syntagmatic or sequential boundaries of the units. As a first approximation we come up with something like this:

Lack — Rightdoing or Favor (saving snake) — Promise of Reward — Deception — Delivery — Reward (lack liquidated)

To see how these higher-level categories might link with the more specific actions that are eidon-variety candidates, we can arrange them in a preliminary fashion as follows:

Lack	Lack of wood Search Failure Explanation of failure Search
Rightdoing or Favor	Encounter with snake Saving of snake
Promise of Reward	Inquiry about problem Revelation of treasure Instructions Reporting to mother
Deception	Problem arises Friend recruited for assistance Friend deceives
Delivery	Friend unable to realize reward, unknowingly delivers it to boy
Reward	Transformation of charcoal to money

After examining the other stories yet to come, we decided that Rightdoing or Favor could be split into two parts: the first called Encounter, and the second joined with Promise of Reward to constitute Transaction or Favor. Thus a revised sequence for "The Snake's Treasure" looks like this:

Lack — Encounter — Transaction — Deception — Delivery — Reward

There is some question as to whether Deception should be divided into Task and Deception. The Task is usually something assigned to the protagonist, not the villain. But we shall tentatively make the division. Thus "Problem arises" and "Friend recruited for assistance" will be linked to a Task eidon, and "Friend deceives" to Deception. The sequence in its further revision becomes:

Lack — Encounter — Transaction — Task — Deception — Delivery — Reward

This sequence has some similarities to another story Shas told us, "The Comadre." It is about a man who went to hell and back. The story starts with a lack (poverty), and the lack is again liquidated by the transformation of charcoal into treasure.[9]

The Comadre Story

Well, now I am going to tell another one I heard when I used to go to the finca. I was still a young boy, and I went along with older people. I listened to what they said. Once, I went to the Finca Alwees. Well, they talked a lot at night when we were lying down before sleeping. They said, "It's no good to be sad. It's no good for one's heart to be preoccupied with too many things in the face of poverty, because once a man did that. He had many children, perhaps as many as twelve, and he didn't have enough to feed them. The children were always crying because of their hunger. He couldn't find work. And he was continually unhappy because of his poverty. 'Ah, if only there were money somewhere. If ever I knew that money was in hell, or if it were only talk, I would go there. I would go to seek it. I would go to earn money there if there were any.'"

Well, to be sure, his words were heard. As soon as it dawned he asked for a little warm water to wash his mouth out with. He washed his mouth and then drank the warm water. Since he had nothing to eat he just took the water.

And then he went out. "I'm going to look for a little work, to see if there isn't work somewhere. Perhaps I can find someone somewhere to work for."

"Very well," said his wife. So he went off.

After perhaps a league or kilometer from his house, he had come to a small mountain when he saw a ladino come out of the trees who then approached and stood in front of him on the road. "Ah, where are you going?" he said to him.

"I'm just looking for a little work because I don't have any. I just want a little money," he replied.

And, certainly, the ladino must have heard what he said [earlier], because he knew about it. "Is it true that you would go to look for money if the money was in hell, as you said? Is it true that you want to go?" said the ladino to him.

"I would indeed, if one could obtain it. I *would* go, because my life is very hard, I don't have anything to eat and that is what I am looking for."

"Well, all right then, come with me. You can earn money with me, I have money. So if you like, come with me. I will give you money, you will work with me," he said.

"All right, I'll come," he said.

"Very well, then, close your eyes. You must close your eyes, and I'll tell you when you can open them again," he said.

"All right."

He closed his eyes, and when he came to, he was in a large house.

"Well, now you have come, you are going to work with me, but I don't have hard work. The work is not difficult. It's just here with a mule. I have a mule. All you have to do is to bring us wood with this animal, because the wood is needed. So just go to fetch the wood with her [the mule]. Put on a harness, and don't be afraid. You must make the wood heavy. You must put on plenty of wood, thus it will be good. You must not be afraid to put on a heavy load, and if she kicks you suddenly because she doesn't want to have such a load, don't be afraid. Just take one of the sticks and hit her right on the head, and even though you hit her in the face, don't be afraid. That way she will accept her load," the ladino said to him.

"All right," he said.

He went with the mule to look for wood. He came to a plain. "Hopefully, there will be wood here." But there wasn't any wood. There were no trees. The land was pure field. There were no sticks, but there were bones. Who knows what kinds of bones they were. Just bones were there in the field. So he finally got tired of looking for wood and returned with the mule. The mule just followed.

Then he went to explain to the ladino, to the patron, why there wasn't any.

"And where is your wood?" he said.

"No, because there aren't any trees. I went to look for wood but there wasn't any. If only there were sticks, but I did not find any," he said.

"Ah, no. Mister, what about that wood, what about those sticks that are in the field? That is the wood. Yes, they are bones, but that is what we burn, that is it. That is our wood. Don't be afraid to gather it. But you needn't return now because it is late. You can wait until tomorrow. You must go to sleep. Tomorrow you must go early, go early to fetch the wood with the animal," he said.

"Just the bones you must gather, and you must place them on top of the animal, and she will carry them," he said.

"All right," he answered.

And when it dawned, he ate, or certainly must have, I didn't hear that part. And then he went with the animal. And then he went to gather the bones. He tied the bones with a rope, surely he tied them well. And he put the load on the animal. The mule did not receive her cargo, and how she kicked the man! Well, the ladino had given him the instruction, not to be afraid even though it was the head of the animal that he hit with the stick and even though it was across the eyes that he hit with the stick as the patron had told him he should do it, so that the animal would accept the load.

"Very well," the man had said.

Well, that's what happened. The animal didn't want to receive her cargo, and just kicked and kicked. So he grabbed a piece of "wood" that he had nearby, grabbed it with both hands, and with all his might, hit her across the eye with the bone. With one stroke he smashed the eye with the stick. The animal shouted. The animal cried. And the animal spoke to him because it was a human being. In truth, it was not an animal, but a human. The woman was his comadre. She had to suffer for a sin she had committed. She had to pass on to a different place, she had to stay with the mountain because she had had intercourse with a priest. She accepted the words of the priest, the priest had made her fall in love, and she had relations with him. Because of that sin, she didn't go to God, but rather to the other place, because it is a sin if you women have [sexual] communications with a priest.

That's what the men said. I only heard what they said.

Well, so he put the cargo on the animal, and the animal spoke to him.

"What's this, compadre?" because she was his comadre, although she was a mule, she was still on earth, she had not yet died, but her soul was already in jail, it already was in punishment there in the mountain.

"What is this, compadre, I am hurt by you. You have damaged my face, don't you recognize me then? I am your comadre," the animal said to him.

"Well, how would I know? And then why was it that you didn't want to accept your cargo? Why were you just kicking me if you knew I was your compadre?" he said.

"No, I am, pardon me, I am doing you a favor, because I have no sin for being here, but it was when I was a little girl, when I was little, that the padre seduced me, and I spoke with him. Well, that is my sin, and thus I am here. I won't be able to leave. Surely my bones will end here," the woman said to him.

"But in the end, it's not important, you must pardon me if I kick, but it is because I was very tired, I act that way every now and then under a load, and it is very tiresome, I am already very tired," she said.

"But do me a favor, because I will in turn give you some advice. But do me a favor. Don't give me much of a load. Measure it out lightly. Don't obey the patron. Just give me a light load, and I will give you some more advice, because poor you, you came here. Here you have caught up with me, what it is I am doing, and you must do the same because you must come back to pay for it; to pay for what it is they will give you. You must return to pay for it here. If you take money, well, you must come back to pay for the money. If you take the spirit of the animals you must return to pay for it. If you take the spirit of a horse, you must return to pay for it. You must come to pay for it here. Also, if you carry the spirit of money, you must return to pay for it, no matter what it is. And already they put on your shoes, but our shoes will never wear out because they are of metal and metal does not die. Never will metal wear out. You just have to come to an end here, you just have to remain here. You won't be able to leave until the metal is worn out, but when does the metal get worn out? Of pure metal are your shoes, that is the deception that has been done by the patron. But I'm going to give you some advice. When you see that I am ready to urinate, place your foot and shoe in my urine. Then it will wear out rapidly. That is the favor I do for you. Don't have fear. If you do that, then you will be able to leave soon. But if on the other hand the metal does not wear out rapidly you will remain here. But I will bestow a blessing. I will bestow a kindness. It is my soul's reminder. But that is so you will not overload me, only do it carefully," said the animal to him.

"Very well. It is good then."

"So when your shoes are worn out, then you say to him, 'Well, my shoes have worn out, and our contract is that I can go only after they have worn out. Well, they have worn out. So certainly I must go,' so you will say to the man.

" 'All right, then. So you go, but now you should take your money, because that is our contract, that you take either your money or the spirit of one of the animals. Which of the treasures do you want to carry with you, because here there are treasures of animals and there are treasures of money; which do you desire to carry? Choose.'

"That's what he will say, but don't you do it. Don't go and touch! Instead, just say, 'All I want to take is the little bag that is over the fireplace, only that I want to take down. That I want to take with me if you will do me the favor, you will give me some food for the road and I'll carry it in the little bag,' you must say to him. But he will say, 'Of course, but do take the money.' You must answer, 'No, I never will take it. I never will touch it, but excuse me.' You must tell him, 'Only the little bag.'

" 'All right, then, take it,' he will say. Then you take it down and just put it underneath your arm.

"Then he also will say, 'Which of the animals do you want to take? Which of the animals is your desire? Choose one,' he will say to you. 'Will you take off on a goat or take off on a coyote? Which of those will you take? They will carry you and take you to your place,' he will say to you.

" 'No,' you tell him. Don't wish for it, because you will never arrive. Don't mount the goat, don't mount the coyote because they will take you to a different place, and you will never reach your home. Don't wish for it.

"The man will say, 'Which animal will you leave with? Perhaps the black-headed vulture will take you.'

"But, no, you don't want that. Then he'll say, 'Perhaps the vulture can take you.' But you must again say no, you don't want to, because the animal will take you far away. That animal will not come out into daylight, but will take you far away. You must instead say, 'Please do me the favor of letting me take that little animal that is white. Let me have this,' you must say.

"Then you get on that animal, the heron; that animal will take you to your own place again.

"Well, all right, but it is only a remembrance of my soul I will give to you: take the little bag; when you arrive home, you must ask your wife for a jar and put the little bag inside and close it up. Then you can turn to speak a little with her, and after you have talked, and you must measure about an hour, then go and uncover it. And you'll just see what comes out of it," said the woman to him.

"Very well," he said. And he did everything he was told. He wore out the shoes and then went to the patron.

"My shoes are worn out now, so I must leave, because that was the contract that we made," he said to the patron.

"Ah, very well, then, you go, but you must take your money. What do you want, or would you rather take the treasure of a cow, or the treasure of a horse, or the treasure of money? Which do you want, look for it," he said to him.

"Ah, no, no sir, if you'll do me the favor then give me a present: just the little bag I'm going to take, the one above the fireplace. Only that one I will take with me," he said.

"Ah, what good will that do you, it's nothing but soot, it's not good for anything, it's useless. What good is it? But the money is, because that's what you should take, the cow, that's what you should take," he said.

"No, thank you, but I don't want to take it. Only that, if you give it to me, I will take."

"Ah, it's not important. Take it. Would that it served for something," he said only.

So he took down the little bag over the fireplace.

After he took it down, the man said, "Good, and which of the animals do you want to ride? Which of the animals will take you to leave you off? Point out the one you want, the one that will take you to your place again," said the man to him.

"Do you want the goat to deliver you? Or will you ride the coyote?"

"No, no."

"Then which one of all do you want to take you, or would you like the black vulture to take you?" he said.

"No, no."

"Well, what then? Or would you like the vulture to take you?" he said.

"No, no, I don't want it. Only that animal I will ride. That little bird of the white color. It will take me and leave me," he said.

"Ah, well, all right then, ride that animal then."

So he climbed on the back of the heron and then left flying. But it was like before, because he also had his eyes closed, he didn't have his eyes open; they were closed. Then when he arrived at his place, right where he had left, when he had encountered the ladino, the animal said, "Open your eyes."

"All right, good." He opened his eyes just in time to see the animal flying into the sky, going up high above, it ascended, it left the man in the light before it ascended. It flew into the sky. The man remained there and he carried his little bag. Then he came to his house, and certainly it must have been some ten days, or who knows how many days, since he had left. And he arrived at his house.

"Look here, I am finally home, I have arrived; it's no good to be thinking about things because of poverty. I encountered a ladino and went into a place and who knows whether our comadre is there or whether she was not there. Find me a little jar: I'm going to put this little bag inside," he said [to his wife].

"Good," said she. She looked for a jar, and he put the little bag inside and closed its lid. Then he sat down and began to talk with her. After an hour passed, he uncovered the jar, and a baby rose out of the jar, it uttered a cry, and it went right away straight up into the sky. Up it went. And then he looked into the jar, and there was money. The money filled about half the jar. A good quantity of money was there. He had put the little bag in, and it no longer was there, but had been transformed into money, and also the little child. Because the little bag also turned into a child and it was a baby, one of the poor babies who are stillborn, it went straight to heaven. They go to the mountain. It is said that that is what the people there eat. Well, it was hung above the fire, and that is what he took with him; that is certainly what he took down because when it awoke, it went straight to the sky leaving the money.

Then he said, "I already went to see; it's no good that you women get involved with the padre. It is very dangerous because our comadre is there. I already went there. I went there and saw her, and there she was, if only she were still human, but rather she is a mule! I spoke with her, and I went to place a load on her. I went to look for wood, and there wasn't any wood, only bones, and that's what we had to put on the poor thing. Is she still there, or is it that she has died?" he said to his wife.

"She is there, but only that she is very sick. One day she eats and another day she doesn't eat. Now she can't keep her food; also her face is swollen up," said his wife to him.

"Ah, the poor thing, were it not for her favor when I went there, I would not be here now. I would not have come back. I would have remained there. But thanks to her who did me the favor, she remained there, she is working there, but also she went to do me the favor. She was the one who did me the favor so that I could come back here again, thanks to her. Let's go to see her a little, then. Let's visit the poor thing; let's take her a little drink, let's take her a little of *trago* [rum]; let's go to see her, let's visit her a little, the poor unfortunate thing. Thanks to her; she did me the favor," he said to his wife.

"Very well, let's go," she said.

Since he now had money, lots of money, surely the money reproduced itself inside the jar, he carried bread and food to the poor woman, he went to give it to the poor woman as a gift.

Well, he didn't speak; he only listened. He only looked, and when he arrived, one side of the face of the poor woman was black and blue, and she couldn't see because her eye was closed, because he had hit her there, and her face was damaged once and for all there and it was the same for her on earth.

Well, that is because it is a sin to talk to the padre, it is unlucky because that's what happened to his comadre, and she had to go to the mountain. But because of her favor, he improved, he got money, because of her. But it was because he had become sad, and his heart thought of many things because of his poverty, but if it hadn't been for his comadre, then he never would have returned. He would have remained there in that place in the mountain [with the mountain spirit]. If his comadre had not been there, but she was there to do him the favor and so his shoes wore out rapidly, and he returned right away.

Only that is what I heard, what I listened to. I only heard what the old men said, the ancient men were those I heard tell it, when I went to the finca; well, that is all, I have it in my memory, I have it in my mind, it is not forgotten, it is in my mind. And it is for that reason that I tell it a little, so that you may know a little bit how it was, or how the ideas of old were. It was long ago, it isn't something that exists now; it hardly is now, it hardly happened recently, but rather it was long ago. Some of the ancient people talked that way in earlier times; that is what was possible; this is what was done, they said. Well, only that is what I have in my memory, only that.

This is another moving story that focuses on empathy and kindness. The comadre wants to help her compadre even after he has struck her. A question occurs to us that we cannot answer without further comparative study: is the emphasis on kindness and sympathy a result of Shas's tendency to select and remember such stories because of his own predilections? Or is the selection of stories Shas has given us similar to the repertoire of other storytellers? In "The Comadre," some of the elements that stand out the most are similar to those in "The Snake's Treasure":

Lack — Transgression (contracting with the devil) — Contest — Release — Reward — Ending Commentary (about the comadre)

A more detailed list of events follows:

Action	*Eidon candidate*
Lack of food and employment	Lack
Expresses willingness to go to Hell for money	Transgression
Encounter with ladino (deity)	Encounter
Agreement to work in Hell	Transaction
Transport to the Underworld	Transference or captivity
Given task of gathering wood	Task
Failure to find wood	Task outcome
Hitting the mule and discovering that it is his comadre	Encounter
Comadre asks for a light load	Favor
Comadre urinates on iron shoes	Precaution
Protagonist engages in contest of wits with devil	Contest
Protagonist returns home	Release
Money appears in jar	Reward
Visits sick comadre	Favor
(Death of comadre assumed?)	Death
Commentary	—

In our first approximation of this sequence, we included a second Transgression, hitting the mule, because we were inclined to be shocked at the man's brutality with the mule (the more so on learning that the mule is really a person). In the overall plot structure, however, Transgression typically leds to some form of punishment, and the incident with the mule has no such consequence. On the contrary, the mule, now revealed to us and the protagonist as his comadre, forgives him, asks a favor of him, and saves him from eternal captivity in the Underworld from which she herself has no hope of escaping. The more likely function for the hitting of the mule is highlighting; it serves to increase one's pity for the poor comadre and to dramatize the line between the human and the animal form of the human's soul in the Underworld (as represented by the later comment that before her death the poor woman had a black eye just where she had been hit as a mule). Moreover, this meanness is immediately followed by concern and compassion on the part of the man, who then disobeys his boss and gives the poor mule a very light load.

Narrative function, whether of a highlighting kind or a basic plot structure kind, is the key to eidochronic analysis; in the earlier stages it helps us to identify eidons and, to some extent also, to sort out the levels of abstraction. In the beginning it is necessary to range back and forth between higher-level categories and lower-level ones. As we have already mentioned, it is sometimes just as difficult in the beginning of analysis to differentiate category levels as to distinguish category boundaries. The thematic sequences, being more predominant, are usually what we see first. They tend to organize more of the details for us and, as focal organizing nodes, seem to have a higher position in our hierarchical framework of narrative categories. However, as we have already pointed out, there are sometimes metonymic characteristics in this relationship, where a more specific (and lower-level) element stands for a higher-level category. By considering higher-level functions, we can partially solve the problem of level sorting. If, for example, we define a story as a narrative that describes a problem and a response to that problem, then all stories would have two components, a Problem and a Response. The point at which options occur—at which not all categories are obligatory— is a major dividing line for levels. In the Ixil stories we have been examining, it looks as though the obligatory level extends one level below that of Problem and Response. The obligatory level has four categories, which at this point we will label Motivation, Preliminary Action, Main Action, and Outcome:

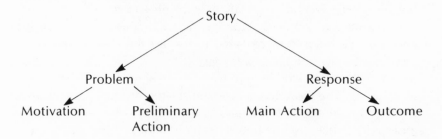

Below these levels selection occurs. Therefore, we define a well-told Ixil story as one that selects at least one eidon from each of the four categories—Motivation, Preliminary Action, Main Action, and Outcome.

The rules for the obligatory categories are quite simple:

Rule 1: Story→Problem + Response
Rule 2: Problem→Motivation + Preliminary action
Rule 3: Response→Main Action + Outcome

There is sometimes a kind of Coda at the end of the story, where attention shifts from the main character to a secondary one. This option will be examined as we proceed further in the analysis.

We are now ready to draw up a list of all the eidon candidates that seem to fit best the six stories we have so far examined:

Motivation Eidons
1. Lack
   a. Wood lacking, suggesting a generally impoverished circumstance ("Comadre," "Snake")
   b. Wife lacking ("Markaao")
2. Transgression
   a. Offense of farmer against the shepherd deities of the Mountain-and-Valley God, instigated by damage to farmer's crop by animals ("Mountain-and-Valley God")
   b. Contract with the Devil ("Comadre")
   c. Eavesdropping on Our Father ("ʔAanhel")
   d. Witchcraft performed against the protagonist ("Fish Merchant")
Preliminary Action Eidons
1. Transference (later changed to Enter Captivity; see Appendix B)
   a. Transference to abode of the Mountain-and-Valley God ("Mountain-and-Valley God")
   b. Transference to Underworld ("Comadre")
   c. Transference by Wind God to Skyworld ("ʔAanhel").
   d. Transference by whale to Skyworld ("Fish Merchant").
   e. Transference to room of lover ("Markaao"; later changed to secondary eidon—see Appendix B)
   f. Transference of bones to urn ("Markaao")
2. Transformation
   a. Transformation into a hummingbird ("Markaao")
3. Encounter
   a. Encounter with a god or gods, a person, or an animal with whom some interchange of favors or information eventually takes place ("Markaao," "Snake," "Comadre"; if the meeting occurs in the dwelling of a god, it is classified as hospitality)
   b. Discovery by gods in the Skyworld ("Fish Merchant")
   c. Discovery that animal is a person ("Comadre")
4. Information
   a. Questioning of the protagonist to learn who he is or why he was transferred to captivity ("Mountain-and-Valley God," "Fish Merchant")

    b. Asking of the protagonist what his problem is ("Snake")

    c. Questioning of people to learn how they survived a rain of fire ("ʔAanhel")

    d. Questioning of daughter about her behavior with a man ("Markaao")

    e. Asking and receiving of information on the whereabouts of a person ("Markaao")

    f. Overhearing of the plans of Our Father ("ʔAanhel")

    g. Warning by plants that cry out ("Fish Merchant")

    h. Revelation of a treasure to be given to the protagonist ("Snake")

    i. Revelation through a sky window of events on earth ("Fish Merchant")

5. Transaction or Favor

    a. Favor, exchange of favors or selling of information ("Markaao," "Snake," "Comadre")

    b. Bringing of sick former wife into the household ("Fish Merchant")

    c. Visiting of sick comadre in her house ("Comadre")

6. Hospitality

    a. Feeding of protagonist while held captive ("Mountain-and-Valley God," "Fish Merchant")

    b. Purification or bathing ("Fish Merchant," "Markaao")

    c. Hospitality of neighbor ("Fish Merchant")

7. Precaution

    a. Precaution against impending destruction ("ʔAanhel")

    b. Measures to deceive the Devil ("Comadre")

Main Action Eidons

1. Task

    a. Gathering of bones ("Comadre"); cutting of anuses of gods of the Skyworld ("Fish Merchant")

    b. Task that is not expected to be completed ("Markaao")

    c. Task given to deceptive friend ("Snake")

    d. Watching over urn of wife's bones ("Markaao")

2. Attack

    a. Attempts to destroy by sending floods, rains of fire, or lightning ("ʔAanhel," "Markaao")

    b. Attempts to destroy by suffocating in sweat house ("Markaao")

    c. Shooting at bird with blowgun ("Markaao")

3. Facilitation

    a. Provision of magical means to complete a task ("Markaao")

    b. Instruction as to how to fool the Devil ("Comadre")

    c. Instruction in what choices to make in a contest with the Devil ("Comadre")

4. Contest

    a. Necessity for choices that will determine whether protagonist will escape from captivity and gain wealth ("Comadre")

5. Noise (or Appeal)

a. Attempt to release protagonist through the beating of drums ("Mountain-and-Valley God")
6. Deception
   a. Deception by someone who seeks to gain the protagonist's treasure for himself ("Snake")
7. Flight
   a. Flight from angry father ("Markaao")
8. Impedance
   a. Inability to escape through a small opening ("Markaao")
   b. Diversion by a feast of blood ("Markaao")
9. Violation of Interdiction
   a. giving way to curiosity and opening of urn against instructions ("Markaao")

Outcome Eidons
1. Delivery
   a. Delivery of treasure to friend ("Snake")
2. Task Outcome
   a. Completion of task ("Markaao")
   b. Botching of task ("Fish Merchant")
3. Escape
   a. Escapes from attacker ("Markaao")
4. Revival
   a. Revival after being "killed" ("Markaao")
5. Reunion
   a. Reunion with wife who has been tranformed into the animals and insects of the world ("Markaao")
   b. Partial reunion with former wife (becomes a servant rather than a second wife) ("Fish Merchant")
6. Bestowal
   a. Giving of characteristics to insects ("Markaao")
   b. Giving of red head to woodpecker ("Markaao")
   c. Bestowal of attributes on animals created from wife's bones ("Markaao")
   d. Assignment of ?aanhel to watch over humans and report on their behavior to Our Father ("?Aanhel").
   e. Changing of wife into servant ("Fish Merchant")
7. Release
   a. Release from captivity in a supernatural realm ("Fish Merchant," "Mountain-and-Valley God," "Comadre").
8. Death
   a. Killing by father ("Markaao")
   b. Death (assumed, not explicitly stated) because soul is being punished as an animal in Purgatory or Hell ("Comadre")
9. Reward
   a. Receipt of money ("Comadre," "Snake")
10. Marriage

    a. Gaining of the bed of lover ("Markaao")
    b. Remarriage ("Fish Merchant")
11. Creation-Transformation
    a. Turning of bones into animals ("Markaao")
Coda Elements
  1. Sickness in someone other than the protagonist ("Fish Merchant," "Comadre")
  2. Various other eidons

REFINEMENTS BASED ON PARALLELS WITH ESKIMO NARRATIVES

In going over the sequences of the six stories as categorized by this eidon candidate list, one is struck by further parallels with the eidon characteristics of the Eskimo study. Several categories of Eskimo folktale eidons functioned as plot-support elements rather than as major elements of the plot structure itself, and therefore were called secondary eidons. The functions served by these eidons included scene change, conveyance of information, prolongation, and episodic transition. Some of these, such as prolongation, were clearly highlighting elements. The sequencing of these secondary eidons was not as simple as that of the main plot eidons; it looked as though they participated in a manifold of systems, such as highlighting, cohesion, and disjunction, that related to the main plot system in a variety of ways. We judged it difficult to work out rules for their appearance without going into a much more extensive study of a wider sample and also, possibly, of the texts in the original language.

In looking at similar functions in the eidon candidates for the Ixil stories, the following (still tentative) eidons can be seen as secondary: Transference, Information, Instruction, Facilitation, Observation, and Impedance.

Another parallel with the Eskimo analysis lies in the higher-level categories. The Eskimo results can be diagrammed as in figure 5.1. In addition to Preliminary Action and Main Action, these other higher-level categories also apply to the Ixil stories. In the Eskimo stories, Immediate Motivation had to do with some abrupt event that galvanized the protagonist into action—for example, the abduction of his wife; in the Ixil stories, the abrupt action may be the protagonist's transgression, which moves the gods to action. Value Motivation, in the Eskimo stories, concerned certain pervading values or conditions

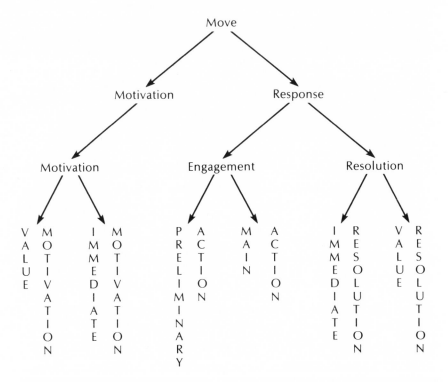

Figure 5.1. Derivational diagram showing Eskimo categories above the eidon level.

of basic importance to the people, such as the need to be strong, to be a successful hunter, or to have one or more wives. A frequent expression of such motivation is Lack. Lack is also found as motivation in the Ixil stories. It is with some reluctance that we come to this understanding, because we have made such a point of the uniqueness of each eidochronic solution to a particular genre and culture-using group. In any event, the parallels do not mean that Ixil and Eskimo narratives have the same eidochronic structure, but rather that they have more similarities at the higher levels than we had at first expected.

With this new insight, we can use an analysis sheet to help us visualize the eidochronic structure. Leaving out the secondary eidons as we did in our work with the Eskimo folktales, and separating the primary eidons according to higher-level categories, we can list the primary eidons in the order they follow in each of the six stories. Our transference eidon candidate seems, on the basis of the Eskimo stories, to be a scene-change eidon and hence secondary in nature. Looking at the Ixil thematic sequence, however, with all its emphasis on imprisonment or sickness, or both, it seems that Entering Captivity should be a primary eidon. We shall thus change the title of Transference (see outline earlier in the chapter) to Enter Captivity and drop one eidon variety (e, "Transference to room of lover"), retaining it under the name "Transference" as a secondary eidon variety.

The advantage of analysis sheets is that they give an immediate picture of the plot flow. Each sheet lists all the main eidons of the Ixil eidon inventory (still a preliminary and incomplete list), with circles drawn in where a particular eidon occurs for a story. This list in the analysis sheets thus represents the latest revision in the course of the analysis; that is, up through the analysis of the previous six tales. Arrows connecting the eidons give an easy visual reference to the flow of events from one eidon to the next and indicate the number of "loops" back through the sequence. The analysis sheets for the six stories we have already discussed, plus one still to come, are given in Appendix B.

To work out the rules for the higher-level categories, we can begin by listing their sequences (with each category abbreviated—for example, Value Motivation is VM), as shown in figure 5.2. From this listing, we see that looping back never occurs in either of the two Motivation categories, but only after the Main Action category has been realized. We also see that events sometimes go from Preliminary Action directly to a resolution, omitting a Main Action event. We thus see the Preliminary action and the Main Action categories as distinct from the Motivation category. So, instead of Problem and Response as in Rule 1 (see the rules for the obligatory categories earlier in the chapter), we have Motivation and Response, just as in the Eskimo stories. The revised first rule is as follows:

Story → Motivation + Response

Further, since we have distinguished two kinds of Motivation, we may revise Rule 2 as follows:

Rule 2: Motivation → [(Immediate Motivation) (Value Motivation)]

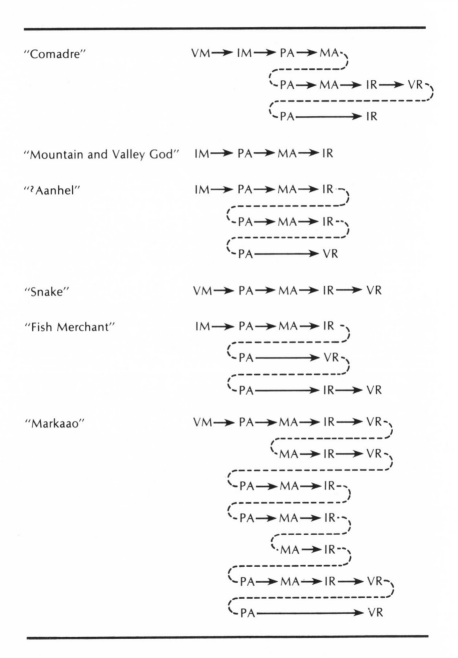

Figure 5.2. Sequencing of higher-level categories for six folktales.

The difference between our first obligatory category rules and the current ones, then, is a moving of Preliminary Action out of Motivation and into the Response category. Earlier we regarded the state of captivity as part of the motivating problem, which is why we had first lumped Preliminary Action with Motivation. However, since Value Motivation and Immediate Motivation occur only once per story while Preliminary Action occurs much more frequently, and since we no longer regard Captivity as part of the Motivation, the change seems justified. Since Motivation occurs only once per story in the Russian and Eskimo samples also, it may well be a universal characteristic for such a genre. Rule 3 may now be rewritten as follows:

Rule   3: Response → Engagement + Outcome

and Rule 4 added:

Rule   4: Engagement → Preliminary Action + Main Action

The Eskimo results also influenced our new view of the final category. In the Outcome category we distinguished Immediate Resolution, Value Resolution (just as it was done for the Eskimo stories), and Coda (which did not exist in our Eskimo samples), a terminal sequence in which the focus shifts to someone other than the main protagonist. Thus, Outcome in Rule 3 is changed to Resolution:

Rule   3: Response → Engagement + Resolution.

Rule 5 is as follows:

Rule   5: Resolution → [(Immediate Resolution) (Value Resolution) (Coda)]

The remaining rules are as follows:

Rule   6: PA → [(Transformation) (Encounter) (Transaction) (Entering Captivity) (Hospitality) (Precaution)]
Rule   5: MA → [(Task) (Attack) (Contest) (Noise) (Deception)]
Rule   8: IR → [(Delivery) (Task Outcome) (Escape) (Release) (Death) (Revival) (Creation Transformation)]
Rule   9: VR → [(Reward) (Marriage) (Reunion) (Bestowal)]
Rule   10: CODA→[(Preliminary Action) (Immediate Resolution) (Value Resolution) (COM)]

TESTING THE GRAMMAR

Now we are ready to test our system with still another story, "The Č'iʔla Naq" or "Bad Men." This is a "real-time" test in the sense that, until we had finished writing the previous section and the rules given above, we had translated but not analyzed "Bad Men." The test is thus a partially blind one. Instead of presenting the finished analysis, with a parsimonious set of rules, eidon definitions, and eidochronic sequences, we have tried to preserve this real-time procedure as a means of explaining better how one might go about doing an eidochronic analysis. We must remember that eidochronic analysis is in its earliest development; we have a long way to go before we will know whether there is a limited set of grammar types among the societies of the world and whether the underlying eidos or cultural logic of a narrative population can be determined clearly enough to provide the foundation for cross-cultural studies. Everything depends on how well the results test out.

What, exactly, constitutes a good test? First of all, we believe that it is important to account in some fashion for all the main events and circumstances of the stories. The first criterion, then, is exhaustive accountability, an exhaustive matching of eidon candidates to all major events of the story. Second, as is implied by the very term "grammar," we must have rules that account for all the sequences. Thus the second criterion is a sequence of eidons that follows all the rules. With these criteria in mind, let us look at the new story, the longest and most complex of all the stories Shas has given us. Because of its length, the story will be followed by a synopsis.

The Č'iʔla Naq Story

God Kub'aal did nothing against Our Uncles (they are Our Uncles because at first all men were gods, they say.) But he made them envious by what he did, because it was he who created the world. And that is how the fight against god Kub'aal all began, for no other reason.

When we first appeared we were only earth. Nowhere else did we appear. Nor were we carved from wood . . . we were only mud. When the story began, when the world appeared, and became fertile; when the trees appeared Kub'aal said, together with the others who were also creating the world, "Now shall the children appear" . . . The ones with him were older brothers who had preceded Kub'aal. So he was the younger brother, while they were the older brothers. And since they were very angry with him, they picked a fight with Kub'aal when we appeared.

It happened when our ancestors appeared. It's an old story. Kub'aal said to those who were with him in the meeting, "Let's do this: let's form round balls, let's make *pixtones* to create the daughters, to create the sons, our worshipers at daytime, our worshipers at dawn. Yes." And they rolled balls, they made their daughters and sons. But their daughters and sons never stood up. They never answered. And they were in the world— we were not yet there because we belonged to the Kub'aal. Their creations turned into snakes and frogs. Under the trees they went, into the water, whatever type the animal was. Those are the ones who appeared first. So the snake was created but it did not answer, it did not speak.

Then they said to Kub'aal, "All right, friend, make yours of what we were using, do yours. Who among us will win?"

So Kub'aal went to get mud. He made round balls, and he moistened them in his hands and stood them up. As the others looked on, the soul entered the person, already there was a small girl. It stood up, already it greeted, "Hello, Father, hello, Mother, hello, Sir, goodnight, Sir," it said.

When the children were greeting, when the children were saluting, the gods tumbled over. They fell out of their seats. The bad men fell over because of the greeting. Because already the little girls greeted, and when they greeted, the evil gods fell down. They fell over backwards. That is how the fight began; it began with us. The bad men said, "Why is it that he is so smart that his children stand up and answer while our children are animals who cannot speak? We will kill him, *jodido*," they said.

The fight began against god Kub'aal; Kub'aal fled. He ran away. They chased god Kub'aal.

In his flight, he came to our father San Antonio, who is a rich man. He lived in the mountain, and there it was that Our Father started to work as a shepherd.

He herded cows, horses, and sheep. He also had merchandise. As a shepherd he did everything. He made leather bags; he made rods for weaving; he made yokes.

And they were sold by San Simon, the stuffed man whom they hang over the entrance of the church when Our Father dies and they nail him up (during the Holy Week ceremonies). He was his assistant.

When the bags were finished, the man went to sell them in the market, like now on Sundays. Kub'aal made the yokes and the man went to sell them—the people bought them from the man, and he brought back the money that he had earned. He made everything; he made hats, he made bags, he made weaving rods, they say.

Then the bad men noticed it, because they were walking around the market when the man came with all the merchandise. The man came to sell it and little by little they asked him questions. "Ah, from where does it come?" or "Are you the one who makes it?"

"I am the one who makes it," (because Kub'aal had said, "Don't tell them what it is that I am doing and don't ever give me away to them.").

"Well, tell us, friend, tell us where it comes from, who makes it. You are not the one who makes it. You are not the one who makes it but only the servant for selling it. So tell us who is the one who really makes it?" they said. They persuaded him: "We will give you money, we will pay you" (the way we do it with him as we already did when we were being filmed, when we explained everything that came out of the tape recorder, just as he does, so it was that they did).[10] So they said, "We will pay you, we will give you money, don't be sad, we have money. And we will give you as much money as you want if you tell us, if you will show us where it is that the rods are made, where he makes them . . . who is the man who really makes them?"

So the bad men questioned the man, the helper of the Kub'aal. The man revealed nothing. "No, I am the one who makes it," he just replied. But they did not believe it. Every Sunday they came to wait for him in order to ask him questions. They showed money to him; they did everything in front of him. They threw dice. They won money for themselves at one throw. They gained money, they gambled, all at once they won.

He did not want to participate; he did not want to play. But little by little, he thought, "If I could do it, if I could do it, it might turn out well," he thought. "It seems like they are winning lots of money. If only I could do it," he thought, "I will ask Kub'aal for a penny," he kept thinking. He returned with the money on that Sunday. "Well, if only, Pap, you would do a favor and give me a little money for the die that some men are throwing. They gamble a lot, it is great fun. There are men there who win money right off. I would like to do that. I can win away their money. Do give me some money." So he kept asking Our Father.

"Leave them alone, son, what do you want from them? What they do is no good. They are not honest. Perhaps they only give it [to each other] in front of you; don't bother with them," said Our Father to him. But he would not listen.

"No, it's all right, because I am sure I'll win. I'll win the money," he kept saying.

"Ah, what for, man? Well, I will make your craving pass and give you a few small coins," said he.

"Thank you."

He counted out two coins. As they always came on Sundays, he, too, came on a Sunday. He came to sell the merchandise, no doubt. When he came to sell the merchandise they asked him again the same way. He was just watching when they played with the dice and everything they did when gambling. So then, "Could I play with you—perhaps I can do it."

"Ah, come, friend, come, friend." They put their arms around him. "Come, do join us."

He handed over his money and went to roll the dice. And what happened to his money? He just tossed it among them. He did not win. He handed them another *real*, and the same thing happened. He won nothing. That way he lost the two reales, and left. He was smart and hid himself. He did not show the way he went. He was smart, and hid from them. But he was followed, and after a while they lost him. He was different because he surely was a god of old. It was not difficult to hide among the trees and houses. No doubt, he hid there, because little by little he had spent his money.

"And where is the money you won?"

"It is all gone."

"Why?"

"They took it from me," he said when he came back to Our Father. "They just took my money, I could not win."

"Just as I told you, what do you want from them, don't mix with them, don't look at them so that they stay away, so they stay there," said Our Father.

But he did not listen.

"Ah, but no, Pap, I will win money from them. For they have money with them and I will be able to get it from them. So give me more money, perhaps you should give me a *tuxtun*. Give me the money, and I will go. Surely I will win, it was only because I used up my money that I had to stop," said he.

"Oh, but you make me lose my patience, man, you'll never win, man. You just give them the money as though it were a gift."

"Oh, no, no, I will win, this will make my desire pass."

"All right, here you are." He gave him one tuxtun. The same thing happened again: he again went on Sunday. He joined them to spend his money. He didn't win anything. Among themselves they won all his money, as though he had distributed the tuxtun.

"Tss, too bad!"

"It's nothing, I don't care."

"But we will give you your money, if you tell us where he is, if you show us where he lives, the person who does the work. Just tell us since you are not the one who does it. You are only hired to sell," they said.

"Ah, no, man, no. I am the one who does it." But he got tired of being asked questions by them and he told them, too bad.

"But you better show us, we will give you money."

"All right, give me my money, then I will tell."

And who knows how much money they gave him. Too bad.

"Well, here is how it can be done, because he takes his lunch at noon and I am the one who brings in his meal. I am the one to carry his meal. You just watch where it is that I go." If we point with our lips, it is bad manners toward the person who is there. If we point at him with our mouth, it's bad for him because we betray his image. This is what the man did.

"I will only show you the place. I will show it with my mouth," said he.

"All right."

And they followed him, they sniffed his footsteps as do some dogs. They were stopping over his footprints. They met at noon for the lunch. They were there on guard.

But he was different, he was a God, Our Father—no one could defeat him. He already knew about it. He knew what it was they were doing and what they had said to the man. So when the man entered with his food he was not in his place at the table. "Where is he who belongs on this seat? He is not at his place."

As there was a window just like this, he just left through the window. They joined a group as do the soldiers of the "commission." With a group they entered and when they got there no one was there. Our Father had left quickly, he ran off, he hurried along.

But they followed him. They went, they chased after to catch him. He was chased by them, being tracked as dogs do. His track was followed wherever he passed, wherever he went, wherever the sun set. Our Father suffered great torment for us, only for us; not anything else, but only for us. He fled to every place wherever there was a place.

Well, it is bad if we lie about the errands. If there is some errand you are going to do, or work you are going to get; if one of your younger brothers or sisters asks, "Where are you going?"

"I am going to get some wood," you answer, if it is really wood that you are fetching. But if you are going to your maizefield: "I am going to my maizefield." Truthful should your word be about what you are doing, and thus it is good. But if, on the other hand, we hide our word about the work that we are going to do or answer, "I am only going there," then it is not good. Only because of our words do we hide the truth and thus we "take away its face." We betray the truth. This is what a person of old times did, he must have been a *meal k'aol,* I suppose.

Surely towns had appeared, so Our Father passed near someone who was sowing his field. He did not know that it was the Kub'aal who passed near him because sometimes he looks like a Chiquimula [non-Ixil Indian], other times he looks like us, and other times he looks like a ladino. He just changed his appearance every day. So he passed there where the man was sowing his maizefield.

"What are you sowing, friend?" said the Kub'aal.

"Ah, only some stones, Pap, I am sowing some stones," he said.

"Ah, thank you, it is all right. When some men come by here they may ask you whether you saw a man pass by. Tell them, 'Oh yes, he passed by but it was long ago that he passed because I was sowing the stones when he passed. Very small was the size of my stones then.' "

That is why the milpa [maizefield] did not grow any more. The stones had become cliffs and rocks as large as mountains and houses. Huge mountains sprang up from the ground because of what the man had said, "stones," and at once a magical blessing was bestowed on the stones. Thus the stones were created, because it was left blessed by Our Father. For it was indeed Our Father who brought the strength to the world with the mountains at the very beginning of the world.

"Didn't a man come by here?" said one of the gods to the man.

"He did pass by, but when he passed I was sowing stones. But small was the size of the mountains when he passed," said the man to them, because there were big cliffs there.

"Jodido, man, what can we do, where did he go? Let's go, let's see if we can find him."

They left, they followed after him, he was hunted by them. When he spoke, right away the thing was grown in a single day whenever the people sowed anything, immediately the maizefield ripened, instantly ripened the stones. He magically blessed the seed. It was not difficult to do because it was the way of a god surely, to give the blessing.

And in one story, he passed near another man, he passed again near a man who was good because he spoke the truth. Therefore, when he came by the same thing happened. The man was sowing his field, too. He sowed beans and he sowed squash when [Our Father] arrived.

"What are you sowing?" asked Our Father of the man.

"Ah, I am sowing my cornfield, Pap, a few squash here, a few beans there. That's all I'm doing," said the man. He spoke the truth.

"All right, very well, my son, you have respect for me. Soon some men will pass who are chasing me, soon they will pass. Tell them when they come inquiring about me, 'It was when I was sowing my cornfield, I think, and now it has already dried and here am I, already harvesting what I sowed when the man passed; but long ago; much time has passed since; it was at the time I was planting, already I am harvesting,' you must say," said our Father.

And sure enough, they came by and the same thing happened. The maizefield was already dry. Lots of beans were dried already, beans and squash. Really fat were the squashes under the maize that he had sowed. And so they appeared.

"Have you seen a man pass by here?"

"He passed, but it was when I was sowing my cornfield when he passed, while I was sowing my cornfield, and look at the field, it is dry already, I am already harvesting it," answered the man.

So they said, "Let's go, let's see," they said, and again left.

Great was the trouble our Father suffered, he wandered all over the world. He came and went on. He came to another man who had two little lambs and five mother sheep that he was guarding, tending in the meadow when our Father passed by.

"Well, then, friend, wouldn't you like to give me for a present one of your small animals? It will help me if you take its meat and eat the meat because only its intestines will be useful to me."

"All right. It is all right, Pap, take yours," he said. He must have been very kind. "Choose one for yourself, then whichever one you select I will give you."

"Thank you."

He caught one of the lambs and took out the intestines and piled them up on the ground. "Soon some men will pass by here. The reason they cannot catch me is that their intestines fill up their stomachs too much. They cannot walk because of it. They cannot climb the mountains because those things are too much. It would be better if they would take them out because then they will immediately be able to travel as I do because I don't have intestines," he told the man.

But it was the intestines of the lamb that he had taken out. "When they appear, when they show up and ask you, 'Was there not a man who passed by here?' tell them, 'He passed but I had only five mother sheep with one lamb when he passed and look at all my animals now—who knows how much time has passed since he came by, I can't count it, because I can't remember what day it was that he passed through.'"

How many were the sheep which were standing there? Perhaps it was a thousand which crowded the meadow very much because they were fat sheep, they were pressing against each other.

"As to me, I am just traveling down the road," said he. "Tell them, and see what they will do."

"All right."

Sure enough, they appeared, and the man repeated Kub'aal's words to them: "Why can't they catch up with me, I wait for them and they can't find me. They'd better take out their intestines, because their intestines fill their bodies too much. It would be better if they took them out and left them near mine so that they can catch me soon," he said, so the man spoke, "and that is his tripe over there," said the man to the men. It was the tripe of the lamb, because he had finished his magic words.

"Friends, that is so, perhaps it's true. We can't travel with the water in our stomachs—let's take ours out." Whoever of the men who followed the advice, who obeyed the order (who knows how many of them there were who took theirs out) died immediately, but one of the men suddenly grew afraid and said, "No, what you are doing to yourselves is of no avail. We'll see whether you come out better for it!" And sure enough who knows how many men took theirs out and died. They did not live, and on dying their blood streamed out and from it there appeared trees, trees with a milky sap called yab'c'a. That is it, that is the blood of those men there, the trees, the milky trees, that is their blood, the yab'c'a, or witchcraft trees.

[Listener, Maria, asks]: *Do you mean the milky trees from which we get skin eruptions?*

Yes, that is why, and the tree is not a good tree, we must not touch the tree, it is taboo. That is their blood, so they say. Also, there are thorns which some trees like the yab'c'a have. The branches are clustered at its base. It has many thorns so that it is not possible for us to touch the tree.

So the others left again, they went on . . . surely he was resting, surely he went ahead of the men. He was able to keep away from them. They never caught him because it was his power, because he was the God, Kub'aal. And so they went and they never could overpower him. Never did they win over him. That wasn't the reason that it happened, that the whole thing came to an end.

What happened was that he went everywhere, he passed by everyplace, and he got bored from walking so much. He got tired of walking: "Oh well, I am tired, I got tired." He met some ʔaanhel, who belong to God, who answer to him who is God. They are the ones he met, with the god of the winds: "Why not wait, rest a little bit, wait! When they come we will overpower them. You better wait and give them to us," said the gods to Kub'aal. "Give them to us," said the ʔaanhel. "Ah, but it's a little good and a little bad that their blood flows, because it is useless. I'd rather they take out my blood, because if my blood doesn't flow, then there won't be any food left for the daughters, there won't be any drink left for the sons' drink. So I am the one whose blood should flow.

"It might be asked what will become of it? Well, it shouldn't be theirs that appears. Because if it is the evil men's blood which flows it is very dangerous. There will be no strength for the day, no strength for the dawn; no daughter, no sons will eat. So it's better they won't die, never mind, may they get over their desire for me," said the Kub'aal. And he was caught. They arrived, those who were behind him. They caught him. But there came the god, Santiago, together with St. Michael with the Sword, and they drew their swords, with great haste [terrible noise] they arrived. What anger they felt, and therefore many people got killed. Many people got destroyed, many were lost.

"Ah, never mind, never mind, stop it! Don't punish them! Don't kill them, because it is a sin. Never mind, I'd rather give myself up to them, let them catch me!" His strength had ebbed. He was tired of walking. They caught him. They looked for a house for him. It was the house of his burial at the Calvario. It is where they went to bury him. When they had caught him, they made a cross.

So that is how the dangerous days came about, so began the days of taboo.

Who knows how many years ago that it happened, that the good Fridays began. Who knows, perhaps thirty-six years after the quarrel began and he was hunted by them, continually hunted. When they found him, no matter what they did, he would escape again, and they kept on chasing him. After they finally captured him, the fight was over. Finished was, as I said, his patience. They put him into prison. Four men, the ones who are in the book (but if only we could read) guarded him. "We will guard him." And they put him into prison. Then they watched, they sat down . . . And that is when the headaches appeared, and the eye diseases appeared. All the sickness which began was caused by them. Perhaps we cannot sleep, perhaps we seem to get sick. Some of us have a headache, some of us get sick eyes. Some of us have earaches. Some of us have sick stomachs. So that is why the sicknesses appeared. And they almost did not win because he made the men get sick. At midnight they became really sick. They were awake, then at 3 or 4 in the morning slowly their sickness subsided, their sickness stopped, they became sleepy and fell asleep. When the morning came god Kub'aal was not there anymore, he had fled again. They awoke, he was not there. It was great trouble which god Kub'aal suffered a long time ago for us when the eyes of the world appeared. So it was, so it happened, and there was still more . . . and when it stopped, god Kub'aal surrendered, they killed him. They did everything to him, just as it is done to the people here who commit treason, that is what they did to him, and his strength weakened. They caught him, they captured him. They put him in prison. They did everything to him. But it was our fault, because of us, it was not anyone else's fault but only because we appeared on earth, that they become envious of him. Only for us it was that god Kub'aal got hurt and suffered pain.

But fortunate was god Kub'aal, because he died only for three days. And if he had not died we would not die either. What he taught us was how to die; because if we would not die the world would not suffice for us. Therefore we die, there are dead people every day. So death does not exist for nothing, it has a reason. Because when we die we don't multiply anymore. There is arrival, there is departure; arrival and departure. If we would never die then there wouldn't be enough space for us and we would kill each other or there wouldn't be any food. But he was fortunate because it was only three days that he was dead, and then his soul returned. Only three days did he die, and that is what happened when he died: they went to bury him, but they only said so. But they did not really bury him because he was still alive. So they burned him. They did everything to him. They put firewood, they started the fire on him. How loud it crackled when those—don't you know those weeds which are tangled up—*c'ini* is what we call them . . .

Not those, Pap, that have a flower on them which we use?

It grows together with it, but it is white, it is only used as mere decoration, but it looks just like its leaf. But it's green, it grows in the brooks, it grows at the riversides, it appears at the rivers' edges. Well, that is the one which god Kub'aal created surely.

Great was the crackling noise of those bushes. But it really was not he who was burning. He had already fled from under the fire, from under those bushes which were left behind, and they were the ones which kept crackling loudly. "Ah, he is already exploding, friends," they said. It was only the bushes which were left to burn, and he had already gone. Where god Kub'aal had been, he was not anymore. They looked for him, and all there was were some bushes the roots of which were scattered around in the fire. It was real trouble he went through. "Papa, never mind, may they kill me": He had his father, of course. To be sure, there is god Kub'aal, and there is another god Kub'aal, whose son is god Kub'aal.

So, "Never mind, Papa, I may as well die—three days I'll be dead, never mind, let them go through with it, may they finish it, may they remain in this place," he said. He had entered the prison and they talked, I suppose, as those of us do who have to go to prison. And one of our friends arrives at the prison and we ask questions about what he, our visitor, knows about the prison. That is how it must have been with him, and the words got to him in the prison. "Never mind, that I die—never mind, whether they lose interest—or stay here, I am not interested in them," he said, while he was secretly planning what to do. And he died, but he was not really dead. He was alive, of course. He was there in heaven.

He just left behind the knowledge of death for us. It is for that reason that we die, because he taught us death. After he had met his end, as they all said, as they all thought (while he was really alive), the god Kub'aal . . . God Kub'aal, the "Eternal Father," who is the lord of the world, said: "Well then, my sons, well then, never mind," he said, "your younger brother is killed. Well then, never mind, let it be."

[But before his death] it seems that they created the rum: it did not appear by itself but it appeared because they made it appear. They did not fetch it from anywhere else. It was their own urine. They poured it into a glass and wished that god Kub'aal would lose his mind, that he would not have power so that they would be able to overpower him, so they thought. Those men were the ones who came to him, and brought it to him. "Drink some rum," they said. "Drink a little rum. Revive yourself."

"Thank you, thank you, thank you, if you would be so kind and give me a little, good," said god Kub'aal. Of course, since he is God, he uttered a blessing for the rum, and the rum turned into pure wine. So great was its sweetness that one could not call it either rum or alcohol, so different was the alcohol. Because he had blessed it, it was pure wine.

After he had drunk the alcohol, well, he was stronger. Even more strength came to him. Instead of having fewer ideas he was stronger.

The ones who created the alcohol, who made it appear, were transported to their home again, the place where they always go.

After they had left, after the day had passed that Kub'aal died before them, as they thought, and therefore had gone, Kub'aal [the Eternal Father] said: "Well, well, my sons, how worthless is the earth here, it's just not good here. There are many trees and many stones, you walk with difficulty up and down the hills. You get hurt by the rocks because the rocks will fall on you and hurt you. So it's bad that there are mountains. But there is a place, a town, which I will show you, that is much better. It is very flat."

Was god Kub'aal the speaker of this?

Yes, it was god Kub'aal, the "Eternal Father" as I said, but as to god Kub'aal, he was guarded because he was sick. He was sick because of being killed by them, he had been wounded by them, so he was sick and he was kept [in seclusion]. He was not visible, not to them. But it was god Kub'aal's father, the Q'esla Kub'aal most surely, who said the words. He was the one who found the town for them.

"You will see, you will understand that there is another place, another town which is much better, without mountains, without valleys, which is better, which is much flatter," he told them.

"Well, perhaps it is true, friends, since it is his magic, so it's all right, let's go and see, let's go by and visit," said they.

A marimba was called. The marimba began playing, the big drums came in, everything, whatever there was, the rum which had appeared. Their

rum was in a jug, a huge fat jug of the old days. And they had their help-
ers, since they were gods, they had their pourers for the rum, just for that,
just like in the church. Just as it is done with the church where the doors
are opened, the windows are opened, for one to enter. And good was the
fiesta, good was the music, good was the dancing, whatever there was,
when surely he [Q'esla Kub'aal] was serving that rum. "Drink your rum,
drink your rum, don't be sad, since it is such a gay place," he said.

"Yes," they said. "Drink your rum, drink your rum." They greeted each
other with the rum. They came as they are gods, to their place in a short
time, they opened the door. They went through it and began to drink.
They began to get drunk, they ended up falling down. They got drunk,
and some fought with each other, while already the door had been closed
again. So they stayed for good.

When is it that they touch their mouth, when is it that their faces are
seen? That is what happened, and the fiesta was over. It is, as I say, only
for three days that the windows are opened a little bit. It surely exists, who
knows where? We don't know where it happened, where it was. We only
hear the story.

The windows are opened just a little when the tabooed days arrive.
Three days, only for three days the rays of the sun enter a little at their
place and they can see, surely, and as they see each other, they begin to
quarrel, they begin to fight. There is no daylight where they are, there is
neither wood nor fire, nothing is there, nothing, there is absolutely nothing. Ah, but cold is that place! The sunlight never reaches inside. They
have only their lights on, just as if this light [pointing to the light bulb]
were on all day. Only in that way is it illuminated. Nor will they ever see a
little fire, because they committed the crime. That is how the fiesta ended.
When the fiesta ended the [ceremony of the] sacrament was celebrated.
"Now is when god Kub'aal goes up to heaven," people said.

During the sacrament?

During the sacrament; because he walked around after he got well. He
came to visit each town again. He passed through every place. He passed
by and gave advice. He came to give away little gifts. He passed to give
some advice how to do our work: which is the way we can work, how we
can eat, how we can find our money; he left the knowledge of our ceremony, but with the people on the other side of the ocean because that is
true that knowledge was left with them.

That is the reason they made the metal tools, for instance. Who was it
who made them, who was it who discovered those things? Never could a
person discover it who lives on this side of the ocean. Nobody could invent them. Rather it is only from the other side of the ocean that they
came from. Those people did not live in the water, but surely just like our
creation, so was the creation of their towns. All the towns appeared at the
same time. And so appeared the ladinos, and whatever other people appeared. Because there is only one mother, only one father, only one creator on earth. But it is only our language that got changed. Because if our

words would be understood we would fight. Because if there is some person who derides us it enters into our head and we hear it. "What did I do to you that you deride me?" And even if it were another town, the fight would start. "Why is it that you mistreat me?" we say. God had foresight because our languages are not the same as theirs. So there is only one Kub'aal, only one creator for us on earth, only one who feeds us. But the only reason we each have our language is that for only one of our languages to remain would be bad, because we would kill each other. This is what god Kub'aal said when he made his plans a long time ago.

With good reason, because when they drink whiskey, then they fight.

Already we behave badly, already we start fighting because so it was from the very beginning of the world, as I say. It was he himself who gave the blessing amongst them who were created first: "They will remain who love me at the moment of light, at the break of dawn." Because whatever bit of sickness there is, whoever it is who caused the trouble, then it is with this, when it is given to them, that they shall lower their heads about it. The one who forgives, the one who finishes the day, the one who starts the day, he is the one who gave his blessing to the liquor. And therefore, whatever is your fault you should offer a small bottle and say, "Please, comrade, forgive my sins, for a little mouthful here." And after he has drunk a small glass it is all over and he has forgiven.

Yes.

Yes, so it is, so it began and so it remained with the liquor. Hm. That is all of it, young girl.

That is all?

That is all, that is all.

Thank you very much, Sir.

You are welcome.

SYNOPSIS OF THE Č'IʔLA NAQ MYTH

An initial statement about how Kub'aal (Our Father) made his older brothers envious when he created the world, which is how the fight all began.

At first man was just mud.

Then Our Father and his brothers decided to create "the children" (mankind).

The brothers try first and fail.

Their results turn into snakes and frogs.

Then they ask Our Father to try and see who among them can win.

Our Father succeeds in creating a young girl who can talk.

The brothers fall over backward in astonishment and defeat.

Then they try to kill Our Father.

Kub'aal flees and goes to San Antonio.

He works there as a shepherd, making bags and other items.

San Simon sells Our Father's products in the market.

San Simon has instructions not to give away the hiding place of Our Father.

The Č 'iʔla Naq (older brothers) see San Simon in the market and ask questions of him about Our Father.

San Simon does not give away Our Father's hiding place.

The Č 'iʔla Naq try to bribe him, but without success.

Then they get him interested in gambling with them.

When he is back with Our Father, San Simon asks him for money to gamble with.

Our Father at first refuses and advises him against gambling, but eventually gives him the money.

Back at the market, San Simon gambles with the Č 'iʔla Naq.

He loses but still keeps from giving away Our Father's hiding place.

Again he asks Our Father for money, again Our Father at first advises him against it but finally gives him the money.

He gambles and again loses.

The Č 'iʔla Naq bribe him with money.

Simon takes the money and informs them about Kub'aal and his habit of taking a noon lunch which Simon serves to him.

Simon tells the Č 'iʔla Naq to watch him and see who he points to with his lips.

The Č 'iʔla Naq follow Simon back to where Kub'aal is.

But Kub'aal flees, escaping out of the window.

The Č 'iʔla Naq arrive to find an empty place.

They chase after Kub'aal.

Kub'aal passes a man in a maizefield.

Kub'aal asks the man what he is sowing.

The man answers, stones.

Kub'aal gives the man instructions about how to answer if the Č 'iʔla Naq come by and ask him about Kub'aal.

Kub'aal makes the stones grow quickly into large boulders and mountains.

The Č 'iʔla Naq come by and ask the farmer if he saw Kub'aal.

The farmer replies as instructed, that yes, but it was when he was first sowing the stones.

The Č 'iʔla Naq, thinking that such large boulders and mountains took some time to grow, are deceived into thinking that Kub'aal had passed by a long time earlier rather than just the previous day.

Again Kub'aal comes to a farmer; this time he is sowing beans and squash with the maize.

Again as before, Kub'aal instructs the farmer how to reply when the Č 'iʔla Naq come by.

He then magically causes the maizefield with its squash and beans to mature instantly.

The older brothers come by, ask the farmer, and are told that Kub'aal had come by, but when he was sowing his crops.

Again the Č̓ 'i^ʔla Naq are deceived.

Again Kub'aal escapes.

The next time, Kub'aal comes to a shepherd tending sheep.

He asks the shepherd to give him one, to take out the intestines and leave them there.

He instructs the shepherd to tell the Č̓ 'i^ʔla Naq that the intestines belonged to Kub'aal, that he took them out to lighten himself and travel faster.

Kub'aal then multiplies the sheep so that the entire meadow is full.

The Č̓ 'i^ʔla Naq come by and are told by the shepherd what Kub'aal instructed him to say.

Some of the Č̓ 'i^ʔla Naq are deceived and try to take out their own intestines.

As a result they die.

They turn into thorn trees with milky sap (representing their blood), which are associated with witchcraft and are taboo to the Ixil.

Kub'aal again escapes, but the remaining brothers continue the pursuit.

Kub'aal meets the wind god and other gods who want to help him and get rid of the older brothers.

Kub'aal does not want them to. He would rather be killed so that the children can live. It is better that his blood be shed than that of his older brothers, because the blood of his older brothers will not sustain the earth for the children.

Nevertheless, there is a fight and many people get killed.

Kub'aal tires of it all and gives himself up.

He is put into prison with four guards.

As a result of the imprisonment, sickness comes into the world.

Then Kub'aal is put to death; he is dead for three days.

With his death, death comes into the world. The children become mortal. A benefit of death is that the world does not become overpopulated.

When they go to bury Kub'aal they find that he is alive. So they try to burn him. However, Kub'aal flees.

The Č̓ 'i^ʔla Naq create rum from their urine.

They wish that the rum will make Kub'aal lose his mind and power.

They give him the rum.

Kub'aal turns the rum into sweet wine.

He drinks it and becomes stronger and causes the creators of the rum to be transported back somewhere.

Then Kub'aal, the Eternal Father, tells the Č̓ 'i^ʔla Naq about another town where everything is flat, where there are no mountains and valleys. He holds a fiesta with marimba, drums, and rum. The Č̓ 'i^ʔla Naq get drunk and start fighting in the building. While they are fighting Kub'aal has the doors closed and they are imprisoned.

Three days each year the windows of the building are open to the sun and they begin to quarrel. The rest of the time the place is devoid of fire or warmth or sunlight.

Kub'aal goes to heaven.

Then he visits all the towns on earth.

He gives advice and gifts, tells them how they should live.

Kub'aal also creates the ladinos on the other side of the sea where they make metal implements and speak a different language. The reason for having different languages is to avoid quarrels.

Kub'aal also gives a blessing to the rum so that it can be offered to ask for forgiveness.

The events in this story can be represented in an analysis sheet, as shown in Appendix B. Not unexpectedly, we have postulated some new eidons (indicated by an asterisk): Loss and Victory. Since they are only single occurrences, we list them tentatively.

In looking over the higher-level categories, we see that the grammar holds, as shown in figure 5.3. Looking at the eidochronic level, we see that the order of the eidons holds and that all looping crosses higher-level boundaries; that is, there is no looping within (if there are several eidons together in the same category, they follow the correct sequence). This has been the case for the previous six stories, with the exception of the Bestowal element in "Maria Markaao."

CONCLUSION

Eidochronic analysis differs from other narrative analyses in its "bottom-up" approach (rather than a top-down imposition of some postulated story structure) and in its goal of approximating cognitive systems, particularly in the natural chunking and linking of narrative ideas, as well as testing them. It is our feeling that only Propp, among all the others, has successfully dealt with the phenomenon of narrative chunking. We do not see Propp as merely a forerunner to European structuralism, for that removes him as a rival *alternative* approach.[11] Another area of narrative analysis also concerned with scientific procedures is the work of psychologists (Rumelhart, 1975; Kintsch, 1977; Mandler and Johnson, 1977) and psychologically oriented anthropologists (Rice, 1978, 1980). The very readable and ethnographically interesting literature of symbolic anthropology, which emphasizes performance setting and "thick description" (Geertz, 1973), rarely includes distributional analyses, formal procedures, or testable models but nevertheless provides a different kind of validity through context description. Symbolic anthropology has always included the study of metaphor, for example in the work of

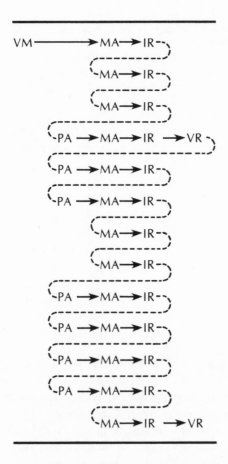

Figure 5.3. Sequencing of higher-level categories for the Č'iʔla Naq story.

Fernandez (1971). Recently the more cognitively oriented analysts in anthropology (Quinn, 1979), linguistics (Lakoff and Johnson, 1980), and psychology (Ortony, 1979) have directed their attention toward metaphor.

All these related areas of burgeoning interest tie in with what we feel is the central empirical phenomenon called eidochronic, which Propp discovered and which we have examined further in our studies of Eskimo and Ixil narrative. We hope we have demonstrated that, for a small collection of Ixil stories, it is possible to construct a cultural grammar that (1) accounts for the plot structure and content and (2) tells us something about the cultural logic the storyteller draws upon. This logic, which includes metaphoric equations, will be discussed further in Chapter 7. We suspect that very similar grammars will apply to stories told by other Ixil as well; in fact, a study of narratives told by other Ixil is likely to reveal further regularities as yet unrecognized in the stories recorded here.

At this point we make no claim to having written a definitive grammar. Strictly speaking there will never be a definitive grammar. We can only approximate a cognitive system, if for no other reason than that cognitive systems are in a continual state of flux. We would have been happier with a much larger sample of stories to analyze. A study of stories told by other Ixil will undoubtedly involve revision of our grammar and its components.

In considering our results, we find ourselves going back to Benedict in spite of all the objections to her work that we raised in our first chapter. Her main contribution was the concept of a systemic philosophy (Benedict, 1934) or, in Bateson's terms, an eidos that pervades many sectors of social life. The problem in the past has been that the mechanisms behind such observations were not determined, and much of the description was subjective and general. If Benedict's characterizations had been more genre-specific and detailed, they would probably have been less disputed.[12]

If, with the folk narratives discussed here, we are indeed close to a high-level organizing principle, will not the study of other sectors of Ixil cultural phenomena also lead to the same organizing principle? This is a question we will examine in the next chapter.

6
IXIL
DIVINATION

Different societies have different means of describing and interpreting human behavior in everyday life. Proverbs, old saws, myths, folktales, divinations, and numerous other cultural devices summarize human situations in useful ways. Such devices reduce the great complexity of human motives and circumstances to a conceptually manageable size. Interposed between individuals and their raw environment, they act as intellectual prosthetic devices, just as material artifacts enhance or amplify our physical abilities.

In divination the client uses a specialist's knowledge in order to attain a state of health or well-being or to gain needed information—the meaning of a dream or a prediction of the future. Though the actual curative power may have the characteristics of a placebo, there nonetheless is often an effect. The ritual therapy Shas talks about in his philosophy text may easily be just as effective, if not more so, than psychotherapy. Modern biological science has shown that there is no clear-cut line between placebo or psychosomatic effects and purely physical or biological ones. Immunological response is affected even at the cellular level by differential hormonal output in the brain which, in turn, is influenced by external stress and how it is coped with. Divination provides a sense of personal control that reduces the effects of stress and hence can have real curative power. Of equal importance with the curative effects of divination are the other consequences: divination and its associated beliefs regulate social relations and encapsulate a view of the social world and a moral order.

As in the previous chapters, we are interested here in learning about an active system—how it is used and what it produces—rather than in presenting a static structural account of symbolic oppositions and similarities. We will begin with a general ethnographic description of the divination process as we have learned about it from Shas and others.

Divination among the Ixil is used for determining the cause and cure of sickness, interpreting dreams, recovering lost or stolen objects, and determining times and places for ritual. Its chief element is the 260-day ritual calendar of twenty day names and thirteen numbers. Each day of the calendar is represented by a deity with special attributes, which are used in getting a divinatory reading or diagnosis. The day gods reveal the underlying cause of a sickness or misfortune to the daykeeper, and he passes this information on to the sick person.

According to Shas, each day reigns from dawn until after midnight. Usually the ceremonies for a particular day begin the previous day and continue through dawn. Thus the days are often thought of in pairs, and the special ceremonies span the change of days.[1]

According to Shas, each of the twenty days has an office corresponding to one of the positions in the civil government of Nebaj: alcalde, regidor, mayor, síndico, secretario, and policía (or comisión). Though Shas named some of the office correspondences easily, he listed others only after reflection, and some with stated uncertainty. We have no data on whether or not these offices of the days parallel the local political offices as a result of some pre-Columbian principle. If such a principle did exist, it might be of possible use in reconstructing pre-Columbian political systems from hieroglyphic texts. (After the conquest there were never four alcaldes, but at one time there were two alcaldes in the towns of Guatemala.) Shas's list (with Čoo not placed—he could not remember) is as follows:

Government offices	Names of days
Alcaldes	Noʔq, ʔliq', Čee, ʔEe
Regidores	ʔImuš, Kamel, B'aac', ʔAama, K'ač, Q'anil, Č'iʔ,C'ikin
Mayores	Tiaš, ʔAq'b'al, Kan, ʔAa

Síndico	Kaoo
(alguacil)	
Secretario	ʔ|ʔ§
Comisión	Hunaapu

Use of the ritual address for each day in prayers indicates that the days are considered deities. Some days (for example, B'aac') are considered good, others (for example, Č'iʔ) are considered bad, while still others are closer to neutral. Along with the offices are one or more attributes representing a domain of interest or aegis for each day god. The literal meaning of the day names is not always a direct representation of the attributes. B'aac', for example, means "howler money" but has no direct connection with monkeys. It is the day for marriages and for praying for wealth. C'ikin means "bird"; it is the day of praying for wealth and good fortune. (It may be of significance that figures of monkeys occur on murals and ceiling designs in Chajul and that woven bird designs appear on the blouses of women in all three dialect areas, but we were unable to elicit any direct exegesis for these symbols.) Hunaapu is associated with the household deity at the shrine of every Ixil family and the saints in the church. Q'anil is related to the growing of corn, while ʔAama represents the corn ear itself. Č'iʔ is the day on which envious persons may seek to bring supernatural displeasure upon their enemies.

These associations constitute a standard list of day-god attributes that can be reeled off by any daykeeper. Such a set of attributes does not have its elements temporally ordered except through association with the days. Instead of an eidochronic sequence, then, what we have is an *array*, a conventionalized pattern in the form of a list which may be drawn upon for some combinatorial purpose.

The numbers associated with the days relate primarily to positive, negative, or neutral valences. The numbers 9 and 13 are generally negative; when they appear with a strong day, such as an ʔAlkaalte day, the reading can result in a grave prognosis. In some cases day numbers give a quantified meaning. For example, the occurrence of the number 12 with Kamel (Death) means that the client has a long time ahead of him before his death, while a lower number would indicate less time. Again, K'ač (Transgression) has the literal meaning of "net," such as the net used for gathering maize ears during the harvest, and is conceptualized as a container for one's sins. The occurrence of a large number with K'ač means that the sin is correspondingly large.

For Shas, day numbers did not appear to represent distinct deities, as Lincoln reported for the Ixil and Thompson thought to be true of the Classic Mayans. However, Shas did link the number one to Santa Teresa "Avaquila" [Ávila?] and San Ignacio and the number seven to San Juan and San Vicente, but not in connection with divination.

There are various combinations of days and numbers that seemed to be salient for Shas. Whether this could be attributed to his own life experiences or to the way the system works we could not determine. For the record, some of the salient combinations are as follows:

For interpretations in general:

    13 Čee: envy
    4 or 8 B'aac': very good luck
    9 or 13 with one of the four ʔAlkaaltes: very bad

Good days for dreams:
    C'ikin 6 or 8 (mostly 6)
    ʔImuš
    12 Kamel
    12 Kan: good not only for dreams but for anything else
    ʔAq'b'al

Other days and numbers:
    K'ač 13, 9, and 11; envy
    ʔAlkaalte days, or 13 or 9 days, are days for paying fines
    8, 5, and 10 are generally good
    ʔAama, ʔAq'b'al, Čoo, and Č'iʔ and 5, 6, and 8 are good for Calvario (i.e., praying in the small church building on the east edge of Nebaj)

A positive number before Kan (fortune): wealth; a negative one: poverty. (However, a positive Kan in the last talking position with but a single seed: wealthy, but through stealing)

Shas usually did his divinations in his own house. On good days, such as B'aac' or ʔIʔš, or days beginning with an 8 or a 6, he might have as many as three or four clients in a single day. Sometimes, however, only three or four clients would come in a week, or a week to ten days might go by before a client appeared. People rarely came on a bad day unless the sickness was a serious one. Less frequently Shas would go to the house of the client, but this only happened once or twice a month and only with people he knew well, who were *contento* and did not have "two hearts" (hidden dislike or bad intentions). When the client came to Shas's house, he had a better chance of a good reading. When Shas took his divining material to another house, he always left some of them at home as a safeguard, and this, he believed, was why such divinations did not go as well. Moreover, the clients themselves preferred to go to the house of the daykeeper rather than have their neighbors know about it. (Such diagnostic consultations are to be differentiated from the times when Shas went with clients to perform rituals to cure sickness or to perform dawn ceremonies.)

THE READING

One can think of the diagnostic readings as being part of a larger story in which half of the motivating element is supplied by the problem that the client brings to the divination. The reading constitutes the other half, going backward from the problem, or sickness, to its cause in order to determine the solution to the problem. After the diagnostic reading has been performed, another reading is done to work out the necessary steps to placate the supernatural being who has caused the trouble. In the widest sense these two readings are not the whole story, because the outcome of the story is whether the sick person gets well or dies.[2]

When Shas was consulted by a sick client, he would lay out his divining bundle in front of the household shrine. The bundle consisted of a cloth, a handful of quartz crystals, and a number of seeds of the coral tree.[3] Usually at least two layouts of the seeds are made, the first for diagnosis and the second for deciding when the prescriptive rituals should be made. Shas would gather a handful of the seeds and lay pairs of them out in rows and columns. The number of rows would vary from one layout of the seeds to another; Shas did not know how many seeds there were in his hand as he laid them out. Similarly, the number of columns would vary (for no reason that we could determine); usually there were six, but sometimes there were as many as seven or eight.

After the seeds had been laid out, Shas would count from left to right, usually beginning with the day of the reading or the day of the onset of the sickness, and calling the names of the days and their numbers. The seed pairs in the extreme right-hand column and in the last position of the count were usually the "speaking days," although occasionally other seeds elsewhere in the layout would speak if they were especially salient days. Sometimes the last position would be a pair of seeds, sometimes a single seed.

As an example of an interpretation, we shall take a divination made on June 16, 1970, in one of a series of hypothetical cases we tried out with Shas when he was staying with us in California. This case was on the day 10 B'aac' in the Ixil calendar. We arranged the first three rows in six columns of seed pairs, and the fourth row in five columns (figure 6.1). We then asked Shas how he would interpret them.

The four speaking days are circled in the figure. The first speaking pair is ?Aama, which represents ancestral souls and female figures. Shas read this as the client's mother, who was dead. The next speaking pair is 8 ?liq', which represents male figures, the earth god, and quarrels. Shas identified this male figure as the client's father, also

10	11	12	13	1	2
B'aac'	?Ee	?Aa	?I?ş	C'ikin	?Aama

3	4	5	6	7	8
No?q	Tiaš	Kaoo	Hunaapu	?Imuš	?liq'

9	10	11	12	13	1
?Aq'b'al	K'ač	Kan	Kamel	Čee	Q'anil

2	3	4	5	6
Čoo	Č'i?	B'aac'	?Ee	?Aa

Figure 6.1. A hypothetical layout of counted divination seeds interpreted by Shas on the day 10 B'aac'.

dead, and said that these two figures once quarreled. His preliminary reading was as follows:

2 ʔAama: The dead one is among the souls.
           It is the mother of the man, the sick client.
8 ʔliqʼ: [A quarrel]. Also, the mother is with the Earth Lord because of the day ʔliqʼ.
           His father is with the Earth Lord too.
           The mother has entered prison.
1 Qʼanil: She [was angry] and fought with his father in former times.
           The speaking pair, 1 Qʼanil, is again the mother.

[At this point, we asked Shas what the father and mother had fought about. He said he didn't know. In response to further questioning, he said that the speaking pair 6 ʔAa indicated that the argument was brought to the courthouse, because one of the attributes for the day ʔAa is that of mayor (bailiff), who summons people to be brought before the ʔalkaalte. The number 6, together with the fact that the last speaking position was a pair, indicated a favorable outcome for the client if he remembered his parents with the proper ritual.]

6 ʔAa: The matter was brought to court.
           A favorable outcome (because of the number 6, and the fact that the final position consists of a pair.)

The preliminary reading represents an artificial situation in which we asked Shas explicitly to key the interpretation to individual speaking days. When asked for the whole reading again, Shas presupposed some elements of the preliminary statements, especially the quarrel, since he had already discussed them:

The son has lived well. He eats and drinks at his home. But he does not place candles or offer prayers. He does not remember his mother's soul. He just fills his stomach. "But the sickness will improve," the dead parents say, "if he honors us. If he realized that he should place a candle and offer food and drink," say the souls, "then we will let him go free. If he doesn't give us food or drink, it's better that he come and help us, because we are in prison. He'll come to help us in prison," [that is, become ill and die], say the holy souls.

It seems that Shas would have had relatively little opportunity to control (consciously or unconsciously) the actual speaking days. He was unaware of how many seeds were in his hand; the day of divination (or of the beginning of the illness) restricted the possible outcomes; and the laying out of seeds was accompanied by praying, which would have made it difficult for him to count to himself. Still another obstacle is that the seeds were read in a different order from that in which they were laid out. The seeds were usually laid out from right to left; when Shas went to count the seeds, however, he moved in the other direction: from left to right all the way across for all the columns that were complete. When he got to an incomplete row, he moved from right to left.[4]

Some control might nevertheless have been possible. The beginning day might have given some control if Shas could, previous to the layout, have calculated in his head what the speaking day would be six, seven, or eight days hence (depending on the number of columns used). The number of columns, varying from six to eight, could have provided another means of control. Since no three bad days or numbers occur in a row, possibly during the first row or two he could have consciously avoided a bad day. In fact, he might have done an entire divination in his head beforehand with sufficient practice. However, Shas strongly denied that he ever did such a thing, saying that it would be a sin to do so. Because of the unknown and varying number of seeds taken up, replanning could only be done for the first few rows.

While Shas had no control over the number of seeds, simply grasping a large handful of seeds would give a "richer" set of speaking days. Moreover, the fact that the days themselves are rich in attributes would have made combination easier, widening the pool of possibilities from which to select a good match. Finally, there were times (though rare) when speaking days appeared elsewhere than the usual end positions. We do not have sufficient data to discover any rules for unusual positions, but we would guess that interpolation has to be done in the absence of salient speaking days that could fit with the possibilities of the client's situation. This is not to suggest any dishonesty, however. To be sure, we have interviewed people who seemed real charlatans, including one Ixil, often dressed as a ladino, who would consult a little man next to his ear, invisible and inaudible to us. The little man would advise him about how much we might have to pay for his services. In the case of an honest person like Shas, however, the question is more one of how much accommodation occurs, in cases where one of several possible readings fits more closely the perceived situation. To Shas's way of thinking, divination is a communication from the gods. We would think, therefore, that if the system were to produce several different messages, the daykeeper's job would be to see which was the most appropriate to the client's situation as the daykeeper understood it. This message, then, would be considered the one intended by the supernatural forces.

Generally, the reading itself does not have much to do with the biological etiology of the sickness. However, there may be some underlying classification of disease types. Shas reported that measles, whooping cough, fever, and skin eruptions are frequently caused by the *tiiš,* while growths or tumors are caused by the Earth Lords, and fever and spasms or cramps by the ancestral souls. Finally, fright, broken bones, cuts, and fainting are caused by the *Č'iˀla Naq* (the "bad men" of the folktale), who, incidentally, never figured in the divinatory readings we collected. The chief objective is to identify the god who is causing the sickness in order to determine what kind of ritual should be done and where.

It is possible for a day to have two different meanings. For example, in one instance 8 ˀliq' (ˀAlkaalte) was read "the days are in the client's head" (that is, the client, a woman, has been chosen to be a daykeeper).[5] Later in the reading, the same day was used to designate the client's father. Sometimes a day will have a number prefix with a valence that does not fit the story being constructed. If some of the other day positions are especially salient or appropriate to the story, rather than rejecting the story the daykeeper may play down or ignore the significance of the number. It sometimes happens that the same object in the story is indicated by two different days. For example, if a fine of money is paid, Čoo (fine) and C'ikin (money) can both stand for the payment if they are both in speaking positions.

Usually the constituents of the readings are derived from the speaking days. Sometimes, however, one or more of the constituents is simply assumed. For example, a transgression or wrongdoing can sometimes be presupposed if another concept, such as revenge, is salient. For example, in a situation where the client is a woman who once rejected a suitor, and the suitor then spitefully asked the gods to make her sick, the reading may just say that an angry person has influenced the gods to punish the client.[6] The reason for the anger may then be supplied not from the speaking days but from the general presupposition that a woman typically makes the man angry by rejecting him. This idea is spelled out in a passage of Shas's philosophy text (see Chapter 4). If the woman is a devout person who performs rituals frequently, she is likely to be immune to this request to the gods that she be punished. However, if she has been neglectful of her religious duties, the rejected suitor may succeed in bringing the gods' attention to her neglect. All this may happen years after the act of rejection.

Though the gods do not require food as mortals do, they depend on rum, incense, and candle smoke for sustenance. Usually, if one can identify the being that has caused the sickness, bringing about a cure is simply a matter of burning more incense and candles, sprinkling rum, and saying the appropriate prayers. The details of the actual ritual that must be performed as a result of the diagnostic reading are determined in a second casting of the seeds.

DAY-GOD ATTRIBUTES

There are three principal tasks that a client can present for divination: (1) determining the meaning of a dream, (2) explaining the client's current situation and telling the client's fortune, and (3) diagnosing the cause of a problem, usually sickness, that the client or client's relative has. The nature of the task determines what to look for as a starting node for the story being constructed. If the divination task involves determining the cause of a problem (sickness or victimization of some kind), then the focus is usually first on the most negative speaking day. Since most divinations are for sickness, the analysis that follows will assume that the case being discussed is a sickness.

Each of the days can be described as a cluster of attributes. The attributes, in turn, can be seen as a mix of terms and predicates. The various attributes or properties of a day are sometimes thematically related to each other, but just as often they appear to be arbitrarily lumped. We suspect that, just as the most frequent verbs in many languages are the irregular ones (redundancy and other communicational requirements shape the irregularity of such terms), the seemingly arbitrary clusterings may reflect aspects of the system's usage that we do not understand.

Table 6.1 is a list of the most important attributes of the days. It

Table 6.1. List of day names with kernel meanings, participant classes, and associated events.

Day	Kernel meaning[a]	Participant class	Event or state
No?q	?Alkaalte, Earth God*	Father, grandfather (animal)	—
Tiaš	Earth God	Sinner, enemy, male envy	—
Kaoo	Earth God	—	Transgression, envy
Hunaapu	Tiiš (Sky God)	Tiiš, male	—
?Imuš	House God	House, females clothes*	Penance
?liq'	?Alkaalte, Earth God*	Father	Quarrel
?Aq'b'al	Night God	Woman	—
K'ač	Transgression	The (measured) transgression, enemy	—
Kan	Fortune	Male	—
Kamel	Death	Departed relative	—
Čee	?Alkaalte	Father	—
Q'anil	Maizefield	Female, maize	—
Čoo	Fine	The fine, enemy	Anger
Č'i?	Anger	Evil deed, enemy	Anger
B'aac'	Wealth	Person, female	Economic success
?Ee	?Alkaalte	Enemy, male	—
?Aa	Youth	Young person, object	Youth
?I?š	Scribe	Person	—
C'ikin	Money	Money, livestock female	—
?Aama	Soul; Harvest	Female, soul, maize	—

a. Asterisk indicates items of lower frequency or secondary importance.

represents a composite of texts, interviews, and readings that Shas has given us. There are three types of attributes, some overlapping: the *kernel meaning* concerns the most salient attribute of the day god—the day god's office, classification, or aegis; the *participant class* includes both the objects and the human (living or dead) participants in the reading; the *event or state* concerns the state of transgression, a response of anger to it, or a positive state, such as economic success.

To get a reading, one takes an attribute from each day cluster and strings them together to make a story. Each attribute can figure in many possible stories and thus could relate to many possible schemata in memory. Two main constraints, however, limit the possibilities. The first constraint concerns the other days in the layout: if we have days A, B, and C, each with five attributes, some of these attributes will not fit in any logical way with the others and must be excluded. The second constraint is the real-world situation: the final reading obviously has to match the real world if it is to be taken seriously. The fact that some possible readings would not match the real world did not, we think, bother Shas, who sincerely believed in the efficacy of what he did. His task was to find which of several possible readings was the true intention of the supernatural forces at work. The mental representation had to mesh with what he imagined the client's situation to be. These mental representations were not, of course, directly accessible to the outside observer. Though Shas described the attributes of the day gods for us, we do not know how he encoded his observations of the client's situation. We can infer the imagined client situation to be either isomorphic to the day-god attributes or directly related to it through some transduced cognitive coding. The constraints are thus in the form of matchings. We use the total set of all attributes of the twenty days as an inventory of the client-situation characteristics.

Certain aspects of the reading, as we have seen, may derive from a filling in of items other than the day-god attributes simply because they are part of "the way the world is." This component, which is not specific to divination but underlies all thinking, we call the presuppositional component. If we generate divinations on the basis of the three divination-specific components—day-god attributes, client-situation characteristics, and rules—the remaining part that has to be filled in is, by definition, the underlying presuppositional component. But this last component is by no means an insignificant, residual category. The kernel meanings, participant-class meanings, and events or states for the twenty days are just the tip of the iceberg; the presuppositional component is the part that lies underneath. It is an entire epistemology of the natural and supernatural world, the attitudes of gods and people, and the typical behaviors of each. There is also a deontology of obligations and mores. The divinatory system thus taps into the very core of Ixil cultural beliefs and values and involves the most salient and typical preoccupations of the people. A large part of this presuppositional component has been made explicit and conventionalized for us in Shas's philosophy text.

TOWARD A SPECIAL THEORY OF SHAS'S DIVINATION

We are ready to suggest a cultural grammar of Shas's divination readings and a modular decision model that ties in with it. Both the grammar and the decision modules are approximations that have been tested against our data, but the modules have required the postulation of cognitive elements that are neither explicit in the data nor derived from some analytical procedure. These postulated cognitive elements could probably be elicited through special interviewing or through some task of symbol arrangement. Unfortunately, we cannot do this with Shas. Nor is the task readily done through observation; it would require being with the daykeeper during consultations and taping not only the divination itself, but also the conversations with the client before and after the ritual. Questions would have to be asked concerning what the daykeeper knew about the client beforehand. In addition, the daykeeper should provide a "stream of consciousness" account of his thinking during the process. Needless to say, only a very unusual daykeeper would be willing, or able, to do that. Yet there are enough daykeepers still active among the Ixil for such a study, and the grammar and model we give here will perhaps provide some guidance for it. Thus the decision modules may help to get the job done, but—as with similar postulations in artificial intelligence—they need to be further shaped or modified by empirical findings.

Other clues may come from archaeological and ethnohistorical data. Ixil divination is not as complex as that which is depicted in the ancient Mayan codices, which presumably are explicit chartings of the kinds of attributes displayed in our tables and frames. However, we suspect that in broad outline they are the same.

The Client Situation

Before the divination ritual itself takes place, there is a discussion between the daykeeper and the client or the client's representative. Sometimes the person who talks with Shas does so on behalf of a wife or child or some other person. If the sick person and the talker are different people, we shall designate the sick person rather than the talker as the client. The talker explains the nature of the problem and the daykeeper inquires into various details—when the sickness first began and so on.

It is during this time that the client's situation is first assessed. We suggest that in the absence of any particular information (which is probably never the case) there is a general, stereotyped idea in the mind of the daykeeper of what the client's situation is likely to be, what the possibilities in the client's history are. In artificial intelligence work these would be called "default" attributes. These possibilities are eliminated or made more likely as the daykeeper receives more information. The general attributes of the client situation stereotype are listed below:

Has spouse
Had a past of changing relationships in courtship or previous marriages
Has children
Has other relatives living and dead
House contains a shrine for ritual
Is in an average economic position
If man: is a maize farmer
If woman: works in the house

For the decision module we postulate a set of standing and occasional attributes that can modify the stereotype, together with likely problems that are associated with each of the attributes (table 6.2).

Added to this Attribute-Problem Linkage List is a set of salience rules ("Client Situation Salience Rules") that assign numerical salience values to the problem areas associated with the attributes:

1. Assign a salience value to each problem associated with an attribute of the client. The salience value is determined by the linkage of the problem to an attribute as follows:
   a. Each ascriptive attribute problem: 1
   b. Each circumstantial attribute problem: 3
   c. Each occasional attribute problem: 2
2. Aggregate all the problems in a list. If a problem is linked to more than one attribute, it is listed only once but the salience weight is incremented for each attribute link according to the values indicated in rule 1.
3. Arrange all problems linked to the client attributes in a Problem Salience List in order of descending salience.

Table 6.2. Attribute-problem linkage list.

Attributes	Associated problems
Standing attributes	
Ascriptive	
Adult	Adultery, neglect of ritual, quarreled, broke an engagement, abandoned spouse, target of envy, stole, sold inheritance
Man	Neglect of maize ritual observations, failure to support family
Woman	Neglect of household duties, spurned a suitor
Child	Quarreling or transgressing parents (with the above associated problems of adults)
Circumstantial	
Alcoholic	Alcoholism, failure of support, loss of wealth, can't get a spouse
Quarrelsome	Quarreled, can't get a spouse
Rich	Target of wealth envy, neglect of ritual
Poor	Stole, neglect of ritual, failure to support family
Occasional attributes	
Got married	Jealous in-laws or former lovers, target of love envy
Got divorced or separated	Angry former spouse, quarreled, alcoholic
Rejected suitor or broke an engagement	Angry suitor or fiancé
Built a house	Cut trees without proper ritual
Sold property	Sold inheritance

The salience rules act on the client situation information to bring out an ordered list of plausible or likely causes of the sickness. The use of a salience index and list represents what we think of as a cognitive foregrounding, where the more likely causes have a higher degree of neural excitation. A ranking of possibilities approximates what we think actually happens in the mind of the diviner just prior to carrying out the ritual. An example of how to arrive at such an ordered list is shown in table 6.3.

The Grammar

At this point Shas performs the divination ritual and arrives at a set of talking positions. This is where the grammar comes in, for the

Table 6.3. Application of the salience rules to the client situation attributes and their associated problems.

Client: A separated woman who is known to be quarrelsome

Application of Client Situation Salience Rule 1 results in a salience value or weight for each problem associated with an attribute of the client:

Adult:	adultery	1
	neglected ritual	1
	quarreled	1
	target of envy	1
	stole	1
	sold inheritance	1
	broke engagement	1
	abandoned spouse	1
Woman:	neglected household duties	1
	spurned suitor	1
Quarrelsome:	quarreled	3
	can't get a spouse	3
Separated:	angry former spouse	2
	quarreled	2
	alcoholic	2

Application of Client Situation Salience Rule 2 aggregates the above:

adultery	1
neglected ritual	1
quarreled	$1 + 3 + 2 = 6$
target of envy	1
stole	1
sold inheritance	1
broke engagement	1
abandoned spouse	1
neglected household duties	1
spurned suitor	1
can't get a spouse	3
angry former spouse	2
alcoholic	2

Application of Client Situation Salience Rule 3 results in a Problem Salience List:

quarreled	6
can't get a spouse	3
alcoholic	2
angry former spouse	2
adultery	1
neglected ritual	1
target of envy	1
stole	1
sold inheritance	1
broke engagement	1
abandoned spouse	1
neglected household duties	1

reading follows the conceptual syntax of the grammar. Yet the actual construction of the reading does not follow a fixed sequence; the construction may begin with Punishment, or it may begin with Transgression. In any event, the final conceptual syntax will be something like the following: A transgression or problem of the client causes some supernatural being to punish him by causing sickness. An optional element is that the transgression causes an injured or offended person to communicate with the punishing being about the transgression. This three-eidon sequence is shown in figure 6.2, along with reading paths containing three decision modules for the choice of the actual eidon varieties.

The Decision Modules

In the actual divination process it is unlikely that a fixed path is followed. Thus unlike decision trees and flow charts, which follow path alternatives in a given sequence, the three decision modules for divination (figure 6.2) can be "entered" in any order. The organization of the end product is provided by the divination grammar. The decision of which module to enter first is determined externally by the salience of likely problems (the Problem Salience List) and the salience of the speaking days.

Highly salient talking positions can bring out some particular element first, and then the remainder of the reading process is a matter of building around that element. Or it may be that some outstanding element of the client's situation is highlighted so that the link to some particular talking position, however inconspicuous, is the one that is taken first. This is where the grammar comes in. The expansion of the three main elements, Transgression, Communication, and Punishment, need not follow any particular order. It is the highlighted element that catches the daykeeper's eye and provides the point of departure.

Let us assume that a variety of the Transgression category has been highlighted, so we shall begin with that. There is one frame for each transgression variety. The decision model indicates what particular variety, and hence frame, to choose as follows:

Take the talking positions and examine the kernel meanings that are associated with them in table 6.1. All those kernel meanings that are transgression varieties are held as candidates. In addition, those

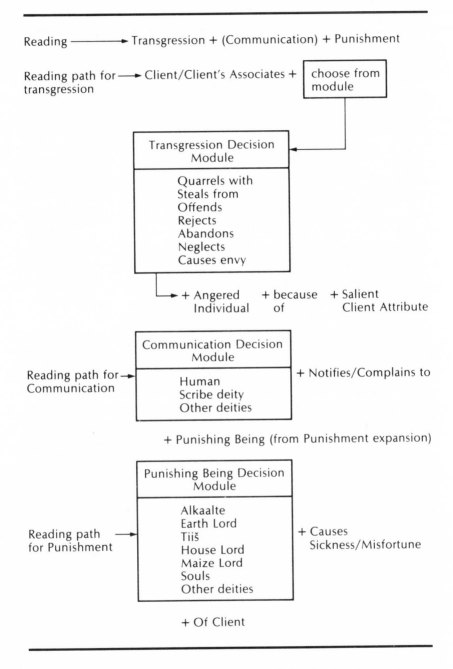

Reading ⟶ Transgression + (Communication) + Punishment

Reading path for ⟶ Client/Client's Associates + choose from
transgression module

Transgression Decision Module
Quarrels with
Steals from
Offends
Rejects
Abandons
Neglects
Causes envy

⟶ + Angered   + because   + Salient
Individual   of   Client Attribute

Communication Decision Module
Human
Scribe deity
Other deities

Reading path for ⟶
Communication

+ Notifies/Complains to

+ Punishing Being (from Punishment expansion)

Punishing Being Decision Module
Alkaalte
Earth Lord
Tiiš
House Lord
Maize Lord
Souls
Other deities

Reading path ⟶
for Punishment

+ Causes
Sickness/Misfortune

+ Of Client

Figure 6.2. Reading paths and decision modules for the three primary eidons of a divinatory reading.

days without transgression varieties as kernel meanings are then matched with the being in table 6.4 (on page 246) to get the associated transgression varieties there. If the kernel meaning is not a being listed in table 6.4, get the participant class in table 6.1 for that day (either living human or departed ancestral soul) and go to the being of table 6.4 for the transgression variety.

Each transgression variety candidate from this combined group is then assigned a Talking Position Salience Value according to the rules below:

1. Assign all talking positions (and the transgression varieties associated with them) an initial salience value of 1.
2. Add to the initial value any additional amounts that accrue from the following attributes of the talking day:
   Number prefixes
      6, 8, 9, or 13:   add 2
      4, 12, 5, or 11:   add 1
   Kernel meanings
      ʔAlkaalte: add 2
      Earth Lord, Tiiš, Soul,
      Death, Anger, Transgression,
      Fine, Wealth, or Money: add 1

The talking position transgression varieties are then matched with the transgression varieties in the Problem Salience List, and the two salience values for each matching pair are combined. The transgression variety with the highest combined salience value is then chosen as the predicate.

Once the predicate has been determined it is necessary to obtain the associated terms, which we refer to as participants. The first participant term is the *actor*, the transgressor or injuring person. The actor for this predicate must be human. Usually the actor is the client or sick person (sometimes, when the client is a child or wife, the head of the household may request the divination on his or her behalf). Sometimes, however, the actor may be a relative: the client may be sick because one of his parents was the transgressing person. Since the transgression always happened sometime prior to the divination, it is possible that the relative did some injury and later died. The actor, therefore, must be human, but he may be either living or dead.

The next participant is the *injured party*. This can be either another human, relative or nonrelative, or a supernatural being.

The Stealing variety of Injury takes a third term, namely, the *object stolen*, whether animals, money, or clothes. This term typically comes from the participant classes (for example, No?q = animal; C'ikin = money, livestock; ?Imuš = clothes; see table 6.1).

More specific rules for participants as terms to a transgression predicate can be kept in the particular transgression variety frame. Since we already described an envy variety frame in Chapter 4, we shall take a modification of that as an example, as shown in figure 6.3.

Thus for each speaking day the associated participants are taken from table 6.1 and added to a participant pool. The appropriate

---

ENVY PARTICIPANT SELECTION FRAME

Actor (envious person)	Target (envied person)	Envy-causing attribute
adult male	adult female	love relationship with another male
adult female	adult male	love relationship with another female
adult, poor	adult, rich	wealth

Rule: Choose above triad that matches best with knowledge of client history and with the participant types of the speaking days (from Table 6.1).

Figure 6.3. Envy participant selection frame.

transgression variety frame contains instructions on what types of participants should then be attached to the predicate. In the case of envy, one must find a speaking day to represent the envious person, one to represent the envied person, and one to represent the reason for envy.

Since a supernatural being or another person is injured or offended by the transgressor, the supernatural being punishes the actor, or else the injured party communicates with the supernatural through ritual and asks him to punish the actor for his sin. The ancestral souls also are frequently cast in the role of informers, particularly through ?Aama (Souls), which is so salient a story ingredient that it often speaks out of position. Sometimes several individuals notify each other: for example, the injured party may notify the scribe deity, who in turn will notify one of the ?Alkaalte deities, who then does the punishing. Apparently the gods are not omniscient and can miss things going on in the world if they are not watching. In some of the stories we examined in the previous chapter, a god asks the protagonist how or why he was transferred to the supernatural realm.

Whether the communication category is used depends in part on the predicate. If the predicate involves an angry or envious person, that person can be the communicator; or if one of the days represents the scribe deity, the scribe is the communicator.

Determining the punishing being is usually a matter of salience in the speaking position. However, if there is no highly salient punishing being (such as an ?Alkaalte), one can proceed backward if the transgression variety has already been determined. Since every transgression variety falls under the aegis of some deity or causes anger on the part of the souls, the chosen transgression variety can be matched with the transgression varieties in table 6.4, and then that variety is matched with those kernel meanings in table 6.1 that are represented by the speaking days.

Testing the Model

We can show how this system works by testing it against an actual case, one of the few divinations witnessed and recorded in its entirety. The case was observed by John Berrueta-Clement (field notes, 1968). The client was a Quiché Indian woman who grew up in Nebaj, had been married for the past eight years, and had a place in the market where she sold salt, chile, and other foods. On the day 10 Čoo this woman, whom we shall call Juana, had what was probably an epileptic attack. She and her husband consulted Shas; they both had known him for a long time and had seen him about earlier problems. Perhaps one reason they chose Shas was that he could speak Quiché. The first layout of the divination began with the day 10 Čoo (the day of the attack) and had three speaking days: 3 C'ikin, 12 ʔliq', and 6 Čoo. Shas's reading was that there was an envious person in the plaza who noted that Juana always had money.

Applying our model, we first list the problems associated with the ascriptive standing attributes of "adult" and "woman." We then add the problems associated with the circumstantial standing attribute of "rich" and those of the occasional attribute, "got married." These problems are all aggregated and salience values assigned to them. The problems are then matched with the transgression variety candidates derived from the three speaking days. The transgression varieties are taken from tables 6.1 and 6.4 and given talking position salience values. The matching transgression variety with the highest salience value (the combined values for the talking position and client attribute associated problem) is "envy for wealth," a confirmation of the model.

Knowing what we do now about divination, we would use a frame approach for any future collection of divination case studies. Going back to our discussion of frames in the earlier chapters, we would develop a question-and-answer frame:

```
Q and A frame
  1. Identification _____

  2. Position _____

  3. Choice _____

  4. Reason _____

  5. Process _____

  6. Contingency _____
```

Of these relation slots, the third one, *choice,* is active during a second layout, when the focus is on which particular deities and super-

naturals need to be placated, when, and at which localities. The remaining five slots are all foci of the diagnostic task in the first layout.

The gist of the reading in the first example (figure 6.1) is that the
sick client has, through ritual neglect of his dead parents' souls,
caused them to want him to join them in the Underworld; this they
are doing through the day gods, who are making him sick prepara-
tory to causing his death. The souls of his parents are themselves
being imprisoned by the Earth Lords because of their quarreling in
life. This information can be placed in five of the six slots as follows:

Identification:
  a. The sick client
  b. The client's parents' souls
  c. The punishing day god
  d. The Earth God
Position:
  a. Prison of the Earth Lords
Reason:
  a. Client is sick because he has neglected ritual duties toward parents'
     souls.
  b. Souls are in prison because they quarreled
Process:
  a. Souls have complained to ʔAama about the neglect
  b. ʔAama has caused the client to be sick
Contingency:
  a. If the client performs ritual, he will get well

These slots are a means of organizing the information that is encoded. The answers to each question have been written out in natural language sentences. They could be further coded to facilitate a
question-and-answer procedure or to accommodate a more formal
treatment, but that would not serve our present analytical purpose.
What is of interest to us here is how the slots can be conceptualized
to approximate what actually exists in the constructed schemata. In
an earlier section, "The Client Situation," we listed the general attributes of the client situation stereotype. This is the "default" situation assumed, we suggest, by the daykeeper in the absence of specific information. But with specific information one can go from the
default stereotype to a client situation frame, as shown in figure 6.4.

The lists in table 6.4 (which could be represented as still another
kind of frame) amount to fragments of cultural sentences that are
associated with particular meanings. Sometimes it is a combination
of kernel meanings that provides the basis for the transgression

```
┌─────────────────────────────────────────────────────────┐
│ ┌─────────────────────────────┐                          │
│ │ CLIENT SITUATION FRAME      │                          │
│ └─────────────────────────────┘                          │
```

CLIENT SITUATION FRAME

Name: _____

   Sex _____

   Age _____

   Marital status _____

Household members:

   Adult females _____

   Adult males _____

   Children _____

   Departed souls _____

   Č'eš (namesake) _____

Salient attributes of client or household members:

   Heavy drinking _____

   Quarrelsomeness _____

Salient past events

   Sold property _____

   Left wife _____

   Rejected suitor _____

   Built house _____

Economic situation:

   Rich _____

   Poor _____

   Average _____

Figure 6.4. Client situation frame with slots unfilled.

Table 6.4. Transgression predicates associated with categories of deities and humans.

Being	Transgression or offending action	Punishing or controlling action
Earth Gods	Cutting wood without license; gathering relics without license; adultery	Punishes
Tiiš	Neglect of shrine, cross, or saints in church	Controls destiny of client, punishes
ʔAlkaalte	Any transgression; not accepting call to be daykeeper; performing ritual when not qualified	Notes transgression, punishes
Maize God	Maizefield neglected	Punishes
Ancestral souls	Quarrels; squandering inheritance; other misbehaviors	Communicates with gods
Living humans	Rejection of suitor; envy of wealth, happiness, or love; stealing	Communicates with gods
House God	Spouse abandoned	Punishes

predicate. For example, a combination of House + Souls expands to a rather specific type of problem, a squandering of inheritance or a family quarrel. Here we see how the client situation can determine the final choice: if the client has sold a house, the ancestral souls might well be concerned about it; if, on the other hand, there has been no sale, it is more likely a matter of family discord. The choice may also be determined by the other speaking days. For example, family discord might be confirmed if ʔliq' (concerned with quarrels) appears in one of the other speaking positions.

If the combination were House + Woman, then a marital problem or quarrel might be indicated, and again the choice would depend on other speaking days and on the client situation. Clearly more refinements could be added to the decision modules, but much more data would be needed to test such refinements in a useful way. At least with our current model we know what kinds of data are required.

CONCLUSION

This description of how we think Shas does his divinations might be thought of as a focused model of a role system—that is, we have focused on the most important activity of the daykeeper role, divination, and presented a description of that activity. There are, of course, many other aspects of the daykeeper role. Most of these aspects have been covered more discursively in the earlier chapters. The more formal description has been given primarily in these last two chapters with our analysis of two kinds of cultural productions, both of which organized the world conceptually for Shas in an epistemology in which relationships to gods, ancestral souls, and people are closely interwoven. Included in this epistemology is a kind of ethnopyschology about what typically motivates people—what moves them to become angry, to seek wealth, and so on.

The divination model could be further formalized by writing an actual computer program. Indeed, this was done during an earlier stage of our study (Colby and Knaus, 1974). The major empirical problem is that we do not really have much control over how the client situation is conceptualized, nor how the presuppositional component—the beliefs and values given in the philosophy text (Chapter 4)—is cognitively organized and accessed. In short, we have gone about as far as possible through analysis and description. We have already introduced "engineering" into the system; that is, we have moved into an artificial intelligence mode as is found in the work of Schank and Abelson, where plans, memory organization points, and scripts are postulated but tested only through introspection (Schank and Abelson, 1977; Schank, 1979). The great advantage of doing this, however, is that we are forced into specifying the divination process in enough detail to get some kind of result that approximates what actually happens.

We are far from completion in our efforts to understand parts of the Ixil world view or eidos. We find ourselves on unfamiliar ground. Ethnographic studies usually have not involved the kinds of analyses we have been trying to do here. Why should we do them? We think such an approach is crucial for an understanding of cultural processes and the further development of cultural theory. We will address this wider question in the remaining chapter.

7
THEORETICAL
AND METHODOLOGICAL
STRATEGY

The analysis of Shas's texts has proceeded concurrently with our development of a pattern-schema theory. This development can be thought of as having two aspects: an informal, discursive theory of a broadly encompassing set of notions about cultural processes; and a somewhat more formal aspect consisting of two ethnographic theories that model major productions of Shas's cultural system, the tales and the divinations.

We have characterized this theory of culture as a simple equation for expository convenience (see Chapter 1). But we have not brought it into a formal theory with quantitative measurements. Cultural phenomena are complex and comprehensive; they are not readily reduced to a single, all-encompassing formal theory. We must rest content with a discursive general theory which can provide a context for smaller, special theories or models that can be formal. Our two special ethnographic theories for the tales and divinations should be sufficiently precise to allow a formalization or, less stringently, a computer simulation, should any purpose be served by it. Further, we have chosen those two areas for more precise analysis because they were focal parts of Shas's Ixil cultural system.

While precision in selected areas is important, ethnography also needs "thick description" in the manner described by Geertz (1973), where emphasis is on discursively detailing the manifold ways in which different aspects of cultural life are interrelated and contextualized. No matter how detailed and precise the specification of some small domain of special focus may be, there will always be underlying presuppositions and contextual linkages that remain unspecified in the analysis, which a more discursive description can bring out. Further, thick description helps us to better enjoy the poetry and beauty of cultural productions by providing an interpretive background for them.

At the same time, we can be more scientifically ambitious in areas previously covered only by discursive description because they were thought to be opaque to formal analysis: dreams, feelings, philosophy, folktales, context, and metaphor. The new approach requires standards for data collection and analysis that include a detailed specification of what seems to be going on, along with an expectation that cultural grammars and decision models be tested against new data, or at least previously unanalyzed data, wherever possible. There is cause for optimism in this approach as long as we recognize some of the consequences that will result—among them being that we are going to require extensive data from single individuals on a scale that previously has characterized ethnographic study only rarely.

If we think of cultural productions and constructions or construals of reality for the individual as being produced by cognitive systems in interaction with external patterns, the emphasis has to be on the identification and analysis of those external patterns. Since the systems ultimately derive from pattern components held in short-term memory as images, either as they are perceived or as they are constructed from schema systems in long-term memory, we must speculate on the nature of those images and schemata. But since all we have to go on are the external patterns, we should try to model those cognitive systems by writing cultural grammars and decision models that approximate cognitive reality well enough so that behavioral patterns produced by those systems are accounted for.

CULTURAL GRAMMARS AND DECISION MODELS

The purpose of a grammar is to define well-formed patterns of some particular genre of cultural phenomena and model the systems that shape them, but not to predict the actual choice of a pattern or pattern sequence. The purpose of a decision model is to determine the necessary input for a choice to occur and to predict the actual choice. The main difference between a grammar and a decision model is what is done with a given cultural production. The input to a grammar developed by the analyst is a string or arrangement of behavior already produced, which is judged by the grammar to be well-formed or not. The input to a grammar is the finished production; the output is a judgment as to whether the production matches some combination of rules and elements in the grammar. The output is a yes or no answer about the grammaticality of the production examined. The key process is one of *matching*. A decision model, on the other hand, *simulates* the production process. The cultural production is the output. The input to a decision model is a set of conditions or situations and a value, and motivational, system. How a cultural grammar and a decision model can work together was suggested in the analysis of divination in the previous chapter.

The reason cultural grammars are useful in the context of our pattern-schema theory is that they identify the patterns of a particular genre or domain. The elements of a cultural grammar represent a cultural code that has been successfully deciphered through a distributional study of the external patterns. This study includes the testing of the coding and the rules with new instances of the phenomena covered by the grammar. Thus the analyst with a successful grammar has been able to do consciously what natives of a social group do unconsciously.

Grammars lay bare the patterns. They are approximations to schema constructions in the mind and are used to identify patterns and describe what is "legal" or normal in the (external) domain covered. They do not predict the content of a pattern, only its form. As Kronenfeld states, a grammar does not try to describe what is likely or what has actually occurred but rather "all and only the universe of what might possibly occur (within its specified area of concern)" (Kronenfeld, forthcoming, p. 6). Grammars further must always claim to be "emic," to represent a configuration that made a psychological difference to the people using the patterns. The descriptive adequacy of a cultural grammar is in its prediction of emic form.

Decision models, on the other hand, do not *always* require that a code be discovered or that hidden patterns be delineated and highlighted. It is not the form that is attended to as much as the content.

Many different kinds of variables can be used in a decision model, and they need not always be emic. For some purposes, they can just as well be "etic" variables of the outside world as observed or measured by the ethnographer. For some studies virtually anything can go into the hopper of a decision model as long as it is relevant to the decision. Different kinds and levels of categories and processes can be used. The main criterion of adequacy for a decision model is whether a decision is correctly predicted. But since it is *sometimes* necessary to have an emic decision model, we will distinguish two types, emic and etic decision models.

In our study of divination we need to have an emic output, which means that a grammar is necessary to identify correctly the output patterns. Thus an emic-type decision model requires that a grammar be hooked up to it. Conversely, some types of language grammars are beginning to include decision components. Recent work in augmented transition networks (Woods, 1970; Wanner and Maratsos, 1978) is moving in this direction.

We must be guided by the special nature of our data. Here we rest content with two separate approaches: the first is that of the cultural grammar, the second that of the decision model. The interlinking of the two occurs because we restrict some of the input and all of the output of the divination decision model to emic patterns. We therefore need a grammar to identify the emic "legality" of the patterns.

PATTERNS OF METAPHOR

Language, though a very dynamic process at the micro-level, is—for most purposes—a shared phenomenon. But more is shared than just systematic rules and semantic features; certain underlying beliefs about the world and behavior must also be shared in order to communicate. Even people of different backgrounds acting different roles and with opposing goals share common ideas about how the world operates. Wallace (1961) demonstrated that individuals need not share exactly the same mental structures in order to interact with one another. But successful communication *does* require certain shared expectations and beliefs about how the world works. It is this common, shared belief structure that is encapsulated by organizing metaphors.[1] We speak of such encapsulating metaphors as "organizing" because they serve as a rallying point for interpretation. They carry a heavy functional load.

We think we have demonstrated that there are common infrastructures or systems that are organized around such metaphors. Organizing metaphors have many entailments, those that are direct consequences implied by the metaphor and those that are indirect. The exposition of organizing metaphors and their entailments, especially as they are manifest in systemic patterns, is a primary ethnographic task. But it is best done from individual to individual, or by cultural productions located in time and space, since our idea of culture is radically different from the standard view of cultures as bounded, countable units.

The description of organizing metaphors in a social group is likely to be a key objective of future ethnographic study, particularly in text linguistics. We see the organizing metaphors of a people as an essential part of their world view. It ties in with a behavioral logic which a people (however grouped) share.

The organizing metaphor of Ixil culture that we have been most concerned with here is the equation of sickness with imprisonment. The clearest expression of this metaphor was in Shas's dream in which he was given the keys to the jail to be able to release prisoners. This dream motif occurred immediately after he dreamed of speaking with the four daykeepers in the cemetery, when he was officially given an appointment as daykeeper.

The entailments of this metaphor focus on the goal of being released from prison and the goal state of staying out of prison. A thematic sequence is tied to this goal—a mechanism for release: *transgression* → *imprisonment* → *appeal* → *release*. But the appeal must take an object—a being to appeal to—and that is one of the tasks of divination. The metaphor and its entailments are shown below:

ORGANIZING METAPHOR: SICKNESS=IMPRISONMENT
   ENTAILMENTS:
      GOAL: RELEASE
      ACTION: APPEAL TO X TO FORGIVE Y FOR Z
         where X=punishing being
               Y=transgressor
               Z=transgression
      Divination decision process: determining x, y, and z

The tales Shas gave us can be seen as variant outcomes of the state of imprisonment. The imprisonment side of the equation rather than the sickness side is predominant because that is the area of religious elaboration. In many cases sickness is assumed, not stated, though there is an explicit linkage in the "Comadre" story where the imprisoned mule with a wounded eye in the nether world (due to the protagonist's hitting of the mule with a stick) is linked directly with the sick and dying comadre in this world, who also has a wounded eye.

The various eidochronic sequences of the tales represent different scenarios in the behavioral logic of Ixil thought, a logic that is tied up with a metaphoric organization of the world and of the typical processes that occur in that world. Lakoff and Johnson (1980) have suggested how metaphor guides our thinking unconsciously, and Quinn (1979) documents how a metaphor can organize the way one conceptualizes marriage and deep-seated human relationships. One way to trace out these relationships is in the myths and folktales that people have grown up with and have organized their more abstract thinking around, especially in areas of highly charged emotional concern such as sickness, death, and marriage.

The fish merchant and mountain god stories are two very clear statements of how transgression (not always by the protagonist) transports an individual to the supernatural world as captive.

Interestingly enough, the Maria Markaao story, which is primarily another metaphor concerning marriage relations, is still part of the same eidochronic system—a different pattern produced by the same cultural device. Thus several thematic sequences can be generated by the same cultural grammar.

SITUATIONS AND FRAMES

Our earlier work focused on grammars with the idea that a successful grammar marked a successful conclusion of the ethnographic task. It should be clear why we now see the grammar as just the beginning: we also must work out control, or decision models, which concern the outcomes of actions and events together with their social contextualization. In the process, we have suggested how it may be helpful to use frames (for example, frames of situational assessment, valence determination, temporal and spatial ordering, and role relations). A frame need not be limited to an analyst's representation of what he thinks to be the cognitive state of a "native"; it may also be used for studies of groups of people, of entire societies. Frames can include statistical figures and economical facts as well as symbols and meanings. Because of this flexibility, a frame can be used for macroanthropological studies as well as microethnographic ones. It is still, however, a representation, albeit the analyst's own, which he constructs to match the social phenomena he studies.

Frames may be narrowed down to particular frames representing specific pattern elements, and thus may be referred to as eidonic frames, situation frames, or even eidons and situations when the context renders superfluous the distinction between cognitive or perceived reality and the observer's approximate representation of it. Control frames can include decision procedures based on matches of situations and future possibilities with actions and desired goal states. There are many different ways in which frames can be used in cognitive models.[2]

The use of these techniques means that almost anything described in language can be modeled in a computer system. This "sky is the limit" implication is of strategic import. Because of this lack of constraint on what can be modeled, the questions of relevance and theoretical purpose gain a special urgency. Chief among the things to focus on, then, has to be the overall architecture. Figure 7.1 shows—only in the barest outline—an architecture of our approach to the components of the grammars and the decision model for the material Shas Koʔw has given us. Not all of these components have been mapped out. Episodic memory structures and other types of knowledge structures are postulated, but the way in which they are formed must be determined through external pattern analysis.

THE TASK OF ETHNOGRAPHY

As we see it, the first task of ethnography is to identify cultural patterns that have special significance. For emic studies this means writing cultural grammars that account for these patterns. Subsequently, one can develop decision models that predict their generation. In the absence of a theory to test (or a special interest the ethnographer brings to the field), special significance is not always easy

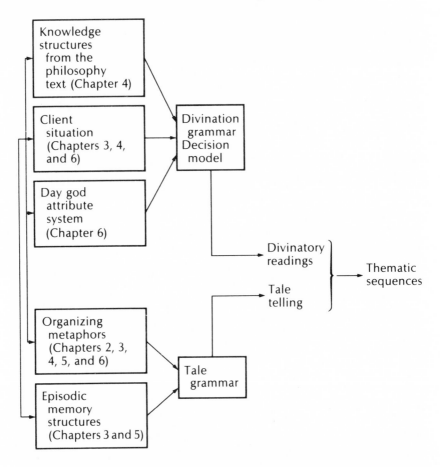

Figure 7.1. Types of ethnographic information and their interrelationships as inputs for the decision model and two grammars.

to decide upon. But if the main ethnographic purpose is to attain maximal understanding of the cultural system, emic studies should be included. One way to do this is to seek out thematic sequences and organizing metaphors and gather data on the phenomena associated with them. Once grammars and decision models have been developed that attain acceptable levels of testing, they can be related to a more comprehensive, discursive theory of culture. Though relatively few cultural grammars have been published (Faris, 1972;

Watt, 1966, 1967; Colby, 1973), there are a large variety of decision models (Geoghegon, 1971; Gladwin, 1979; Quinn, 1976; Fjellman, 1976; Randall, 1977).

It is encouraging that through our microethnographic study of Shas's texts we have developed a conceptual framework that we think can apply equally as well to macroethnographic studies. The link between the two kinds of studies is in the interaction between the exigencies of the external situation and the selection of what the individual native judges to be the most appropriate cultural patterns. The concept of role occupies a pivotal position in this linkage. From one perspective—the one we have adopted here—roles consist of schema systems and behavioral patterns, as we have suggested in the divination model; from another perspective, roles occupy places in particular settings and situations. These situations can be organized by political, economic, and other institutional criteria. In choosing to look at roles from the perspective of an individual rather than from that of an institution and in emphasizing the religious rather than the economic aspect, we do not argue that symbols and meanings are primary and economics only secondary. If we were to examine the events of Shas's life or other aspects of Ixil life in general, we would find just as many cases in which economics and other macroethnographic subjects should have center stage.

In an earlier study, *Ixil Country* (Colby and van den Berghe, 1969), we analyzed some of the political and economic effects influencing the lives of the Ixil. Here we have emphasized religion because it was the dominant force in Shas's life. However, for Shas's children the economic and political situation has become much more of a significant force for change. In future studies one might wish to work out decision-making models as to when and where maize is planted, when a person decides to hire himself out as a laborer, and how politicization occurs in a group of people who used to vote for the incumbent. In later years television will also become a significant influence. At the moment the strongest agents of change are the intrusions of private, national, and international economic interests, as we mentioned in an earlier chapter. Extremely harsh political and military actions have included the killing of thousands of political opponents of the government. These actions have increased social stress markedly for the entire area since the time we gathered our data. History may repeat itself and the Ixil may once again harbor rebel soldiers in self-defense as they did in the time of Rufino Barrios. Shas Ko?w's death in 1976 spared him from witnessing the worst of the recent events.

While our focus here has been at the microethnographic level, even in the study of a single individual the links to a regional and national perspective are quite evident. We see these links as Shas leaves his homeland, goes to the lowland coffee plantations, and describes how his life was influenced by political decisions made at the national level. We also can form impressions of what plantation work was like and the authoritarian personalities of those in command. The boss who offered to hunt down Shas's wife was clearly doing so for expressive reasons rather than out of any wish to help Shas. Much of this information comes only in bits and pieces, but the great advantage in using such texts is that they have been selected by the narrator rather than by the outside observer.

THE IMPORTANCE OF STEREOTYPED BEHAVIOR

Nevertheless, as outside observers we do have our own special interests. We have been concerned in this book with productive processes, from very broad ones to quite detailed particulars. Attention has been directed toward the interplay between a person's idiosyncratic experience and those experiences that are culturally mediated through sterotyped forms present in the society as a whole. The balance in this interplay is different for the different production types and for different individuals and situations.

The attempt to understand cultural processes rests ultimately on our success in decoding the cognitive chunks or elements of which cultural patterns are made. The goal of decoding or discovering cognitive chunks has been spurred in the past by the analogy of linguistics, but more recently the quest for the equivalent of phonemes in nonlinguistic areas of culture has been replaced by the quest for higher-level organizations of the mind, somewhere between linguistic phenomena as traditionally defined and the larger cultural system of beliefs and presuppositions about the world.

Just as psychologists seek out a controlled experimental situation in the laboratory, we seek out stereotyped behavior patterns for study in the field. Such patterns include systems of "prepackaged" thought, such as proverbs, omens, folktales, and other kinds of stereotyped cultural productions which, in their functional capacity, we have referred to as cultural devices. These productions are revealing of cultural eidons, especially when analyzed with techniques such as distributional and frame analysis.

If the patterns of these cultural productions have enough repetition in them for us to spot their regularities and enough variation to reveal key choice points, then we are on our way toward discovering cognitive chunks and approximating the rules for their combination. However, stereotyped phenomena need not be restricted to traditional forms like proverbs and folktales. In modern society there are innumerable situations that can be reduced to a set of rules or, as Hasan describes them, structural formulas (Hasan, 1978). Asking for an appointment on the telephone (Hasan, 1978), ordering a meal in a restaurant (Schank and Abelson, 1977), and teaching children in a classroom (Mehan, 1978) all have routinized cultural patterns that are amenable to analysis.[3]

Further, the functions that these patterns have in modern as well as traditional societies can be better understood when the systems that produce the patterns have been worked out. Sometimes these patterns are understood by a manipulative minority in society, whether they be magicians and shamans or whether they be modern psychologists working at the service of corporate advertising (Jordan and Goldberg 1977). But for the most part patterns function in ways that are largely unconscious for us. Highly patterned folk productions function as many different kinds of devices—prosthetic (La Barre, 1964), randomizing (Moore, 1957), learning (Roberts and Sutton-Smith, 1962; Moore and Anderson, 1968), and assuaging (Vogt and Hyman, 1959; Roberts and Sutton-Smith, 1962; Ridgeway and Roberts, 1976). The analysis of these functions and the highly patterned systems involved with them are leading to a new frontier of anthropological study, chiefly pioneered by John Roberts and his colleagues (Roberts, 1964, 1965; Roberts, Chiao, and Pandey, 1975; Roberts and Chick, 1979). Most of this work has been in the area of games because these cultural productions are clearly and explicitly identified in all their essential particulars. We now need to develop means of seeing the patterns in other cultural productions, which is often difficult because cultural productions evidence varying degrees of systematization or routinization. The same type of device may be differently formed—that is, formed by different principles—

in different societies. The success of the Eskimo narrative grammar in accounting for previously unexamined, unpublished stories suggests that the Eskimo folktale system, at least in traditional Eskimo groups, has been highly coherent. Ixil folk narratives seem to be more complex, but until a large collection of stories told by other Ixil is analyzed there are still many unanswered questions concerning eidochronic details.

One of the difficulties in studying the lives of interesting people, however, is that schemata are sometimes too dynamic, too protean in expression for their patterned realizations to emerge clearly or with certainty in an analysis. Only with the use of traditional or highly routinized forms can we see sequential patterns clearly enough to construct grammars for the systems that produce them. Thus our theory would hold that *described* cultural systems not only vary from one society to the next, but vary because of different kinds of cultural limitations on what can be described. That is, the folktales of one society may be so conventionalized as to be readily analyzed into eidons and rules for their sequencing, whereas in other societies they may be so idiosyncratic and unconventional that eidochronic analysis is next to impossible. What is highly routinized in one society may be quite variable in another. Even so, areas of routinization in one society tell us, at least at higher levels of abstraction, much about the same areas in other societies where there may be much less routinization; they also tell us about basic cultural dynamics and about a society's "trajectory" through recent time.

In short, a successful model for how one person combines chunks and rules in the traditional cultural productions of some genre will provide our chief clues to less stereotyped, nontraditional behavior within a similar genre in other societies. Determining the mechanisms of routinized behavior may well be the best and most rewarding approach that can be taken toward this end. These regularities, through the very nature of their regularity, are indications of a type of cultural relevance and have a strong hold on the people who generate them. Anything that we do often enough will become routinized. If it creates a permanent record—written, iconic, or three-dimensional—we have a chance of being able to work out a grammar for it that can account for new samples from the same population.

Much of the recent work in artificial intelligence has been concerned with the representation of cultural knowledge, particularly in routinized areas of behavior such as the roles of waiter and customer in a restaurant. The scriptlike patterns used in such routines allow us to act without much conscious thought. In a project at the University of California, Irvine, on how people go about solving everyday mathematical problems, Jean Lave and Olivia de la Rocha have worked out a precedence scale for the kinds of thought processes people will undertake. Somewhat like Zipf's law of least effort, their study postulates that anything that can reduce inferencing is given higher precedence. A similar principle holds in all other activities. Routine activities are performed with some sort of script structure in mind. If inferencing is required, then scripts must be replaced by some kind of plan construction in which inferences about goals establish a connection between actions and the achievement of the goals (Schank and Abelson, 1977).

Though artificial intelligence has influenced our own approach, one must remember that artificial intelligence systems are usually ad hoc, generally working from the top down rather than, as in linguistics, from the bottom up. Cognitive chunks should be demonstrated to exist through distributional analysis, not simply established by fiat and imposed from above, as is done in artificial intelligence and in European studies of text grammar (and sometimes even in psychology, though at least categories are subsequently tested through experimentation in this field). With our Ixil data we have worked from the bottom up whenever possible. We have immersed ourselves in a repertoire of cultural forms, both intermediate and full-length: divination, folk narrative, hortative advice, life story, and prayer.

Above all, our descriptions must be relevant; they must focus on patterns discerned in the environment that have special valence either to the observer or to the people the observer seeks to describe. If some aspect of the natural or sociocultural environment is entirely neutral with respect to what the analyst is interested in, if it is not criterial for anything of concern to the analyst, then there is less need to include it in the description. It is the valence that counts. There are so many pieces of information available that only the most significant information, that which has a valence that relates to the analytical purpose, should be utilized.

This is where the notion of salience is crucial. In an earlier chapter we brought up the issue of how information and default categories are two opposing bases for defining salience. In anthropological writings salience is usually meant to indicate a basic, more frequently used category (Dougherty, 1978; Burton and Kirk, 1979). But the idea of a basic category is itself poorly defined. High-frequency, more redundant elements carry less information and, in that sense, can be thought of as having a lower salience. Psychologists have also grappled with the notion of salience. Tversky (1977) defines salience as a mix of intensity and diagnosticity. Diagnosticity is the discriminability of one object from others with which it is usually grouped; intensity concerns features that increase the signal-to-noise ratio: brightness, loudness, frequency, clarity, saturation (of a color), and vividness. Ortony (1979) disagrees with Tversky's view that intensity is independent of the object and goes on to argue that salience imbalance is the essence of metaphoricity, where the first term or topic is one of low-salient attributes while the second term or vehicle (which must be from a different domain than the first term) has high-salient attributes, some of which are applicable in the metaphoric equation and others of which are not. The relation of salience to marking, intensity, highlighting, diagnosticity, and information will have to be more carefully worked out in the future, because the study of cultural patterns will depend on a clear understanding of these phenomena.

Certainly it would be difficult to identify eidons and thematic sequences if they were not salient in some form. A cultural pattern has to be seen as a pattern. One way of identifying a sequence as a pattern is through its repetition. If a particular, noisy-looking pattern appears frequently enough, we see that it must not be a random sequence. But sometimes we do not see these patterns unless they are marked or highlighted in some special way so that their appearance carries more information for us—is more unexpected and, hence, attention-attracting.

For the time being we are content simply to discover these patterns and sequences as they are derived from different kinds of cultural productions, which in turn were created by differing uses of underlying systems. The main example in our Ixil material has been the transgression sequence (transgression → imprisonment → appeal → release). Since this sequence is produced by two different, though interrelated, cognitive systems, it is doubly reinforced.

The description of some delimited activity, such as folktales, makes it easy for models to take on a unified and separate existence. Of course we know that a syntactic grammar for language models only a small part of what happens when we speak; yet too often we slip into habits of thinking that reify the grammar and emphasize the boundaries of our analytical models. Clearly those boundaries do not really exist in the mind. We must recognize that systems that can be modeled in part by grammars, such as Shas's divination system and his narratives, are never independent systems, even though the grammars we write appear to be. That they appear to be independent reflects a failure to identify and model the interconnections with related systems. All the grammars can do is model that part of the system that can be reconstructed from regularities found in the cultural patterns, the data. There are undoubtedly many more seemingly "peripheral" (but, from another perspective, more central) systems that divination and narration both draw upon. Metaphoric systems, for example, are used by both, as are language systems; many other cognitive systems at different levels of integration are certainly used by both. Consequently, though we speak of these systems as distinct but interrelated, we must be prepared to find that boundaries may not always exist, at least in the form we would expect.[4]

Our theory questions the traditional distinctions between culture and cognition and between culture and personality. We treat what has typically been called intelligence (or various aspects of intelligence as measured by IQ tests) and most of what has typically been characterized as personality (which usually involves affective elements) as both being cultural phenomena, though of course with a deep biological base. In many respects we agree with Malinowski, who noted years ago (1926) that although affect has roots in universal biological needs, the shaping, channeling, sublimation, and displacement of biological needs has a strong cultural component with respect both to the cultural systems individuals carry around in their heads and the sociocultural environment they live in. This perspective amounts to a widening beyond the traditional province of cultural systems.

In light of this very general sketch of the chief aspects of our approach and theory, we can see how Shas's situation was advantageous as well as disadvantageous. It was advantageous in that Shas was exposed to a much wider repertoire of behavioral patterns than was usual for Ixil of his time. He did not have a father and mother as role models during his childhood; thus he lacked the intensity of role focus that occurs in a simple family situation over an extended period of time. We can only speculate on the emotional content of this early learning—presumably the time spent with his grandparents was one of warmth and support, but it did not last after his fifth year.

There is no evidence we could see that suggested Shas to be emotionally different from others. That shamans have a deviant personality has been part of a general expectation by anthropologists, although a study by Fabrega and Silver (1970) did not support this view conclusively for the Zinacantan Mayans they studied. In any event, it was perhaps Shas's lack of deep parental attachment that might have made him a seeker—it was important for him to find a philosophy of life and to talk about it. His role-model exposure was broader than it was deep; it was diversified over a number of adults who were significant at different times. Shas had to create his own model of how to live, to think about his life, and to discuss it, but the wide range of behavior patterns he observed could be drawn upon to meet the need. Here is where the religious patterns in particular were of help. Shas turned to those thematic sequences available to him and brought them together for his own guidance as well as for that of others.

Socioeconomic and political conditions determine the availability of cultural patterns to people. Shas did not have available to him the patterns that school children learn when they begin to read. He did, however, have access to the divinatory patterns that led him to take on the role of daykeeper. Since Shas's boyhood there has been much change, and today there is a greater opportunity for education. The current political turmoil is likely to have more far-reaching influences on the availability of patterns to the Ixil, and on the perceived desirability of patterns for them, than anything since the time the Ixil befriended Rufino Barrios, a rebel of the previous century.

As obvious as macrodynamic forces are in their influence on cultural evolution and change, we feel that they must eventually be studied *through* microdynamic processes, which are also evolutionary. The link between the two kinds of forces is readily perceived in a pattern-schema theory with the differential selection and creation of patterns by individuals aggregating in large-scale changes of institutional structures, as shown below:

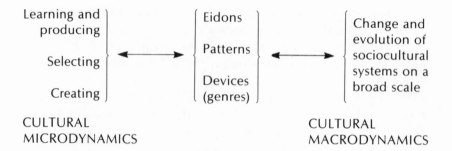

CULTURAL   CULTURAL
MICRODYNAMICS   MACRODYNAMICS

To shift from the microdynamic level of the details of the divinatory system used by Shas to macrodynamic studies might lead to the
prediction of large-scale effects. So far we have taken only the first
step, the working out of two grammars and a decision model. The
next step would be a study of how the elements of the system vary
from one individual to the next, or in one individual over time in different situations. Whatever the focus—be it on an individual, a role,
or on broad political, economic, and evolutionary processes—eventually the relationships and models worked out at the macro-level
should be examined at the micro-level to avoid the loss of empirical
reality control or validation. Further, it is at the micro-level that
mechanisms of cultural evolution operate. Until these mechanisms
are understood and ethnographically treated, we will lack an adequate theory of cultural change and evolution. Culture is not a
"thing of shreds and patches," as Lowie once characterized it, nor is
culture like a blind "grab bag," as Quinn recently stated (1979). The
cultural evolutionary process is more like going through a cafeteria.
Cultural patterns are selected as people choose foods. Later at home
a customer may try to duplicate some new dish first seen at the
cafeteria, and in this fashion the pattern is transmitted.

This process of going through a cafeteria is what programmers in
artificial intelligence must do when working out models of comprehension and behavior—except that the creative part goes into the
program as well as the mind. One of the tasks currently being under-
taken in this field by James Meehan at the University of California,
Irvine, is the simulation of life in a small town. A key part of such a
task is the development of role "packets" (frames with entry conditions, entailments, plans, goals, expectations, and attributes associated with role behavior) for the town's inhabitants, with special

emphasis on family roles. Though Meehan and his colleagues have developed different mechanisms, the output of the simulation model could be likened to the output of Shas's divination. In both cases a story is generated about individuals in a particular situation. This suggests how a model of Ixil divination can be more than a model of the focal activity of the daykeeper role in Ixil society; it is a model of Ixil life itself. The model deals with the major concerns of Ixil life, from maize farming to family relations. Ixil divination, then, is a folk model of Ixil life and culture.

Whatever the aspect of cultural life that seems most important, we hope that we have shown how ethnography will ultimately have to be grounded at the micro-level or the individual level. In doing this the most rewarding strategy for ethnographers looking at cognitive systems is to seek out routinized behavior for analysis. Once the analysis is complete, the question turns to how an individual goes beyond the routines. This going beyond is where the real challenge lies. It may be a modulation on the thematic sequences, or it may be much more. Whether subtle epiphenomenon or basic change, ephemeral or lasting, it is a fundamental aspect of the cultural process.

By widening the idea of culture we give a different and deeper meaning to personality, especially as including a higher level of consciousness that is something above the level of neurotic compulsions and animal-like emotional reactions, something we might call "humanity" as expressed during a person's finer hours. Alternatively, we might borrow the still more nebulous idea of "soul." The human soul would stand as something distinct from both cognitive systems and deeply "wired" emotional reactions.

Our task is nothing so presumptuous as that of understanding the human soul. We instead try to understand what we usually mean by humanity in its nobler aspect and to learn as much as we can about the cultual milieu in which humanity flourishes. We think of culture and humanity as two quite different, but not entirely distinct, phenomena. Curiously, the two are in conflict with each other as often as they are in harmony; Jules Henry even entitled one of his books *Culture Against Man,* meaning culture against humanity (1963). But where would humanity be without culture? Without the peaks of cultural expression in our civilization, our consciousness would not have enlarged to the extent that it has, nor might we even be disposed to reflect upon such matters as these.

In spite of all our philosophizing, our understanding of great cultural achievement and of the ebb and flow of world civilizations is most rudimentary. This challenge, this great wall of ignorance, is an impetus for the use of divinatory systems, myths, and ethical statements that seekers like Shas Koʔw communicate to those around them. Trying to make sense of the world is as basic as anything else in the human endeavor, and try we must—whether we be daykeepers raised in the mountains of Guatemala or anthropologists schooled in the traditions of Western academe.

APPENDIXES
GLOSSARY
NOTES
REFERENCES
INDEX

APPENDIX A
LINGUISTIC NOTES

PHONOLOGICAL ELEMENTS OF IXIL

Symbols used in linguistic transcriptions

Consonants:	p	t	c	ç	č	k	q		Vowels:	i		u
	b′	t′	c′	ç′	č′	k′	q′	ʔ		e		o
			s	ş	š		h				a	
	m		n							ii		uu
	w		l	r	y					ee		oo
											aa	

NOTES ON THE TRANSLATION

Shas's texts were recorded on tape both in Guatemala and during his stay at Irvine and then transcribed into Ixil by young Ixil assistants and by Lore Colby. The English translations are based on the Ixil. However, our assistants also made Spanish translations; the English translations were then checked against the Spanish ones, and

269

discrepancies were cleared up in further interviewing. In cases of ellipsis or where information was presupposed by Shas, we supplied
the missing information and enclosed the words in brackets. In cases
where words were inaudible on tape, they are indicated by ellipsis
points. Some statements, such as the frequent "it was said that he
said" in the folktales, have been shortened (simply to "he said").
"Posiib'le," which occurs with great frequency in prayers (variously
equivalent to "Lord have mercy," "forgive us," or "harken") has
usually been omitted. The Ixil words are rendered in the linguistic
alphabet used by the IJAL. An exception is the name *Shas*, where *sh*
has been used instead of š in order to facilitate reading. Text numbers refer to an inventory of texts to be transferred to microfilm some
time in the future.

APPENDIX B
EIDOCHRONIC CHARTS
FOR SHAS'S FOLKTALES
AND MYTHS

ANALYSIS SHEET FOR "THE ʔAANHEL"

Value Motivation									
Lack (Lck)	–	–	–	–	–	–	–	–	–
Immediate Motivation									
Transgression (Tgn)	0	–	–	–	–	–	–	–	–
Preliminary Action									
Transformation (Trf)		–	–	–	–	–	–	–	–
Encounter (Enc)		–	–	–	–	–	–	–	–
Transaction (Tra)		–	–	–	–	–	–	–	–
Enter Captivity (Cap)		–	–	0	–	–	–	–	–
Hospitality (Hsp)		–	–		–	–	–	–	–
Precaution (Prc)	0	0	0		–	–	–	–	–
Main Action									
Task (Tsk)									
Attack (Atk)	0	0	0		–	–	–	–	–
Contest (Cnt)					–	–	–	–	–
Noise (Nse)					–	–	–	–	–
Deception (Dcp)					–	–	–	–	–
Immediate Resolution									
Delivery (Dlv)					–	–	–	–	–
Task outcome (Tko)									
Escape (Esc)	0	0	0		–	–	–	–	–
Release (Rls)	–	–	–		–	–	–	–	–
Death (Dth)	–	–	–		–	–	–	–	–
Revival (Rvl)	–	–	–		–	–	–	–	–
Creation-Transf (Crt)	–	–	–		–	–	–	–	–
Value Resolution									
Reward (Rwd)	–	–	–		–	–	–	–	–
Marriage (Mrg)	–	–	–		–	–	–	–	–
Reunion (Reu)	–	–	–		–	–	–	–	–
Bestowal (Bst)	–	–	–	0	–	–	–	–	–
Comment (Com)	–	–	–	0	–	–	–	–	–

Secondary eidons: Transference; Information; Instruction; Facilitation; Observation; Impedance

ANALYSIS SHEET FOR "MOUNTAIN-AND-VALLEY GOD"

Value Motivation									
Lack (Lck)	–	–	–	–	–	–	–	–	–
Immediate Motivation									
Transgression (Tgn)	0	–	–	–	–	–	–	–	–
Preliminary Action									
Transformation (Trf)	–	–	–	–	–	–	–	–	–
Encounter (Enc)	–	–	–	–	–	–	–	–	–
Transaction (Tra)	↓	–	–	–	–	–	–	–	–
Enter Captivity'(Cap)	0	–	–	–	–	–	–	–	–
Hospitality (Hsp)	0	–	–	–	–	–	–	–	–
Precaution (Prc)	–	–	–	–	–	–	–	–	–
Main Action									
Task (Tsk)	–	–	–	–	–	–	–	–	–
Attack (Atk)	–	–	–	–	–	–	–	–	–
Contest (Cnt)	↓	–	–	–	–	–	–	–	–
Noise (Nse)	0	–	–	–	–	–	–	–	–
Deception (Dcp)	–	–	–	–	–	–	–	–	–
Immediate Resolution									
Delivery (Dlv)	–	–	–	–	–	–	–	–	–
Task outcome (Tko)	–	–	–	–	–	–	–	–	–
Escape (Esc)	↓	–	–	–	–	–	–	–	–
Release (Rls)	0	–	–	–	–	–	–	–	–
Death (Dth)	–	–	–	–	–	–	–	–	–
Revival (Rvl)	–	–	–	–	–	–	–	–	–
Creation-Transf (Crt)	–	–	–	–	–	–	–	–	–
Value Resolution									
Reward (Rwd)	–	–	–	–	–	–	–	–	–
Marriage (Mrg)	–	–	–	–	–	–	–	–	–
Reunion (Reu)	–	–	–	–	–	–	–	–	–
Bestowal (Bst)	–	–	–	–	–	–	–	–	–
Comment (Com)	–	–	–	–	–	–	–	–	–

Secondary eidons: Transference; Information; Instruction; Facilitation; Observation; Impedance

ANALYSIS SHEET FOR "FISH MERCHANT"

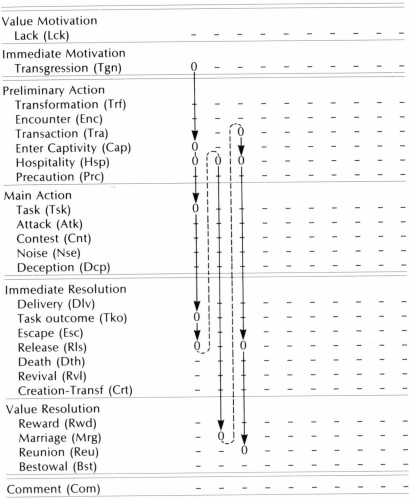

Value Motivation										
Lack (Lck)	–	–	–	–	–	–	–	–	–	–
Immediate Motivation										
Transgression (Tgn)	0	–	–	–	–	–	–	–	–	–
Preliminary Action										
Transformation (Trf)		–	–	–	–	–	–	–	–	–
Encounter (Enc)		–	–	–	–	–	–	–	–	–
Transaction (Tra)		–	0	–	–	–	–	–	–	–
Enter Captivity (Cap)	0	–		–	–	–	–	–	–	–
Hospitality (Hsp)	0	0	0	–	–	–	–	–	–	–
Precaution (Prc)				–	–	–	–	–	–	–
Main Action										
Task (Tsk)	0			–	–	–	–	–	–	–
Attack (Atk)				–	–	–	–	–	–	–
Contest (Cnt)				–	–	–	–	–	–	–
Noise (Nse)				–	–	–	–	–	–	–
Deception (Dcp)				–	–	–	–	–	–	–
Immediate Resolution										
Delivery (Dlv)				–	–	–	–	–	–	–
Task outcome (Tko)	0			–	–	–	–	–	–	–
Escape (Esc)				–	–	–	–	–	–	–
Release (Rls)	0		0	–	–	–	–	–	–	–
Death (Dth)	–			–	–	–	–	–	–	–
Revival (Rvl)	–			–	–	–	–	–	–	–
Creation-Transf (Crt)	–			–	–	–	–	–	–	–
Value Resolution										
Reward (Rwd)	–			–	–	–	–	–	–	–
Marriage (Mrg)	–	0		–	–	–	–	–	–	–
Reunion (Reu)	–	–	0	–	–	–	–	–	–	–
Bestowal (Bst)	–	–	–	–	–	–	–	–	–	–
Comment (Com)	–	–	–	–	–	–	–	–	–	–

Secondary eidons: Transference; Information; Instruction; Facilitation; Observation; Impedance

Appendix B

ANALYSIS SHEET FOR "MARIA MARKAAO"

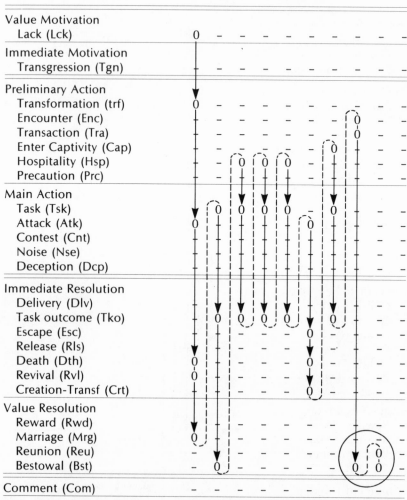

Value Motivation
  Lack (Lck)

Immediate Motivation
  Transgression (Tgn)

Preliminary Action
  Transformation (trf)
  Encounter (Enc)
  Transaction (Tra)
  Enter Captivity (Cap)
  Hospitality (Hsp)
  Precaution (Prc)

Main Action
  Task (Tsk)
  Attack (Atk)
  Contest (Cnt)
  Noise (Nse)
  Deception (Dcp)

Immediate Resolution
  Delivery (Dlv)
  Task outcome (Tko)
  Escape (Esc)
  Release (Rls)
  Death (Dth)
  Revival (Rvl)
  Creation-Transf (Crt)

Value Resolution
  Reward (Rwd)
  Marriage (Mrg)
  Reunion (Reu)
  Bestowal (Bst)

Comment (Com)

Secondary eidons: Transference; Information; Instruction; Facilitation; Observation; Impedance. Circled area indicates exception where looping occurs within a single higher-level category. Possibly Bestowal, being more of a mythic rather than folktale element, does not follow a regular eidochronic sequence and therefore represents a special category.

ANALYSIS SHEET FOR "THE SNAKE'S TREASURE"

Value Motivation
  Lack (Lck)   0   – – – – – – – –

Immediate Motivation
  Transgression (Tgn)   – – – – – – – –

Preliminary Action
  Transformation (Trf)   – – – – – – – –
  Encounter (Enc)   0 – – – – – – – –
  Transaction (Tra)   0 – – – – – – – –
  Enter Captivity (Cap)   – – – – – – – –
  Hospitality (Hsp)   – – – – – – – –
  Precaution (Prc)   – – – – – – – –

Main Action
  Task (Tsk)   0 – – – – – – – –
  Attack (Atk)   – – – – – – – –
  Contest (Cnt)   – – – – – – – –
  Noise (Nse)   – – – – – – – –
  Deception (Dcp)   0 – – – – – – – –

Immediate Resolution
  Delivery (Dlv)   0 – – – – – – – –
  Task outcome (Tko)   – – – – – – – –
  Escape (Esc)   – – – – – – – –
  Release (Rls)   – – – – – – – –
  Death (Dth)   – – – – – – – –
  Revival (Rvl)   – – – – – – – –
  Creation-Transf (Crt)   – – – – – – – –

Value Resolution
  Reward (Rwd)   0 – – – – – – – –
  Marriage (Mrg)   – – – – – – – –
  Reunion (Reu)   – – – – – – – –
  Bestowal (Bst)   – – – – – – – –

Comment (Com)   – – – – – – – – –

Secondary eidons: Transference; Information; Instruction; Facilitation; Observation; Impedance

Appendix B

ANALYSIS SHEET FOR "COMADRE"

Value Motivation										
Lack (Lck)	0	–	–	–	–	–	–	–	–	–
Immediate Motivation										
Transgression (Tgn)	0	–	–	–	–	–	–	–	–	–
Preliminary Action										
Transformation (Trf)		–	–	–	–	–	–	–	–	–
Encounter (Enc)	0	0	–	–	–	–	–	–	–	–
Transaction (Tra)	0	0	0	–	–	–	–	–	–	–
Enter Captivity (Cap)	0			–	–	–	–	–	–	–
Hospitality (Hsp)				–	–	–	–	–	–	–
Precaution (Prc)		0		–	–	–	–	–	–	–
Main Action										
Task (Tsk)	0			–	–	–	–	–	–	–
Attack (Atk)				–	–	–	–	–	–	–
Contest (Cnt)		0		–	–	–	–	–	–	–
Noise (Nse)				–	–	–	–	–	–	–
Deception (Dcp)				–	–	–	–	–	–	–
Immediate Resolution										
Delivery (Dlv)				–	–	–	–	–	–	–
Task outcome (Tko)	0			–	–	–	–	–	–	–
Escape (Esc)	–			–	–	–	–	–	–	–
Release (Rls)	–	0		–	–	–	–	–	–	–
Death (Dth)	–		0	–	–	–	–	–	–	–
Revival (Rvl)	–			–	–	–	–	–	–	–
Creation-Transf (Crt)	–		–	–	–	–	–	–	–	–
Value Resolution										
Reward (Rwd)	–	0	–	–	–	–	–	–	–	–
Marriage (Mrg)	–	–	–	–	–	–	–	–	–	–
Reunion (Reu)	–	–	–	–	–	–	–	–	–	–
Bestowal (Bst)	–	–	–	–	–	–	–	–	–	–
Comment (Com)	–	–	–	–	–	–	–	–	–	–

Secondary eidons: Transference; Information; Instruction; Facilitation; Observation; Impedance

ANALYSIS SHEET FOR "THE Č'I²LA NAQ"

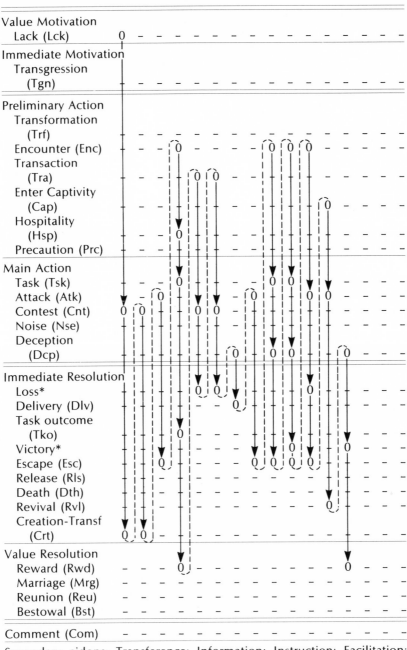

Value Motivation
  Lack (Lck)

Immediate Motivation
  Transgression
  (Tgn)

Preliminary Action
  Transformation
  (Trf)
  Encounter (Enc)
  Transaction
  (Tra)
  Enter Captivity
  (Cap)
  Hospitality
  (Hsp)
  Precaution (Prc)

Main Action
  Task (Tsk)
  Attack (Atk)
  Contest (Cnt)
  Noise (Nse)
  Deception
  (Dcp)

Immediate Resolution
  Loss*
  Delivery (Dlv)
  Task outcome
  (Tko)
  Victory*
  Escape (Esc)
  Release (Rls)
  Death (Dth)
  Revival (Rvl)
  Creation-Transf
  (Crt)

Value Resolution
  Reward (Rwd)
  Marriage (Mrg)
  Reunion (Reu)
  Bestowal (Bst)

Comment (Com)

Secondary eidons: Transference; Information; Instruction; Facilitation;
Observation; Impedance
* Asterisk indicates added eidon candidates

APPENDIX C
DIVINATION
PRAYER

ʔAaq'ii Šas Koʔw's Prayer on the Day 4 K'ač

Hesus Mariiya Hoseewa Kriisto, wentasyon kučuč kub'aal
Jesus, Maria, Joseph, Christ, bestow blessing, sacred gods

Taʔn koq tešlal santa kruus
Through the sign of the holy cross

ʔOʔ ikoloʔkoʔ tuul iq'ab' qaaca qalab'al
[He] who took us into his hand from the time of our birth:

En yooš palaaš i spiiritu santos, ameen: Kriisto.
(in the name) of God, Father, and Holy Ghost, amen: Christ.

Kub'aal yooš ʔaanhel, teče? Muundo posiib'le
Our father, God, Spirit, be greeted, Worldgod,

Kub'aal loq'ola q'ii, loq'ola saq
Our Fathers the Holy Days, the Holy Dawns,

Kat ʔel č'uʔl Wiʔ Čoo, ʔel č'uʔl kub'aal Wiʔ Palaaw Kriisto
Who left from the place of the lakes, who left from the place of the sea,
Christ,

Tiʔ waʔ s qilčeʔ, tiʔ qab'ileʔ
To watch over us, to listen to us,

Kučuč kub'aal ʔalmikaʔ, yooš ʔaanhel, tečeʔ Muundo,
Sacred gods of heaven, gods and ʔaanhel, be greeted, Worldgod,

Kureey kučuč kub'aal
Our rulers, sacred gods:

Paadre senyoor San Peedro, kub'aal yooš
Father and master Saint Peter, our Lords and Gods

Loq'ola q'ii, loq'ola saq, kučuč kub'aal ʔalmikaʔ posiib'le.
The Holy Days, Holy Dawns, sacred gods of the heaven:

ʔIlaʔ b'a, Kriisto, tuk ėk'učunseʔ, tuk ek'učunsa
It *is* here—Christ, make it show now, make it visible now,

Lenaawitsa te wemeʔal te wek'aol
Reveal it to your daughter, to your son:

Domiingo Peeresʔaʔ posiib'le, Kriisto yooš.
It is Domingo Perez, Christ God.

ʔilaʔ kučuč, ʔilaʔ kub'aal
Here it is, our Mother, here it is, our Father:

Haqb'al kuyb'al, haqb'al liseensya
the petition of favor, the petition of indulgence [from]

Kaʔwaʔltib' meʔal k'aol, yooš ʔaanhel tečeʔ
A pair of children. Gods and aanhel, be greeted,

Kučuč kub'aal b'a teʔ
You are surely our sacred gods:

Pap kub'aal loq'ola q'ii, loq'ola saq
Lords, our Gods, the Holy Days, the Holy Dawns:

Kub'aal kaqwaʔl K'ač
Our God 4 K'ach,

ʔEş kučuč ʔeş kub'aal, Pap, posiib'le
You are our Mother, you are our Father, Lord, forgive,

Soqsa ipaaw u meʔal kʼaol, kaʔwaʔltibʼ čaq ʔoya maayi
Forgive the children's fault, the pair of Mayi offspring:

Domiingo Peeres ʔilaʔ tukʼ was ameʔal akʼaol aʔ, posiibʼle
It is Domingo Perez here with your daughter, your son, —please

Posiibʼle ʔeş kučuč ʔeş kubʼaal bʼa
Forgive, —you are our Mother, you are our Father for sure,

Pap, loqʼola qʼii loqʼola saq,
Lord, Holy Day, Holy Dawn

Kʼubaal ʔoʔwaʔl Kan
Our God 5 Ķan

ʔEč koq tuk ekʼučunsa tuk enaawitsa te was emeʔal ekʼaol, posiibʼle
Could you only make it visible, make it apparent to your daughter and son,

Posiibʼle, kubʼaal yooš
Our masters and gods, please:

ʔEş kubʼaal loqʼola qʼii loqʼola saq, —kubʼaal
You are our Gods, the Holy Days, the Holy Dawns, —our God

Pap ʔoʔwaʔl Kan, mayuul, tečeʔ kučuč kubʼaal
Lord 5 Kan, the officer, be greeted, sacred god:

ʔEč koq tuk ekʼučunsa tuk enaawitsa bʼa
Could you only make it visible, make it apparent right now,

Posiibʼle Kriisto, kam paalta pees
Forgive, Christ—what is the fault then

Te kʼašʼkʼo tiʔ čaq meʔal kʼaol
For the difficulty with the children [who are]

Şeʔ was etoq, şeʔ was eqʼabʼ.
At your feet, at your hands.

ʔeş kučuč ʔeş kubʼaaleʔ, Pap
You are our Mother, you are our Father, Lord—

ʔAteş tuul enimal ebʼalaleʔ Kriisto diooš
You are present inside your dominion, your dwelling, Christ god,

Siib'le kub'aal, kučuč kub'aal, Mariiya santiisima
Forgive, our Masters, sacred gods, Maria santissima,

Kučuč kub'aal ʔaanhel
Sacred god and Father Nazarene,

Salwadoor muundo, paadre eteerno, ʔiiho de la gwaardo
Savior of the world, eternal father, son of the guard,

ʔomb're werdadeero, rewentoor muundo, kreadoor i rewentoor
True man, redeemer of the world, creator and redeemer:

ʔEš kučuč kub'aal
You are our sacred gods,

Milaagro kub'aal yooš ʔaanhel, pap posiib'le
Our miraculous masters, gods and ʔaanhel, Lords,

Tečeʔ b'a, Kriisto, tuk unhaq u kuyb'al, tuk unhaq u liseensya
Be greeted then, Christ, I am asking the favor, I am asking permission

Tiʔ wik'učunsaleʔ: ma yeʔl u maq paalta, ma yeʔl u maq k'ašk'o
For its revelation: is there any penalty, is there any hardship

Tiʔ u meʔal tiʔ u k'aol
For the daughter, for the son?

Haqb'al kuyb'al liseensya tiʔ u ʔoya maayi
Petition of favor, of indulgence for the Mayi offspring:

Petroona Maarkos ʔilaʔ
Here is Petrona Marcos:

kučuč kub'aal, yooš, Pap, soqsa kupaaw, ʔeš kučuč ʔeš kub'aal b'a, po-siib'le
Holy deities, gods, Lords, forgive our sins, you are our sacred gods,

Kuhaq u kuyb'aleʔ: ma yeʔl u maq ʔil
We pray for the favor: is there not a danger,

Ma yeʔl u maq caʔl
Is there not a peril

Tiʔ u meʔal, tiʔ u k'aol
For the daughter, for the son?

Kub'aal diyoos, ?ila? b'a, Pap
Our masters and gods, here it is then, Lords,

Tuk wab'i b'a s ete
I am asking you:

?eyene? seşe? ?eş kučuč, ?eş kub'aal
The truth is there with you, you are our Mother, you are our Father:

Santa la Waara, ?Aana siila, ?Aana meesa
Katarina the priest, Katarina the diviner,

?Antoonyo siila, ?Antoonyo meesa
Antonio the priest, Antonio the diviner,

Paaskwaal siila, Paaskwaal meesa, teče?, kučuč kub'aal, reey:
Pasqual the priest, Pasqual the diviner, be greeted, holy deities, kings:

Kub'aal San Marčoor, San Warkasaal
God Saint Melchor, Saint Baltasar,

Milaagro kub'aal, paadre senyoor San Peedro
Miraculous Gods, Father senyor Peter,

San Peedro Maartin, San Peedro Apooštol
Saint Peter the martyr, Saint Peter the apostle,

San Peedro Wiirhin, San Peedro Luupa
Saint Peter of the Virgin, Saint Peter of Guadalupe,

?I San Peedro las glooriya
And Saint Peter of the glory,

Ib'aal u muundo, ib'aal ?almika?
Master of the world, master of the heaven,

Ib'aal laawe tu glooriya, tu syeelo, Pap, posiib'le.
Master of the key to paradise, to heaven, Lord,

Icaeb'al u kub'aale? ib'uq'eb'al kučuč kub'aale?
Place of the departure of our Lord the sun, place of the appearance of the holy deities,

Tu saanto la Rooma, Saantos Paapa
In holy Rome, the holy Pope,

Kaasa Roosa de Čeruusalem
The house of the Rose of Jerusalem,

Kučuč kub'aal
Holy deities:

Reeiy de la ʔEspanya, icaeb'al
King of Spain, place of the departure of

U kučuč, icae(b'al) u kub'aaleʔ b'a posiib'le
Our Mother the Moon, [place of the] departure of our Father the Sun,

(ʔat) koq yeʔ nikaʔy kat
There is nowhere she would not peer into,

(ʔat) koq yeʔ ni tilon kat kučuč
There is nowhere she would not look into, our Mother the Moon,

Koq yeʔ ni tilon kat kub'aal—Pap posiib'le
Where he would not gaze down, our Father the Sun, Lord,

Kaqayil: tuulaq koka tuulaq siwidaad
Everything: in the wilderness, in the middle of town,

Čalaq čaq išikin ʔamaq'
Alongside the slopes of the hills: [that is]

Kat ʔilon kat, kat ʔab'in kat kub'aal
Where our Father observes, where he listens,

Tuulaq koka tuulaq heʔnaq kuʔnaq
Amidst the mountains, amidst the ascents and descents,

Tuulaq koka, siwidad posiib'le
Amidst the mountainous countryside, the cities,

Tuulaq b'ele čolčo, ʔošlaa čolčo,
Amidst the 9 springs, amidst the 13 springs: [that is]

Tilon kat u kub'aaleʔ
Where our Father the Sun observes.

ʔokoq u yoleʔ s ešeʔ
Would the message be received by you,

ʔokoq wunyoleʔ te etoq te eq'ab'
Would my word be received at your feet, at your hands,

Kub'aal paadre
Our God and Father,

Salwadoor muundo, paadre Heesu Kriisto
Savior of the World, Father Jesus Christ,

Paayre Selestiyaal
Heavenly Father,

ʔEš Kub'aal, ʔeš kučuč
You are our Father, you are our Mother,

ʔAteš tuul enimal, tuul eb'alal
You are present in your kingdom, in your power,

ʔEš unčuč unb'aal Kriisto ʔilaʔ b'a, pap
You are my Mother, you are my Father, Christ, it is here, Lord,

ʔeč koq tuk ek'učunsa
Would you make it visible,

ʔeč koq tuk enaawitsa
Would you make it apparent,

ʔIl was emeʔal ek'aol posiib'le
These are your children,

Loq'ola q'ii, loq'ola saq, pap posiib'le
Holy Day, holy Dawn, Lord, please,

Kučuč unb'aal Kriisto, ʔaay diyooš
Holy Mother, my Father Christ, oh God,

ʔEš kub'aal ʔeš kučuč
You are our Father, you are our Mother,

ʔAay pap posiib'le, tečeʔ
Oh Lord forgive, be greeted,

Soqsa tunpaaw
Forgive my sin,

La nimal was icii u meʔal k'aol
Will you honor the children's plea,

Tuk qab'i b'a ti? u me?al, tuk qab'i b'a posiib'le
We do listen for the daughter, we do listen now:

?Ab'iste? u paaw ti? was ica?l posiib'le
What is the cause for her debt toward the gods?

?A?e? wa? nihaqe? u ame?al k'aol—teče?
This is what they are asking, the children of yours, be greeted,

Kučuč kub'aal ?almika? yooš ?aanhel
Holy deities of heaven, Gods, spirits,

?Eš unčuč ?eš unb'aale?, pap
You are my Mother, you are my Father, Lord,

?Ateš tu enimal eb'alal
You dwell in your kingdom, your residence,

Kriisto, yooš Muundo
Christ, Worldgod,

?Ila? b'a kub'aal, loq'ola Muundo
It is here, God, Holy World,

Qaaleb'al, posiib'le, ka?šob' ?ošob'
At our place of worship, the two-cornered, three cornered,

Kaasimaka
Four-cornered room [house],

Wi? pwerta, še? Markoo
The doorstep of the kitchen,

Siinta, cucub'al, šoraal, pe? q'anal kolom
Door rope, gutter, patio, yard inside the patio fence:

Teče? kučuč kub'aal ?almika?, yooš ?aanhel
Be greeted, holy deities of heaven, gods and spirits,

?Ila? pap posiib'le
Take notice, Lords,

Posiib'le kub'aal
Our Gods

Kab'lawal ?aanhel, ?ilol qec ?ab'in qec
12 aanhel, who see us, who hear us,

Kab'lawal santos ʔaanimas—posiib'le
12 holy souls,

Kučuč kub'aal, ʔaanima de las ʔispriitu
Holy deities, souls of the spirits,

ʔIlol qec, ʔab'in qec, kučuč kub'aal
Who see us, who listen to us, holy deities,

Imool kub'aal tiʔ tel č'uʔl Wiʔ Čoo
Our Lord the Sun's companions when he leaves the Place of the Lake,

Imool kub'aal tiʔ tel č'uʔl Wiʔ Palaaw
Our Lord the Sun's companions when he leaves the Place of the Sea,

Tu čaala č'awaʔ tu b'ešla č'awaʔ
In sacred country, in holy country

Kučuč kub'aal
Holy deities

Kab'lawal santos wiirhin
12 holy virgins,

Posiib'le kučuč kub'aal
Holy deities:

Mal icaal u q'ii, icaal u saq
Perhaps the Day has left, the Dawn has left [to watch]

Kamal ʔat umaq kupaaw
If we committed a sin,

Kamal ʔat umaq qil
If there is danger for us

Tuk' meʔal k'aol
With the children:

Diooš, ʔaanhel ʔeš kučuč unb'aal
Gods, aanhel, you are our holy parents,

Kučuč kub'aal ʔalkaalte
Holy deities our chiefs,

ʔAlkaalte kub'aal Kaqay
Chief god Kahay,

ˀAlkaalte kub'aal Kuˀišal
Chief god Kuˀisal,

ˀAlkaalte kub'aal Kučul Č'im
Chief god Kučul Č'im,

ˀAlkaalte Kub'aal Čaˀš B'aac'
Chief god Čaˀš B'aac',

Kuwicil kučaq'alil kub'aal Laawic ˀiqlenaal
Of our mountside, of our valleys, god Laawic, the ruler,

ˀIlol qec, ˀab'in qec b'a posiib'le
Who sees us, who surely hears us,

Kub'aal Čaš Mala, kub'aal yooš ˀaanhel
Our God Čaš Mala, Lord, gods and ˀaanhel,

Kučuč kub'aal muundo: Wiˀ Laham
Holy deities of the world: Wiˀ Laham,

Kub'aal Nimla Č'aab'al
Our God Nimla Č'aab'al,

Kub'aal Payiič ˀAˀ
Our God Payiič ˀAˀ,

Kub'aal Tiin Qowec
Our God Tiin Qowec,

Wiˀ ˀiˀleb'al tu Saakab'
Place of rest at Saakab',

Kub'aal Kampu Santo
Our God of the cemetery,

Komoon ˀAnima, Wiˀ Wayiik'a—posiib'le
Of the house of the souls, of the place of repose,

Kub'aal Wiˀ Čočol, Kub'aal Wiˀ Sib'aq' Wic
Our God Wiˀ Čočol, God Wiˀ Sib'aq' Wic,

ˀAanhel Ciˀ Sučum, šeˀ Kub'aal Huˀil
ˀAanhel Ciˀ Sučum, near our God Huˀil,

Reey San Kaspaar
King Saint Gaspar,

Milaagro kučuč Kub'aal
Miraculous deities,

San Martiin, San Luukas—posiib'le
Saint Martin, Saint Luke, please,

Kub'aal San Marčoor, San Warkasaal
Our gods Saint Melchor, Saint Baltasar

ʔEş kučuč, ʔeş kub'aal
You are our Mothers, you are our Fathers.

Paayre San Hwaan, Mariiya santiisima
Father Saint John, Maria the holiest,

Mariiya de glooriya, Mariiya del syeelo
Maria of the glory, Maria of Heaven,

Tan ʔeş kučuč, ʔeş kub'aal
Because you are our holy Mother, you are our holy Father,

ʔAteş tuul enimal, eb'alal
You are present in your kingdom, your residence,

Kat koq yeʔ nekaʔy kat
There is no place from where you cannot observe us,

Kat koq yeʔ netilon kat
There is no place from where you cannot see us, [you],

U kub'aaleʔ s ʔalmikaʔ tu glooriya syeelo
The Lords of Heaven, in the glory, the sky:

ʔIloʔ ʔatoʔ wac u muundoeʔ, ʔatoʔ wac u č'awaʔ
Here we are who face the world, who face the earth,

ʔAtoʔ wac u ʔalmikaʔ
Who face the sky,

Paleb'al ʔoʔ k'uʔl
We, the cause of disturbance,

ʔOʔ č'onsan awiʔ, ʔoʔ č'onsan asikin
We who hurt your head, we who hurt your ear,

ʔAtoʔ wac u muundo
We who are facing the world,

Tečeʔ Muundo, lesoqsa wunpaaw
Be greeted, Worldgod, would you forgive my sins,

Letaleʔ, la ʔoq'ayeš
Will you talk, will you reply?

[The day count begins]

Kub'aal kaqwaʔl K'ač
ʔOʔwaʔl Kan
Waašil Kamel
Wuqwaʔl Čee
Waašaqil Q'anil
B'eluwal Čoo
Lawal Či ʔ
Kučuč kub'aal pap posiib'le
Holy deities, Lords,

Lawal Č'i ʔ
Hunlawal Kub'aal B'aac', posiib'le
Kub'aal Kablawal ʔEe
ʔOšlawal ʔAa
ʔUmaʔl ʔIʔš, pap
Kaʔwaʔl C'ikin
ʔOšwaʔl ʔAama
Kub'aal ʔOšwaʔl ʔAama
ʔUmaʔl Noʔq
Kaawaʔl Tiaš
ʔOšwaʔl Kaoo
Kaqwaʔl Hunaapu
ʔOʔwaʔl ʔImuš
Waaqil ʔliq' ʔAlkaalte
Wuqwaʔl ʔAq'b'al
Waašaqil K'ač
B'eluwal Kan
Lawal Kamel
Hunlawal Čee
Kab'lawal Q'anil
ʔOšlawal Čoo
ʔUmaʔl Č'i ʔ
Kaʔwaʔl B'aac'
ʔOšwaʔl ʔEe

ʔAlkaalte soqsa kupaaw
Chief, forgive our sin

ʔOšwaʔl ʔEe
3 ʔEe

ʔEš kučuč, ʔeš kub'aal, Pap
You are our holy Mother, you are our holy Father, Lord

ʔAteš tenimal, teb'alal
You who are present in your kingdom, in your residence:

Teče? yooš ʔaanhel, posiib'le soqsa umpaaw
Be greeted, gods and spirits, erase my sin,

Leb'an b'aʔnil, leb'an čečil
Will you do the favor, will you give the sign,

ʔEč koq ek'učunsa taq
You should make it visible,

ʔEč koq enaawitsa taq
You should make it apparent,

U b'aʔnil, u čečil te was emeʔaleʔ, te was ek'aoleʔ
The favor, the sign, for the daughters, for the sons of yours,

Kučuč kub'aal, ʔilaʔ pap, posiib'le
Holy deities, there it is, Lord,

Haqb'al kuyb'al, haqb'al liseensya
The petition of favor, the petition of indulgence

Kaʔwaʔl tib' u meʔal k'aol, čukb'al tib' u ʔoya maayi
(For) the pair of children, the couple of ʔoya Mayi,

Haqb'al kuyb'al, haqb'al liseensya
Petition of favor, petition of acquittal

ʔOq'ayoq čit eš, etal taq—posiib'le
Do answer, tell us

Kam u paalta kam u k'ašk'om
What the fault is, what the displeasure is,

Ma hit u maq č'oʔm ma ʔat u maq yaab'il
Whether there isn't a sickness or some weakness,

Kam paalta la ileq unq'a meʔal k'aol—posiib'le
Which fault will the children encounter:

ʔAʔeʔ tuk qab'i, ʔaʔeʔ tuk kuč'oti wac u tiiš, tiʔ u kub'aal
This is what we listen for, this is what we ask facing the altar, from the gods of

Loq'ola q'ii, loq'ola saq Pap
The Holy Day, Holy Dawn, Lord.

GLOSSARY

THEORETICAL TERMS

cognitive system A system of schemata. A cognitive system can consist of the productive mechanisms of observed behavior pattern sequences and arrangements and of the controlling or choice mechanisms for selecting them, which include evaluations and motivations. It also includes the perceptual systems needed for the recognition of patterns.

cultural grammar An approximation to some part of a cognitive system for conventionalized behavior, usually within some genre, in terms of a set of elements and production rules.

cultural pattern A sequence, arrangement, or other regularity perceived in an artifact, process, or situation that results from a cultural production or from human behavior. While cognitive schemata are drawn upon in the perception of regularity, pattern is theoretically treated as external to the individual.

cultural production Any physical result of human behavior generated by a cognitive system that has, in turn, been developed through interaction with prior cultural patterns. Productions include artifacts, performances, meetings, games, and rituals. Cultural productions are communicated to another person who takes cognizance of the object or behavior by recognizing its significance, that is, by seeing some regularity or pattern in it and attaching some value to it. Cultural productions are thus vehicles for cultural patterns.

eidon An element of a cultural pattern that can be identified through the comparative analysis of different examples of the genre exhibiting the pattern. It is the basic "chunk" of the pattern and is part of a hierarchy or system of chunks that facilitates processing in the short-term memory system. Eidon varieties can be events, concepts, or design elements.

> **process eidon** An eidon that constitutes one of a sequence of eidonic chunks through time or in serial order. Process eidons may be referred to as eidochronic elements.
> **arrangement eidon** An eidon that constitutes one of several eidonic chunks arranged spatially, as the constituents of an iconic or pictorial design or the parts of a letter in the alphabet. Arrangement eidons may be referred to as eidospatial elements of an arrangement pattern in two- or three-dimensional space.

frame The analyst's rough approximation to either a perceived world or a mental system including data structures and procedures.

frame network A series of frames interconnected by access pointers for retrieving data or procedures.

image A short-term memory representation of some aspect of the world through either a match of schemata to what is perceived, or through schemata alone (as called up in dreams, for example).

model The analyst's theoretical description of a more encompassing type than frame or grammar.

schema Representation of elements, events, and relationships in the mind of an individual. Schemata include the means to construct the following cognitive phenomena which, in turn, are also schemata: (1) a mental representation of a prototype: (2) a generalization of a pattern and its context(s); (3) a set of rules for carrying out various operations on patterns and their contexts; (4) an element of a generative system. See Bartlett (1932), Piaget (1962), and Becker (1973) for more detailed and variant descriptions.

thematic array A repeated or conventionalized pattern of significance which organizes cultural experience in the form of a series, list, or ordered arrangement that is not temporal (in contradistinction to a thematic sequence or eidochronic sequence). The day god attribute list is an example.

thematic sequence A recurrent and significant pattern that organizes cultural experience. It is a sequence of ideas, a chain of events, a motif, or simply a proposition about the world that occurs frequently. A thematic sequence is usually a more abstract or higher-level representation of an eidochronic pattern; but it also may be a lower-level "prototype" representation in a metonymic relationship. One example is the sequence from transgression to imprisonment (sickness) to appeal and release found both in the folk narratives and the divination process.

IXIL AND SPANISH WORDS

ˀ**aab'oola** One who carries skyrockets.

ˀ**aakun** A person who practices witchcraft.

ˀ**aama** People. Regarded as sentient.

ˀ**aanhel** Deities who act as intermediaries between the high god, Kub'aal, and mortals. Among the many ˀaanhel are lords of the mountains and springs.

ˀ**aanima** Soul.

ˀ**aaq'ii** A calendar specialist and diviner; one of the types of Ixil priests who specialize in divination and knowledge of the Mayan calendar. The term ʔaaqʼii is used when the daykeeping function is stressed, ʔaameeša when the divination function is emphasized.

Acción Católica A lay Catholic organization, "Catholic Action," engaged, among other things, in the "reconversion" of Guatemalan Indians. Members are sometimes referred to as "catequistas" (cate-chists).

ʔalmikaʔ Sky, heaven.

alcalde (Ixil: ʔalkaalte) The mayor or highest municipal official. When spelled with a capital, signifies any of the four day gods which can start a New Year in the Ixil calendar.

alguacil (šeempoobʼal) A municipal official in charge of menial chores, sometimes called **mayor,** but not to be confused with the four mayores of a higher-level office.

bʼaal Father; owner.

bʼaal mertoma Leader or "father" of the mayordomos of a religious brotherhood.

bʼaalwactiiš Prayersayer, "father before god."

bʼaal wic (Supernatural) owner or lord of a hill or mountain; an ʔaanhel.

bʼaʔnil Blessing.

bʼaqʼ mič Seeds of the **mič** or palo pito (coral) tree.

bʼaša rišitol The highest Indian municipal official in Nebaj, who holds the position of second **regidor.** (In Ixil **bʼaša** means first.) Earlier when all the officials were Indians, this term was used for the first regidor.

bʼoʔqʼol bʼaalwactiiš The Ixil high priest in Nebaj who, like the ʔaaqʼii, keeps the day count. He decides on the dates of ceremonies and has an important function at cofradía ceremonies and community-wide ceremonies, such as the celebration of the Ixil New Year.

b'o²q'ol tenam   The Ixil leader of the principales in Nebaj; a kind of **primus inter pares** among "elder statesmen."

cantón   A section of a town; a neighborhood.

caporal   A foreman; on a plantation, it is the lowest-level supervisor, often an Indian.

ča²šla q'ii   `Favorable day for ritual.

catequista   An Indian who has been "reconverted" to orthodox Catholicism, a member of **Acción Católica.** Sometimes such a person is militantly opposed to traditional forms of Ixil ritual.

chilacayotes   Whitish melonlike fruits (*cucurbita ficifolia*).

č'i²la naq   Bad men; in Ixil mythology the evil older brothers of Kub'aal, Our Father. Sometimes referred to as "Our Uncles of old."

cofradía   A religious brotherhood centered around one of the saints; the most important type of religious association in Ixil society.

colono   A person who contracts to live and work on a finca (plantation) for a period of time.

compadre (Ixil: Kumpaale)   Literally, "co-father"; a reciprocal term of address and reference used between a person's godparent and his biological parents; its feminine form is **comadre,** or "co-mother." In the Cotzal dialect of Ixil it refers to a daykeeper or prayersayer, including the four ranked "official" daykeepers.

contratista   A labor recruiter, usually a ladino; also known as **habilitador.** The term **contratista,** emphasizing the contractual aspect in which indebtedness is limited, is preferred by ladinos.

čo²unši²   (My) wool blanket.

cuerda A measure of an area equal to 32 square **varas** (33 inches), between one-fifth and one-sixth of an acre.

čusul (maestro de coro in Spanish) An Indian church official who officiates at important cofradía ceremonies, burials, and other religious activities traditionally associated with the church.

-ešlal (Visible) sign.

finca A land estate or plantation.

güisquil Vegetable pear or chayote (*sechium edule*).

huipil Indian blouse, usually with woven designs.

ʔil Trouble, danger.

ʔiqaʔl Slingshot.

jornalero Wage worker on a finca.

juzgado Tribunal or courthouse; the term used in Nebaj to designate the town hall, which is formally known as the **Alcaldía Municipal.**

Kub'aal Our Father, an honorific which, with Kučuč, goes with most deity names, but when used alone without a prior referent usually denotes the supreme god.

Kub'aal q'ii The supreme god in the Ixil pantheon; literally, "our father sun," or "day."

Kučuč Mariy The highest ranking cofradía in Nebaj, that of the Virgin Mary of the Assumption, the patron saint of Nebaj.

maestro de coro See **čusul.**

manzana A measure of area equal to 16 cuerdas, or 10,000 square varas.

mayor (Ixil: **mayuul**)   One of four ranked municipal officials below the status of regidor, but above that of alguacil and policía.

mayordomo (**mertoma** in Ixil)   One of ten ranked office holders in an Indian cofradía.

mertomil   A shortened form of **mertomail,** which is derived from the Spanish **mayordomo.**

mič   The palo pito tree from which seeds for divination are obtained; also used to refer to the divination bundle.

municipio   A subdivision of a **departamento;** a district or county including a town and its rural hinterland. **Municipios,** in turn, are divided into **aldeas.**

meeša   The divining bundle; the power of divination.

piškal (**fiscal** in Spanish)   In colonial times, a religious official who was the right hand of the parish priest. Current functions are similar to that of the čušul and involve cofradía ceremonies, funerals, and other activities associated with the church.

policía   The police; in Nebaj, the unpaid Indian youths whose main duty is to patrol the streets at night.

pom   Incense, from tree resin in disk form, usually wrapped in corn husk or packages. The best grade is called "cuilco" (from the town it used to be made in).

principal   An Indian "elder statesman" who has occupied high political or religious office.

Q'esla Kub'aal   The supreme god in the Ixil pantheon; "great father," "ancient father."

regidor   A municipal councillor ranked from one through six or seven according to the number of council members.

sacristán A parish official who combines custodial, caretaking, and ritual functions.

saqb'ičil Dawn ceremony, lasting usually from early evening through the early morning of the next day. There is music and prayer. During the ceremony people talk, eat, drink, and dance. There are also one or more rituals carried out by one or more baal-wactiiš.

šaqal One of four assistants of the **maestro de coro** and **fiscal**. Duties include ringing the church bells during processions.

señora Ladina; female deities may take the form of a ladina.

síndico An official of the municipal council whose functions include registering land transactions.

tarea A day's work; about one cuerda cleared of trees, bushes, or weeds. In 1910 about one peso was paid per tarea.

tiiš God; saint statues in church.

vara (Ixil: **waara**) Measure of length equal to 836 mm (32 or 33 inches); a ceremonial staff of approximately that length carried by officers of municipal councils. Also used to refer to the sacred divining bundle of the ʔaameeša.

Wiʔ ʔAama Prayer hut at the cemetery.

Wiʔ Kamnaq Cemetery.

wiʔ šokomil šiʔ Chamarra, a coarse wool jacket.

NOTES

1. BEGINNINGS, METHODS, AND ISSUES

1. The letter "x" in Ixil was used by the early Spanish missionaries to represent a sound lacking in Spanish but which comes close to the English *sh*. The chief indicator of conservatism among the Ixil is that they have retained more elements of the pre-Columbian calendar than other Mesoamerican groups (Miles, 1952; Nash, 1957).

2. In the linguistic alphabet, Šas Koʔw.

3. Pap is an honorific term, something between Mister and Sir.

4. Lévi-Strauss's writings stimulated public interest, but the chief novelty was in his style and rhetoric. His earlier, more theoretical work on kinship is in dispute and has not affected neighboring social science disciplines, nor does it approach the comprehensive theory of cultural mechanisms and processes that we have in mind. See Thomas, Kronenfeld, and Kronenfeld (1976) and Kronenfeld and Decker (1980) for a critique from the viewpoint of cognitive anthropology.

5. The tapes and transcriptions are on file at the Laboratory of Anthropology, School of Social Sciences, University of California, Irvine. We plan to have them microfilmed to facilitate use by other scholars.

6. Strictly speaking, if the term "culture" is used at all there is naturally some binding, if only at a high level of generality. But for our purposes we speak of such usages as unbound. Thus unless culture is described as bound, the context will have to suffice for meaning variations or for implicit bindings at higher levels of generality. Binding culture as a variable therefore gives us a way out of the dilemma caused by traditional notions of culture as a homogeneous unit with coincident linguistic, political, and religious boundaries.

300

7. Rice (1978, 1980) has recently carried out some experiments in this area, basing her work on an anthropological perspective such as we have taken here. Her results are suggestive for further theoretical studies.

8. For example, Susan Tax Freeman (forthcoming) in her studies of Spanish village life interrelates the values and concerns of the people with folk poetry and saying; Sebeok and Ingemann (1965) have made an extensive analysis of the forms of such devices and their interrelationships in an ethnographic context among the Cheremis; Bascom's study of Ifa divination (1969) and Jacobs's study of oral literature (1959) are further examples. For a general overview of folk productions see Edmonson (1971b).

9. We think that artificial intelligence and anthropology have much to offer each other. Text comprehension programs in artificial intelligence are cumulative and provide many useful formalisms for characterizing belief systems, contexts of situation, and behavioral sequences. What is lacking, however, is the overall theoretical sophistication concerning cultural phenomena that anthropologists might be able to supply, along with their primarily ethnographic interest of representing how a group of people view the world and act in it. In spite of the natural affinity of these two disciplines for each other, their practitioners have only recently become aware of such possibilities. Significant work by anthropologists has already begun. In addition to the earlier Ixil divination computer program, Werner, Sailer, and their associates at Northwestern (Werner, n.d.; Werner and Topper, 1975) have made some interesting studies. In the summer of 1979 Naomi Quinn organized a Social Science Research Council conference which brought together anthropologists, psychologists, and artificial intelligence researchers. At the University of California, Irvine, we have established a Laboratory for Text Ethnography where artificial intelligence techniques are being applied to the content analysis of narrative and expository texts (James and Colby, 1979).

10. In our work we have drawn upon cognitive science (Rumelhart, 1975; Mandler and Johnson, 1977; Schank and Abelson, 1977), philosophy (Popper, 1966a and b, 1968; Searle, 1969; Husserl, 1973), semiotics (Watt, 1975, 1978a and b), and linguistics (Hymes, 1959, 1974; Halliday, 1967–68, 1977; Longacre, 1968; Quillian, 1968; Grimes, 1975) as well as the writings within anthropology on ethnoscience (Werner, n.d.; Werner and Topper, 1975), propositional analysis (D'Andrade, 1976), information processing (Horton and Finnegan, 1973; Hinz, 1978; Kronenfeld, 1979), decision making (Barth, 1967; Quinn, 1975, 1976), metaphor and symbolic content (Fernandez, 1967; Sapir and Crocker, 1977; Quinn, 1979), psychobiological anthropology (Laughlin and D'Aquili, 1974), and evolutionary anthropology (Carneiro, 1973). The way in which the developments cited above have influenced our thinking is not always spelled out in the chapters that follow. Our purpose is not to review them; we cite them here by way of general acknowledgment only.

2. HISTORICAL AND RELIGIOUS BACKGROUND

1. From text #315, p. 52, tape 45, 2nd side.
2. From text #208.
3. There is some interesting linguistic evidence. There are a number of Quiché loanwords in Ixil speech, and some of them, such as the calendar names, may possibly have been adopted before the conquest. Terrance Kaufman thinks, however, that at least some of the borrowings are post-conquest, which suggests a number of possibilities, among them that control over the Ixil was maintained by Quiché troops who were loyal to the Spanish; another possible reason is that Ixil spent a considerable amount of time outside Ixil country as merchants among Quiché speakers. We know that much later they had contact with Quiché speakers as wage laborers in the lowlands. Shas Ko?w spoke some Quiché himself. However, he says that at an earlier time very few Ixil could speak Quiché
4. Photographs and drawings of these murals will be published in a subsequent monograph on a Dance Drama of Chajul.
5. From text #321, tape 48, 2nd side.
6. These supermen were credited with the building of houses that reached up to the sky; they owned treasures of gold and jewelry; and they possessed other superhuman qualities.
7. The Ixil *komoon* is a loanword from Spanish. It is also used to refer to the communal praying house in the cemetery, which is used for rituals addressed to all the souls.
8. From text #209B.
9. A reconstruction drawing was made of the site by Proskouriakoff (1963).
10. If the religious system is so central in the Ixil area (at least it has been in the past), we might look at the Catholic alternative to the current syncretic tradition deriving from the early colonial period. Here again there is a difference. In Zinacantan there was no resident priest when we were there. The attitude of the priest who visited Zinacantan was one of continual exasperation at the people's traditionalism and backwardness. This attitude contrasts with the much more sustained effort of the missionary priests from Spain who live in the three Ixil towns. There is a much closer and more personal relationship between the priest and the converts and a close-knit camaraderie among the converts themselves. Though the priests change frequently and there is little understanding by some of them of the subtler points of Ixil traditional belief, there has been an increasing willingness to make accommodations.
11. An interesting contrast between Zinacantan and Zapotec witchcraft beliefs is that in the Zapotec group Selby studied, witchcraft candidates are sociologically distant (1974, p. 120). But this is less often the case in Zinacantan. In our field experience we knew of one Zinacantan person who suspected his own father. Though the Ixil believe that sickness is often caused by the souls of fathers and other close relatives, it is not the

result of direct action by these souls but rather their sense of injustice being passed on to the gods, who then cause the sickness. Moreover, the reason is quite different. We do not know of any Ixil cases in which sickness was attributed to envy on the part of an ancestral soul (though envy as a motive is frequently attributed to living people).

12. It is curious that when Pap Shas's purpose is didactic, in situations where he wants to impart his knowledge, advice, or admonitions, his style vacillates between the formal and more casual modes, as will be seen in his "philosophy text" of Chapter 4. This mixed style is also present in some of the more religious folktales, especially when there is conversation between gods and humans.

13. One can see how this would facilitate the learning of a text. However, the more formalized a text the more ellipsis there is, the more the semantic load is carried by certain presuppositions that are not stated (which a specialist with highly esoteric knowledge would not have to state). This means that without a rich body of myth and folktales, and particularly without an active use of an astrological system such as Shas's divinations, much of the information alluded to indirectly in the prayers can be lost. This is why it is so difficult to derive an understanding of the religious system from the prayers alone, often the only really rich material that remains among more acculturated Mayan peoples.

3. SHAS KO²W'S LIFE HISTORY

1. An Ixil child will receive an Ixil name combination chosen from the grandparent generation, including great-uncles and great-aunts. The child is supposedly the present or future replacement of the person whose name he carries. The Ixil term č'eš means "replacement"; in Quiché it also has the association of "repayment." There are often close ties between the two family members joined by a č'eš relationship. The older person will pay special attention to his younger namesake while he grows up, for instance, protecting him against small punishments or injustices within the family. After the death of the older person the namesake is expected to remember the departed č'eš in prayers and rituals.

The first part of the Ixil name and the Spanish first name have a one-to-one relationship; it may consist of an Ixil name or a well-assimilated Spanish first name. The second part of the Ixil name combination is an Ixil name. It is the whole combination that is passed on in the č'eš naming pattern, and children of the same family may all have a different combination. The Spanish surname is passed on by the father to his children, and the school-educated generation adds the mother's name following the Spanish pattern.

2. Text #219.

3. To be buried away from home is a great misfortune. The soul has to

travel a long distance when it is called in prayer in the hometown, and then it has to travel back to the place where it is buried.

4. Text #234.

5. Text #219.

6. Date of earthquake: 1908.

7. San Augustín near Tešlal Č'awaˀ.

8. Text #2.

9. Text #19.

10. Mazatenango.

11. About 3 meters.

12. Mala is the Ixil name for San Sebastian, Department of Mazatenango.

13. This alludes to the Christian idea of selling one's soul to the devil for money and riches and neglecting one's spiritual obligations—in this case one's obligation to the ancestors who have to be attended to in their own homeland.

14. Ladino figures in dreams and mythology stand for supernatural beings such as day gods, or the Earth God in one of his many ˀaanhel manifestations.

15. Women from Cotzal are taller than Nebaj women and carry themselves erect, according to Shas.

16. A distance of 50 meters looking out of the interviewing room in Guatemala where the recording took place.

17. The woman is a symbol of the fertile, beautiful lowland place that Shas occupied.

18. "Have you come?" "Yes, I have arrived," is a standard exchange when someone expected arrives.

19. The sacred bundle is the professional "instrument" of the day-keeper.

20. Earth God: the generalized manifestation of many particular deities associated with specific locations such as rivers, springs, caves, mountains, or land one lives on. This god appears in dreams and folktales in the shape of a ladino of wealth, sometimes armed, sometimes on horseback.

21. The grandfather's displeasure refers to Shas's absence during the ceremonial remembrance of the ancestors in his hometown of Nebaj.

22. The knowledge of the day count will be received, and one becomes a b'aalwactiiš.

23. *Meeša* (from the Spanish *mesa*), the table where the seeds are laid out, is another symbol for divining with the sacred bundle of mič seeds.

24. Wiˀ Sul ˀAˀ, a hamlet in the district of Sumal.

25. Šeˀ Kampaaro Wic, a mountain in the district of Sumal.

26. "Certain knowledge" is an allusion to the ability to cure sickness as well as being able to cause it.

27. Falling from a sitting position: metaphor for jealousy.

28. Kaqay: name of one of the four Alcalde crosses at the four corners of town.

29. *Wec-k'aol:* term used between Ixil men from Chajul and Nebaj who have a special visiting privilege relationship with each other. Each can stay overnight and receive meals in the other's house.

30. *Saqb'ičil tec ʔokeb'al wac q'ii:* dawn ceremony for the novice daykeeper to present himself to the Days.

31. *Čaʔ ṣ pap* is a greeting directed toward an old person or one of higher rank.

32. The white head shawls mean a high-status ritual position; the white wrappings mean the people are dead; the address "kumpaale" is the term used in Cotzal for one of the four official town daykeepers as well as more generally for *compadre* or co-father, a Catholic ritual relationship based on baptism. In this context it means that Shas is recognized as being a daykeeper, as being of equal status with the four other daykeepers.

33. "Good things" means praise for helping people; "bad things" means gossip from envious people, especially witchcraft accusations.

34. He would gradually find the seeds to make up his "sacred bundle."

35. *Tal suʔt* means "small napkin," a traditionally striped woven napkin; here to wrap the seeds in.

36. "Talking days" are the ones that show up in the final position of a row laid out in a divination pattern.

37. "Died (for me)" means she went out of his life: because she did not understand his concerns, he left her. Shas did not want to give a detailed explanation at the time.

38. The Ixil believe that small children's souls detach easily from their bodies and linger in places where one has lived for some time. The child becomes sad and even sick.

39. ʔAn would borrow from the *patrón* just as Shas did and repay the loan with her own work.

40. ʔAn enjoyed her work and did not want to lose her source of cash. Shas wanted her to work with him, and not incur a debt of her own.

41. Text #238.

42. The carpenter was a former *b'oʔq'ol tenam* and was used to giving advice. He suggested dividing the land between brother and sister. After Sin refused he counseled: "She is not the only woman in the world. You are without your own land, you are *nothing* in her eyes!"

43. The soul of the mother is believed to be strongly concerned about the land she left to her children. She is capable of causing misfortune if her will is not respected.

44. "My soul wandered" means "I was sad; I suffered."

45. A posse was made up of the lowest ranking officials at the city hall.

46. Perhaps since Sin did not remarry she thought it important for the little boy to live with his father. ʔAn did not let Shas's first son go, but she had remarried very soon.

47. Taa did not take anything from Shas when they separated.

48. The alcalde here is the mayor of the plantation.

49. Text #239.

50. *Mojado* means "moist from intercourse."

51. Bridal money is offered by the groom or his family.

52. To be buried away from home is a great misfortune (see note 60), and to be aware of it while dying might be very sad.

53. Funeral customs include a celebration with food and drink that may last for half a day or more.

54. The fiesta of San Antonio takes place in June; change of cofradía house takes place in the night exactly one week later. The fiesta of Santa Maria occurs on August 15.

55. The Mountain God (*wic, ʔaanhel,* loq'ola lugaar) is the lord of a particular location; "Earth God" is the general manifestation of many similar deities.

56. Chiquimula is associated with "foreign, non-Ixil, usually Indian" people.

57. Preparation for taking part in a procession during a fiesta is an important event.

58. Text #239.

59. Text #219.

60. The grandfather had kept the sheep for his grandson; the mother's complaint must have been legally justified and the old man had to go to jail—although it was only a day or two before influential friends got him out. But his pride was deeply hurt—after all, he was one of the principales—and as an ancestral soul he made Shas's mother pay for her affront: she had to die away from home and be buried in foreign soil. Shas had to suffer, too, because he was the cause of the quarrel, and he thought his unhappy choices of wives were inflicted on him as punishment. The mother, after this first experience in the courthouse, was afraid to go the next time when she should have demanded Shas's rightful share of the land at his grandfather's death. So Shas suffered doubly from the unfortunate incident.

61. Text #223.

62. Just as a ladino figure in a dream or myth often stands for a supernatural being, a *sanyoora* (*señora*) stands for a benevolent heavenly being, Shas's interpretation for *Kučuč,* Our Mother, whose place of worship is the church.

63. *B'eluwal q'ii* means "nine days," a ritually important number of days.

64. In a small town such as Nebaj family situations are freely discussed, and Shas's problems must have been common knowledge. To have "lost" as many wives as Shas did had to be a punishment for something in the past, a fine he had to pay in order to regain the goodwill of the gods. In note 60 Shas analyzes his predicament in more detail.

65. "It's difficult because of what I'm doing" refers to Shas's activities as a daykeeper, which often kept him away at night and curtailed normal sexual relationships during times of vigils. This led to mistrust and quarrels and finally to breakups of his marital relationships.

66. The dealings with the courthouse were not judicial, but only clerical.

67. Kurus ʔlᶘoq or Kruus ʔlᶘoq.

68. There was a simple hut made of sticks on his land with a place to keep his maize, because Shas mentioned living there with his fourth and fifth wives.

69. This line is not clear. It may refer to "remaining in the world of the dead" before being sent back to the world of the living—or to another level within the world of the departed souls.

70. Continuation of text #219.

71. The Ixil term for daykeeper is *ʔaaq'ii*. The prefix, *ʔaa*, is a role designator; *q'ii* is day. Thus one way to inventory recognized roles in Ixil society is to look for this prefix. For example, the person who carries skyrockets (*b'oola*) is designated in Ixil as *ʔaab'oola;* a scribe is *ʔaacib'.*

72. These studies have begun to move in interesting directions with more sophisticated techniques. Semantic studies by Burton and Kirk with multidimensional scaling techniques suggest how one's life roles can influence semantic attributes and the evaluations of other roles (Burton and Kirk, 1977; Burton and Kirk, 1979).

73. The question of salience for particular lexemes is different for *types* of lexemes. The term "salience" has been used to mean different things. In Brown (1979) and Burton and Kirk (1979) it is used to mean the concept that is most readily used or presupposed in, for example, an unmarked-marked pair such as "actor and actress," where the unmarked item can sometimes be used to cover the full range of designata while the marked one covers only a narrower range. However, one could argue for a different usage of the term "salience." In a pair such as "actor and actress" the marked item (actress) carries more information content, since it is the less frequent of the pair. When it does appear it is a salient item; it highlights or marks some special attribute (in the example, that of being female). By "salience" we mean something that is prominent, that stands out. But this does not always mean following the second usage. When it comes to *types* of lexemes and more complex concepts such as actions or events, some items may be more salient because their frequency of usage gives their occurrence a regularity or pattern that is more easily spotted. In that case the item that is more readily perceived may, in fact, be a high-frequency, low-information item. We would refer to this as another kind of salience, one that is utilized in the eidochronic analysis of Chapter 5.

4. SHAS KOʔW'S PHILOSOPHY

1. See translation notes in Appendix A.

2. Shas refers to four of seven types of formal prayers he knows (see Chapter 2).

3. ʔIqlenal (president), ʔalkaalte, and ʔaacib' are the most important positions held in the ladino government.

4. The sending forth of moisture (čaqub'), which one finds on the chamarra on awakening, causes sickness.

5. The ʔuq'iib'al, an Ixil version of the standard Catholic introductory blessing, the Our Fathers, and the Hail Mary are often used as an initial part of a ceremonial prayer.

6. Consecration of the staves of office at the "Change-of-Office" ceremonies for government and cofradías can only be done by the head prayersayer, the b'oʔq'ol b'aalwactiiš.

7. Wild animals are protected by the ʔaanhel of a particular location. One should pray to the ʔaanhel, offer gifts, and ask permission before hunting or one may be punished by stumbling over tree trunks; hound dogs are punished by having to die earlier than other dogs.

8. According to Ixil tradition, incense and candles were the original nourishment of the newly created earth and helped to invigorate its infertile soil. (See Chapter 5.)

9. To awaken means "to become mature," "to think ahead."

10. A person's unhappiness may be caused by a departed family member who does not get enough attention through prayers or ritual (for example, lighting candles before the house shrine).

11. Good days to perform ritual are sixteen out of twenty. Some days are particularly suited for certain ceremonies. K'ač is neutral; Čoo, Č'iʔ and ʔAq'b'al are bad.

12. To cry out (in anger) to the gods.

13. To "lose yourself" means to become homeless.

14. Each of the twenty day gods has attributes which he may bestow on the person born on "his" day. Shas does not commit himself about which attribute belongs to which god because he does not want to make a mistake and offend a god with an incorrect attribute.

15. The "children" here are the Colbys, who invited Shas to the United States.

16. Physical handicaps may be attributes bestowed by a particular god on the day of birth, but conditions such as poverty, wealth, or laziness may be part of one's destiny, which is influenced by many factors: one's own behavior toward the gods, attitudes of enemies or ancestors.

17. Uncles of old: the mythical brothers of Kub'aal who in their envy wanted to kill their younger brother and were banned to a dark, distant place.

18. Further details on the procession of the sun are found in text #321 of our data archives.

19. See note 17.

20. Shas alludes to the belief that one may have to remain for a few days only in a place where one is judged; gloria is for the good souls, including honest daykeepers; one may return to earth as a completely different being—or one may have to go to a place of punishment.

21. We shall pay for using witchcraft, striking a younger or an older brother—just like the man Shas witnessed in the dream being tortured as punishment for disobeying God's law.

22. Numbers: perhaps he means the chords or the notes.

23. ꞋOlin C'uꞋm = name of man who operated the bellows; *ꞋOlin* means to move, to swing with.

24. That is, the prayer addressed to the ꞋaanheI.

25. *ꞋOoro* are the stones and crystals kept together with the mič seeds in the sacred bundle. The term is often used metonymically for the entire bundle.

26. He will address his complaints to the gods.

27. *Mulco* is maize with imperfect grains.

28. *T-ual wi-č'awaꞋ:* paper to document rental of land.

29. PaꞋ Micolaš and Ču Lol are the Ixil names of the authors.

30. *Kastiiya* = Castellano = Spanish language.

31. "They" refers to the Europeans who conquered the Indians of the New World. Since there were people who lived across the sea, and Shas flew over water when he came to California, he felt as though he were in the land referred to in his ritual prayers as "across the sea" and "to the East."

32. *MuꞋs* is Ixil for ladino; *ꞋulaꞋ* is the term for a non-Ixil Indian.

33. He is carried in a casket in Good Friday processions in Nebaj.

34. See Chapter 5: we die because he showed us how to die.

35. Father Kayiita: a *češel* or namesake of Kub'aal.

36. *Niiyo Hesus, niiya B'elen, niiya Atoča, niiyo Kapetal* = attributes of the Christ child.

5. FOLK NARRATIVES

1. The Ixil seem to have preserved their narratives better than many other Mayan peoples. When Ruth Bunzel asked the Quiché Mayans of Chichicastenango about myths, they told her that only among the Ixil in Nebaj were myths still known and told (Bunzel, 1959). When the German anthropologist Schultze-Jena went to Chichicastenango with the express purpose of collecting Mayan myths, he was unable, Bunzel tells us, to find a single one. Perhaps partly for this reason, there are few good collections of Mayan tales; notable exceptions are those of Laughlin (1977), Fought (1972), Gossen (1974), and Shaw (1972). Laughlin has also published the first extensive texts of Mayan dreams (1976). It is hoped that other types of Mayan texts will be published as more ethnographers recognize the need for text ethnography. See Fischer (1963) for a review of earlier studies.

2. The Ixil word *Ꞌaanhel,* which represents both the singular and plural forms, comes from the Spanish *ángel.* However, we do not translate this as

"angel" because the actual referent is far from that of Christian beliefs. For the Ixil, ʔaanhel represent both earth deities and sky deities. Only the context indicates the particular class.

3. A probable reference to the pyramids in the area.

4. In a forthcoming study of a Chajul myth (B. Colby, G. Ayres, and A. Palomino) it will be shown how the myth, wall paintings, and a dance drama are closely interwoven. We suspect that many, if not all, Mayan myths have been associated with ritual, including the famous *Popol Vuh* (Edmondson, 1971a), many elements of which appear also in the Ixil material.

5. Technically, one cannot describe the events in a story like "Goldilocks" as eidons without first doing an eidochronic analysis. Such an analysis requires studying a sample of stories all originating from the same population that "Goldilocks" belongs to.

6. Another episode, which was left out of this particular telling, is the task performed by the fish merchant of distributing rain clouds out of a gourd. Too many are released, causing severe thunderstorms and flooding.

7. The names ʔOyew ʔAči and *Mataqtani* do not seem to be natural Ixil names. Could this myth have been borrowed from a Quiché-speaking elite that once had brief dominion over the Ixil—an elite that may have been struggling with the problem of jurisdiction over marital decisions and concern about a competing political-religious and kinship system, as suggested in note 8 below? These are mysteries that may never be cleared up, but they bear thought as new archaeological and ethnohistorical evidence comes in.

8. We cannot refrain from asking some ethnohistorical questions and making a number of speculative asides about this story. If, as we suspect, Ixil ancestor worship is a survival of the Classic Mayan and in some places the early post-Classic Mayan (see Colby, 1976 and the beginning of Chapter 2), why does a story that deals with death not relate in some way to the belief in ancestral souls? Instead, an animal pantheism is represented; the soul of Maria Markaao is dispersed among the animals.

To speculate further, the major theme of the story is a "marriage" that is consummated without the consent of the parents. One of the characteristics of ancestor worshipping elsewhere is the great emphasis placed on lineage and lineage status and the consequent practice of arranged marriages. Marriage for love may cross class lines and be a real threat to a family's lineage status in society. The fact that a story focuses on this problem suggests that it is a serious one. That it is dealt with at all suggests that marriage without parental consent was within the realm of possibility, if not an actuality, at some earlier time and, as we know, happens frequently today (Palomino, 1972). One could read into this story the following statement: "If one disobeys the wishes of lineage, death will result in dispersal of the soul through animals rather than preservation of the soul as a sentient ancestral spirit (watching over human affairs and communicating with deities)."

Of passing interest also is that, while names are absent from most Ixil stories (might the absence be a result of a wish to hide the earlier religion from Catholic converts, or simply a confusion resulting from the numerous different names a single character might have had in pre-Columbian times?) the names for two characters in this one are known, though Shas actually confused the two and indicated he was not sure which was which. Fortunately we know from other variations of the myth, particularly in Chajul, that Maria's father is Mataqtani, and her husband, ʔOyew ʔAči.

9. Perhaps the most European of the stories in Shas's repertoire, "The Comadre" includes Catholic coparenthood, a mule, mention of a priest, and the theme of contracting with the devil. Possibly "Snake" and "Comadre" represent pre-Columbian and post-Columbian ways of dealing with lack—the pre-Columbian way emphasizing positive action (doing favors), while the post-Columbian way is more negatively cast, emphasizing the consequences of sin and the dangers of dealing with the Devil. The evidence for this, however, is not sufficient for anything more than speculation.

10. Referring to Benjamin Colby. Usually when people gave us long texts that were recorded we would pay a day's wage so they would not "lose their day."

11. This is not to say that European studies of narrative structure are lacking in useful insights. Beaugrande (1980) has summarized and synthesized much of the more interesting European work.

12. See Pelto and Pelto, 1978, pp. 23–26 for a summary of the dispute.

6. IXIL DIVINATION

1. This does not mean, however, that all of the days are linked in alternating good and bad pairs, as was reported earlier by Lincoln.

2. The main difference between a sickness case and a case of fortune telling is that the seeds must show something to be wrong in the sickness case. When we were making up hypothetical cases of sickness and layouts of the seeds with Shas when he visited us in California, one of us constructed a positive layout in which there were no negative days or numbers. Shas simply said that it didn't speak. Since the layout was for a sick person, there had to be an indication of a problem somewhere in the speaking positions.

3. The quartz crystals are sometimes used by themselves in a different kind of divination. Shas said that he did not do this other type of divination, which seems to be something like gazing into a crystal ball. The daykeeper looks into the quartz crystals for a reading. Lights, or possibly fig-

ures, in the pieces supposedly reveal something that will offer a solution to the client's problem. These quartz crystals are referred to by the term *?ooro*. This same term is sometimes used to refer to all divination, including divination with the mič seeds. It can therefore be confusing in conversation if the context is not sufficiently precise to determine which of the two meanings is intended.

4. There are other ways of laying out seeds, which were observed by John Clement in Nebaj and Chajul (Berrueta-Clement, field notes, 1968).

5. Ixil women daykeepers are rare. When Shas was younger he knew of at least two. Many people feel that it would be embarrassing (*vergüenza*) for a woman to appear at the crosses where the other prayersayers do their ritual. But women do readings of the mič seeds inside their houses. The two women Shas knew were not living with a man; one was a spinster, the other a widow. A husband would pose a problem because sexual taboos must be observed by those working with the holy days. No intercourse is allowed on days with the numerals 9 or 13 or on *?Alkaalte* days, nor on the day *?I?š* (the scribe deity who records all human deeds), on the day 8 B'aac, during the end-of-year period (*?o?q'ii*), or during Holy Week. A husband lacking knowledge of the calendar would not allow such taboos, and unless the taboos were observed the woman and her family would be punished through poverty and bad luck with animals. Shas's wife did not know the calendar and thought it was a "vergüenza" when other women did.

6. A request like this to the gods is not quite the same thing as witchcraft or sorcery. In the latter case, the witch acts directly upon one's victim through magical compulsion or by transforming himself into a magical animal to do harm. The suitor's action in our hypothetical case is more a matter of persuasion, and he may be seen as having just cause. The line between witchcraft and persuasion of the gods is, however, a fine one. Doing ritual (*čaq*) in anger against someone for some injustice is not usually classified as witchcraft by the Ixil. The person doing the ritual is less often seen as being spiteful than as having just cause. For example, a woman abandoned by her husband can "cry" to the gods (a kind of half singing and half crying, also characteristic of mourning behavior). If this is done during a ritual the gods are likely to respond.

As the texts make clear, Shas is no stranger to the idea of witchcraft, whether by ritual or by animal familiars (the Quiché term *win*). The potential for evil through ritual knowledge is explicit throughout Shas's discussion, and he reports accusations of witchcraft against himself as well as the application of witchcraft of both kinds against him by others. He repeatedly asserts the strength of divine sanctions (early death) against witches. The Ixil generally speak of the use of animal familiars as being more common along the coast, which indirectly suggests that at least this kind of witchcraft belief is more prevalent among the more Hispanicized groups (though it is often noted by anthropologists that outgroups are generally attributed with practicing more witchcraft than the ingroup).

In many of the Tzotzil and Tzeltal Mayan groups of Chiapas in Mexico, which have lost the calendar, witchcraft accusations and even murders of suspected witches are frequent. There is general evidence that the prevalence of witchcraft is indeed correlated with a higher degree of Hispanicization, or at least with a loss of pre-Columbian elements (Colby, 1967). The reason loss of the calendar is related to a greater incidence of witchcraft is probably that the use of the calendar includes strong injunctions against witchcraft (as seen in Chapter 4). with the associated belief that old age is proof of one's good behavior. Further, the calendar is embedded in a strong ethic of positive social attitude, while more Hispanicized areas are often undergoing rapid changes which cause more anomie (in the Durkheim sense), with a resulting negative attitude toward others. Finally, Indians in the Hispanicized areas are more subject to ethnic prejudice, with a resulting decrement in self-image which leads to projections of hostility and blame toward others.

7. THEORETICAL AND METHODOLOGICAL STRATEGY

1. By sharing we do not mean an isomorphic neurophysiological structure. To be so concerned at our level of analysis would clearly be a case of misplaced specification. Rather, by sharing we mean a much higher level of cognitive perception through the process of communication. The most interesting anthropological study of cognitive sharing has been done by Burton and Kirk (1979), who show how the same role terms are linked to different attributes according to the sex of the individual.

2. A useful notation for representing frames has been introduced by Joseph Becker (1973), who refers to them as schemata. Of all the artificial intelligence work to date, we find his approach the most interesting. It includes dynamic processes such as analogic matching, generalization, and differentiation. An important advantage to Becker's system over that of Schank and Abelson (1977) is that a learning process is built into the system. However, Schank and Abelson have much to offer the ethnographer seeking to work out a systematic model, for they make explicit how goals and plans might link up to other knowledge structures, how they might conflict, and so on.

3. In addition to patterns of sequences are patterns of design and arrangement, such as those used for bodily decoration (Faris, 1972) or cattle brands (Watt, 1966, 1967).

4. There is one aspect of systemic interrelation that is still largely unexplored. We must recognize that systems held in the mind can run at cross-purposes to each other so that the resulting productions represent a compromise. This has been demonstrated by W. C. Watt's study of the evolution of the alphabet (1975, 1978a), in which an array of salient cul-

tural patterns has been forged between the trend toward convenience of writing, on the one hand, and the avoidance of reading ambiguities, on the other. There are many other sources of conflicting or competing cognitive, perceptual, and motor demands. A particularly interesting cognitive "battlefield" is a situation where one's self-image as an effective person conflicts with perceived reality or with one's perceived social image (see note 5 in the previous chapter). This brings us to the question of deeper levels of personality and of motivation in general.

REFERENCES

Adams, Richard E. W. 1969. Maya archaeology 1958–1968, a review. *Latin American Research Review*, vol. 4, no. 2, pp. 3–45.

Amnesty International. 1976. *Amnesty International briefing paper* no. 8. London: Amnesty International Publications.

————. 1979. In Guatemala: death or exile. *Matchbox*, November 1979, p. 3.

Anderson, Arthur J. O., and Charles E. Dibble. 1950–63. *Florentine codex. General history of the things of New Spain*, books 1–12. Santa Fe: The School of American Research and the University of Utah.

Antonovsky, Aaron. 1979. *Health, stress and coping.* San Francisco: Jossey-Bass.

Barth, Frederik. 1967. On the study of social change. *American Anthropologist* 69:661–669.

Bartlett, Frederic C. 1932. *Remembering: a study in experimental and social psychology.* London: Cambridge University Press.

Bascom, Williams. 1969. *Ifa divination: communication between gods and men in West Africa.* Bloomington: Indiana University Press.

Bateson, Gregory. 1936. *Naven.* Cambridge, Mass.: Harvard University Press.

Beaugrande, Robert-Alain de. 1980. *Introduction to text linguistics.* London: Longman.

Becker, Joseph D. 1973. A model for the encoding of experiential information. In *Computer models of thought and language,* ed. R. C. Schank and K. M. Colby. San Francisco: Freeman.

Becquelin, Pierre. 1969. *Archaeologie de la région de Nebaj.* Mémoires de l'Institut d'Ethnologie. Paris: Université de Paris.

Benedict, Ruth. 1934. *Patterns of culture.* New York: Houghton Mifflin. (Reprinted by Mentor Books, New York, 1959.)

Berlin, Brent. 1972. Speculations on the growth of ethnobotanical nomenclature. *Language in Society* 1:51–86.

————. 1976. The concept of rank in ethnobiological classification: some evidence from Aguaruna folk botany. *American Ethnologist* 3:381–399.

Berrueta-Clement, John Ramon. 1978. *Ethnic and intra-ethnic differentiation in cognitive characteristics: a study of bilinguals and monolinguals in Nebaj, Guatemala.* Ph.D. dissertation, University of California, Irvine.

Bidney, David. 1967. *Theoretical anthropology.* New York: Columbia University Press.

Black, Mary B., and Duane Metzger. 1969. Ethnographic description and the study of law. In *Cognitive anthropology,* ed. S. Tyler. New York: Holt, Rinehart and Winston.

Brown, Cecil H. 1979. Folk zoological life-forms: their universality and growth. *American Anthropologist* 4:791–817.

Bunzel, Ruth. 1959. *Chichicastenango: a Guatemalan village.* Seattle: University of Washington Press.

Burton, Michael L., and Lorraine Kirk. 1977. Meaning and context: a study of contextual shifts in meaning of Maasai personality descriptors. *American Ethnologist* 4:734–761.

————. 1979. Sex differences in Maasai cognition of personality and social identity. *American Anthropologist* 81.4:841–873.

Carneiro, Robert L. 1973. The four faces of evolution. In *Handbook of social and cultural anthropology,* ed. John J. Honigmann. Chicago: Rand McNally.

Chomsky, Noam. 1957. *Syntactic structures.* The Hague: Mouton.

————. 1965. *Aspects of the theory of syntax.* Cambridge, Mass.: MIT Press.

Colby, Benjamin N. 1963. Folk science studies. *El Palacio* 4:5–14.

————. 1966a. Ethnographic semantics: a preliminary survey. *Current Anthropology* 7.1:3–32.

————. 1966b. Cultural patterns in narrative. *Science,* vol. 151, no. 3912, pp. 793–798.

————. 1966c. *Ethnic relations in the Chiapas highlands.* Santa Fe: Museum of New Mexico Press. (Ph.D. dissertation, Harvard University, 1960.)

————. 1967. Psychological orientations. In *Handbook of Middle American Indians,* ed. Robert Wauchope. Vol. 6: *Social Anthropology,* ed. Manning Nash. Austin: University of Texas Press.

————. 1973. A partial grammar of Eskimo folktales. *American Anthropologist* 75.3:645–662.

————. 1975. Culture grammars. *Science* 187:913–919.

————. 1976. The anomalous Ixil—bypassed by the postclassic? *American Antiquity* 41.1:74–80.

Colby, Benjamin N., and Lore Colby. 1974. Two Ixil myths (Guatemala). *Anthropos* 69:216–223.

Colby, Benjamin N., and Michael Cole. 1973. Culture, memory, and narrative. In *Modes of thought,* ed. Robin Horton and Ruth Finnegan. London: Faber & Faber.

Colby, Benjamin N., and Rodger Knaus. 1974. Men, grammars, and machines: a new direction for the study of man. In *On language, culture, and religion: in honor of Eugene A. Nida,* ed. Matthew Black and William A. Smalley. The Hague: Mouton.

Colby, Benjamin N., and Pierre L. van den Berghe. 1969. *Ixil country: a pluralistic society in highland Guatemala.* Berkeley: University of California Press.

Colby, Lore M. 1980. Ixil text. In *Mayan texts III,* ed. Louanna Fourbee. IJAL-NATS Monograph No. 5. Chicago: University of Chicago Press.

Collier, George A. 1975. *Fields of the Tzotzil: the ecological bases of tradition in highland Chiapas.* Austin: University of Texas Press.

D'Andrade, Roy G. 1976. A propositional analysis of U.S. American beliefs about illness. In *Meaning in anthropology,* ed. K. H. Basso and H. A. Selby. Albuquerque: University of New Mexico Press.

Dougherty, J. W. D. 1978. Salience and relativity in classification. *American Ethnologist* 5:66–80.

Du Bois, Cora. 1944. *The People of Alor.* Minneapolis: University of Minnesota Press.

Edmonson, Munro S. 1971a. *The book of counsel: the Popol Vuh of the Quiché Maya of Guatemala.* New Orleans: Middle American Research Institute of Tulane University, publication no. 35.

——. 1971b. *Lore; an introduction to the science of folklore and literature.* New York: Holt, Rinehart and Winston.

Elliot, Raymond. 1960. Ixil grammar. In *Mayan studies I,* ed. Benjamin Elson. Norman, Okla.: Summer Institute of Linguistics, University of Oklahoma.

Elliot, Raymond, and Helen Elliot. 1966. Ixil. In *Languages of Guatemala,* ed. Marvin K. Mayers. The Hague: Mouton.

——. 1971. Ixil texts. In *According to our ancestors; folk texts from Guatemala and Honduras,* ed. Mary Shaw. Norman, Okla.: Summer Institute of Linguistics, University of Oklahoma.

Fabrega, Horatio, Jr., and D. Silver. 1970. Some social and psychological properties of Zinacanteco Shamans. *Behavioral Science* 15:471–86.

Faris, James C. 1972. *Nuba personal art.* Toronto: University of Toronto Press.

Fernandez, James W. 1967. *Divinations, confessions, testimonies—confrontations with the social superstructure among Durban Africans.* Occasional Papers of the Institute for Social Research, University of Natal, Winter-Spring 1967.

——. 1971. Persuasions and performances: of the beast in every body . . . and the metaphors of every man. In *Myth, symbol, and culture,* ed. C. Geertz. New York: Norton.

Fischer, John L. 1963. The sociopsychological analysis of folktales. *Current Anthropology* 4:235–97.

Fjellman, Stephen M. 1976. Talking about talking about residence: an Akamba case. *American Ethnology* 3.4:671–681.

Fought, John G. 1972. *Chorti (Mayan) texts.* Philadelphia: University of Pennsylvania Press.

Freeman, Susan Tax (forthcoming). The municipios of northern Spain: a view from the fountain. In *Currents in anthropology,* ed. Robert Hinshaw. The Hague and Paris: Mouton.

Geertz, Clifford. 1973. *The interpretation of cultures; selected essays.* New York: Basic Books.

Geoghegon, William H. 1971. Information processing systems in culture. In *Explorations in mathematical anthropology,* ed. P. Kay. Cambridge, Mass.: MIT Press.

Gibbs, Jack P. 1972. *Sociological theory construction.* Hinsdale, Ill.: Dryden Press.

Gladwin, Christina H. 1979. Production functions and decision models: complementary models. *American Ethnologist* 6.4:653–681.

Gossen, Gary H. 1974. *Chamulas in the world of the sun; time and space in a Maya oral tradition.* Cambridge, Mass.: Harvard University Press.

Grimes, Joseph E. 1975. *The thread of discourse.* The Hague: Mouton.

Halliday, Michael A. K. 1967–68. Notes on transitivity and theme in English (parts 1–3). *Journal of Linguistics* 3.1:37–81; 3.2:199–244; 4.2:179–215.

———. 1977. Grammars and descriptions. In *Studies in text theory and text analysis,* ed. T. A. Van Dijk and J. S. Petofi. Berlin and New York: de Gruyter.

Halliday, M. A. K., and Ruqaiya Hasan. 1976. *Cohesion in English.* London: Longman.

Harding, Joseph R., and Dorothy C. Clement. 1979. Regularities in the continuity and change of role structures: the Ixil Maya. In *Predicting sociocultural change,* ed. S. Abbott and J. van Willigen. Athens, Ga.: University of Georgia Press.

Harris, Marvin. 1978. *Cannibals and kings; the origins of cultures.* London: Collins.

Hasan, Ruqaiya. 1978. Text in the systemic-functional model. In *Current trends in textlinguistics,* ed. W. U. Dressler. Berlin: de Gruyter.

Henry, Jules. 1963. *Culture against man.* New York: Random House.

Hewitt, Carl. 1975. Stereotype as an actor approach to solving the problem of procedural attachment in frames. Workshop on theoretical issues in Natural Language Processing, Massachusetts Institute of Technology, Cambridge, Mass.

Hinz, Eike. 1978. *Analyse aztekischer Gedankensysteme; Wahrsageglaube und Erziehungsnormen als Alltagstheorie sozialen Handelns.* Wiesbaden: Franz Steiner Verlag GMBH.

Horton, Robin. 1967. African traditional thought and Western science. Part I: From tradition to science. Part II: The "closed" and "open" predicaments. *Africa,* 37.

Horton, Robin, and Ruth Finnegan. 1973. *Modes of thought; essays on thinking in Western and non-Western societies.* London: Faber & Faber.

Husserl, Edmund. 1973. *Experience and judgment; investigations in a ge-*

nealogy of logic, ed. L. Landgrebe; trans. J. Churchill and K. Ameriks. Evanstòn, Ill.: Northwestern University Press.

Hymes, Dell H. 1959. Myth and tale titles of the lower Chinook. *Journal of American Folklore,* vol. 72, no. 284, April–June 1959, pp. 139–145.

————. 1974. *Foundations in sociolinguistics; an ethnographic approach.* Philadelphia: University of Pennsylvania Press.

Jacobs, Melville. 1959. *The content and style of an oral literature.* New York: Wenner-Gren Foundation for Anthropological Research.

James, Mark L., and Benjamin N. Colby. 1979. The DRS-77 instructional manual. School of Social Sciences, orangeback series. Scientiarum Ancillae 1, University of California, Irvine.

Jordan, Brigitte, and JoAnne Goldberg. 1977. The portrayal of liquor and liquor consumption in popular magazine advertisements in the United States (manuscript).

Kandel, Eric R. 1979. Psychotherapy and the single synapse. *New England Journal of Medicine* 301.19:1028–1037.

Keesing, Roger M. 1972. Paradigms lost: the new anthropology and the new linguistics. *Southwestern Journal of Anthropology* 28:279–332.

Kintsch, Walter. 1977. On comprehending stories. In *Cognitive processes in comprehension,* ed. M. A. Just and P. Carpenter. Hillsdale, N.J.: Erlbaum.

Kroeber, Alfred L. 1948. *Anthropology.* New York: Harcourt, Brace.

————. 1952. *The nature of culture.* Chicago: University of Chicago Press.

Kronenfeld, David B. 1979. Information processing and cognitive structures. Paper presented at the Riverside Conference on Cognitive Anthropology, 17–20 May 1978, University of California, Riverside, California.

———— (forthcoming). Structuralism and sociolinguistics—grammar and statistics: a response to Maranda. In *The language of sociology,* ed. J. Law. Sociological Review Monograph series. Keel, Staffordshire, England: University of Keel.

Kronenfeld, David B., and Henry W. Decker. 1979. Structuralism. *Annual Review of Anthropology* 8:503–541.

La Barre, Weston. 1964. Confession as psychotherapy in American Indian tribes. In *Magic, faith, and healing,* ed. A. Kiev. New York: Free Press of Glencoe.

Lakoff, George, and Mark Johnson. 1980. *Metaphors we live by.* Chicago: University of Chicago Press.

Laughlin, Charles D., Jr., and Eugene G. D'Aquili. 1974. *Biogenetic structuralism.* New York: Columbia University Press.

Laughlin, Robert M. 1976. *Of wonders wild and near; dreams from Zinacantan.* Smithsonian Contributions to Anthropology no. 22. Washington, D.C.: Smithsonian Institution Press.

————. 1977. *Of cabbages and kings; tales from Zinacantan.* Smithsonian Contributions to Anthropology no. 23. Washington, D.C.: Smithsonian Institution press.

Lévi-Strauss, Claude. 1964. *The raw and the cooked.* New York: Harper & Row.

Levy-Bruhl, Lucien. 1910. *Les fonctions mentales dans les sociétés inférieures.* Paris: Falcon. (English edition: *How natives think,* trans. L. A. Clare. New York: Washington Square Press, 1966.)

Lewis, Oscar. 1951. *Life in a Mexican village: Tepoztlan restudied.* Urbana: University of Illinois Press.

―――. 1961. *The children of Sanchez.* New York: Random House.

Lincoln, Jackson S. 1942. *The Maya calendar of the Ixil Indians of the Guatemalan highlands.* Carnegie Institute of Washington pub. 528, contrib. 38.

―――. 1945. *An ethnological study of the Ixil Indians of the Guatemala Highlands.* Chicago: University of Chicago Microfilm Collection.

Longacre, Robert E. 1968. *Discourse and paragraph structure.* Summer Institute of Linguistics, Santa Ana, California.

Lord, Albert B. 1960. *The Singer of Tales.* Cambridge, Mass.: Harvard University Press.

McClelland, David C., W. N. Davis, R. Kalin, and E. Wanner, 1972. *The drinking man.* New York: The Free Press.

Malinowski, Bronislav. 1926. *Myth in primitive psychology.* New York: Norton.

Mandler, Jean M., and N. J. Johnson. 1977. Remembrance of things passed: story structure and recall. *Cognitive Psychology* 9:111–151.

Mehan, Hugh. 1978. Structuring school structure. *Harvard Educational Review* 48.1:32–64.

Metzger, Duane, and Gerald E. Williams. 1963. Tenejapa medicine I: the curer. *Southwestern Journal of Anthropology* 19:216–234.

Miles, Suzanne W. 1952. An analysis of modern middle American calendars. In *Acculturation in the Americas,* ed. Sol Tax. Chicago: University of Chicago Press.

Minsky, Marvin. 1975. A framework for representing knowledge. In *The psychology of computer vision,* ed. P. Winston. New York: McGraw-Hill.

Montessori, Maria. 1963. *The absorbent mind.* Madras, India: Adyar.

Moore, Omar K. 1957. Divination: a new perspective. *American Anthropologist* 59:69–74.

Moore, Omar K., and Alan Ross Anderson. 1968. Some principles for the design of *clarifying* educational environments. In *Handbook of socialization theory and research,* ed. David Goslin. Chicago: Rand McNally.

Murdock, George P. 1949. *Social structure.* New York: MacMillan.

Murray, Henry A. 1955. American Icarus. In *Clinical studies in personality,* vol. 2, ed. A. Burton and R. E. Harris. New York: Harper.

Nadel, Siegfried F. 1957. *The theory of social structure.* London: Cohen & West.

Naroll, Raoul. 1970. What have we learned from cross-cultural surveys? *American Anthropologist,* vol. 72.6.

Nash, June. 1970. *In the eyes of the ancestors: belief and behavior in a Maya community.* New Haven: Yale University Press.

Nash, Manning. 1957. Cultural persistences and social structure: the Mesoamerican calendar survivals. *Southwestern Journal of Anthropology* 13:149–155.

Olrick, Axel. 1965. Epic laws of folk narrative, trans. J. P. Steager. In *The study of folklore*, ed. A. Dundes. Englewood Cliffs, N.J.: Prentice-Hall.

Ortony, Andrew. 1979. Beyond literal similarity. *Psychological Review* 86.3:161–180.

Palomino Ojeda, Aquiles. 1972. *Patrones matrimoniales entre los Ixiles de Chajul, Guatemala.* Ph.D. dissertation, School of Social Sciences, University of California, Irvine.

Pelto, Pertti J., and Gretel H. Pelto. 1978. *Anthropological research; the structure of inquiry* (2nd ed.). Cambridge: Cambridge University Press.

Piaget, Jean. 1962. *Play, dreams and imitation in childhood.* New York: Norton.

Popper, Karl. 1966a. *The open society and its enemies* (5th ed.). Princeton: Princeton University Press.

————. 1966b. *The poverty of historicism* (2nd ed.). New York: Basic Books; Harper & Row Torchbook.

————. 1968. *The logic of scientific discovery* (2nd ed.). New York: Harper & Row Torchbook.

Propp, Vladimir. 1968. *Morphology of the folktale.* Austin: University of Texas Press.

Proskouriakoff, Tatiana. 1963. *An album of Maya architecture.* Norman, Okla.: University of Oklahoma Press.

Quillian, M. Ross. 1968. Semantic memory. In *Semantic information processing*, ed. M. Minsky. Cambridge, Mass.: MIT Press.

Quinn, Naomi. 1975. Decision models of social structure. *American Ethnologist* 2.1:19–46.

————. 1976. A natural system used in Mfantse litigation settlement. *American Ethnologist* 3:331–351.

————. 1979. A cognitive anthropologist looks at American marriage. Paper presented to the 78th Annual Meeting of the American Anthropological Association, November 1979, Cincinnati, Ohio.

Radin, Paul. 1927. *Primitive man as a philosopher.* New York: Appleton.

Randall, Robert A. 1977. *Change and variation in Samal fishing: making plans to 'make a living' in the southern Philippines.* Ph.D. dissertation, University of California, Berkeley.

Redfield, Robert. 1930. *Tepoztlan: A Mexican village.* Chicago: University of Chicago Press.

Rice, Grace Elizabeth. 1978. *The role of cultural schemata in narrative comprehension.* Social Sciences Research Reports, no. 10. Ph.D. dissertation, School of Social Sciences, University of California, Irvine.

————. 1980. On cultural schemata. *American Ethnologist* 7:152–171.

Ridgeway, Cecilia L., and John M. Roberts. 1976. Urban popular music and interaction: a semantic relationship. *Ethnomusicology* 20.2:233–251.

Roberts, John M. 1964. The self-management of cultures. In *Explorations in cultural anthropology; essays in honor of George Peter Murdock,* ed. Ward Goodenough. New York: McGraw-Hill.

———. 1965. Oaths, autonomic ordeals, and power. *American Anthropologist* 67.6(2):186–212.

Roberts, John M., C. Chiao, and T. N. Pandey. 1975. Meaningful god sets from a Chinese personal pantheon and a Hindu personal pantheon. *Ethnology* 14.2:121–147.

Roberts, John M., and Garry E. Chick. 1979. Butler county eight ball: a behavioral space analysis. In *Sports, games, and play,* ed. Jeffrey Goldstein. New York: Halstead Press.

Roberts, John M., and Brian Sutton-Smith. 1962. Child training and game involvement. *Ethnology* 1.2:166–185.

———. 1966. Cross-cultural correlates of games of chance. *Behavioral Science Notes* 1.3:131–144.

Rohner, Ronald P. 1975. *They love me, they love me not; a worldwide study of the effects of parental acceptance and rejection.* New Haven, Conn.: HRAF Press.

Romney, A. Kimball, and Roy G. d.'Andrade, eds. 1964. *Transcultural studies in cognition.* Special publication of the *American Anthropologist,* vol. 66, no. 3, part 2.

Rumelhart, David E. 1975. Notes on a schema for stories. In *Representation and understanding; studies in cognitive science,* ed. D. Bobrow and A. Collins. New York: Academic Press.

Sapir, J. David, and J. Christopher Crocker. 1977. *The social use of metaphor; essays on the anthropology of rhetoric.* Philadelphia: University of Pennsylvania Press.

Schank, Roger C. 1979. *Language and memory.* Paper presented to the Conference on Cognitive Sciences, August 1979, La Jolla, California.

Schank, Roger C., and Robert P. Abelson. 1977. *Scripts, plans, goals, and understanding.* Hillsdale, N.J.: Erlbaum.

Searle, John R. 1969. *Speech acts: an essay in the philosophy of language.* London: Cambridge University Press.

Sebeok, Thomas A., and Frances J. Ingemann. 1956. *Studies in Cheremis; the supernatural.* Viking Fund Publications in Anthropology, no. 22. New York: Wenner-Gren Foundation.

Selby, Henry A. 1974. *Zapotec deviance; the convergence of folk and modern sociology.* Austin and London: University of Texas Press.

Shaw, Mary, ed. 1972. *Según nuestros antepasados: textos folklóricos de Guatemala y Honduras.* Guatemala City, Guatemala: Instituto Linguistico de Verano.

Smith, Augustus Ledyard, and Alfred V. Kidder. 1951. *Excavations at Nebaj, Guatemala.* Publication no. 594. Washington, D.C.: Carnegie Institute of Washington.

Spitz, Rene A. 1945. Hospitalism: an inquiry into the genesis of psychiatric conditions in early childhood. *Psychoanalytic Study of the Child* 2:53–74.

Stoll, Otto. 1887. *Die Sprache der Ixil-Indianer.* Leipzig: Brockhaus.

Termer, Franz. 1958. Apuntes geograficos y etnograficos de la zona de Nebaj. *Anales de la Sociedad de Geografía e Historia,* vol. 31, nos. 1–4, pp. 150–166.

Thomas, Lynn L., Jerrold E. Kronenfeld, and David B. Kronenfeld. 1976. Asdiwal crumbles: a critique of Lévi-Straussian myth analysis. *American Ethnologist* 3.147:173.

Tversky, Amos. 1977. Features of similarity. *Psychological Review* 84:327–352.

Tylor, Edward B. 1958. *Primitive culture.* New York: Harper Torchbooks.

Vittengl, Morgan J. 1979. Where is our plane? *Maryknoll* 73.7:37–42.

Vogt, Evon Z. 1976. *Tortillas for the Gods.* Cambridge, Mass.: Harvard University Press.

———. 1969. *Zinacantan; a Maya community in the highlands of Chiapas.* Cambridge, Mass.: Harvard University Press.

Vogt, Evon Z., and Ray Hyman. 1959. *Water witching, U.S.A.* Chicago: University of Chicago Press.

Wallace, Anthony F. C. 1961. *Culture and personality.* New York: Random House.

———. 1967. Identity processes in personality and in culture. In *Cognition, personality, and clinical psychology,* ed. R. Jessor and S. Feshbach. San Francisco: Jossey-Bass.

Wanner, Eric. 1974. *On remembering, forgetting and understanding sentences: a study of the deep structure hypothesis.* The Hague: Mouton.

Wanner, Eric, and Michael Maratsos. 1978. An ATN approach to comprehension. In *Linguistic theory and psychological reality,* ed. Morris Halle, Joan Bresnan, and George A. Miller. Cambridge, Mass.: MIT Press.

Watt, William C. 1966. *Morphology of the Nevada cattlebrands and their blazons,* pt. 1. Washington, D.C.: National Bureau of Standards (Report 9050).

———. 1967. *Morphology of the Nevada cattlebrands and their blazons,* pt. 2. Pittsburgh: Department of Computer Science, Carnegie-Mellon University.

———. 1975. *What is the proper characterization of the alphabet? I: desiderata.* Social Sciences Working Paper no. 73. Irvine, Calif.: School of Social Sciences, University of California, Irvine.

———. 1978a. *What is the proper characterization of the alphabet? II: composition.* Social Sciences Research Reports, no. 2. Irvine, Calif.: School of Social Sciences, University of California, Irvine.

———. 1978b. Review of *Theory of semiotics* by Umberto Eco and *Contributions to the doctrine of signs* by Thomas A. Sebeok. *American Anthropologist* 80:714–716.

Werner, Oswald. n.d. The synthetic informant model. I: On the simulation of large lexical/semantic fields (manuscript).

Werner, Oswald, and Martin D. Topper. 1975. On the theoretical unity of ethnoscience and ethnoscience ethnographies. Paper presented at the meetings of the American Anthropological Association, San Francisco, November 1975.

Woods, William A. 1970. Transitional network grammars for natural language analysis. *Communications of the ACM* 13:591–606.

INDEX